Know Your Enemy is a must for every American worthy of the name and is especially recommended to those men who hold high offices and are in position, before it is too late, to save the Republic from its traducers. If the Founding Fathers were alive today they would be the first to approve this book and to point with pride at an author with the courage and patriotism to risk everything, as they risked everything, for this our beloved country.

P.A. del Valle, Lieut. General, U.S. Marine Corps (Ret.)

24 feb 2001

Other works by
Donn de Grand Pré

*A Window
on America*
1970

*Confessions of an
Arms Peddler*
1979

Brother Jim Grand Pré (325 PIR) Operation Long Horn – 1952

In Memoriam...

GEN OMAR BRADLEY
GEN BRUCE C. CLARKE
GEN JAMES M. GAVIN
GEN ROBERT H. YORK
GEN MAXWELL TAYLOR
GEN ARTHUR TRUDEAU
GEN SAMUEL WILLIAMS
GEN JOSEPH H. CRAWFORD
COL CHARLES A. LINDBERGH
COL DONN STOWELL
COL EDWARD GRAND PRÉ
CPT EDDIE RICKENBACKER
CPT EDGAR AGNEW
CPT PETER J. MCCABE
CPT CORLISS CAMPBELL
LT COLIN CAMPBELL
LT LOGAN CAMPBELL
LT CHARLES BLOMBERG

Dear friends and gentle people...
All soldiers... once young...
REQUIESCANT IN PACE
Rest in Peace

If the trumpet give an uncertain sound, who shall prepare himself for battle?

I Corinthians XIV 8

CONTENTS

FOREWORD

THE words and pages and chapters of this book are not written to shock the reader. But they do. Here, for the first time in many decades, is a view of the forces that act on our lives as Americans. Here is a case, complete with impeccable historical references, of plans begun many years ago to control the course of human life on earth. And the plans are a continuum – not easy to envision in the every day life of a people born to, and believing in, personal freedom. This book is a measure by which thinking people can see the gradual reduction of the freedoms that were the promise of our national founders.

The author gives us a perspective based on a firsthand knowledge of both time and events, as well as close association with many of the leading characters who willfully assisted the country, our society and its institutions in a downhill spiral leading to the present and ongoing crisis of epic proportions. He was witness to the almost incomprehensible treachery, ineptness and blatant corruption of our chosen leaders, at the highest levels of government, as they dragged this country and its peoples from one unmitigated disaster to another, not only in domestic affairs, but especially in our rudderless foreign policy, which led us blindly into a series of pointless and disastrous no-win wars. What emerged was an almost fatally weakened military force, which has been purposely led astray from its major – and only – mission of defending the constitution, and handed such morale-destroying tasks as humanitarianism, peace-keeping and nationbuilding. As these tragic events unfolded, the deliberate destruction of our culture, morals and mores as a Christian nation was aided and abetted by a subservient and complicit press.

While many people will undoubtedly read this book, a far greater number will be unable to read it, for illiteracy is one of the aims of those who would remove the power of individual opinion. For those of us who have good memories, the progress of group control is obvious. The growing power of the shadowy figures who increase their own domain and little by little eliminate the options of individuals is visible to any who will step back and look, compare, measure. The most frightening aspect of the growing power and control over our daily lives is the sincerity of those who wish to exercise it. They believe with a religious fervor that they are better qualified to manage our lives than we are.

It has often been repeated that freedom is the unobstructed exercise of options. Conversely, tyranny is the absence of human options. As humans, we came into life on this earth complete with the need to make decisions, to find and to choose between one course and another; one object or another; one person or another; one belief or another. These options are being gradually removed and replaced. That is a measurable fact. The only question remaining is whether it is accidental encroachment or a planned one. Col Donn de Grand Pré thoroughly documents his case that it is planned, that the planners' direction is historic and unchanging.

We must finally recognize that there are those among us who have the human characteristic, the need, to control other humans. We must finally recognize that they span generations and lifetimes. We must finally see them for what they truly are. They have many names; Scribes and Pharisees, the Parsees and high castes of India, the myriad of upper bureaucrats in our own and other government, the one-worlders. These are those who cannot abide individual decisions and actions contrary to group thought, for the excitement of individual action is frightening to them. Their needs are the great warm wombs of group thought, group action. Their violent hostility to any thought or purpose other than mass acceptance is evident to any logical observer.

The contest between those who believe in individual rights and actions and those who seek control of other human lives is not a new one. It is an ancient struggle with many dimensions. It is a war between forthrightness and the candor of individual decisions and those who would gain power through stealth and hypocrisy. The forces that act against individual liberty are subtle, gradual, persuasive – and very rewarding to those whose own lack of individual courage and achievement leads them in the group direction. And the pendulum is high on the side of the power-centralizers.

Those who purvey group thought, who pretend to believe in the herd mentality, herd wisdom, can win. But the only path for them to achieve victory is one that dehumanizes and degrades others. Therefore their destabilization of the courts, the insistence on mediocrity in public schools, the constant attacks on religious faith should not come as a surprise. That the majority of the media should support these actions is disgraceful in every sense of the word.

Thoughtful and honorable people who read this book will discover a wake-up call in Col Grand Pré's premises and conclusions. Make no mistake about it – this book is the opening shot in a war that individuals must win in order to have our nation and our freedom restored.

John F. Williams III

Madison, Virginia
April 2000

John F. Williams, a decorated Army officer and Combat Engineer of World War II and of the Korean police action, is a graduate of North Carolina State and Duke Universities, with a BS and MS in Natural Science (Forestry). He is presently a missionary to Guatemala.

A TRUE AMERICAN HERO

Charles A. Lindbergh, a colonel in the US Army Air Corps Reserve, volunteered for active duty 10 Dec 1941, but FDR, who feared and hated him, turned the famous aviator down. In 1944, he traveled to New Guinea, where as a civilian, "Mr. X," he flew P-38 Lightning fighters on 50 combat missions, shooting down three Japanese Zeros and carrying out secret missions for Gen Douglas MacArthur.

In the above Army Signal Corps photo, "Lucky Lindy" is shown being debriefed by Maj Thomas McGuire on the New Guinea airstrip after a combat flight over the Pacific.

PROLOGUE
ON THE EVE OF WORLD WAR III

The barbarians are not at the gates, they are inside the gates –
and have academic tenure, judicial appointments, government grants,
and control of the movies, television, and other media. The question
of the hour – and of the next century – is whether all this can be
turned around.

Dr. Thomas Sowell, 1994

"I am in favor of Bolshevism."

So spoke David Ben-Gurion (born David Gruen in Lodz, Poland in 1886), the first prime minister of the new state of Israel. In a revealing article, "Whose Country Is It?" in the January 1998 *American Spectator*, Tom Bethell puts those stirring words in their proper context. Bethell had just returned from a week in Jerusalem, which may or may not become the first capital city of the World. Bethell writes that when the British controlled Palestine after World War I, Chaim Weizmann and the Zionist collaborated with quotas that prevented most religious or Oriental Jews from immigrating.[1]

"Fifty years ago exactly," Bethell informs us, "the Soviet Union cast its crucial United Nations vote in favor of the new state." He also quotes Yosef Lapid, an editorial writer for *Ma'ariv,* a left-wing newspaper, whose column bore the header: "It Just Isn't My Country Anymore."

This begs the question, just whose country is it – this land once called Palestine? There is a simple answer, but we can feel for the perplexity of this man, Yosef Lapid, as he sees within his country, the steady encroachment of Orthodox and religious Jews, "most of the newer faces from Russia," Bethell says, "almost a million strong" since the collapse of the Soviet Union. They brought with them "a new faith, which is to say the old faith; the God of Abraham and Isaac and Jacob."[2]

Although he doesn't say it, Bethell intertwines several exceptionally close alliances in his article, the United Nations, Bolshevism, the Soviet Union, Zionism, Palestine, the new state (Israel), David Ben-Gurion, Chaim Weizmann....

They are all of a set piece. We will discover in this work just how they interconnect, and how a relatively small band of evil gangster-statesmen contrive unceasingly to erect a world empire under the blue and white banners of the secular humanist governments of the United Nations and the mini-state of Israel.

The cunning tactics and terror techniques of Lenin and Stalin and their Zionist (say Bolshevist) Comrades, headed by such historically significant thugs as "Iron Felix" Dzerzinsky and Leon Trotsky (Lev Bronstein), are today being implemented with a vengeance right here in our own country – the United States of America – once the citadel of liberty and freedom; now, fast becoming the premier fascist police state.

We too may ask the question: just whose country is it?

These latter-day Bolshevists, dedicated conspirators with a fanatical will to power, are seizing the critical levers of government and straining for the ultimate brass ring – a one-world United Nations of absolute despotism.

FLASHBACK 1951

The Korean War was the first large-scale war in American history that began and ended without a declaration of war by the Congress of the United States. It was the first war to be fought under the aegis of the United Nations.

We rushed into Korea with no advance planning, and we stumbled into the ground war in Vietnam with uncertain footing. In neither case did we have any fully thought-out ideas concerning our objectives or the means we would be willing to expend to attain them... There was some excuse for our precipitate action in Korea, but little or none for our somewhat aimless drift into deep involvement in Vietnam. We must not let such situations develop again.[3]

J. Lawton Collins stressed this point in his book, *War in Peacetime*, published in 1969. Known as "Lightning Joe" for his heroic exploits as commander of the VII Corps from D-Day until Germany surrendered, General Collins was Chief of Staff of the US Army from 1950-53. During that time, those brave men doing the actual fighting for the US Army in Korea looked upon *Lightning Joe* as "The Boss." This author was a young combat infantry troop commander in Korea, who had served proudly as a soldier in World War II, a latterday Sir Lancelot on a quest. It was one of his heroes of World War II, General of the Army Omar Bradley, who stated in 1951, "Korea is the wrong war in the wrong place at the wrong time."

After the Korean debacle, the author began to develop serious doubts about the people who were running our country. He thought then... *did we do this... officers such as Generals Ridgway, Collins, Taylor, Williams and Clarke, as well as those of us of lesser rank?* But that thought has been tempered by time; we were the soldiers who carried out the orders; we were in effect the architects and executioners of a failed policy.

Today, the doubts persist.

Here, the author makes his key point, for without it, this book in its entirety is meaningless and a mere exercise in polemics. We are in fact at war. We have an enemy, which can and must be defined from a political standpoint, for war and politics have a symbiotic relationship. While such factors as economic domination, religious differences and ideological disjunction may have a bearing in the political arena, they can never of themselves generate the intensity of mutual antipathy between opposing forces to cause a war to break out.

To wage war, one must have a well-defined enemy. That enemy must constitute a threat to our survival as a nation-state with a clearly understood way of life. This condition leads to the defense of a specific territory.

We can also wage offensive war against an enemy. The purpose must be political gain or an increase in political power. The net result may be an increase in land, booty, slaves and women (as defined in the Old Testament), but concomitantly, there must also be an increase in political power. Otherwise, you may emerge from a war victorious, but suffer a net loss in political power; witness France and Britain after both world wars.

And it is to these two world conflagrations we must now look back, in order to grasp the realities of why they were fought and who actually benefited from the ensuing peace.

We must be able to discern the nature of the propaganda that we are constantly being fed in order to convince the unthinking that a particular war is necessary. Always ask the question: necessary for whom, or for what?

We will be incessantly hammered with atrocities and the barbarous behavior of a supposed enemy; and/or appealed to for humanitarian reasons to gain our support in sending our armed forces to some distant shore to protect some defenseless peoples (usually suffering women and children – Bill Clinton and his handlers perfected this emotional appeal), or to wage war against a personal enemy, a madman, or a dictator (George Bush developed this to an art form, slavering in public over his personal animosity toward Saddam Hussein). These emotional reasons of themselves are meaningless, and are usually based on lies and damned lies, which are propagated on a daily basis by a controlled and compliant media. In every instance, ask *Cui bono*?

Let's not drift from Gen Collins' major point that we are at war.

It is the thesis of this work that those overt wars in which we engaged for whatever reason since the end of World War II have not only been waged unconstitutionally in the truest sense, but that we, the people, as a sovereign nation-state (meaning the United States of America) have suffered a net loss in political power.

And each one was waged in order to divert our time and energies and thoughts away from the true *Enemy within* and toward a contrived enemy outside our borders.... *Cui bono*?

That same "nation" with which we have been actively at war, albeit covertly, since 1933. It was best defined by Theodor Herzl, the "father of International Zionism," in 1902:

> I will give you my definition of a nation, and you can add the adjective 'Jewish'. A nation is, in my mind, an historical group of men of a recognizable cohesion held together by a common enemy. That is in my view a nation. Then if you add to that the word 'Jewish' you have what I understand to be the Jewish nation[4]

The planning for this ideological conflict goes back much further. It makes use of the ancient formula, *Knowledge equals Wealth equals Power* to further its intent of *absolute gain* which equates to *absolute despotism* over all of us...men, women, children, suckling babes, as well as a net gain in land, booty, slaves, sheep, goats and cattle.

A quick overview will reveal that this ideological conflict is purposely embodied in the "constitution" of the United Nations.

LEAGUE TO "ENFORCE" PEACE

The United Nations Charter was purposely designed as an instrument of force. Patterned after the Soviet constitution, it even allowed for a Soviet commander-in-chief of the UN forces. Those who fought in Korea served under that commander. They thought Gen Collins, the chief of staff of the US Army, was "the Boss." He was not. A *Soviet Bolshevik* was.

The UN Undersecretary for Political and Security Affairs from 1949 through 1953, Konstantin E. Zinchenko of the USSR occupied that position. He was in fact "the Boss" and orchestrated the defeat of the UN forces in Korea. None of the men fighting in Korea realized that. Not even Gen Collins or Gen MacArthur was aware until after the "peace" negotiations that our politicians – including Presidents Truman and Eisenhower – had sold us out to a twin-headed monster, the Zionist-Bolshevist and the Fabian Socialist, whose heads occasionally snarl and spit at each other, but in fact are joined to the same body.

Bear in mind that it is not "Jewish," although many of its individual components are in fact Zionist-Bolshevist Jews. Neither is it "Christian," although an equivalent number purport to be Christians. That two-headed monster is comprised of "Jews who are not Jews" and of "Christians who are not Christian," for this *Bicephalous Monster* is in fact satanic. We will go through the courting, the conception, the gestation and the Caesarean delivery of this illegitimate child of Lucifer... the god of light.... O, yes!

The late Representative Usher L. Burdick of North Dakota knew who was in charge. Burdick operated a big cattle ranch in western Dakota. He delivered a scathing speech on 17 Jan 1957 on the floor of the House in which he said:

> The Russians are and will continue to be on the Inside of any Military Action taken by the Security Council of the United Nations. [5]

This is still not general knowledge, for the mainstream press has suppressed it over the years; yet, today, the UN Security Council is the prime instrument for global conquest and establishment of the *New World Order*. And this, of course, is exactly the way the UN founders intended it to be.

Let's look back briefly to a statement by the first Secretary General for the UN, Trygve Lie, who said in his book, *Cause for Peace:*

> Vyshinski was the first to inform me of an understanding which the Big Five had reached in London on the appointment of a Soviet national as Assistant Secretary-General for Political and Security Affairs.[6]

Who sold us out to the Soviets? We can cite the litany of our country's traitors, starting with FDR and those who surrounded him, such as Alger Hiss, Harry Hopkins, Henry Morgenthau, Jr., Bernard Baruch, Samuel Rosenmann, Harry Dexter White (Weiss), *et al,* but it was Edward Stettinius who had agreed in London that the USSR would get that post.

The "Ultimate Dictator" gets his marching orders in Chapter VII of the Charter that says in part under Article 47:

> The Military Staff Committee shall be responsible under the Security Council for the strategic direction of any armed forces placed at the disposal of the Security Council.

This is why we went into Korea without Congressional authority. That august body had, in fact, abdicated their constitutional responsibility (Section Eight, Article I: "...Congress shall have power to declare war").

What does this really mean? It means simply that the UN Security Council – not the Congress of the United States – has now the supreme authority to declare war.

The US Congress ratified that charter, which had been authored by known communists and traitors in FDR's cabinet, including Alger Hiss, Leo Pasvolsky and Phillip Jessup. They are gone. Others have taken their place, such as Henry Kissinger, Zbigniew Brzezinski, Brent Scowcroft, Lawrence Eagleburger, Robert Rubin, and many others who seem to have that same irreverence for the US Constitution and love for the United Nations Charter.

DEFINING THE ENEMY WITHIN

FLASHBACK - February 1991: George Bush's greatest triumph as President was also his greatest failure; that was the fiasco of "Desert Storm." Some of us who at one time were "insiders" in the true sense of the word disengaged ourselves from a corrupt and failing federal government, not because we were Democrat or Republican or independent, but because we saw the nature of the Enemy within. Some of us retired into serenity, senility and pastoral pursuits, while others tried to sound the alarm, most to little avail, for they were reluctant – for whatever reason – to explicitly define the Enemy.

Why did the United States deliberately set out in 1990 to destroy the viability of the once-sovereign nation of Iraq? We can find an answer in the superb work by George Knupffer, *The Struggle for World Power.* Knupffer had the foresight to predict a war with Iraq such as *Desert Storm.* He wrote:

> Before leaving the subject of the enemy's foreign policy, we should note that the significance of Israel and of Jerusalem, the intended capital of the world, is very great. Now it may seem that the Soviets are opposed to Zionist conquests and are backing the Arabs. In fact the

Communists play their usual role of *agent-provocateur*, and they give the Arabs enough arms and encouragement to fight without real hope of victory, thereby justifying further Israeli conquests until they have what they have always wanted – the whole area from the Nile to the Euphrates... But should Israel ever be in real danger then both the USA and the USSR would come to its rescue, being always in collusion. The sooner the Arabs understand the facts the better for them. Their only chance of survival is to work on the lines we propose, while abandoning policies which, for over fifty years, have brought nothing but defeats.[7]

It is perhaps time that we too understand the facts. It is also time to identify and to know our enemy. It is the purpose of this series of papers to identify that enemy. We know that he is already inside the gates.

Another soldier of an earlier era, Colonel Robert R. McCormick, distinguished himself in the Battle of Cantigny in France in 1918. He came home to Chicago and took over the family newspaper, the *Chicago Tribune*, and built it up to be the nation's largest-circulation broadsheet. *The Barnes Review* (Mar-Apr 1998) honored the Colonel in its section "Profiles in History"[8]

In an address at Notre Dame University in 1941, McCormick recalled his World War I experiences and said that American intervention in Europe would bring about a most unfortunate repetition: "The use of our power to strengthen one side of a quarrel – at our expense." For 45 of his 75 years, Col McCormick imparted his message of patriotism and nationalism in the *Chicago Tribune*. He was a brave and fearless messenger.

He was both an American nationalist and an avid midwestern sectionalist. He saw in the power centers of the East a paradoxical alliance of "international capital and international communism." Like Colonel McCormick, others view the United Nations, and its international Declaration of Human Rights, as threats to America's sovereignty. As reported in *The Barnes Review* cited above, McCormick considered the Nuremberg "war criminal" trials to be a lynching rite staged to justify the newly conceived *ex post facto* crime of "waging aggressive war." We will address these fraudulent, and indeed criminal, trials in Chapter 7.

DEFINING "ANTI-SEMITISM"

There is an ancient fable that asks the question: Who will bell the cat? It is the intent of this book to bell the cat. By belling the cat, the author will naturally step on a few toes and will probably be accused of being both "anti-Christian" and "anti-Jewish." There will be those who, rather than addressing the issues, will hurl the poison spear of "anti-Semitism" at the messenger.

A standard Zionist-Bolshevist modus operandi is to scream anti-Semite at anyone who exposes any of their nefarious plans, and to seek the "sympathy factor" by staging "incidents," such as desecration of their own cemeteries or torching their own synagogues and blaming it on "neo-Nazis." They are masters at this kind of deception, dissimulation and propaganda. Because they control 90% of the mainstream media here in the US, as well as in many other countries, they have the added advantage of mass outlets for their deception and outright lies. Two remarkable writers addressed the political potency of the pejorative, "anti-Semite."

That great American scholar and author of Jewish heritage, Alfred M. Lilienthal, in *The Other Side of the Coin*, said:

> Neither the religious nor the lay leaders of the many Jewish organizations wish to lose this potent weapon. Remove prejudice and lose adherents to the faith... This is the conspiracy of the rabbinate, Jewish nationals and other leaders of organized Jewry to keep the problems of prejudice alive.[9]

Ivor Benson, writing in *The Zionist Factor*, said that we would do well "never to forget that it is a chauvinist Zionist ambition that is edging mankind toward the brink of another global catastrophe, and that its most potent weapon is the mind-paralyzing lie of antisemitism."[10]

Israel Shahak, whom Gore Vidal calls "the latest – if not the last – of the great prophets," resides in Israel. In his seminal work, *Jewish History, Jewish Religion: The Weight of Three Thousand Years*, he concentrated on this great and driving need for prejudice and outright hostility toward non-Jews on the part of chauvinist Zionists. In a chapter appropriately titled "Political Consequences," he wrote:

> US support for Israel, when considered not in abstract but in concrete detail, cannot be adequately explained only as a result of American imperial interests. The strong influence wielded by the organized Jewish community in the USA in support of all Israeli policies must also be taken into account in order to explain the Middle East policies of American administrations.... It should be recalled that Judaism, especially in its classical form, is totalitarian in nature. The behavior of supporters of other totalitarian ideologies of our times was not different from that of organized American Jews....
>
> Any support of human rights in general by a Jew which does not include support of human rights of non-Jews whose rights are being violated by the 'Jewish State' is as deceitful as the support of human rights by a Stalinist.[11]

Shahak concludes his monumental work by stating:

> The real test facing both Israeli and Diaspora Jews is the test of their self-criticism which must include the critique of the Jewish past.... The extent of the persecution and discrimination against non-Jews inflicted by the 'Jewishized' Diaspora Jews is also enormously greater than the suffering inflicted on Jews by regimes hostile to them.

The quadripartite countries involved in the Mideast takeover (the US, the USSR, Britain and Israel) continue to use destabilization as a principal weapon. It has destroyed the once-beautiful city of Beirut, known as the "Paris of the Mideast"; the most advanced country, Iraq; and wreaked havoc on the country with the highest per capita income, Kuwait.

The culprit has been and continues to be International Zionism wedded to Fabian Socialism – both with direct ties to Soviet Bolshevism.

Zionism was established as a world political force in 1897 in Basel, Switzerland. Its aims since then have been centered on setting up a one-world government with Zionism in control of worldwide finance and therefore "Lord of the World." Knupffer points out in *The Struggle for World Power* that the driving force is

"Messianic Finance Capitalism that actually brought about Soviet Bolshevism."

A quote from Edward Gibbon's *Decline and Fall of the Roman Empire* is pertinent: "The enslavement of man usually begins in the economic sphere."

Dr. Theodor Herzl, the father of Zionism, stated in a proposal to the Rothschild family council in 1881:

> We are a people – one people. When we sink, we become a revolutionary proletariat, the subordinate officers of the revolutionary party; when we rise there rises also our terrible power of the purse.[12]

Bolshevist Zionism is but one of two heads. The other – Anglo-Saxon – is Fabian Socialism. The victims – those who are mauled and devoured by this monster – are both gentile and Jew, that make up the patriotic and freedom-loving peoples of America, England, Israel, Russia, and, in fact, of the world over. This is not a religious issue, but one of power politics which is built on the foundation of money monopoly, coupled to monopoly of the media for monetary and mind control. Ask yourself a simple question: who – or what group – controls both money and the media, as well as other levers of power, in the United States?

That's what it's all about. It doesn't matter who is backing whom in the Mideast or other regions around the world; the end result, after destabilizing the region, is control of the resources and the real estate, especially the *choke points*. We saw this so clearly when we dispatched our troops into Somalia in 1993. Check your world atlas, and notice that Somalia and its tiny neighboring country of Djibouti are separated from the Arabian Peninsula by the strategically vital strait of Bab el Mandeb. Another critical choke point which the US and Britain control with carrier task forces is the Strait of Hormuz, separating the Persian Gulf from the Gulf of Oman. In fact, we have had a naval task force stationed at Bahrain, off the north coast of Saudi Arabia, since 1973. The choke point most threatening to the US is that of the Panama Canal. Under a Panamanian 50-year lease beginning on January 1, 2000, China took possession of the ports of Cristobal on the Atlantic and Balboa on the Pacific. "Doomsday" proclaims

Admiral Thomas H. Moorer, former Chairman Joint Chief of Staff, now retired. "The Chinese are in a position today to…use Panama as a launching point for missiles to attack the US."

BEATING THE KETTLE DRUMS OF WAR

In a *Time* magazine report, "As Washington Burns…" (9 Feb 1998), Bruce Nelan writes about Secretary of State Madeleine Albright's trip to Europe and the Mideast to seek "allied" support in the bombing – one more time – of the Islamic country of Iraq, and to persuade Saudi Arabia and Bahrain to allow US planes based there to take part in any anti-Saddam offensive. "So far," Nelan says, "only Britain, which has sent an aircraft carrier task force to the Gulf, stands firmly with the US on the use of force."[13]

Nelan explains that the US has plenty of land and carrier based planes and missiles in the Gulf to give Saddam's military a pounding. He continues, "But such attacks would not wipe out all of Iraq's hidden poisons and gases, because the US does not know where they are."

Therein is the heart of the dilemma; we have had UN inspection teams combing the backwaters of Iraq for over seven years looking for what Madeleine and others call "weapons of mass destruction." These teams have found nothing even remotely resembling "weapons of mass destruction"; no rockets, no poisons, no gases, no nothing… zip… zilch… still we look – and demand the right to continue to look. Saddam, in effect, has said, "enough is enough" and balked at further checking. Even the so-called leaders of the Grand Old Party in Congress shook the mailed fist, wanting to go in and kill somebody, if not Saddam himself, then his Republican Guard; if not the Iraqi military, then the civilians, including women, children and suckling babes. As Sen John McCain pontificated: "If we can take him [Saddam], out clearly we want to take him out. That's far different from assassination."[14]

Yes, far different. In fact, it would be mass murder. President George Bush performed similar surgery on Iraqi women, children and suckling babes in 1991 during Desert Storm. Our public loved it, by jingo!

In his article Nelan stated that Clinton has a double standard:

> He relentlessly pursues Saddam's weapons of mass destruction while saying nothing about the atom bombs everyone assumes Israel has stashed in its basement.

This is a courageous statement on Nelan's part, albeit an understatement. As Seymour Hersh revealed in his book, *The Samson Option,* Israel has stockpiled weapons of mass destruction in underground caverns in the Negev Desert for at least 30 years; weapons equipped with not only nuclear, but chemical and bacteriological warheads, all ready to go.

Do they have the will or power actually to use these weapons? Perhaps they already have. There is the danger, however – certainly recognized by Hersh – that they, like Samson, could pull the temple down upon themselves. In order to grasp this concept fully, we must turn once more to Israel Shahak's monumental work, *Jewish History, Jewish Religion.* Shahak, who arrived in Palestine in 1945, became an admirer of David Ben-Gurion. He explains how he became his dedicated opponent:

> In 1956, I eagerly swallowed all of Ben-Gurion's political and military reasons for Israel initiating the Suez War, until he (in spite of being an atheist, proud of his disregard of the commandments of Jewish religion) pronounced in the Knesset on the third day of the war, that the real reason for it is 'the restoration of the kingdom of David and Solomon' to its Biblical borders.[15]

Shahak defines those borders as being all of Sinai and a part of northern Egypt; all of Jordan and a large chunk of Saudi Arabia; all of Kuwait and a part of Iraq south of the Euphrates; all of Lebanon and all of Syria; together with a huge part of Turkey; and the island of Cyprus.

Is this vast territory still the ultimate goal of Israeli expansionism? Shakak further states that in May 1993 Ariel Sharon formally proposed in the Likud Convention that Israel should adopt the *Biblical borders* concept as its official policy. Shahak sees the alternatives that face Israeli-Jewish society:

It can become a fully closed and warlike ghetto, a Jewish Sparta, supported by the labour of Arab helots, kept in existence by its influence on the US political establishment and by threats to use its nuclear power, or it can become an open society.

The second choice is dependent on an honest examination of its Jewish past, or the admission that Jewish chauvinism and exclusivism exist, and on an honest examination of the attitudes of Judaism towards the non-Jews.[16]

BARBARIANS INSIDE THE GATES

In a sidebar, also in *Time* (9 Feb 1998), Lisa Beyer writes under a banner "Getting Ready for War" that Israel has developed plans for battling the Palestinians anew, including one code-named Field of Thorns, which calls for the retaking of the West Bank cities:

Both sides know two things in advance of another fight: Israel will win it, and it will be horribly painful. 'It'll be much bigger than last September,' says an Israeli commander. 'Much crueler, much bloodier, much more complicated'.[17]

Therein, in that succinct statement, is the heart of the troubles and misery of "civilization" over the past 3,000 years, all perpetrated by a biblical band of outcasts which history records as the tribes of Judah and Benjamin with their maniacal thirst for destruction and revenge forever.

A prolific American writer, Robert Kaplan, whose prose appears in the liberal *Atlantic Monthly* as well as the conservative *Wall Street Journal,* produced a superlative book in 1996, *The Ends of the Earth*, in which he argues that "democracy" is the source of many problems affecting third world nations. Kaplan claims that "the barbarians are not only at the gates, but may already be inside the gates in the shape and form of faceless gigantic multi-national corporations."[18]

The shape and form of *the Barbarians Inside the Gates* is actually that of a bicephalous monster – two heads, one body. Far from being faceless, it is in fact two-faced, one being branded "Zionist Bolshevism," the other, "Fabian Socialism."

This then is the *Barbarian Inside the Gates.* Has he in fact taken over?

HAS THERE BEEN A DE FACTO COUP?

Edward Luttwak, formerly a student at the London School of Economics, published *Coup d'État - A Practical Handbook*, first in England in 1968 and later by the Harvard University Press (1979). This work has since been published in all major languages and received wide distribution about the globe. The *Times Literary Supplement* stated that *Coup d'État* was "an extraordinarily competent and well-written work, displaying very wide knowledge of the ways in which coups, both successful and unsuccessful, have actually been organized."

Writing the foreword for this amazing piece, Walter Laqueur stated:

> Once upon a time the commander of a tank brigade in a Middle Eastern country was at least a potential contender for political power. This is no longer so, partly as a result of centralization in military command, partly because the political police have become more effective. But if in these parts coups have become less frequent they are still the only form of political change that can be envisaged at the present time.[19]

Which brings us to the here and now, not only in the Middle East, but especially here in the United States. We must ask the question: Have the *Barbarians* already pulled off a *de facto* coup?

Here is a most pertinent passage from Luttwak's *Coup d'État:*

> If we were revolutionaries, wanting to change the structure of society, our aim would be to destroy the power of some of the political forces, and the long and often bloody process of revolutionary attrition can achieve this. Our purpose, however, is quite different: we want to seize power within the present system, and we shall only stay in power if we embody some new status quo supported by those very forces which a revolution may seek to destroy. Should we want to achieve fundamental social change we can do so after we have become the government. This perhaps is a more efficient method (and certainly a less painful one) than that of the classic revolution.

Though we will try to avoid all conflict with the political forces, some of them will almost certainly oppose a coup. But this opposition will largely subside when we have substituted our new status quo for the old one, and can enforce it by our control of the state bureaucracy and security forces. This period of transition, which comes after we have emerged into the open and before we are vested with the authority of the state, is the most critical phase of the coup. We shall then be carrying out the dual task of imposing our control on the machinery of state, while at the same time using it to impose our control on the country at large. Any resistance to the coup in the one will stimulate further resistance in the other; if a chain reaction develops the coup could be defeated.[20]

Our major point to ponder as we go through *Barbarians Inside the Gates* is that if a de facto coup has already taken place, then, in order to avoid a bloody revolution for change, a counter-coup may be necessary in order to restore the machinery of state and gain control once more of the critical levers of power.

Think about it seriously, for time is fast running out.

LAUNCHING A MILITARY OPERATION

It is always wise before launching a military operation to review where you have been in a particular campaign. Here, briefly, is a "thumbnail sketch" of certain momentous events we will enlarge upon in the following chapters of *Barbarians Inside the Gates.*

There were two gigantic propaganda campaigns launched in 1945; one was designed to make the people throughout the United States, Canada and the United Kingdom aware of something called "anti-Semitism." The other, closely related to the first, was to seek the sympathy of these peoples for the Nazi crime of "Jewish extermination." The staging of the Nuremburg Trials was the instrument used to accomplish both.

Each of these campaigns was based on a colossal blitz of such astounding proportions that, had it been any other group in the world, save Talmudic Zionism, each of these hoaxes would have been laughed out of existence.

These events of 1945 are now culminating in the ongoing campaign, which is really the third and final phase of world conquest on the part of Talmudic Zionism wedded to Fabian Socialism. At this writing, we have the major effort concentrated in three geographic areas and centered in Russia, Israel and the United States. This in fact is a major military operation, with command headquarters occupying two principal locations – New York City and Washington, DC.

The groundwork was laid by the mathematical manipulation of the election process in order to place Bill Clinton in the White House by setting up a "three-way" race. An identical ploy was used to get the Princeton Professor, Woodrow Wilson, in as the first Bolshevik "premier-dictator" in 1912.

Wilson was maneuvered and manipulated on a daily basis, from 1911 until his death, by Edward Mandell House (Huis), Bernard Baruch, Louis Brandeis, Chaim Weizmann, Stephen Weiss, Jacob Schiff and Paul Warburg. The go-between for most of the political intrigue was House's brother-in-law, Sidney Mezes, who worked with Theodor Marburg of Baltimore, Maryland on the details of a "League to Enforce Peace."

The goal (Phase One) was three-fold, all predicated on a world war: (1) to destroy the Russian monarchy and Christianity in Russia; (2) to establish a "world government"; and (3) to lay the groundwork for the establishment of a Jewish "homeland" in Palestine.

The goal of Phase Two (World War II) was also three-fold: (1) to occupy Palestine; (2) to set up the "United Nations"; (3) to spread "Communism" throughout Eastern Europe.

The financial/political operations center shifted from Europe to the United States during and after Phase One. A quadrilateral of "premier-dictators" was chosen to bring the goals of Phase Two to fruition: Franklin Roosevelt, Winston Churchill, Adolf Hitler and Josef Stalin. The "advisers" shifted somewhat, with the "elder statesman," Bernard Baruch, playing the lead and supported by Herbert Lehman, Felix Frankfurter, Samuel Rosenmann, and James Warburg.

As was the case during Phase One, the "advisers" were actually running the government of the United States, but in concert with the Supreme Soviet and the Fabian Socialists in Britain. This "orchestration" continued after World War II and was enlarged by bringing in the newly created Jewish "Nation of Israel." Thereafter, by shifting crises and chaos from the Middle East to Eastern Europe at will over the next four decades; i.e., playing "Zionism" against "Bolshevism," the "elder statesmen" created confusion, economic instability and political unreliability in the countries of Europe and especially in the United States.

While a rather quick thumbnail sketch of the momentous events of this century, this sets the scene for what is currently happening. In the ensuing chapters we will get a closer look at these events and the people who purposely and cunningly brought them about, i.e., the *traitors* – several at the highest pinnacle of government – who deliberately sold us out to the bicephalous monster with one head labeled Bolshevist Zionism, and the other, Fabian Socialism.

WHAT IS A TRAITOR?

A nation can survive its fools and even the ambitious. But it cannot survive treason from within. An enemy at the gate is less formidable, for he is known and carries his banners openly against the city. But the traitor moves among those within the gates freely, his sly whispers rustling through all the alleys, heard in the very halls of government itself. For the traitor appears not a traitor; he speaks in the accents familiar to his victims, and he wears their face and their garments, and he appeals to the baseness that lies deep in the hearts of all men. He rots the soul of a nation; he works secretly and unknown in the night to undermine the pillars of a city; he infects the body politic so that it can no longer resist. A murderer is less to be feared.

Cicero - 45 BC

CHAPTER I

WE ARE AT WAR
(And We Are Losing)

"If the trumpet give an uncertain sound, who shall prepare himself for battle?"

I Corinthians XIV 8

PART ONE
SEARCH FOR DUTY – HONOR – COUNTRY

MY friends, we are at war... and have been unceasingly since 1933. The major problem is that we don't realize it. We have become so accustomed to being under siege by the enemy within that we don't realize that we are in fact in a war to the death.

And we are losing... not only the war, but our country.

We now must define that enemy within, his history, his tactics and his techniques, chief among them being mass manipulation, coupled to physical and psychological acts of terror.

The enemy within now dominates six of the seven M's – Money, Media, Markets, Medical, Mind, Morals. He desperately needs the seventh M – Muscle – embodied in our military and its primary function, to defend the Constitution of the United States of America against all enemies, foreign and domestic.

Without getting wrapped around the flagpole, that Muscle has slowly and systematically been sabotaged, first by the murder of our first Secretary of Defense, James Forrestal (a calculated act of terror similar to the "removals" of Sen Joe McCarthy and Gen George Patton), and then by thrusting that military into UN wars of attrition – no-win wars of both psychological and physical defeat as planned by that amorphous group of self-aggrandizing and self-promoting one-worlders who are slowly, slowly strangling us and our freedom with the binding chains of despotic World Government. And who have done so steadily since the assassination of President McKinley in 1901 by one of Emma Goldman's "Eastern European émigrés." Thus began what many knowledgeable historians call "the Jewish Century."

Let's highlight certain current events that point unalterably and unequivocally to the facts that we are at war and that we are losing.

It is not only the muscle that is atrophying, but the brain and the guts as well: the intestinal fortitude. We will discover the breakdown in our moral and ethical outlook in Chapter 11, which concentrates on brainwashing and mind control. These are tried and true techniques being used by such as Morton Halperin and his colleagues in the Institute for Policy Studies (IPS), to switch the role of our military from the "common defense" of the States to such tasks as "peacekeeping," "nationbuilding" and "humanitarianism." They have envisioned, ever since the founding of the IPS in 1963, that the US military will become surrogate global enforcer of their coming one-world Socialist/Bolshevist government.

Ask yourself a simple question: Is such a blatant act of subversion a part of a larger scenario for eventual world conquest?

INTERLOCKING SUBVERSION IN GOVERNMENT

To put subversion in the proper context of what is happening to us as a nation here and now, let's consider the unanimous Senate confirmation of two appointments made on 22 Jan 1997, namely Madeleine Albright as Secretary of State and William Cohen as Secretary of Defense. One year later (29 Jan 1998), Albright traveled to Paris to convince the French that it was time to bomb the Iraqis back into the stone age...once more, while her cohort in crime, Cohen, addressed Congress – our very own Forum – about the need to pound the peasants of Iraq back into the stone age to prevent their developing "weapons of mass destruction."

Here is an astounding fact: the only country in the Middle East possessing weapons of mass destruction is the tiny theocracy of Israel. Mordechai Vanunu, one-time engineer at Israel's top secret nuclear complex at Dimona, was kidnapped and returned to Israel in 1986 for blowing the whistle to the London *Times* on his government's clandestine nuclear weapons program: he was sentenced to serve 18 years in solitary confinement at Israel's Ashkelon prison. Couple that observation with the fact that the bulk of the reigning elite of the Bolshevik regime presently in power there are "Jews who are not Jews," but descendants of a Turko-Asiatic tribe – the Khazars – who converted *en masse* to Judaism in the seventh century. There is not a drop of Semitic blood in their veins.

Dr. Alfred M. Lilienthal took his stand as a patriotic American when, in 1948, he wrote *Israel's Flag is not Mine*. Since then, he has produced a string of blockbusters, such as *The Zionist Connection*, *The Other Side of the Coin*, and *What Price Israel?*

In a typically hard-hitting article entitled "What Price Holocaustomania?" (*The Washington Report on Middle East Affairs* – April 1998), Dr. Lilienthal points out:

> Even Arabs can be labeled 'anti-Semitic', although they are in fact Semites and do not have to link any claim to the Holy Land to descent from seventh century converts to Judaism, as do the Ashkenazi Jews of Europe from whom half the Israelis and most American Jews, including this writer, are descended.[1]

In that same scholarly piece, Lilienthal also speaks of "America's 'Israel First' approach to the Middle East":

> The simplistic 'Get Saddam' solution to our resulting troubles there flourishes with the help of media-drawn similarities to Hitler and the crying need of opinion molders and politicians to find a new villain, now that the Evil Empire no longer exists.[2]

Lilienthal points out that Iraq "certainly poses no threat to the United States"; yet, it was Secretary of State Madeleine Albright who in January 1998 toured the Arab countries to win support for a US military strike against Baghdad. Lilienthal called her efforts "an abysmal failure."

He stated that the Arabs questioned obvious US double standards "seeking to punish Iraq for having defied one United Nations Security Council resolution while condoning 50 years of innumerable broken UN resolutions by Israel, which also makes no effort to conceal the fact it possesses all three forbidden categories of weapons of mass destruction: nuclear, chemical and biological."[3]

To comprehend fully what is in store for us, not only in the Middle East, but in the Balkans as well, let's look back at a very similar period of history when our nation was purposefully dragged into deadly conflict and internal turmoil during the 1960s – that is, our ever-increasing commitment of men and materiel to the meat-grinder war in Vietnam. We who served at fairly high levels within the Pentagon at the time knew that such a war was unwinnable – and was meant to be – from the beginning.

A book, *The Living and the Dead*, subtitled "Robert McNamara and Five Lives of a Lost War," by Paul Hendrikson, brings this out clearly. In the Epilogue, "Because our Fathers Lied," he writes in part:

> This above all – To thine own self be true. He [McNamara] wasn't. It was his greatest lie. He was motivated to help create rational utopias, and the world disappointed him. Why weren't they more like he was? What he lacked, or lost, was intuition. He was not without American virtues and ideals. But he was terribly ambitious and he was terribly proud and he became sooner than later terribly arrogant.[4]

This author was momentarily puzzled by the title of his epilogue "Because our Fathers Lied." His daughter, Doneva, always knowledgeable, solved it by referring him to the February 1997 issue of *Vanity Fair* and a red-bannered *fin de siecle* [end of an era] piece by Christopher Hitchens titled "Young Men and War." It had to do with the recent discovery of the body of Rudyard Kipling's son, John, in Northern France some 80 years after he died in the Battle of Loos. Having volunteered when the war broke out in 1914, John was rejected because of poor eyesight, but Rudyard used his influence to get the boy a commission in the Irish Guards. He lasted but a few weeks of the murderous trench warfare which in the span of fifty months of *the Great War* butchered at least ten million soldiers of Britain, France, Germany, Russia, Turkey and the United States, to say nothing of civilian losses.

> On the first day of the Battle of the Somme, July 1916, the British alone posted more killed and wounded than appear on the whole of the Vietnam memorial. In the Battle of Verdun, which began the preceding February, 675,000 lives were lost.[5]

Hitchens tells us that after Kipling was informed of his son's death at age 18, his personality as an author underwent a deep change. "At different stages, one can see the influence of parental anguish, of patriotic rage, of chauvinistic hatred, and of personal guilt. A single couplet almost contrives to compress all four emotions into one:

> If any question why we died,
>
> Tell them, because our fathers lied. [6]

Of course, there are lies, damned lies and statistics. It was Stalin who said, "To kill one man is murder, to a kill a million, a statistic." Much earlier, in 400 BC, Sophocles opined: "Truly, to tell lies is not honorable; but when the truth entails tremendous ruin, to speak dishonorably is pardonable." Even Adolf Hitler addressed the subject of lying in *Mein Kampf*: "In the size of the lie there is always contained a certain factor of credibility, since the great masses of the people will more easily fall victims to a great lie than to a small one."[7]

All of these quotes are directly pertinent to the subject at hand. The art of lying which is now practiced on a daily basis not only by our government in Washington, DC, but in all the courts throughout the land, gained credence with "the great masses of the people" here in the United States following the assassination of John F Kennedy in 1963 and in the subsequent *Warren Report,* and the conduct of LBJ's war in Vietnam. This author was a first-hand witness to all those lies and damned lies, as well as the statistics, throughout the 1960s from his vantage point in the Pentagon, where he served as Director, Ground Weapons Systems, under Deputy Secretary of Defense, International Security Affairs (ISA), John McNaughton.[8]

Robert Strange McNamara gave President Johnson (LBJ) a 22-page document "Future Actions in Vietnam," on 19 May 1967. Essentially, the paper said that the US could not win the war and should seek the least unsatisfactory peace.[9]

> The picture of the world's greatest superpower killing 1,000 noncombatants a week, while trying to pound a tiny backward nation into submission on an issue whose merits are hotly disputed, is not a pretty one.[10]

The memo acknowledged that "the enemy has us 'stalemated' and has the capability to tailor his actions to his supplies and manpower...the enemy can – almost certainly will – maintain the military stalemate by matching our added deployments as necessary."[11]

Two months later to the day, 19 July 1967, John McNaughton, his wife and youngest son were killed in a freak air accident when their commercial 727 collided over North Carolina with a twin-engine general aviation aircraft. Unfortunately, he was replaced as head of ISA by Paul Warnke, a member of the Marxist/Leninist IPS. He would bring on board such colleagues as Morton Halperin, Leslie Gelb and Adam Yarmolinsky.

A few days before the 19 May memo, McNaughton sent a short blurb up to McNamara: "a feeling is widely and strongly held (around the country) that the Establishment is out of its mind."[12]

Most of the military types who worked for McNaughton were not reluctant to voice such an opinion – that the Establishment was indeed out of its mind – going way back to 1963, following the murder of JFK and the escalation of troop commitments to another unwinnable land war on the Asian continent.[13]

They were overruled and often overwhelmed by the Harvard and Rhodes scholars who had infiltrated the inner workings of the Establishment, especially the Kennedy entourage, many who lingered on and reinforced "our crowd" of internationalists, Fabian Socialists, fellow-travelers and outright Bolshevists such as the Bundy brothers (William and McGeorge),

Walt Whitman Rostow, Morton Halperin, Paul Nitze, Harold Brown, Paul Ignatius, Alain Enthoven, John Deutch, Phil Goulding, Sol Horowitz, Adam Yarmolinsky, Henry Glass, and the Chairman of the Joint Chiefs, Lyman Lemnitzer. At least 90% of the top echelon was comprised of "Jews who were not Jews" and "Christians who were not Christian." Each was also a member in good standing of the prestigious Council on Foreign Relations (CFR).

Here – 35 years later – are just a few names plucked from the dominant news media during one month in 1998: Albright, Cohen, Berger, Rubin, Glickman, Greenspan, Wolfensohn, Feinstein, Freeh, Barshefsky, Liebermann, Morris, Kantor, Magaziner. During that same month, Steve Grossman, formerly head of America-Israel Public Affairs Committee (AIPAC) became Chairman, Democratic National Committee (DNC), Marvin Rosen became finance chairman of the DNC, and Eli Segal became chief DNC fundraiser. All were members of the CFR.[14]

"We wage war to bring peace." So bragged the inimitable Henry Kissinger in 1971 (when Nixon's National Security Adviser). This Orwellian doublespeak prevails today in our culture-distorting society. We can call it: Bleeding for the Bosnians.

Unfortunately, this disease infected our military leaders during the Vietnam debacle as well. One who saw through it was Colonel David Hackworth, our most decorated veteran of that misbegotten era.

In 1969 Hackworth returned to Vietnam for his third tour. He waged a lonely battle against the Viet Cong in the Mekong Delta, accounting for over 2,700 enemy killed in action (KIA), with a loss of less than 25 of his soldiers in his all-draftee infantry battalion.

Yet, he knew the war was being badly bungled and so informed his bosses, Generals William Westmoreland (CFR) and Harold K Johnson (CFR). They stonewalled him. Later, he would say:

> Why did all these colonels and generals who knew the truth…
> who knew the war was not winnable, that there was no objective, that
> tactics were wrong, why did they keep sending men into a chain saw to
> be ripped apart? Why didn't somebody say, 'enough is enough?'[15]

Unfortunately for our Country, the colonels and generals were not in charge. The Internationalists were, and those selfsame high-ranking officers lacked the guts to do what a few German officers attempted in 1944… to knock off Hitler.

McNamara published "The Essence of Security" on the day he resigned as Secretary of Defense (29 Feb 1968). The journalist, Ward Just, wrote (12 Sep 1968) in the *Washington Post:*

> It is somehow indecent that the man who bestrode the
> enlargement of the war for seven years and was now ensconced in the
> World Bank could cobble together a collection of his speeches and
> statements, call it a book, and barely mention Southeast Asia and what he
> had done there.[16]

Years later, David Halberstam, author of *The Best and the Brightest*, wrote:

> … Robert McNamara, one of the most disturbingly flawed civil
> servants of this era. In truth, McNamara lied and deceived the senate and
> the press and the public. He consistently lied to the nation about the
> levels of increment of troops. But his greatest crime, like that of his
> colleague, McGeorge Bundy, was the crime of silence.[17]

In 1983 McNamara (then 67) appeared on a panel following an NBC TV movie called "The Day After," a drama about a town in Kansas after a nuclear attack. Hendrikson writes: "Of all the panelists – Henry Kissinger, Carl Sagan, Elie Weisel – McNamara seemed to me the most human and humble."[18]

The movie was a total farce and the panel a cross between Dante and Disney…three Jews and a contrite fallen-away Catholic. The theme, of course, was the threat and the promise, right out of the Babylonian Talmud.

McNamara never comprehended that he was being sorely used, just as they had used him from the moment he became the Secretary of Defense in 1961 until he walked away from it in February 1968…the culpable goy. The fact is that such people as McNamara and Dean Rusk, Bill Rogers and Mel Laird, as well as LBJ and Nixon, were subverted by a cohesive group who had burrowed within the government with but one mission in mind; to render ineffective that government and its Constitution – and its military, whose only mission is to defend that Constitution from all enemies foreign and domestic.

Whittaker Chambers in *Witness* aptly describes how these people inveigle themselves into the policy-making apparatus of the government and gradually take over the inner workings, as did Alger Hiss and Harry Dexter White (Weiss).

Chambers' former Communist colleague, Elizabeth Bentley, in 1953 stated in testimony to a special sub-committee of the US Senate on internal security that the espionage agents with whom she had been in contact had been working for the Soviet NKVD (secret service) and that they were "primarily employees of the United States Government stationed in Washington DC." She named individuals within State, Treasury, Defense, the OSS (later CIA) and the Securities and Exchange Commission.[19]

Senator Homer Ferguson asked: "What were your avenues for placing people in strategic positions?"

Miss Bentley:

> I would say that two of our best were Harry Dexter White and Lauchlin Currie. They had an immense amount of influence and knew people and their word would be accepted when they recommended someone.

Ferguson asked her if there were others.

Bentley:

> Yes, I mean whomever we had as an agent in the Government would automatically serve for putting someone else in. For example, Maurice Halperin was head of the Latin American Section in OSS, and we used him to get Helen Tenney in. Once we got one person in he got others, and the whole process continued like that. [20]

In the sub-committee report to the Senate Judiciary Committee, titled "Interlocking Subversion in Government Departments" (30 Jul 1953), such other names were included as

Nathan Silvermaster, William Ulman, George Silverman, Victor Perlo, John Abt, Sol Leshinsky, George Perazich, Harold Glasser, Julius Joseph, Michael Greenberg and Bernard Redmont. The sub-committee stated:

> They (the Communists) used each other's names for reference... They hired each other. They promoted each other. They raised each other's salaries. They transferred each other from Bureau to Bureau, from Congressional committee to Congressional committee. They assigned each other to international committees. They vouched for each other's loyalty and protected each other when exposure threatened.... [21]

The Sub-committee stated that "virtually all were graduates of American universities. Many had doctorates or similar ratings of academic and intellectual distinction...some were teachers."[22]

The identical situation prevails today; only the names have changed. Check your President's close advisers and his Cabinet appointments. Make a list of the key people who are featured in the mainline media "news" for just one week.

These are not the sons of Erin!

PART TWO
THE McNAMARA *MEA CULPA*

THE *Washington Post* ran a semi-adulatory piece on former Secretary of Defense Robert McNamara and his new self-critical memoir, *In Retrospect: The Tragedy and Lessons of Vietnam* (9 Apr 1995). Because this author worked directly for McNamara and his Deputy Secretary of Defense for International Security Affairs (ISA) as the Director for Ground Weapons Systems during those hectic and tragic years, he has a personal and abiding interest, not only in what the *Washington Post* might have to say about it, but in the McNamara "confessions."[22]

Why was McNamara, at age 78, spilling his guts and apparently taking the blame for those misbegotten years of committing our military forces into the bottomless pit of a no-win war on the mainland of China? Let's look more closely at the article for clues. Is he magnanimously taking the blame on his own shoulders for simply carrying out the edicts of the real perpetrators? Or, is he guilt-ridden to the point where he just might don sackcloth and ashes, enter a monastery and do penance for the rest of his life?

Bear in mind that during the early part of the so-called Vietnam War, McNamara constantly questioned our commitment, and finally resigned during the latter part of the Johnson Administration, leaving Secretary of State Dean Rusk and LBJ himself to carry the torch for "Communist containment in Asia." They in turn passed that torch to Nixon and his national security advisor, Henry Kissinger, to pursue the no-win policy for another eight seemingly unending years.

Is McNamara now absolving all those culpable, including our premier traitor, Henry Kissinger?

The *Washington Post* states that McNamara assigns himself "much of the blame for the most tragic international misadventure in this nation's history."[23]

According to McNamara: "The war could and should have been avoided and should have been halted at several key junctures after it started." He states that other senior advisers to LBJ, as well as himself, "failed to head it off through ignorance, inattention, flawed thinking, political expediency and lack of courage."[24]

This just doesn't wash. He is speaking of "the best and the brightest," others who, for whatever reason, were playing a major role and who devoted nearly every waking hour to ever-greater commitments of troops and resources into the Vietnam quagmire. They, such as Paul Warnke, Paul Nitze, Mort Halperin, Adam Yarmolinsky, the Bundy brothers, Walt Whitman Rostow, and Dean Rusk; and such paratroopers and combat troop commanders as Max Taylor, William Westmoreland and Bob Gard, were all members of the Council on Foreign Relations (CFR).

Here is more from that *Post* article. Please sprinkle liberally with salt:

> Even when he and Johnson's other aides knew that their Vietnam strategy had little chance for success, according to McNamara, they pressed ahead with it, ravaging a beautiful country and sending young Americans to their deaths year after year, because they had no other plan.[25]

Let's pause a moment and contemplate this statement, for it continues to represent a gross cover-up. Our role in the area known as French Indochina really began in 1945, as WW II wound down.[26] We were simply following a bloody set of footprints laid down by our first imperial president, Franklin Delano Roosevelt. As these bloody prints wend their way down a rocky road to a global government under a "United Nations," the imperialists (Universalists) needed to establish a global UN army which could – and would – use maximum force and advanced technology to utterly destroy sovereign nations and their military forces. To get there, it became necessary to involve our military in another no-win war on the Asian mainland. Its calculated purpose, as carried out by LBJ and his chief foreign policy duo – Secretary of Defense McNamara and Secretary of State Rusk – was to defeat and humiliate that military.

Perhaps the most difficult factor to comprehend about Bob McNamara – especially for those of us who worked directly for him during those crucial years of our unsavory commitment to another undeclared war on the mainland of China – was his almost overnight conversion from the chief war hawk of the administration to a fluttering peace dove. Some attributed it to the sudden illness of his lovely wife, Margaret, and her subsequent death; others wondered if it was just another act in an ongoing tragedy staged by those who would control the world.

To grasp the significance of all this, we should be aware of another top secret paper prepared by the Hudson Institute in 1963, entitled *Report From Iron Mountain*. It relates directly to the carefully planned and executed no-win war in Vietnam from 1964 to May 1975. Secretary of Defense McNamara commissioned the study. The Hudson Institute, located at the base of Iron Mountain in Croton-on-Hudson, New York, was founded and directed by Herman Kahn, formerly of the Rand Corporation. Like McNamara, he was a member of the CFR. The 15 "fellows" who produced the study – including Henry Kissinger (Heinz Kissingen) – were also members of the CFR.

The overall purpose of that study, as emphasized by G. Edward Griffin, author of *The Creature from Jekyll Island*, "was to analyze different ways a government can perpetuate itself in power, ways to control its citizens and prevent them from rebelling."

The major conclusion of the study, according to Griffin, was that, in the past, war has been the only reliable means to achieve that goal:

> Only during times of war or the threat of war are the masses compliant enough to carry the yoke of government without complaint. Fear of conquest and pillage by an enemy can make almost any burden seem acceptable by comparison. War can be used to arouse human passion and patriotic feelings of loyalty to the nation's leaders. No amount of sacrifice in the name of victory will be rejected. Resistance is viewed as treason. But, in times of peace, people become resentful of high taxes, shortages, and bureaucratic intervention. When they become disrespectful of their leaders, they become dangerous. No government

has long survived without enemies and armed conflict. War, therefore, has been an indispensable condition for 'stabilizing society'.[26]

Griffin then outlines the new definition of "peace," which was embodied in the report. The "fellows" who produced the report predicted a time when it would be possible to create a world government in which all nations will be disarmed and disciplined by a world army, a condition that will be called peace. The report says: "The word peace, as we have used it in the following pages... implies total and general disarmament."

Griffin, who published his work in 1994, accurately predicted the events that have taken place, and are currently taking place, in smaller sovereign states about the world:

> Under that scenario, independent nations will no longer exist and governments will not have the capability to wage war. There could be military action by the world army against renegade political subdivisions, but these would be called peacekeepers. No matter how much property is destroyed or how much blood is spilled, the bullets will be 'peaceful' bullets and the bombs – even the atomic bomb, if necessary – will be 'peaceful' bombs.[27]

The study was eventually published in 1967, under the title, *Report from Iron Mountain on the Possibility and Desirability of Peace.* The participants considered whether there could ever be a suitable substitute for war. They concluded that there can be no substitute for war unless it possesses three properties: It must: (1) be economically wasteful, (2) represent a credible threat of great magnitude, and (3) provide a logical excuse for compulsory service to the government.[28]

The study examined "the time-honored use of military institutions to provide anti-social elements with an acceptable role in the social structure... the incorrigible subversives, and the rest of the unemployable are seen as somehow transformed by the disciplines of a service modeled on military precedent into more or less dedicated social service workers... Another possible surrogate for the control of potential enemies of society is the reintroduction, in some form consistent with modern technology and political processes, of slavery...the logical first step would be the adoption of some form of 'universal' military service."[29]

The study also emphasizes that if a suitable substitute for war is to be found, a new enemy must be discovered that threatens the entire world:

> Allegiance requires a cause; a cause requires an enemy...the enemy that defines the cause must seem genuinely formidable...that power must be one of unprecedented magnitude and frightfulness.[30]

The final candidate for a useful global threat was pollution of the environment, according to Griffin. "It might even be necessary to deliberately poison the environment to make the predictions seem more convincing. In this fashion, it would be possible to focus the public mind on fighting a new enemy, more fearful and cruel than any invader from another nation – or even from outer space."[31]

The study stresses that truth is not important in defining a substitute for war; it's what people can be made to believe that counts. "Credibility" is the key, not reality. This is perhaps the key to understanding the seeming dichotomy of a man such as Bob McNamara. After all, he did not don sackcloth and ashes after his mea culpa regarding the Vietnam War. Instead, he was offered – and eagerly accepted – the presidency of the World Bank following his resignation as Secretary of Defense.

Perhaps most telling about the man and his internationalist associates is a speech made by David Rockefeller, founder and director of the World Bank, at the farewell dinner for McNamara when he stepped down from that exalted position:

> The world that we have worked to construct is threatened. The gravity of this moment, when Mr. McNamara and others are about to leave their posts while a new administration re-examines American foreign aid policy, is great. If we are going to save the international institutions we have put in place, the moment is now or never, for the struggle between the old guard and the new is going to go far beyond the reduction of capital appropriations. It is going to endanger the new world order which we have based on the alliance between Wall Street and Washington. While we men of firms and banks organize international channels of economy and raw materials, the government is now building its own diplomatic and economic bridges between Washington and foreign governments. By our methods, our governments contribute to the stability and economic growth of the world, our multinationals benefit,

and when it is necessary, they contribute their political support. Now radical conservatives are attempting to destroy all that in seeking first and foremost to serve the national interests of the United States.[32]

All of these seeming contradictions and dichotomies relate directly to the carefully planned and executed no-win war in Vietnam from 1964 to 1975. It was all a set piece. They had no other plan because they didn't need another plan. It is as simple as that.

WHAT WAS THE MILITARY OBJECTIVE?

This fact is better explained in the writings of L. Fletcher Prouty, Colonel, USAF (Ret). A pilot in Africa and the Middle East during World War II, Prouty would later become the chief liaison between the Defense Department and the CIA. He was the real-life role model for the character of Mr. X in the Oliver Stone film *JFK*. Prouty reveals the real story behind McNamara's "Book of Confession" in an article carried in *The Barnes Review* (Dec 1995) and a later issue (May 1996) in which he discloses the fatal connection between "The Military-Industrial Complex and the Gulf of Tonkin Resolution."[33]

Prouty states that, as taught in the war colleges, the most important of the nine classic principles of war is the "military objective." If the commander-in-chief has no positive attainable military objective, no victory can be achieved. This was evident from the start of the fracas in Vietnam, and was the driving reason behind JFK's decision to get our troops out. What we see unfolding in Kosovo, Serbia, today, under the sorry misdirection of Bill Clinton, is a repeat of this sad scenario. To echo Col Hackworth's succinct question: "Why didn't the generals say 'enough is enough'?"

Nowhere is this more in evidence than in a column by another retired colonel, Harry Summers, featured in the *Washington Times* (28 Apr 1999):

> The ongoing debacle in the Balkans begs the question: 'How could Gen Shelton and the Joint Chiefs of Staff, and Gen Wesley Clark, the NATO commander, be party to this obviously unplanned,

uncoordinated and unfocused fiasco? ... In so doing, they have done neither their soldiers, their country, nor their president any favor by their failure to speak up...[34]

There is no better evidence that we violated (on purpose) that cardinal principle of war than that contained in Clark Clifford's remarkable book *Counsel to the President* wherein, as Secretary of Defense, Clifford met with the then President Lyndon B. Johnson, Secretary of State Dean Rusk, the military advisor to the president, Walt Rostow, and the Chairman of the Joint Chiefs, Earle Wheeler, on 21 May 1968. Clifford told the illustrious assemblage:

> With the limitations placed on our military – no invasion of the north, no mining of the harbors, no invasion of the sanctuaries – we have no plans or chance to win the war.[35]

As Prouty states in his article:

> Clifford, a most experienced man in the ways of Washington, as well as the Secretary of Defense, had to ask the president, the commander-in-chief, what the military objective of our presence in Vietnam was. Lyndon Johnson gave him no substantive reply.[36]

That particular trail of deceit wends it way back to a most important document issued by President Kennedy on 11 Oct 1963, the National Security Action Memorandum (NASM) #263. In this document – virtually ignored by McNamara in his book – are "Conclusions and Recommendations" which state that the military campaign in the Northern and Central Areas should be complete by the end of 1964, and in the Delta by the end of 1965, when "the essential functions performed by US military personnel can be carried out by Vietnamese... It should be possible to withdraw the bulk of US personnel by that time."[37]

Alas, there were other forces at play, best described by Prouty with a quote from the renowned book by Alexis de Tocqueville, *Democracy in America* (1835) in which war is predicted:

> The inevitable growth of democracy [will] also lead to despotism and militarism. While peace is peculiarly hurtful to democratic armies, war and all its popular passions gives them advantages which cannot fail in the end to give them victory.[38]

De Tocqueville clarified this point with a statement that is most pertinent to any definition of "modern" war. It was not only the driving force behind the Vietnam War, but is most applicable today with the United States government (now an Imperium) actions in several staged "hot spots" about the globe, particularly in the Middle East and in the Balkans. Here is de Tocqueville:

> The secret connection between the military character and that of the democracies was the profit motive. [39]

In his subsequent article on the contrived "Gulf of Tonkin Resolution," Col. Prouty enlarged on this aspect, stating:

> The case of Vietnam serves as a textbook example of the manner in which wars are manufactured. Beyond the question of how – or whether – the US should have fought the war, other questions of great national import are involved. Insider manipulations at the highest levels ensured the conflict's escalation into a protracted, extremely costly venture in terms of both blood and treasure. As brave young Americans died by the tens of thousands, well-connected politicians, financiers and industrialists made fortunes, while their own sons stayed home, safely ensconced in institutions of higher learning.[40]

Prouty points out that at the time of JFK's assassination there were less than 16,000 military personnel in Vietnam, "of whom fewer than 2,000 were military advisors; an involvement that had begun with a series of CIA-controlled covert operations."[41]

NSAM #263, which Kennedy published just prior to his death, stipulated, among other things, that 1,000 servicemen would be brought home by Christmas and that all US personnel (not limited to military personnel) would be out of Vietnam by the end of 1965.[42]

So, what happened? Prouty states:

> [T]hey wanted him out of the way, because they felt that he would be re-elected in 1964, and would then be in a position to carry out his NSAM #263 policy. So the president's murder was ordered to be done by a professional 'hit team'. This was also LBJ's conclusion as expressed shortly before his death in an interview published in the 19 Jul 1973 issue of *Atlantic Monthly*.[43]

President Johnson completely reversed the Kennedy policy less than four months after assuming office. On 16 Mar 1964, LBJ signed NSAM # 288 that stated:

> We seek an independent non-Communist South Vietnam.... Unless we can achieve this objective in South Vietnam, almost all of Southeast Asia will probably fall under Communist dominance. Thus, purely in terms of foreign policy, the stakes are high.[44]

How high? Prouty states that the usual "all up" figure given for the cost of the Vietnam War is $570 billion.[45]

In retrospect, McNamara admits that had that war never been fought, Communism would have prevailed in Asia, and the international strategic position of the United States would be no worse than it is today. That is a true statement, and today we are paying the price in spades for losing not only the Vietnam War, but our country.

McNamara tells us that he has grown sick at heart witnessing the cynicism and even contempt with which so many people view our political institutions and leaders. Let's not immediately acknowledge this calculated "sympathy factor" until we look at other "political institutions and leaders." McNamara did not bring about the Vietnam holocaust all by himself.

There is a truism, the Peter Principle, that if you stay long enough (in either military or civil service), you will eventually be promoted to a level beyond your competence. This is especially true within the bureaucracy of the United Nations.

The unalterable fact is that the formation of a United Nations, and the League of Nations before that, was instigated by a very powerful political alignment between International Zionism and Fabian Socialism with the stated purpose of forming a one-world government under a "League of the Just" (which had commissioned the *Communist Manifesto*) and to create an all-powerful military force under that government for "peacekeeping."

All of this leads to the conclusion that little has changed since the issuance of the 1953 Senate Internal Security report

"Interlocking Subversions in Government Departments." That report concluded:

> There is a mass of evidence and information on the hidden Communist conspiracy in Government that is inaccessible to the FBI and to this subcommittee because persons who know the facts of the conspiracy are not cooperating with the security authorities of the country.[46]

Alas, since that time, these very same "security authorities" have been badly subverted as well, not only the FBI and the CIA, but the jack-booted thugs in the Bureau of Alcohol, Tobacco and Firearms (BATF) which has become the willing and criminally culpable handmaiden of the Israeli Mossad and British intelligence.

"LOSING THE WAR"

This is the title of a hard-hitting article in the February 1997 *American Spectator* by Tom Bethell which blasts complacent conservatives who, according to Bethell, are blind to the evil forces in our midst. He says:

> Most conservatives – by which I mean normal people – have little conception of the aggressive and revolutionary force that confronts them. It is a revolutionary force, in the sense that it seeks to overturn the existing order, but it differs from the spirit of Marx and Lenin in that it never proclaims itself openly.[47]

Here in the US, Bethell tells us, "most people don't understand that they are in a war" and "normal Americans who do sense the conflict shrink from the fight." Why is this? He outlines some interesting reflections contained in an issue of *Heterodoxy*.

> They note the unwillingness of most conservatives to play offense. The left is constantly the aggressive force. Confronted with the threat of this fury, the conservative instinct is to retreat, to back off, to retire into the gated community, into private life, to withdraw from the public school and to teach children at home, to retreat to the rural eyrie. They want to be left alone and most would gladly settle for that.[48]

Bethell points to the remote mountain top of Ruby Ridge, Idaho, whereon the Weaver family was pursued and gunned down by federal agents, as being a better symbol of the war we are in than is Oklahoma City. "They want to leave us no place to hide."[49]

Where is the counter-reformation? Where are the leaders who will be needed to launch a counteroffensive? Think of Bush and Dole and weep...[50]

How can we win this war we are in – and are surely losing, just as we lost the war in Vietnam – when so many of our would-be warriors shun the fight? Let's go back to the guidance of the warfare experts, such as Claustwitz, Tsun Tsu, and, yes, even Thomas Aquinas; first we must define the enemy, then marshal our forces, go on the offensive and overwhelm him in the cultural arena and on the political battlements.

"WHY DID WE LOSE?"

In a gut-grabbing commentary (*Washington Times* 30 May 1999), B. K. Eakman asks that question, then pointedly answers it:

We lost because we failed to apply the strategic lessons of warfare to the attack on our culture. We lost because we gave away the psychological environment. We spent 30 years playing by our opponents' rules of engagement instead of forcing them to play by ours.[51]

In his exceptionally revealing book, *Cloning of the American Mind*, Eakman also asks the question: "How did we lose?"

We lost by basing our strategy on wishful thinking instead of the realities of war, by allowing turf battles to split our alliances, by treating our allies like competition instead of welcoming them as friends. If we are to save our way of life in the coming century, individuals of principle will have to don the mentality of the resistance fighter. We no longer have the luxury of time for righteous indignation.[52]

In sum, we have two choices: we can surrender unconditionally to the enemy within; or we can fight. There are no other choices, and time is fast running out. If we choose the latter, we had best unsheath our swords and join Horatius at the bridge.

DWIGHT DAVID EISENHOWER

ABILENE, KANSAS

Senatorial Appointee, Kansas
"Ike"

Corporal, Sergeant, Color Sergeant; A.B.,
B.A., Sharpshooter; Football Squad (3, 2),
"A" in Football; Baseball Squad (4); Cheer
Leader; Indoor Meet (4, 3).

*"Now, fellers, it's just like this. I've been asked
to say a few words this evening about this business.
Now, me and Walter Camp, we think—"*
—*Himself*

THIS is Señor Dwight David Eisenhower, gentlemen, the terrible Swedish-Jew,
as big as life and twice as natural. He claims to have the best authority for
the statement that he is the handsomest man in the Corps and is ready to
back up his claim at any time. At any rate you'll have to give it to him that he's
well-developed abdominally—and more graceful in pushing it around than Charles
Calvert Benedict. In common with most fat men, he is an enthusiastic and
sonorous devotee of the King of Indoor Sports, and roars homage at the shrine of
Morpheus on every possible occasion.

However, the memory of man runneth back to the
time when the little Dwight was but a slender lad of
some 'steen years, full of joy and energy and craving
for life and movement and change. 'Twas then that
the romantic appeal of West Point's glamour grabbed
him by the scruff of the neck and dragged him to his
doom. Three weeks of Beast gave him his fill of life
and movement and as all the change was locked up at
the Cadet Store out of reach, poor Dwight merely
consents to exist until graduation shall set him free.

At one time he threatened to get interested in life
and won his "A" by being the most promising back in
Eastern football—but the Tufts game broke his knee
and the promise. Now Ike must content himself with
tea, tiddledywinks and talk, at all of which he excels.
Said prodigy will now lead us in a long, loud yell for—
Dare Devil Dwight, the Dauntless Don.

DWIGHT DAVID EISENHOWER
"The Terrible Swedish-Jew"
The Howitzer Westpoint Yearbook
1915

CHAPTER II

SHOWDOWN AT HIGH NOON
(Selecting a Military Traitor)

United by the strongest bonds of organization, always in closest and quickest touch with one another, situated in the very heart of every business capital of every State, controlled by men of a single and peculiar race, they are in a unique position to manipulate the policy of nations.

J. A. Hobson in *Imperialism: A Study* (1902)

PART ONE
MONEY - MEDIA MONOPOLY

IN blatant violation of Article 1, section 8 of the Constitution of the United States, the Congress of the United States adopted the Federal Reserve Act (HR 7837) on 23 Dec 1913, thereby transferring the power to borrow money on the credit of the United States, and the power to coin money and regulate the value thereof, from the Congress to a cartel of international bankers.

By this illegal act, the financial destiny of America was removed from the control of its citizens to that of a coterie of arch-criminals who have assumed total control of the nation's financial system.

In a previous chapter we discussed the need to control the seven levers of power in order to take over a country and its peoples. When any group for whatever reason grabs for these seven levers of power they actually commit an act of political warfare. In later chapters, we will see how the Bolsheviks practiced the art of grabbing and centralizing all power, not only in Russia in 1917, but especially in the United States in 1933.

In order to assume total control, these "gangster-statesmen" must create monopolies. Those of you who have played Parker Brothers' famous game of *Monopoly* understand that the driving force behind it is the accumulation of money in order to purchase properties, then to construct houses and hotels, until the winner ends up not only with all the play money, but all the properties as well. It's a fun kind of game to while away a quiet evening at home by the fireside, and whether you win or lose you can retire to a warm bed and a satisfying sleep.

To understand how the game of Monopoly is played in real life, one must understand the Money Power and how it plays the game. This tightly knit group is an international network whose sole goal is gain. These international financiers know how to play *Monopoly*, for they wrote the rules, and even now, make periodic adjustments to those rules, always to their collective benefit.

The monopolists are driven by their innate need to accumulate and dominate. They seek to monopolize trade by instituting "free trade" – first of goods, then of money – represented by the trading in stocks and bonds, as well as the selling of money at usury.

This group recognizes that to create a monopoly, they must first buy and control a triad of organizations:

1) The governing power, whether prince or president, a political coalition or party, as well as all the visible power brokers, the law-makers, the law interpreters and related bureaucracies.

2) The media, including the whole spectrum of means to manipulate the minds of the masses...press, periodicals, radio, TV, movies....

3) The money market, including a stock exchange, a commodities market, and a central bank, used not only to print the currency, but also to set its value and control its distribution.

With the help of Professor Carroll Quigley and his voluminous 1966 epic, *Tragedy and Hope: A History of the World in Our Time,* we will look first of all to France, for as that once-great country rose and fell by the machinations of the money changers, so are doing these once great United States (currently well on the way to the financial and fiscal bottom).

Quigley calls it financial capitalism. While we should be leery of statistics, they do have a place. He outlines the statistics on the issuance of fraudulent securities during the 1850s in France. There, the excesses perpetrated by the Money Power were worse than in Britain or Germany, "although they were not to be compared with the excesses of frenzy and fraud displayed in the United States."[1]

Quigley reveals that between 1854-55 a total of 457 new companies, with a combined capital of one billion francs, were formed in France. By early 1856 the losses to security buyers were so great that the government had to prohibit temporarily any further issues.

WHY FRANCE FELL

Gross thievery and systematic monetary and market manipulation were the real causes of the fall of France in 1940.

In a period of 30 years – from 1899 to 1929 – over 300 billion francs were stolen by the Money Power from the French people by manipulation of worthless securities. The identical ploy is currently being used against the US people by issuance of junk bonds and the overvaluation of stocks, along with wild manipulations of commodity prices.

Quigley explains how it was done to the French. During that period of what he calls financial capitalism, approximately 40 families owned the ten largest private banks that, in turn, controlled the central bank of France.

Two banks dominated; one Jewish, the Banque de Paris et des Pays Bas (Paribas), controlled by the Rothschilds and their cousins, Rene Mayer and Horace Finaly; and the Union Parisienne, founded by a non-Jewish bloc in 1901.[2]

Within this banking brotherhood, these two giants cooperated in matters monetary; however, as their influence spread into the commercial/industrial fields, competition was severe, which led during the period 1932-40 to a death struggle for pre-eminent power. It was also one of the leading causes of the planned conflagration known as World War II.

The Jewish group went after shipbuilding, communications, transportation, public utilities; the non-Jewish group emphasized iron, steel and armaments.

Here we get a glimpse of the embryo of what became the "Bicephalous Monster" in our own society – one head Anglo-American, the other Jewish.

Picture the early rivalry of the two groups as they went after worldwide control of petroleum products. Basically, Paribas (Rothschild) allied itself with Standard Oil (Rockefeller), while Union Parisienne (Union Comité) controlled Royal Dutch Shell.[3]

The oil combine today, under the Bicephalous Monster, is known as the "Seven Sisters." They control oil production worldwide, and brought about the Yom Kippur war in October 1973, with the consequent and planned skyrocketing price of crude. This put the squeeze on Japan and Western Europe, especially, and brought about hyperinflation and runaway interest rates in the United States under Carter and his "boss," Paul Volcker.

It is highly important to recognize at this time that during the first half of the twentieth century, the international (Jewish) cabal gradually took over control from their "allies," the Anglo-Saxon, Freemasonic Money Power, and subverted finance from constructive projects – industrial development – to destructive ones – war making. This was a continuation of nihilism (nothing can be known, for nothing exists); of bloody revolution as practiced against the Russians by the Zionists, with the aim of completely destroying existing institutions.

Warning! This philosophy is still alive and well! To date, with the exception of the inner cities, it is non-bloody here in the

US. This could undergo a radical shift following the year 2000, to coincide with a major market crash.

In France (and later, in the United States) the two blocs vied for control of government in such arenas as director of finance, and governor of the Bank of France. In order to monopolize control over labor, they fought for control of the various trade associations.

In similar moves, using intermarriage and integration by family alliances, along with interlocking directorates, the blocs gained control of the coalfields and railroading. In this latter area, the Rothschild railroad monopoly extended into the US, where the Harrimans were brought into the fold.

Here is another statistic, just to give us order of magnitude. In 1936 there were about 800 firms of any import in France, most of them registered on the Paris stock exchange. Paribas controlled 400, while Union-Comite dominated 300.[4]

Paribas gained absolute control over communications, which included the media. Quigley explains that:

> Havas was a great monopolistic news agency, as well as the most important advertising agency in France. It could, and did, suppress or spread both news and advertising. It usually supplied news reports gratis to those papers that would print the advertising copy it also provided. It received secret subsidies from the government for almost a century (a fact first revealed by Balzac) and by late 1930 these subsidies from the secret funds of the Popular Front had reached a fantastic size.
>
> Hachette had a monopoly on the distribution of periodicals and a sizable portion of the distribution of books. This monopoly could be used to kill papers that were regarded as objectionable. This was done in the 1930s to Francis Coty's reactionary *L'Ami du Peuple*.[5]

Without getting deeply mired in the politics of the times which led to World War II and the rapid defeat of France as a viable power, we must take a look at Paribas (Rothschild) and its support of the leftist Popular Front, particularly of Rothschild money being funneled into Soviet Russia (Jewish-controlled from the top down, from 1917 to date) and to the Loyalists – that is to say, the Bolshevists – in Spain.

The Rothschilds were not alone in their financial support of Bolshevism and subsequently Communism under the Third International; such Money Powers as the Warburgs of Germany and the US, as well as the Schiffs, fed millions of marks and dollars into the coffers of the collectivists.

William Shirer, a foreign correspondent who lived in France and Germany during World War II and the prior years of the 1930s – and who leans left, as opposed to what he frequently calls the Radical Right – gives us remarkable insights into the collapse of the Third Republic (an inquiry into the fall of France in 1940), as well as the rise and fall of the Third Reich.

In the foreword, he talks of how all the savagery came about; he dumps it into the lap of Christianity, which is as good a scapegoat as any. We still have active elements of this school in the US. If nihilism is to prevail – and at this writing, it appears that it will – Christianity must be destroyed. Shirer says:

> I wrote of the rise and fall of Nazi Germany and how it came that a cultured Christian people lapsed into barbarism in the midst of the 20th century, gladly abandoning their freedoms and the ordinary decencies of human life and remaining strangely indifferent to the savagery with which they treated other nations, other races. [6]

He quotes the famous French poet-diplomat Paul Claudel, who once observed, "It is not enough to know the past, it is necessary to understand it."

DE-CHRISTIANIZING FRANCE

It was Exalted French Grand Orient (Masonic) Potentate Leon Blum, Zionist and one of the principal architects of the Popular Front coalition, who emerged as premier after the 1936 elections, which saw the Socialists and Communists win a strong majority in the Chamber of Deputies.

Thus, we set the stage for what Quigley calls the fantastic size of the secret funds that the Popular Front poured into Havas, the great monopolistic news agency that could and did manipulate and suppress the "news." This, coupled with the driving need of the Rothschilds and their various cousins to form an alliance with

Soviet Russia and support the Communists in the Spanish Civil War, brought about the deep divisiveness in France which led to early defeat in 1940.[7]

Let's leap back quickly to the beginnings of the Third Republic in 1872, where we see the concerted effort to de-Christianize France (a practice currently ongoing in the US).

Led by a coalition of Socialists and Radical Republicans in Parliament, a well-organized effort to destroy the influence of the Catholic Church was launched. The first target was education, administered mainly by the Church.

Jules Ferry began the persecution in 1880s, by introducing a series of legislative enactments that prohibited religious education in the public schools (do you see any parallels?). Members of religious orders were banned from teaching in the public schools. At that time, half the boys and nearly all the girls attended parochial schools. One wonders whether they taught *les innocents* such subjects as sex education and secular humanism.

In most of the villages the only schools were Catholic, and in the few public schools most of the teachers were nuns, monks or priests. At this time, Ferry cut off all public funds to the parochial schools.[8]

In 1901 the Association Act, which was designed to curb the influence of the religious orders, was passed. This was aimed especially at the Assumptionists, an articulate and vocal anti-republican religious group. Waldeck-Rosseau, the Premier, did not wish to attack the religious orders, but was overridden by the coalition. He resigned and was replaced by "a man of a different stripe," Emile Combes, a fanatical radical.[9]

Combes was a fallen-away Catholic who had once studied for the priesthood. Three weeks into office, he shut down all primary schools for girls run by the religious sisters. A month later, he gave the 3,000 parochial schools eight days to shut down for good.

He then tackled what he considered the main enemy, the congregations or religious orders. With a stroke of the pen, he dissolved all 54 of them. Some 20,000 monks, brothers and priests fled France for other countries.

The curtain was coming down on Christianity in France. Hostility against Christianity was the order of the day. (We see the same sort of virulent hatred expressed openly and covertly in the US today.) Shirer wrote: "Freemasonry helped to keep the fires burning."[10]

In an effort to wipe out Catholic influence in the army, the Republican Minister of War, General Andre, enlisted the aid of the Masonic lodges to weed out all Catholics from the officer corps.

"In many ways the army proved more difficult to deal with than the Church," says Shirer. "The great military chiefs, with scarcely an exception, were Catholic and Royalist. To expel all of them would have weakened the army fatally."[11]

And so, in France, the way was paved for the fall. First, by destroying the absolutes, along with the influence of the Church, then fostering the rise of the new religion – secular humanism – part and parcel of the new majority in Parliament, the Socialists.

From all this emerged, as planned, "the war to end all wars," the first war to make the world safe for democracy, followed by the also-planned and brilliantly-executed market manipulations leading to the Great Crash of 1929, and the depression which destroyed the middle class of several countries, not the least France.

From this agglomeration sprang the two socialist totalitarian dictators, once partners, Adolf Hitler and Josef Stalin, whose rise to power was financed by the same oligarchical *hofjudean* families, especially those in the United States and Germany. Of course, Stalin (Steel) also robbed banks.

And simultaneously came the rise to supremacy in the world financial markets of the international Zionist oligarchy, the now-dominant head of the Bicephalous Monster – the destructive head.

These events led naturally to the second war to make the world safe for democracy, which not only brought about the heinous butchery of civilians as well as soldiers, but the massive and heretofore unimaginable destruction of entire cities.

It also brought about the "New Order," the entrenchment of Bolshevism, then spreading like a cancer from Soviet Russia throughout the world.

Why? Initially for the bottom line – the pure profit motive, but then, shifting gradually and inexorably to the insatiable thirst for power – absolute despotic control. The first defined "master race" in recorded history referred to the Chosen Few, who will reign supreme as Lords of the World. And all the rest, the goyim, or cattle, will be enslaved. It's in the book!

The inviolable formula remains constant: Knowledge equals Wealth equals Power.

And what of the other head, that of Anglo-American Establishment elitism? The constructive head still clings tenaciously to the mistaken hypothesis that they will share in the new world order with the Money Power.

MONOPOLY CONTROL OF THE MEDIA

We must address an endemic problem that aided the fall of France in 1940 and even now threatens the United States. The very forces that have controlled the "evil empire" since its capture by them in 1917 are also the power behind the throne here in the United States, as well as in Britain, Canada and Israel.

For the most part this powerful cabal is anonymous and its collective face is more often than not hidden from the general public, that is to say, kept out of the media. In order to do this successfully, year in and year out, this cabal must also control all facets of the media.

The Rothschild-controlled firms of Havas and Hachette held absolute sway over newspaper publication, books, periodicals and radio. They also controlled the government Office of Communications, thereby assuring a monopoly, for it is a truism that without government intervention and/or support there can be no monopoly in anything.

The medium of control was generally the doling out of advertising. To go up against the system by developing an "independent" editorial policy, or to refuse to carry their gratis "news" service, was to invite failure by having the highly lucrative advertising sources cut off.

It is important to recognize the ties between and among the Money Power, the politicians and the collective media. They are the legs of a tripod supporting the State. It is a three-pronged back scratcher, for the State can guarantee perpetuation of the monopoly, and the Money Power, together with the media moguls, can guarantee perpetuation of government policies, both foreign and domestic, regardless of the party in power.

In the case of a democracy, such as we are purported to be, and in the case of a republic which we once were – and as France was before the onset of World War II – it becomes doubly important to control the media, for by the manipulation of the written and spoken word, one can win, if not the hearts and minds, at least the votes of the citizens of any given country.

Of course, in a true totalitarian state, the governing force doesn't have to concern itself with influencing 51% of the voters; and yet, there too, for obvious reasons of control and prevention of uprisings, there must exist both media control and media manipulation, as well as a curb or check-rein on the military.

PART TWO
HAS OUR MILITARY BETRAYED US?

ONE can look back through history and discover several instances where the military forces of a country caved in and the country was ultimately destroyed from within. This was especially true of Rome where the military leaders lost their pride and honor, succumbed to bribery, and left the defense of its empire to *Barbarians* who had been allowed inside the gates.

We need only go back to 1917, when Russia was invaded by alien hordes, albeit small in numbers. Prof. Quigley explained this anomaly in his epic work *Tragedy and Hope*. Two passages are especially pertinent, for it depicts what is currently happening to our own military:

> The Bolsheviks had no illusions about their position in Russia at the end of 1917. They knew that they had formed an infinitesimal group in that vast country and that they had been able to seize power because they were a decisive and ruthless minority among a great mass of persons who had been neutralized by propaganda...
>
> In the course of this chaos and tragedy (famine 1921-22) the Bolshevik regime was able to survive, to crush counterrevolutionary movements, and to eliminate foreign interventionists. They were able to do this because their opponents were divided, indecisive, or neutralized, while they were vigorous, decisive, and completely ruthless. The chief source of Bolshevik strength were to be found in the Red Army and the secret police, the neutrality of the peasants, and the support of the proletariat workers in industry and transportation. The secret police (*Cheka*) was made up of fanatical and ruthless Communists who systematically murdered all real or potential opponents. The Red Army (under Trotsky) was recruited from the old czarist army but was rewarded by high pay and favorable food rations. Although the economic system collapsed almost completely, and the peasants refused to supply, or even produce food for the city population, the Bolsheviks established a system of food requisitions from the peasants and distributed this food by a rationing system that rewarded their supporters...[12]

SELECTING A MILITARY TRAITOR

To bring into sharp focus the current spider-web of intrigue, corruption and criminal betrayal of our country and its Constitution at the highest pinnacle of government under the Clintonistas, let's skip back in time and place to Seattle, Washington, to the Olympic Hotel, and to a special dinner arranged by the hotel owner for a group of military officers from nearby Fort Lewis in the fall of 1940.

The honored guests from the East were John and Anna Boettiger; she the only daughter of Franklin and Eleanor Roosevelt, who had been previously married to Curtis Dall (who would later found Liberty Lobby). Among the officers from the 3d Infantry Division at Fort Lewis was a lieutenant colonel from the 15th Infantry Regiment, Dwight David Eisenhower.

During the evening, Lt Col Eisenhower monopolized the attentions of Anna Roosevelt Boettiger. Observers, overhearing much of the conversation, emphasized that Eisenhower constantly sang the fulsome praise of her father, how wonderful he was, how great.

> Early the next morning Anna was on the telephone to her father in Washington. "I've found the man," she said. And she proceeded to tell the abnormally vain FDR what a hero-worshipper of his, and what a genius, she had discovered in an army uniform. Within days – although the incident is completely and understandably ignored in Ike's own account of this period in his ghostwritten autobiography, *Crusade in Europe* – Lt Col Eisenhower was ordered to Washington for an interview in the White House.[13]

And then the meteoric rise of the man through the ranks, which led John Gunther to observe in his 1951 book, *Eisenhower: The Man & the Symbol*, "There is no record quite like this (Ike's rise in rank) in the American Army."[14]

It is there, for all to see in the first few pages of *Crusade in Europe*. Back from the Washington interview, Ike was made chief of staff of the 3d Infantry Division (Dec 1940), and in March 1941 he was promoted to colonel and became chief of staff of the entire IX Army Corps. In June he was made chief of staff of the Third

United States Army with headquarters at Fort Sam Houston in San Antonio where he oversaw army maneuvers at a ranch south of Monterey, California. By September 1941, he supervised the maneuvers at Camp Polk, Louisiana and was duly promoted to brigadier general.[15]

General George Catlett Marshall, chief of staff of the United States Army, pulled the new brigadier general into Washington, DC on 14 Dec 1941, where, by 16 Feb 1942, he was made assistant chief of staff of the War Plans Division. On 9 Mar 1942, he became the first head of the Operations Division of the War Department, and was promoted to major general. On 11 Jun 1942, he was given command of the European Theatre of Operations, and soon, in London, he fell into the habit of having luncheon with Winston Churchill at 10 Downing Street every Tuesday and dinner with Churchill at the latter's home every Thursday.[16]

In July 1942, Ike was awarded the three stars of a lieutenant general. Seven months later on 11 Feb 1943, less than two years from the time he had still been a lieutenant colonel, Eisenhower became a full general.[17]

Ten months later, although he had never seen a battle, General Eisenhower was made commander in chief of all the Allied forces in Western Europe.[18]

Ike was foreordained in that position as supreme commander to assist the Soviets in their advance into Western Europe, to the detriment of the United States, and to the further glorification of one-world bolshevism as personified by FDR in the United States and his bosom Bolshevik, Josef Stalin, in Soviet Russia. These two traitors, jointly and severally, provided Ike with his guidance for the sell-out of Western Europe to the so-called Communists, who were, in fact, Zionist Bolsheviks.

From the past, one case can suffice, if only to set the pattern for the ongoing sellout of our country and its Constitution by Bill Clinton as commander-in-chief and his immediate subordinates. A news clip taken from the *Boston Herald* (17 Jul 1970), is highly pertinent:

> WASHINGTON (UPI) - Allied military documents made public last week show Gen Dwight D. Eisenhower alone made the decision that allowed Soviet armies to reach Berlin first during World War II.
>
> New light was thrown on the decision made in 1945 by the release of Anglo-American chiefs of staff documents, which had been classified top secret for 25 years.
>
> Among the documents were cables from Eisenhower, the supreme Allied commander in Europe, to Washington and to Soviet Premier Josef Stalin which indicated Eisenhower felt Berlin was not an important military target.
>
> Stalin, in one exchange of documents, said he agreed with Eisenhower that Berlin had lost its strategic importance. He said his high command intended to allow only 'secondary forces in the direction of Berlin'. Allied forces were halted at the Elbe River and the Red Army took Berlin May 2, 1945. The German high command surrendered six days later. A similar decision was made with respect to Prague, the capital of Czechoslovakia.
>
> Eisenhower in both instances was fully backed by the US chiefs of staff and former President Harry S Truman. British Prime Minister Winston S. Churchill and his chief military advisers objected.
>
> Nikita Khrushchev (Perlmutter), in purported memoirs published earlier this month in the United States, quoted Stalin as praising Eisenhower's 'decency, generosity and chivalry' in the decision on Berlin. Stalin said that 'if it hadn't been for Eisenhower, we wouldn't have succeeded in capturing Berlin.'
>
> The Memoirs said that if Eisenhower had not held back as Germany's Western front crumbled, 'the question of Germany might have been decided differently and our position might have turned out a bit worse.'[19]

Many observers have held since World War II that the decision on Berlin had been a political one, possibly made months before. The chiefs-of-staff documents appear to dispute this.

As early as 1951 when the leading journalist of Britain, if not the world, Douglas Reed, was penning *Far and Wide*, he stressed:

> It fell to Gen Eisenhower to obey orders to make the Anglo-American advance in Europe, in 1944-45, conform with the Soviet

advance from the east, so that in the end Communism swallowed half of Europe. The Anglo-American military commanders, left to pursue purely military ends, could have averted that calamity by pressing right through Germany, and beyond. Gen Eisenhower repeatedly mentions recommendations by Mr. Churchill in some sense, but says he had to oppose them because they were 'political', where he was tied to 'military' considerations. However, the supreme order to let the Red Armies get to Berlin first was the greatest political one of these 1951 years, in my judgment.[20]

DID IKE HATE THE GERMANS?

Ike sent a message to the Combined Chiefs of Staff of Britain and the US on 10 Mar 1944 recommending an entirely new class of prisoners – Disarmed Enemy Forces (DEFs). At a press conference in Paris on that date, Ike said, "If the Germans were reasoning like normal human beings they would realize the whole history of the United States and Great Britain is to be generous towards a defeated enemy. We observe all the laws of the Geneva Convention." Soon after, he sent a letter to his wife, Mamie, in which he said, "God, I hate the Germans! Why? Because the German is a beast!"[21]

A year later, the International Red Cross, with over 100,000 tons of food stockpiled in Switzerland, sent two trainloads into the American Zone of Germany. Under Ike's orders, the military governor, Gen Lucius Clay, sent the food back. Clay referred to the Morgenthau Plan and its requirement for a "Carthaginian Peace" for Germany. On 11 Apr 1945, on the eve of his death, FDR told Morgenthau in Warm Springs, Georgia, "Henry, I am with you 100%." When Truman took over, he continued Morgenthau's "Carthaginian Peace" for Germany, which Ike, the Supreme Commander, continued to implement.

On 17 Apr 1945, the American forces opened the enormous Rheinberg prison camp, with no food or shelter whatsoever. The Bingen camp, near Bad Kreitznach in the Rhineland, was holding nearly 400,000 German POWs, with no shelter or medicine and little food and water. Fatalities among the prisoners in these US prison camps were 30%, according to a US medical survey.

Ike became military governor of the US Zone in Germany in July 1945. He continued to turn back all relief teams from Switzerland and the US. A French Army under Gen Rousseau took over the Dietersheim camp near Mainz from the Americans on 10 Jul 1945. He found 32,000 men and women of all ages in a moribund state... "a vast mire peopled with living skeletons, male and female, huddled under scraps of wet cardboard."[22]

The International Red Cross, on 26 Jul 1945, proposed to Ike that mail service be restored to German POWs. He rejected the request, and on 4 Aug 1945, ordered that all remaining German POWs be stripped of their rights under the Geneva Convention, thus reducing them to DEF status. On 27 Aug 1945, British Gen Littlejohn sent a memo to Ike informing him that 1,550,000 Germans who were supposedly receiving US Army rations were receiving nothing. Ike ignored the memo, and the death toll continued to climb.[23]

Ike returned to the States in December 1945, and the US Army allowed the first relief shipments to enter the American Zone.

THE FORGING OF A MILITARY POLITICIAN

Ike states in *Crusade in Europe* that soon after he completed the War College in 1928, he worked as special assistant to the Assistant Secretary of War. The consummate politician stressed:

> The years devoted to work of this kind opened up to me almost a new world. During that time I met and worked with many people whose opinions I respected highly, in both military and civil life. Among these an outstanding figure was Mr. Bernard Baruch, for whom my admiration was and is profound. I still believe that if Mr. Baruch's recommendations for universal price fixing and his organizational plans had been completely and promptly adopted in December 1941 this country would have saved billions in money – possibly much in time and therefore in lives.[24]

So we see this political pattern which would later emerge in 1948 when "extreme left-wingers" were plugging Ike for the Democratic nomination for president. His chief backer, Leonard

Finder, then decided on a strategy to make Ike the Republican candidate. His agent for this "change" was a Socialist New Yorker, one Stuart Sheftel. Ike sent a letter to Finder (dated 22 Jan 1948), stating that he was not a candidate.[25]

Among the faithful pushing Ike for the Democratic candidate in 1948 were Bernard Baruch, Adlai Stevenson, James Roosevelt, Franklin D. Roosevelt, Jr., Helen Gahagan Douglas, David Dubinsky (who had raised American money to help the Bolsheviks in the Spanish civil war), Eleanor Roosevelt, Drew Pearson and Sidney Hillman.[26]

Now, shift the scene to 1952 and look closely at those (besides Finder) who were pushing Ike for the Republican nomination: Bernard Baruch, Oscar Hammerstein, Moss Hart, Richard Rodgers, Arthur Shwartz, Quintin Reynolds, Arthur Loew, William Zeckendorf, Max Kriendler, Jacob Potofsky, Humphrey Bogart, Lauren Bacall and Michael Straight.[27]

The belabored point in this instance is that all of Ike's backers, whether "Democrats" or "Republicans," were known Bolsheviks and Bolshevik sympathizers who saw clearly (as FDR had seen early on) that Dwight David Eisenhower was one of their own. He would do their bidding. They were not disappointed.

To comprehend the extent of this soldier's betrayal of the military and his country fully, one must study his ghost-written autobiography, *Crusade in Europe*, and compare it to the factual work by Robert Welch, *The Politician*, for – give the man credit – Eisenhower, while not much of a soldier, was a consummate politician.

Question: How many of today's top military brass have sold out the Constitution and the country?

PART THREE
WHO CONTROLS THE VOTES?

TO set the stage for the ongoing vote fraud being perpetrated here in the United States, we must journey back to the beginning of this century. President McKinley was assassinated by an Eastern European émigré in 1901, which placed the popular Anglophile and descendant of Sephardic Jews from Holland, Theodore Roosevelt, in the highest office. He was followed by a reasonable Republican, William Howard Taft, who would run for a second term in 1912. It was pre-ordained that he would lose.

A gathering of key agents in 1910, backed by their international financial controllers, chose the next president, who would reign over the United States for eight years and serve as their puppet to assure our entry into the planned Great War.

The chief president-maker was Edward Mandell House (Huis), aged fifty. He had attended schools in England, where prominent members of the Fabian Society captivated him. A man of great personal wealth, his family fortune was made during the War Between the States. His father, T. W. Huis, was the confidential American agent of the Rothschilds.

One of his leading henchmen was Rabbi Stephen Wise (born in Budapest, as were Herzl and Nordau), who in 1910 told a New Jersey audience:

> On Tuesday, Mr Woodrow Wilson will be elected governor; he will not complete his term as governor; in November 1912 he will be elected President of the United States; he will be inaugurated for the second time as President.[28]

Bear in mind that, at this time, neither House nor Wise had ever met Wilson. As House stated: "I turned to Woodrow Wilson...as being the only man...who in every way measured up to the office...."

Did he mean that Wilson was also the best man for the office? House said:

> The trouble with getting a candidate for president is that the man that is best fitted for the place cannot be nominated and, if nominated could not be elected. The People seldom take the best man fitted for the job; therefore it is necessary to work for the best man who can be nominated and elected, and just now Wilson seems to be that man.[29]

Without rehashing the role of Teddy Roosevelt and the Bull Moose Party in assuring Wilson's election in 1912, let's go to House's 1912 novel *Philip Dru: Administrator* (a word right out of the *Protocols....* The *Administrators* whom we shall choose...). The chapter "The Making of the President," which, as we build up to another farcical presidential election, is important enough to read again.

Douglas Reed, in his *Controversy of Zion*: (1956) describes the technique:

> The secret of Mr. House's hold over the Democratic Party lay in the strategy which he had devised for winning elections. The Democratic party had been out of office for nearly fifty unbroken years and he had devised a method which made victory almost a mathematical certainty. The Democratic party was in fact to owe its [victory in] 1916, as well as President Roosevelt's and President Truman's victories in 1932, 1936, 1940, 1944 and 1948 to the application of Mr. House's plan.

> In this electoral plan, which in its field perhaps deserves the name of genius, lies Mr. House's enduring effect on the life of America; his political ideas were never clearly formed and were frequently changed so that he forged an instrument whereby the ideas of others were put into effect; the instrument itself was brilliantly designed.

> In essence, it was a plan to gain the vote of the "foreign born," the new immigrants solidly for the Democratic Party by making appeal to their racial feelings and especially emotional reflexes. It was worked out in great detail and was the product of a master hand in this particular brand of political science.[30]

The House strategy was, as we today know so well, to concentrate its efforts on the "swing vote," the minority of undecided, uncommitted voters.

Is this diabolical electoral plan part of a gigantic conspiracy? FBI Director J. Edgar Hoover, in *The Elks* magazine, August 1956, states:

Yet the individual is handicapped by coming face to face with a conspiracy so monstrous he cannot believe it exists. The American mind simply has not come to a realization of the evil which has been introduced into our midst. It rejects even the assumption that human creatures could espouse a philosophy that must ultimately destroy all that is good and decent.[31]

MANIPULATING THE 1952 ELECTORAL PROCESS

The chief manipulator of the 1952 election process was Bernard Baruch. Truly to understand Baruch, the "Elder Statesman," and what his intentions and motivations were, one must consider his relationships with other "elders," particularly after World War II. He was a man who understood full well not only the first and second secrets of the Protocols, but the need to form a "super government" and, of course, always the "terrible power of the purse."

Oscillating between running Ike as a Democrat or Republican, his cohorts manipulated the electoral process in 1952 to give us a "false" Republican, Dwight Eisenhower, over Republican Bob Taft.

Thus it was that in 1952 Dwight David Eisenhower, an avowed "internationalist," was chosen over Taft as the standard-bearer for the GOP in that fateful election.

He was programmed to win, just as Jimmy Carter, George Bush and Bill Clinton were foreordained to win in their elections...and by the same group, namely, the Zionist masters. And just as Clinton was spotted early on by his future handlers (and shipped to Oxford for brainwashing in "social" skills), so was the young Eisenhower spotted in an academic environment.

It was Bernard Baruch who spotted Eisenhower, marking him for future "greatness." Ike was a student of the Army War College at Fort McNair in 1928. Baruch had been granted the "honor," as an "elder statesman," of being a guest lecturer at this most prestigious military school. Apparently the young Eisenhower asked the right questions, especially of Baruch.

Later this same Dwight David Eisenhower – who had never seen a day of combat – rose to five-star rank. After the war and before he became president, he spoke to a gathered group of American Legionnaires, telling them among other things that for a quarter century he "had the privilege of sitting at Bernard Baruch's feet and listening to his words."[32]

A more apt word would be "groveling." In GI parlance, we call this ass kissing. It works…sometimes. It got Ike the presidency of the United States.

COMPARING TWO ELDER STATESMEN

One of Baruch's comrades was the notorious Ben Hecht, who gave us a verbal view of the elder statesman:

> One day the door of my room opened and a tall, white-haired man entered. It was Bernard Baruch, my first Jewish social visitor. He sat down, observed me for a moment and then spoke. 'I am on your side,' said Baruch, 'The only way the Jews will ever get anything is by fighting for it. I'd like you to think of me as one of your Jewish fighters in the tall grass with a long gun. I've always done my best work that way, out of sight.'[33]

Douglas Reed, in his suppressed opus, *The Controversy of Zion*, informs us that Hecht was one of the most extreme chauvinists in the US. He openly endorsed violence:

> One of the finest things ever done by the mob was the crucifixion of Christ. Intellectually it was a splendid gesture. But trust the mob to bungle. If I'd had charge of executing Christ I'd have handled it differently. You see, what I would have done was have him shipped to Rome and fed to the lions. They never could have made a saviour out of mincemeat.

Baruch attempted to portray himself as a great public-spirited citizen and a patriotic American, as well as a generous philanthropist, when his life was devoted to personal aggrandizement and advancement of the Zionist conspiracy for worldwide Talmudic despotism which would be brought about by controlling a "supergovernment." Baruch, and others of his select circle of power, called this yet-to-be-formed colossus The United Nations as early as 1940.

According to Reed, Baruch submitted a Plan for control of atomic weapons to the UN AEC (14 Jun 1946):

> He spoke with the voice of the Levites' Jehovah, offering "blessings or cursings," alluded to the atom bomb as the "absolute weapon," and used the familiar argument of false prophets, namely, that if his advice were followed "peace" would ensue and if it were ignored all would be "destroyed." This threat of nuclear annihilation then became the centerpiece for what was dubbed the "Cold War" which is Talmudic in its concept of eternal revenge.[34]

Let's look closely at his "promise" and his "threat," as stated in Baruch's Plan, which is diabolical in its cunning. Remember that the man speaking these words "advised" (say, controlled) six presidents, starting with Woodrow Wilson:

> We must elect world peace or world destruction...we must provide immediate, swift and sure punishment of those who violate the agreements that are reached by the nations. Penalization is essential if peace is to be more than a feverish interlude between wars.... The United Nations can prescribe individual responsibility and punishment on the principles applied at Nuremberg by the USSR, the UK, France and the US – a formula certain to benefit the world's future... We represent the peoples of the world... The peoples of these democracies gathered here are not afraid of internationalism that protects; they are unwilling to be fobbed off by mouthings about narrow sovereignty, which is today's phrase for yesterday's isolation.[35]

Those two phrases, "internationalism that protects" and "yesterday's isolation," would have a profound effect on the election process in 1952 and guarantee that Baruch's (Zionism's) man would become President.

Baruch proposed that "an Authority" with a monopoly of atomic energy be set up, which should be "free from all check in its punitive use of atomic energy against any party deemed by it to be deserving of punishment."

In this one profound statement, we catch a glimpse of the strivings of 3,000 years on the part of a "chosen people" to rule the earth by sheer brute force and terror, by promising "peace," but threatening "destruction."

And now possessing the "absolute weapon."

ROBERT A. TAFT – TRUE AMERICAN

Here are excerpts from the 1952 book, *A Foreign Policy for Americans*, by another elder statesman, Robert A. Taft.

The result of the Administration policy (Democratic, 1933-52) has been to build up the strength of Soviet Russia so that it is in fact a threat to the security of the United States.... Russia is far more a threat to the security of the United States than Hitler ever was....

Fundamentally I believe the ultimate purpose of our foreign policy must be to protect the liberty of the people of America... I feel that the last two presidents have put all kinds of political and policy considerations ahead of their interest in liberty and peace...

It seems to me that the sending of troops without authorization of Congress to a country under attack, as was done in Korea, is clearly prohibited.... The European army project, however, goes further... It involves the sending of troops to an international army similar to that which was contemplated under the United Nations charter... I was never satisfied with the United Nations Charter...it is not based on an underlying law and an administration of justice under that law...

I see no choice except to develop our own military policy and our own policy of alliances without substantial regard to the non-existent power of the United Nations to prevent aggression....

The other form of international organization which is being urged strenuously upon the people of the United States, namely, a world state with an international legislature to make the laws and an international executive to direct the army of the organization...appears to me, at least in this century, to be fantastic, dangerous and impractical...

Any international organization which is worth the paper it is written on must be based on retaining the sovereignty of all states. Peace must be sought, not by destroying and consolidating nations, but by developing a rule of law in the relations between nations...[36]

Compare the words of these two elder statesmen, Bernard Baruch and Robert Taft, as they should give you a better insight as to how we ended up with a Bill Clinton as president in 1993 and again in 1997. Coupled with that is the fact that by not choosing Bob Taft in 1952 as the Republican candidate, we, as a nation, lost our last chance to halt the inexorable march to a one-world super government.

IKE'S SUPPORT OF ISRAEL

Dwight David Eisenhower was born 14 Oct 1890, in Denison, Texas, the son of Jacob David Eisenhower and Ida Stover. Ida named her son after the American evangelist, Dwight Moody.

Shortly after his nomination in 1952, Eisenhower told Maxwell Abbell, president of the United Synagogue of America, "the Jewish people could not have a better friend than me [*sic*]... I grew up believing that Jews were the chosen people and that they gave us the high ethical and moral principles of our civilization... my mother reared us boys in the Old Testament."[37]

Reed points out in *Controversy of Zion* that all Jewish papers carried the quote. Reed also reveals that in the 1952 election campaign, "the only passage of any vital meaning in the 'foreign policy programmes' adopted by the two parties related, in each case, to Israel."

The Republican Party programme, on which Eisenhower was unanimously elected candidate, said: 'We regard the preservation of Israel as an important tenet of American foreign policy. We are determined that the integrity of an independent Jewish state shall be maintained. We shall support the independence of Israel against armed aggression.'

The Democratic Party programme said: 'The Democratic Party will act to redress the dangerous imbalance of arms in the area created by the shipment of Communist arms to Egypt, by selling or supplying defensive weapons to Israel, and will take such steps, including security guarantees, as may be required to deter aggression and war in the area'.[38]

Insofar as the Zionist State is concerned, Reed stressed:

In those years the little state misnamed 'Israel' proved to be something unique in history. It was governed, as it was devised, set up and largely peopled, by non-Semitic Jews from Russia, of the Chazar breed. Founded on a tribal tradition of antiquity, with which these peoples could have no conceivable tie of blood, it developed a savage chauvinism based on the literal application of the Law of the Levites in ancient Judah. Tiny, it had no true life of its own and from the start lived only by the wealth and weapons its powerful supporters in the great Western countries could extort from these. During these years it outdid the most bellicose warlords of history in warlike words and deeds. Ruled by men of the same stock as those who wielded the terror in Poland and Hungary, it daily threatened the seven neighboring Semitic peoples with the destruction and enslavement prescribed for them in *Deuteronomy* of the Levites.[39]

According to author Gregory Douglas, in *Gestapo Chief, Vol. II*, Ike's brother Milton Eisenhower, while maintaining a high position in the Department of Agriculture was listed as a Soviet sympathizer.

Here we are in the new millennium, and the relationships of our leading politicos – regardless of party affiliation – vis a vis the Zionist mini-state have not deviated an iota since the founding of "Israel" in 1948. Can this obsequious groveling in front of the altar of Mammon be renounced as treason, or have we in fact sold our birthright for a mess of pottage?

TAKING OUT ISRAEL'S ENEMIES

Let's journey back in time to a relatively small signpost flagging our direction on the rough roadway to destruction of our national sovereignty, of our Constitution, and of our very way of life. The man who erected the signpost was a soldier in that he looked like a soldier, dressed like a soldier and occasionally – but not that often – acted like a soldier, Dwight David Eisenhower. He was really not a soldier; he was a politician and an opportunist of the first magnitude. His fellow soldiers often referred to him as Dwight David *Kerensky,* denoting not only his Jewish family lineage, originally from Sweden, but especially his conduct in high office when chosen by the very few to wear the ermine mantle. The all-important question becomes: are top military commanders also betraying their country to international Bolshevism under the crooked and traitorous Clinton administration in 1999?

Following the Suez debacle, on 5 Jan 1957, President Eisenhower asked Congress for standing authority to use the armed forces of the United States against "overt armed aggression from any nation controlled by international communism in the Middle East."[40]

What did Ike's handlers have in mind when they penned these words for their "premier-dictator"?   Bear in mind that the man himself wrote very little in his lifetime... not even a word of *Crusade in Europe*, which was written in its entirety by a known communist and subversive, Joseph Fels Barnes.[41]

Before and after the attack on Egypt by the combine of Israel, France and Britain, the international press accused one Arab nation after another of being "controlled" by international communism.   Ike's request to Congress, under the guise of extirpating communism, was actually an attack not on communism but on the Arabs.

One example will suffice about the lock step of the complicit media picking up the drumbeat of a "communist-controlled" enemy in the Middle East, which ultimately came to mean the entire Muslim world.   The *New York Times,* which ostensibly prints all the news fit to print, in its 2 Dec 1956 issue, published photos of "Russian tanks captured by the Israelis" during the attack on Egypt.   A military officer's objection led the paper to admit that the tanks were in fact American.[42]

The curious twist under Ike's request centered on the fact that Egypt was widely declared by the international media to be the "aggressor" in the October 1956 attack on itself.   The aggressor in the Middle East, then and now, was and is the tiny theocratic state of Israel.   Had Ike meant those words of Jan 1957, and had he spoken them but six months earlier, it would have been incumbent on the American forces, on Egyptian request, to repel the Israeli attack.

Another curious twist emerged following the publication of Moshe Sharett's personal diary in 1979.   As Livia Rokach writes in *Israel's Sacred Terrorism*:

> On October 1, 1955, the US Government, through the CIA, gave Israel the "green light" to attack Egypt.   The energies of Israel's security establishment became wholly absorbed by the preparations for the war which would take place exactly one year later.[43]

Perhaps the most telling of Sharett's personal diary entries, as reflected in Rokach's work, deals with the concerted efforts on the part of the Israeli "hard-liners" to use force, violence and sheer terror to drive out all of the Palestinians and then destroy Egypt as a military force in contention with Israel for Middle East dominance.

> The basic motivation was also clearly stated.... The use of force was 'the only way' for Israel to become the hegemonic power in the region, possibly in alliance with the West. Nasser had to be eliminated, not because his regime constituted a danger for Israel, but because an alliance between the West [and Nasser] would inevitably lead to a peace agreement, which in turn would cause the Zionist state to be revitalized as just one of the region's national societies.[44]

Sharett's diary entries in March 1955 make frequent reference to Ben-Gurion, Dayan and Lavon pressing to present Egypt with an ultimatum: either it evacuates all the Palestinian refugees from Gaza and disperses them inside Egypt, or else....

> It is easy to imagine the outrage and hate and bitterness and the desire for revenge that will animate them (the Palestinians)...and we still have 100,000 of them in the Strip, and it is easy to imagine what means we shall resort to in order to repress them and what wave of hatred we will create again and what kind of headlines we shall receive in the international press.[45]

What Sharett feared most was Western reaction. On 14 Apr 1955, he wrote:

> Reports by US embassies in Arab capitals, studied in Washington, have produced in the State Department the conviction that an Israeli plan of retaliation, to be realized according to a pre-fixed timetable, exists, and that the goal is that of a steady escalation of the tension in the area in order to bring about a war.[46]

Ben-Gurion made a public speech (8 Aug 1955) in which he blasted Prime Minister Sharett's "timidity," asserting that his policy was aimed only at pleasing the gentiles. At that time, the West had refused to provide Egypt with defensive weapons and John Foster Dulles' commitment to help Egypt in the construction of the Aswan Dam had faded into thin air, while Israel executed a devastating attack on Gaza and continued to prepare for all-out war.

"These factors contributed to extinguishing Cairo's last illusions. By the end of September, Egypt signed an arms deal with Czechoslovakia intended to secure its survival and self-defense." (Rokach.)[47] These activities led to the following entry in Sharatt's diary, dated 1 Oct 1955:

> Teddy [Kollek] brought in a classified cable from Washington. Our "partner" named [in code] 'Ben' [Kermit Roosevelt of the CIA]...describes the terrible confusion prevailing in the State department under the shock of the Nasser-Czech, i.e., 'Russian' deal.... If, when the Soviet arms arrive, you will hit Egypt – no one will protest." (Kermit Roosevelt's words in the cable)[48]

To heighten Sharett's understanding of US government backing for the coming attack on Egypt, he makes the following entries on 3 October:

> "If they really get MiGs [declared Ben-Gurion]... I will support their bombing! We can do it!" I understood that he read the cable from Washington. The wild seed has fallen on fertile ground....

> Isser [Harel, Shin Bet chief] likewise concludes that the US is hinting to us that as far as they are concerned, we have a free hand and God bless us if we act audaciously.... Now...the US is interested in toppling Nasser's regime...but it does not dare at the moment to use the methods it adopted to topple the leftist government of Jacobo Arbenz in Guatemala [1954] and of Mossadegh in Iran [1953].... It prefers its work to be done by Israel.[49]

Thus, we are afforded a glimpse of the background leading up to Ike's supposed outrage regarding the attack on Egypt and the Suez Canal the following year. Here is Rokach's studied view:

> Precisely one year later Dayan's troops occupied the Gaza Strip, Sinai, and the Straits of Tiran, and were arrayed along the shore of the Suez Canal to watch the spectacular French and British aerial bombardments of Ismailia and Suez, accompanied by the rapid landing of troops in the Canal Zone. Six months before, as a result of a personal decision by Ben-Gurion, Sharett had been eliminated from the government. The premiership had been resumed by the Old Man (Ben-Gurion) in November 1955, one month after the US 'green light' for an Israeli invasion of Egypt...

> At the moment of the Suez offensive the US feigned surprise, and even indignation. But it made a clear distinction between England and France – the beaten rivals in the inter-imperialist struggle for

influence in the Middle East – and Israel... With the CIA authorization in its pocket, Israel was granted the mitigating circumstances of 'security needs' in world opinion's judgment on that criminal war."[50]

THE POWER OF TRUTH

Was this particular issue as regards the Middle East but an aberration on the part of our Republican President, D. D. Eisenhower? No indeed! In 1963, Robert Welch published a book about Ike, called *The Politician.* He quotes Daniel Webster:

> There is nothing so powerful as truth, and often nothing so strange.[51]

In a telling chapter, "The Word is Treason," Welch details the absolute and documented truth that Eisenhower was a traitor for, among other reasons, his gag order preventing the *House Un-American Activities Committee* from revealing Communists in government. This gag order brought about unrestricted immigration, particularly of "refugees" from Eastern Europe. Welch quotes Madame Roland: "Humanitarianism – what treason is committed in thy name!"[52]

This is the same Ike who ordered our troops in Europe to drive back into the arms of his Communist colleagues (the Soviets) all – I repeat, all – of the people who had fled the Communist menace to the "safety" of the United States forces in Germany (1945). This was Ike's infamous "Keel Haul" directive, which was mass murder on a grand scale.

You can ask, what in God's name was the purpose of his criminal acts? For now, a quote from Welch will suffice:

> For six years Eisenhower and his associates have carried on a persistent and energetic campaign to break down the independent sovereignty of the United States, and to submerge that sovereignty under international agreements and the control of international agencies.

> The open boasts of the United Nations crowd...that there is a day-to-day de facto surrender of American sovereignty to the UN are well justified. And Eisenhower's support of this transfer of sovereignty by installments is continuous. He has emphasized over and over, for instance, that our troops are to be used, in implementation of the

Eisenhower Doctrine, under the control of the United Nations Security
Council. [53]

Thus began the current and ongoing utter destruction of
Israel's enemies in the Middle East on the part of the armed forces
of the United States in their role as the *force majeure* of the United
Nations Security Council, now embodied in a sub-UN group
(NATO) which has become the world's police force. Over the
ensuing years, we see how Ike's words have been expanded
outward to include the use of armed forces of the United States
against any nation for any reason. We do not need to recite the
litany of our violations of the sovereignty of many once-
independent countries about the world. In fact, today we, the
United States, as the muscle behind the United Nations, have
combat troops in over one hundred nations about the world.

IT'S DÉJÀ VU

His name is Wesley Kanne Clark; he is a cardboard cutout
of Dwight David Eisenhower, and was, until relieved in July 1999
and replaced by Gen Joseph Ralston, the supreme commander of
NATO forces. Gen Eisenhower was the first commander of that
organization, which was set up after WW II with but one mission –
to defend Western Europe against the further encroachment of
Soviet Bolshevism. We saw earlier how FDR, in 1940, selected
Ike, then a lieutenant colonel, for rapid advancement to the
ultimate position of Supreme Allied Commander in Europe
(SACEUR).

With a little help from the *New York Times* (3 May 1999),
we see that it is *déjà vu* all over again. It was President Bill
Clinton who spotted Wesley Clark early on, arranged for his rapid
promotion to 4-star general, and placed him in the position of the
commander of NATO's "new and improved" military operations,
which are now built on the old military axiom that "the best
defense is a good offense."

The banner over the Clark story in the *New York Times*
stated: "His Family's Refugee Past is Said to Inspire NATO's
Commander." Here is the lead:

The American general who is leading NATO's military operation...discovered as an adult that he is the grandson of a Russian Jew who fled his country to escape the pogroms there a century ago. Gen Wesley Kanne Clark was raised as a Protestant in Little Rock, where he was brought up by his mother and step-father, Victor Clark. He was ignorant of his ancestry, which disappeared from his life with the death of his father, Benjamin Jacob Kanne, when Wesley was five years old. He learned of his ethnic background when he was in his 20's and embraced the discovery, according to several family members....[54]

The *New York Times* article likened the forced exodus of Albanians from Kosovo to the "expulsion of Jews from Russia and the Nazi mass murder of Jews during the Holocaust in Europe." (Of course, overlooking the forced exodus of Palestinians from Israel.) Some of Clark's relatives say that the general was inspired by the story of his grandfather's persecution and escape from his native land, and that his determination to defeat Milosevic is fed in part by his empathy for the victims of Serbian ethnic purges.

The article stated that the general's grandfather, Jacob Nemerovsky, fled Russia in the late 1890s in fear for his life, and found safety in Switzerland where he obtained a false passport under the name of "Kanne," which he used to immigrate to the United States.[55]

So much for a backgrounder on the NATO commander, but who is he, really? Here is a telling lead from another source:

"WASHINGTON - May 5 - The real Gen Clark is a vain, pompous, brown-noser, say those who have served with him in the armed forces," according to a report by *Counterpunch*, a Washington-based newsletter.[56]

"Bill Clinton's pal from Little Rock, Arkansas – a Rhodes scholar who, like Clinton, also went to Oxford – is a typical 'political general' whose promotions came only because of his White House pull," according to the article. He is facing the gloomy prospect of becoming the fall guy for NATO's disastrous failure to bring the Serbs to heel.

"Who is responsible for an air offensive that is building anti-American anger across Europe without breaking the Serbian regime's will?" asks Robert Novak, a nationally syndicated columnist (5 May 1999). He answers his own question. "The blame rests heavily on Gen Wesley K. Clark, the NATO supreme commander."[57]

After pointing out that Clark's belligerency toward Serb civilians has stunned even his defenders in the national security establishment, Novak concludes: "The president and the general are collaborators in a failed strategy whose consequences cast a long shadow, even if soon terminated by negotiation."

To understand the reasons for such failures, one must look at the general's past, and the way he rose to power. "Clark is a perfect model of a 1990s political 4-star general," Novak observes. "Clark's rapid promotions after Dayton (the agreement which ended the war in Bosnia) – winning his fourth star to head the Panama-based Southern Command, and then the jewel of SACEUR – were both opposed by the Pentagon brass. But Clark's fellow Arkansan in the White House named him anyway."[58]

His NATO subordinates call him, not with affection, "the Supreme Being." Recognizing the fortunes of war and the adroit maneuvering of political generals, perhaps Wesley Kanne Clark will, like Dwight David Eisenhower, rise to the pinnacle of power and become both president and commander-in-chief. A major war – call it World War III – could cause it to happen. Does Bill Clinton want it? Does Wesley Clark want it? Most important: Do their fearful masters want it? If the answer to these questions is yes, then the subsequent question must be, Why?

What with NATO's unprovoked attack on the sovereign nation of Serbia, the only nation whose sovereignty is sacrosanct seems to be Israel. This "nation within nations" has striven ever since its benign captivity in ancient Babylon to take over the world and govern it in absolute despotism.

How did such a situation evolve? The history is long and sordid; however, by examining a part of it, namely, the takeover of Russia by a "minority," who referred to themselves as Bolsheviks (the majority), we will be able to comprehend how we ourselves –

citizens of the once-Republic of the United States of America – were also bolshevized, that is, enslaved.

Can we somehow reverse this bolshevization, or is it, in fact, too late? If there is still a chance that we can regain our liberty, what must we do to restore our Republic and its Constitution?

I consider that the immediate suppression of Bolshevism is the greatest issue now before the world, not even excluding the War, which is still raging, and unless as above stated, Bolshevism is nipped in the bud immediately, it is bound to spread in one form or another over Europe and the whole world, as it is organised and worked by Jews who have no nationality, and whose one object is to destroy for their own ends the existing order of things.

M. Oudendyk, 1918

CHAPTER III

BOLSHEVIKS RULE RUSSIA
(Enslavement of a Nation)

The objective of strategic deception is to paint a false picture of the entire political climate in which the Soviet Union operates among both friend and foe alike – disguising their objectives and ultimate ambitions.... [It] succeeds not so much because of the ability of the Soviet propaganda and agents of influence to deceive us, but because of our tendencies to deceive ourselves.

Dr John Lenczowski, *Soviet Strategic Deception*, 1987

PART ONE
RULE BY THE "MINORITY"

IN an article in *The Atlantic Monthly* (Nov 1945), "Einstein on the Atomic Bomb," *Time Magazine's* anointed man of the century, Albert Einstein speaks of the "minority" then ruling in the Soviet Union, to wit:

> While it is true that in the Soviet Union the minority rules, I do not consider the internal conditions there are of themselves a threat to world peace. One must bear in mind that the people in Russia did not have a long political education and changes to improve Russian conditions had to be carried through by a minority for the reason that there was no majority capable of doing it.[1]

Just who are the Barbarians, that "minority" who ruled in the Soviet Union from 1917 until the present millennium? What "changes to improve Russian conditions" were actually carried through by these Barbarians whom Einstein laureled?

The pattern of confusion, chaos and conquest created in Russia from 1917 onwards was identical to that of the War Between the States (1861-65) and of other major revolutions, such as the English civil war (1642-48) under Oliver Cromwell, culminating in the beheading of Charles I in 1649; and the French Revolution (1789-94), resulting in the beheading of Louis XVI in 1793.   Each of these major historic events was fomented by "outside forces."   Each had its roots in Talmudic terrorism and revenge. This pattern is prevalent here in the United States today, for in each instance aliens had to inveigle their way inside the gates in order to poison the well of public opinion while simultaneously taking over the reins of finance and government.

What was the nature of these crimes committed under the Bolsheviks and, most important, just who were those criminals?

We can turn briefly to the recent writings of an erudite American scholar who revealed much about both: *Russia Under the Bolshevik Regime* by Richard Pipes.   Pipes, a noted Harvard professor, published his work in 1995. He served as Director, East Europe and Soviet Affairs for the National Security Council under President Reagan (1981-82). Suffice it to say, the man knows his subject.

WHO WERE THE BOLSHEVIKS?

Pipes explain that Jews undeniably played in the Bolshevik Party a role disproportionate to their share of the population; "the number of Jews active in Communism in Russia and abroad was striking."[2]

The Bolshevik Party was organized as a conspiratorial group for the specific purpose of seizing power and making a revolution from above, first in Russia and then in the rest of the world.   It was the prototype for all subsequent totalitarian organizations, especially Fascism and National Socialism (the Nazis). While they were virtual carbon copies of the Soviet police state, both were much more benevolent, meaning that they murdered and imprisoned far fewer of their people.

The Russian Revolution, the murder of Czar Nicholas II and his family, and the civil war that followed absolutely devastated that country. In many ways it followed what the Northern forces did to the South in our own fratricidal conflict. In both instances alien "invaders" brought chaos and conflict, death and destruction to the native inhabitants.

In the 13th century, Russia had been caught in the grip of the Mongol hordes. Now, it was another invasion of the "Khazarians" – descendants of the warlike Turko-Asiatics who had converted to Judaism in the eighth century – who committed a series of unspeakable atrocities, slaughtering millions by a frightful combination of bloody combat, fierce and unending cold, hunger and starvation.

As that great British journalist and author of the long suppressed, *The Last Days of the Romanovs*, Robert Wilton, would report from Moscow in 1918, it was alien Jews who had Russianized their names and now headed the Red Army, the dreaded Cheka secret police and the Soviet, who had masterminded the diabolical takeover. Their continuing aim throughout this century – and especially is it true today as we near the millennium – is to bring about "revolutionary universalism."[3]

Wilton knew his Bolsheviks.

So did Winston Churchill. In a lengthy article, "Zionism versus Bolshevism," in the London *Sunday Herald* (8 Feb 1920), he remarked:

> There is no need to exaggerate the part played in the creation of Bolshevism and in the bringing about of the Russian Revolution by these international and for the most part atheistic Jews. It is certainly a very great one; it probably outweighs all others.[4]

A top official in the British foreign office, Sir Eyre Crowe, commenting on pogroms carried out in Russia in 1919, wrote:

> What may appear to Mr Weizmann (Chaim Weizmann, head of international Zionism) to be outrages against Jews, may be – in the eyes of the Russians – retaliation against the horrors committed by the Bolsheviks who are all organized and directed by the Jews.[5]

What we know as the Bolshevik Party was the creation of Lenin; both Mussolini and Hitler merely copied the model. The Party, whether called Bolshevist or Communist or National Socialist or Fascist, was the instrument used to take over the state as Lenin had done earlier. To enforce total compliance with their dictates, each of the three developed an all-pervasive secret police. These are the recognizable marks of a totalitarian regime.

US Presidents and their handlers are today using the identical tactics to destroy the sovereignty of the United States. All that is lacking at the moment is a major catastrophe, such as the collapse of the currency, and/or a controlled disintegration of both the economy and the culture. Revolution, civil war and mass starvation will surely follow, as the identical instigators of the Russian Revolution are now in charge here in the United States and are set to implement their final step in "revolutionary universalism."

CHURCHILL WARNS OF BOLSHEVISM

There was a time when Winston Churchill was very candid about the dangers of Bolshevism, as he called Communism. The unalterable fact is that he sold out to them prior to 1939. As we will discover in Chapter 4, our four-term President FDR, had sold out much earlier. Together and separately, they sold out both Britain and the United States to international Bolshevism.

Little known revelations of about Roosevelt, Churchill and a clandestine group of Jewish European financiers, known as the Focus Group, can be found in David Irving's historic book *Churchill's War*. Irving chronicled that European banking interests approached Churchill, paid off his estate mortgage, and arranged conferences with Roosevelt for the purpose of jarring the US as an ally of England into waging a war with Germany. This was to be accomplished via the "back door." Japan, Italy and Germany were joined as the axis allies in a treaty where in the event one country was attacked, the others would come to its defense. Subsequent to the conferences, President Roosevelt shifted the US naval fleet into the South Pacific and began the grueling embargo of strategic materials to Japan, including scrap iron and oil. Just as German U-boats sunk the *Lusitania*, to commence World War I, Roosevelt employed this strategem to entice Japan into sinking a US naval vessel by tightening the embargo noose. Japan refrained from biting the bait. In desparation, the bulk of the Pacific naval fleet was stationed at Pearl Harbor – an inviting target for Japanese Zeros to strike. For further research, one should read Professor Tansill's *Back Door to War* and *Pearl Harbor: The Story of the Secret War* by George Morgenstern.

Continuing: Churchill, who took over the War Office in 1919, had an anti-Communist stance, rather than anti-Russian. He regarded Communism as "unadulterated evil, a satanic force"; he referred to Bolsheviks as "animals" and "butchers." He stated September 15, 1919:

> It is a delusion to suppose that all this year we have been fighting the battles of the anti-Bolshevik Russians. On the contrary, they have been fighting ours and this truth will become painfully apparent from the moment that they are exterminated and the Bolshevik armies are supreme over the whole vast territories of the Russian Empire.[6]

Here are other "Winnie" quotes, circa 1920:

> It would almost seem as if the gospel of Christ and the gospel of the anti-Christ were designed to originate among the same people and that this mystic and mysterious race had been chosen for the supreme manifestations, both of the divine and the diabolical....

> It (the worldwide Bolshevik takeover) played, as a modern writer, Mrs. Nesta Webster, has so ably shown, a definitely recognizable part in the tragedy of the French Revolution. It has been the mainspring of every subversive movement during the nineteenth century; and now at last this band of extraordinary personalities from the underworld of the great cities of Europe and America have gripped the Russian people by the hair of their heads and have become practically the undisputed masters of that enormous empire.[7]

The British Government churned out a white paper in 1919 called "Russia No.1, a Collection of Reports on Bolshevism." It included a statement made by the Netherlands minister at St. Petersburg, M. Oudendyke, which was sent to former Prime Minister, Arthur Balfour in London in 1918:

> The danger is now so great that I feel it my duty to call the attention of the British and all other governments to the fact that, if an end is not put to Bolshevism at once, the civilization of the whole world will be threatened.... I consider that the immediate suppression of

Bolshevism is the greatest issue now before the world, not even excluding the war which is still raging, and unless, as above stated, Bolshevism is nipped in the bud immediately, it is bound to spread in one form or another over Europe and the whole world, as it is organized and worked by Jews, who have no nationality and whose one object is to destroy for their own ends the existing order of things. The only manner in which this danger can be averted would be collective action on the part of all the Powers. I would beg that this Report be telegraphed as soon as possible in cipher in full to the British Foreign Office in view of its importance.[8]

At the same time, the US ambassador in Moscow, David R. Francis, reported back to Washington: "The Bolshevik leaders here, most of whom are Jews and 90 percent of whom are returned exiles, care little for Russia or any other country but are internationalists and they are trying to start a worldwide social revolution."[9]

Time to recall the famous – or infamous – words of David Ben-Gurion spoken as he took over the newly created state of Israel in 1948: "I am in favor of Bolshevism."

Robert Wilton, correspondent for the London *Times,* was stationed in Moscow at that time and was witness to the bloody revolution. He provided what was to become the official report; the *Official Bolshevik Lists.* Wilton included the names of every individual involved. Subsequently, many of them changed or Russianized their names to conceal their true identity. The report consisted of the following ethnic makeup:

Central Committee of the Bolshevik Party: 9 Jews, 3 Russians; Central Committee of the Executive Commission: 42 Jews, 19 Russians, Letts, Georgians and others; Council of People's Commissars: 17 Jews, 5 others; Moskow Cheka: 23 Jews, 13 others.[10]

Douglas Reed, badly wounded as a British soldier during WW I, returned to Germany before WW II as a correspondent for the London *Times* (of all WW II correspondents, Reed was the highest salaried). He reported: "Among the names of 556 high officials of the Bolshevik state officially published in 1918-19 were 458 Jews and 108 others. Among the other Socialist parties were 55 Jews and 6 others."[11]

The composition of the two short-lived Bolshevik parties outside Russia (in Hungary and Bavaria) was similar. This is substantiated by Professor Pipes, who writes: "In Hungary, they [the Jews] furnished 95% of the leading figures in Bela Kun's dictatorship [and were] disproportionately represented among the Communists in Germany and Austria, and in the apparatus of the Communist International."[12]

Here is Reed's startling but factual analysis. Such facts hold true today, not only in Russia, but here in the United States:

> Taken according to numbers of population, the Jews represented less than one in ten; among the commissars that rule Bolshevik Russia, they are nine in ten; if anything the proportion of Jews is still greater. This was plain reporting and if the report had related to "Ukrainians," for instance, instead of "Jews," none would have objected; the mere act of reporting a fact became the ground for secret denunciation because the fact related to Jews…hence, anti-semitic.[13]

COMING OUR WAY – THE UNITED NATIONS HORROR

Bolshevism of itself is meaningless without a force behind it. That force today is embodied in the United Nations. That same force is currently active in a gigantic effort to subvert our Constitution and our "muscle," namely, the US military, and put it under the control of the UN.

This is the ultimate betrayal.

In his classic work *Modern Times*, Paul Johnson cites the beginning of the modern world as 1905 when Einstein introduced to that world his theory of relativity. This led, according to Johnson, to the belief, for the first time at a popular level, that there were no longer any absolutes; of time and space, of good and evil, of knowledge, above all of value. Mistakenly but perhaps inevitably, relativity became confused with relativism.[14]

He points to a trio of imaginative German scholars who offered explanations of human behavior: Marx described a world in which the central dynamic was economic interest. To Freud, the principal thrust was sexual.

Nietzche also was an atheist; however, he saw God not as an invention but as a casualty. He wrote in 1886, "The greatest event of recent times – that God is dead, that the belief in the Christian God is no longer tenable – is beginning to cast its first shadows over Europe."[15]

The "Will to Power," as Nietzche believed, was a more tenable ... plausible explanation of human behavior. So, of course, did Lenin and Stalin.

WILL TO POWER = DESPOTIC TERROR

A letter written by Baruch Levy to Karl Marx (1879) predicts the future, which is now:

> The Jewish people, taken collectively, will be its own messiah. It will attain mastery of the world through the union of all the other human races, through abolition of boundaries and monarchies...through the erection of a universal Republic, in which the Jews will everywhere enjoy universal rights.

> In this new organization of mankind the sons of Israel will spread themselves over the whole inhabited world...since they belong all to the same race and culture-tradition, without at the same time having a definite nationality, they will form the lead element without finding opposition.

> The government of the nations, which will make up this universal Republic, will pass without effort into the hands of the Israelites, by the very fact of the victory of the Proletariat. The Jewish race can then do away with private property, and after that everywhere administer the public funds.

> Then shall the promises of the Talmud be fulfilled. When the time of the Messiah has come, the Jews will hold in their hands the key to the wealth of the world.[16]

This letter, written in 1879, served as the springboard for several subsequent events. It is in fact the key linkage of the terrors of the Talmud to the formulation of International Zionism in 1897 as a political tool to accomplish the stated objectives.

The Revolution in Russia by William Eleroy Curtis appeared in the May 1907 issue of *The National Geographic Magazine*. It is a concise documentary comprising his first-hand account of the revolution which began as a result of the Russo-Japanese War, and subsequently led to the 1918 murder of the Czar and his family, and the takeover of all of Russia by the Bolsheviks.

Curtis states that in a wave of unprecedented terror in 1906 (while he was in Warsaw) 7,300 persons were killed and 9,000 wounded, including 123 governors, generals, chiefs of police and other high officials. Thirty thousand revolutionists were arrested and most of them were sent to Siberia, while 221 were executed.

> Twelve railway trains were held up and robbed of government treasure and 400 government liquor stores were robbed and destroyed (chief government source of revenue).[17]

He also stated that of the revolutionary leaders nearly all belonged to the Jewish race and the most effective revolutionary agency was the Jewish Bund (Union).

> The government has suffered more from this race than from all of its other subjects combined. Whenever a desperate deed is committed it is always done by a Jew, and there is scarcely one loyal member of that race in the entire Empire.[18]

"Ethnic Cleansing and Soviet Crimes Against Humanity" by Dr A. B. Kopanski (*The Barnes Review,* Dec 1997), outlines the brutal butcheries by the Soviets who "holocausted" Baltic, Slavic, German, Polish, Caucasian and Turkic peoples during the period 1939-1949.[19]

This above all else – control the money! It was monetary control that made possible the Bolshevik takeover of Russia in 1917. G. Edward Griffin's book *The Creature from Jekyll Island* is a good available source for detailed coverage of this aspect of the takeover of Russia. Read especially his Chapter Thirteen - "Masquerade in Moscow," in which Griffin states:

> One of the greatest myths of contemporary history is that the Bolshevik Revolution in Russia was a popular uprising of the downtrodden masses against the hated ruling class of the Tsars...financing came from outside Russia, mostly from financiers in Germany, Britain, and the United States.... This amazing story begins with the war between Russia and Japan in 1904. Jacob Schiff, who was head of the New York investment firm of Kuhn Loeb, had raised the capital for large loans to Japan. It was due to this funding that the

Japanese were able to launch a stunning attack against the Russians at Port Arthur and, the following year, to virtually decimate the Russian fleet.[20]

SPREADING THE RED TERROR

Stalin ordered the purging of all potential partisans of Hitler's army in 1939, three years before Germany's invasion of Russia, code named "Barbarossa." Hundreds of thousands of "reactionaries and fascists" were "prophylactically" shot or deported to the *Gulag* (*Glavnoye Upravlenye Ispravatelno-Trudovikh Legerei*), Siberian slave-labor camps established in 1934.

Stalin issued a decree (5 Mar 1940) to murder by firing squad 14,736 Polish military, along with 10,685 Poles held by the NKVD in detention camps at Ostashkov and Starobielsk. This document was handed over by Boris Yeltsin to the Polish government in 1992 as an act of "reconciliation." *Smersh,* composed mainly of Jewish commissars, used the technology of mass executions; e.g., in the prison cells of the Soviet steamer *Dzhurma* 12,000 captives froze to death near Wrangel Island; 1,650 Polish deportees died in the winter in unheated and overcrowded cattle cars; 15,000 interned Polish officers, intellectuals, teachers and doctors, disappeared in the Okchotzk Sea.

The killing fields of Katyn Forest were exhumed in 1943 to reveal thousands of Polish POWs butchered by the National Committee of Internal Affairs (*NKVD – Narodnyi Komissariat Vnutriennikh Del.*) Stalin informed Polish Premier Stanislav Mikolajczyk that he had "liquidated" 20,000 Ukrainian nationalists and conscripted another 200,000 suspected Ukrainian enemies of the Soviet Union into the Red Army.

Douglas Reed names names of those who set up "The First Despotic Utopias," among them, Lenin, Kamenev, Stalin, Trotsky, Karl Radek, Iron Felix Dzerzhinsky, Rosa Luxemburg, Plekanov, Latsis.

"The end of the old order, with an unguided world adrift in a relativistic universe, was a summons to such gangster-statesmen to emerge," Reed states. "They were not slow to make their appearance."[21]

Just as Lenin, Trotsky and Iron Felix believed that violence was an essential element of the Revolution, so today our own gangster-statesmen also employ terror and oppressive police power to subjugate the citizens and create the ultimate despotic police state here in the United States.

PART TWO
SETTING THE STAGE FOR CONQUEST

THE fatal linkage between International Zionism and Fabian Socialism was forged in the Zionist-instigated *Treaty of Versailles.* It was designed to destroy Germany as the central power in Europe and to make it ripe for bolshevization, following the rape of Russia. It paved the way for the eternal Jewish dream of global conquest by controlling a "League to Enforce Peace" which came to be known as the *League of Nations.* Congress was wise enough then to prevent our becoming a signatory to that evil scheme for a one-world government. Two other related acts took place in the drama of the "Great War"; one was the Balfour Declaration laying the groundwork for a Jewish homeland in Palestine (1917); the other, creation of a sympathy factor for the "persecuted" Jews.

The sympathy card was dealt after World War I. It was at this time that the idea of a holocaust of six million was hatched. Former governor of New York, Martin Glynn, in October 1919, spoke of "the extermination of 6 million Jews and the holocaust of European Jewry during the Great War."[22]

Because each of these schemes was a necessary adjunct to total world conquest, another war would be staged to put them into place. It was first vitally necessary to spread the poison of Bolshevism across the European continent.

By the use of a strange mix of the "scum of society," fellow travelers, socialists – Fabian and otherwise – ideologues and intellectuals, plus *agents provocateur* and for-hire spies, the Red Terror spread quickly across Europe, penetrating into Spain and Italy, as well as hapless France, thence to the Western Hemisphere, even into the inner sancta of the White House, the Supreme Court and Congress.

These shocking aspects, as Dr. Israel Shahak addresses in his *Jewish History, Jewish Religion: The Weight of Three Thousand Years,* directly relate to The Law as contained in the

Talmud, especially the *Kol Nidre*, or *All Vows* which affords a Jew forgiveness in advance for all of his lies, perjury and transgressions of the coming year. (We will look more closely at the Talmud in a later Chapter.)

"FAT HOLLYWOOD COWS TO BE MILKED"

Who were the liars? Professor Arthur Koestler in *The Invisible Writing* describes how "fascist atrocities" were fabricated in "the lie factory" run by two inspired professional liars, Willi Muenzenberg and Otto Katz, both later murdered on Stalin's orders.[23]

One of Muenzenberg's Communist cronies, then dwelling in absolute splendor in Hollywood, was Stanley Lawrence. In fact, in the 1930s, he and V. J. Jerome, another Bolshevik boss, founded the Hollywood branch of the Communist Party. It was controlled from Party headquarters in New York.

Lawrence and Jerome raised millions from what Lawrence dubbed "fat Hollywood cows to be milked," according to K. L. Billingsley on "Commie Dearest: The Hollywood Ten's 50th Birthday" (*Heterodoxy* Dec 1997).

> One of the most pressing tasks confronting the Communist Party in the field of propaganda is the conquest of this supremely important propaganda, until now the monopoly of the ruling class," said Comintern official Willi Muenzenberg. "We must wrest it from them and turn it against them.[24]

And turn it they did! We now have such current Hollywood Bolsheviks as Stephen Spielberg and Michael Eisner milking (or mulcting) the great American public. When Stalin had Muenzenberg executed – for whatever reason – he certainly didn't kill off the "Lie Factory." It is still alive and well in Hollywood.

PROPTER METUM JUDAEORUM

It was Abbe Augustin Barruel, writing in his massive work on the French Revolution in 1798, "Memoirs Illustrating the History of Jacobinism," who used the expression *propter metum Judaeorum* (for fear of the Jews) in connection with a pair of "secret adepts," Messieurs Turgot and Necker, who had served King Louis XVI as prime ministers.   Both of these skilled gangster-statesmen formed monopolies to manipulate bills of credit and commodities, such as corn.   Both were driven by two all-consuming goals.[25]

At a later date, but still addressing the Jacobins – now called Bolshevists – it was Winston Churchill who addressed the role of Russia in World War I. Give the man credit; he knew the difference between the country called Russia as an historical state and the criminals who hatched the plot to take over Russia and subjugate its peoples under the Soviet Bolsheviks. Churchill's views appeared in another massive work, *The Great War*, published by George Newnes Ltd. Churchill summed up his views in the London *Daily Telegraph* on 4 Dec 1930:

> Those who, like myself, are inveterate opponents of all that Bolshevism stands for whether in subversive corruption or despotic rule, are prone to dwell on its root characteristic. It is unnatural.
>
> A monster has born into our modern world.... It possesses the science of civilization without its mercy, the fanaticism of religion without God, the exploitation of human passions and appetites without any ideal beyond their gratification – and that not achieved.
>
> I have repeatedly warned my Liberal and Socialist friends...that they will never get any satisfaction out of the Russian Communists. We are in the presence of a sub-human degeneration which, if not luckily inherently morbid, would reduce great nations, nay, all mankind to the conditions of the White Ant. Or again, it is a cancer bacillus feeding and spreading itself upon the starving body, thriving by the very process which tortures and destroys its victim.
>
> Undeterred by this advice, many have tried the experiment. All have been disillusioned. All in turn have sought to clasp that clammy hand. All in turn have recoiled, injured, infected, or at least defiled by its chill, poisonous sweat....
>
> ...Will the Soviet Government 'get away with the goods' in Russia? Will they succeed in diverting the wrath of the Russian people at the horrible and utterly needless privations which they are now enduring, into a harmless and imaginary canal?
>
> I am by no means sure that they will not. The combination of the powers of Terrorism without limit or compunction, and of caucus machinery, newspapers, the broadcast, and the cinema, applied to a

primitive people, isolated from all external news and bowed in grinding toil, is not to be measured.

It is by no means certain that, if these forces of soulless barbarism and modern inventions once get us down, we could ever recover or escape.

...My only regret is that Europe and the United States did not make a more resolute effort to rescue the Russian people from the awful fate by which they are now gripped.[26]

Alas, here we are 70 years from Churchill's stirring words sounding the alarm and some 200 hundred years after Abbe Barruel dwelt on that root characteristic... "it is unnatural"; and we find ourselves in an identical strait of abject terror and virtual subjugation. We, in our turn, have clasped that clammy hand – for whatever reason – and now we recoil, "injured, infected, or at least defiled by its chill, poisonous sweat..."

Is there no antidote?

The very tactics and techniques used to enthrone Lenin and his gangster-statesmen, such as Felix Dzerzhinsky and Leon Trotsky, are today being implemented with a vengeance in the United States. A small group of dedicated gangster-statesmen with a fanatical will to power, and backed by international financial oligarchs with absolutely no scruples whatsoever, are seizing the critical levers of power and straining for the ultimate brass ring – a one-world despotic government under the United Nations.

A quick scan of these "elites" in Washington DC and New York City, of the media moguls, of multi-nationalists and internationalists, and especially of the megabankers and investment-house gurus, will put a familiar face on our own gangster-statesmen. What Lenin and his Bolshevist thugs accomplished in a few short months during the Russian "Revolution" is being accomplished at a much slower pace, but just as effectively, here in our country. All we lack at the moment is the Red Terror, but bet on it, it is coming. Can we stop them?

President Bill Clinton announced on 21 Jan 1999 that he is contemplating a Domestic Terrorism Team to be headed by a military commander and funded with a $2.8 billion budget to combat alleged terrorism on US soil. (*New York Times* 22 Jan 99)[27]

The danger of terrorism on US soil stems directly from Clinton's reckless and criminal bombing of six sovereign nations: Yugoslavia, Sudan, Afghanistan, Bulgaria, Albania and Iraq. Such acts of terror and destruction motivated a leading terrorist, Osma bin Laden, to state that all Americans, including "those who pay taxes," are now his targets.

Using terrorism as an excuse, the Clinton administration made extraordinary plans to use military force against American citizens:

• Secretary of Defense William Cohen said in an *Army Times* interview that "Americans soon may have to choose between civil liberties and more intrusive means of protection";

• Deputy Secretary of Defense John Hamre floated the idea of designating some US troops as a "Homeland Defense Command" to impose military rule within the United States;

• The Army War College journal *Parameters* (Autumn 1997) predicted that "terrorism will almost inevitably trigger an intervention by the military" and "legal niceties...will be a minor concern";

• Clinton's Executive Order 12919, "National Defense Industrial Resources Preparedness," gives FEMA dictatorial authority over communications, energy, food, transportation, health, housing, and other resources. Clinton can also invoke "emergency" powers to deal with any perceived emergency.[28]

What we desperately need is a cadre of true patriots well versed in the truths of recent history who are able and willing to expose these gangster-statesmen (say thugs) for what they really are. Coupled with these modern-day penmen, we need courageous publishers and distributors who will get the unvarnished truth into the hands of thinking people throughout the world, who then might rise up and break the binding chains of Bolshevism and slavery.

PART THREE
OLIGARCHS TAKE OVER

BY mid-1999, the long knives were being sharpened in the barracks and cantonment areas throughout Russia by the military officers, particularly those of the elite units. To put it bluntly, they were fed up. They had been pushed to the wall by the Yeltsin regime, first by his two top guns in Moscow, Anatoli Chubais and Boris Nemtsov, who were the principal ministers in the austerity policies demanded by the International Monetary Fund (IMF) throughout 1994-97.

And then carried out, by a not-so-strange alliance between a small group of super oligarchs and international financiers with a clique of bureaucratic bagmen who fought and connived and cheated their way to the very pinnacles of Russian political/economic power; of course, with a continuing and very able assist from their like-minded cronies here in the United States.

One of the top leaders of these not-too-disparate groupings was Boris Abramovich Berezovsky (45) who had risen in the scheme of things from a once low-level position in the government to a car dealership in Moscow, and thence to bank ownership under what is euphemistically called "privatization," to one of the world's richest billionaires.

RUSSIA IS MIRROR-IMAGE OF US CORRUPTION

This author attended a high-level secret briefing on 5 January 2000 at a secure military facility in Northern Virginia where the conference room was "swept for bugs" just prior to the proceedings. A top civilian intelligence officer and Soviet expert from the Defense Department led off the discussions relating to recent happenings in Russia at the close of the century. He was in Moscow just prior to what he called "the forced resignation of Boris Yeltsin and replacement by the hand-picked Vladimir Putin as president."

The briefing officer requested anonymity, hereinafter referred to as Mr. X.

Mr. X stated that Russia, under the control of oligarchs (6 of the 7 are Zionists), has become a mirror image of the political and financial corruption endemic at the highest levels of government here in the United States:

> "It represents a not-so-strange marriage between the financial oligarchs and the media barons, which together, not only control the market place, but the minds of the mostly unthinking public, which can easily be persuaded to vote for a particular pre-selected candidate."

He emphasized that the elections for deputies to the Duma, which took place on 19 December 1999, were tightly controlled from the Kremlin; or, more exactly from Yeltsin's inner circle, known as "The Family," comprised of such newly-minted oligarchs as Boris Berezovsky, Roman Abramovich, Yeltsin's daughter, Tatanya Dyachenko, and a select few thugs, gangsters and opportunists who assisted in placing Yeltsin in the position of president, following the fake coup d'état in 1991 when Mikael Gorbachev was ousted.

Mr. X stressed that many of these same arch-criminals went after seats in the Duma with a vengeance in the 19 Dec 1999 elections, as a win would give them total immunity from prosecution for any and all crimes committed, including murder and grand theft. Both Berezovsky and Abramovich sought and won seats in the Duma; both ran in provinces located far from the capital. Since Berezovsky owned the only two TV stations able to reach across the broad expanse of Russia, he was able to ensure favorable comment for himself and other members of the newly formed Unity party, and to smear or black out any opposition.

In fact, it had been Berezovsky, with his virtually unlimited loot, who had organized the creation of the Unity party in Sep 1999, only three months before the election. Mr. X stated that it was also Berezovsky who had "convinced Yeltsin to fire Stephasin and replace him with the spy chief, Vladimir Putin, a month earlier."

Mr. X then brought up another mirror image. As if on cue, a series of horrific explosions rocked Moscow and two other cities in September, crumbling four multi-storied apartment complexes and murdering nearly 300 people in the middle of the night. Chechen terrorists were immediately blamed. Putin's popularity skyrocketed virtually overnight, as he declared war on the breakaway province of Chechnya.

> ...thinking people in Moscow and St. Petersburg supposed that the FSB had simply taken a page from the FBI and ATF here in the United States, following the blow-up of the Murrah Building in Oklahoma City. The finger of blame was pointed immediately at "terrorists," and by adroit use of the controlled media, the unthinking public – roughly 85% of the population – was convinced. Just as was the case with the federal building in Oklahoma, the Russian government moved its bulldozers onto the bombed sites and buried the debris, thus destroying any evidence that may have implicated the government or its Cheka secret police, the FSB.[29]

Mr. X then quoted General Alexander Lebed, former governor of Russia's largest province. Lebed was featured in a Reuters news report dated 28 Sep 1999 in which he stated that the bombing of Chechnya and the bomb attacks on apartments in Moscow could be a part of a government bid to unify Russia.

This is what we call *quid pro quo*. And, of course, it relates to the statement made by Mr. X that what was happening at the end of the century in Russia was a mirror-image of identical happenings here in the United States, and at the highest levels of government.

So, this Russian spy who came in out of the cold – one Vladimir Putin – has become Mr. Squeaky Clean and will not tolerate criminality or favoritism. Such rhetoric, whether uttered by a Russian presidential candidate or an American wannabe, seems to cry out for further scrutiny... commonly known in the US as a background check.

Such a check was made by Richard C. Paddock of the *Los Angeles Times*, among others, as well as by certain of our Defense intelligence specialists here in the US, including not only Mr. X of previous mention, but two of this author's close associates; one,

Dan Michaels, now retired, was at one time a top Soviet analyst and intelligence officer in the Office of Naval Intelligence (ONI). Dan is fluent in Russian and translates selected Russian newspapers on a weekly basis.   Another, Colonel J. Richard Niemela, USAF (Ret), a former fighter pilot and once head of the US military advisory group in Norway. Gleaning their voluminous data reveals a glaring fact, that Vladimir V. Putin, despite his stated intent to clean house in the Kremlin, is very much a part of the problem, having been an active member of "The Family" for years and a more-than-willing participant in its intrigues, manipulations, criminality and favoritism.

The more things change, the more they remain the same. Consider the following:

A Reuters news report (21 Dec 1999), dateline MOSCOW - President Boris Yeltsin and Prime Minister Vladimir Putin, in line with Russia's current hard-line mood, heaped praise on the Soviet-era secret service, the KGB and its successors. "Several years ago, we fell prey to an illusion that we have no enemies," *Itar-Tass* quoted Putin as telling a meeting of top security officials, marking the Day of Security Bodies (the Cheka), founded 82 years ago, December 20, 1917.

"We have paid dearly for this," Putin said. "Russia has its own national interests, and we have to defend them." On Saturday, Yeltsin sent a special message to security bodies, the Kremlin service said. "The history of the Federal Security Service (the FSB, successor body to the KGB) is part of the country's history. Brilliant victories and bitter defeats are inseparable in it," the message said.[30]

As we have seen elsewhere, what these two dynamic Russian leaders were glorifying was the founding by "Iron Felix" Dzerzinsky of the dreaded Cheka secret police, an organization directly responsible over the years for the murder, deportation and imprisonment in the Gulags of the frozen north of millions of Slavic Russian peoples.

In yet another Moscow dateline, Paddock wrote (*Los Angeles Times,* 4 Jan 2000) that "Tycoon Boris A. Berezovsky likes to say that anyone can become president of Russia – as long as that person has the backing of the wealthy elite and the media. The billionaire Kremlin insider is about to prove himself right."[31]

Paddock stated that Berezovsky has emerged as a pivotal figure in events leading to Yeltsin's resignation and the appontment of acting president Vladimir V. Putin, "a stern, little-known former spy who came to Moscow less than four years ago." He said, "Berezovsky is a key member of The Family, the inner circle of Kremlin advisers revolving around Tatanya Dyachenko."[32]

He quoted Marina Salye, a former Leningrad City Council member: "The Family that has always feared to let the reins of power go all of a sudden entrusts their fate to a man whom they appear not to know at all. Isn't that weird? It is simply not their style; they have never acted so recklessly. So they must know something that allows them to trust Putin fully."[33]

Salye, ten years ago, headed an investigation into alleged improprieties by Putin. He had apparently improperly issued licenses for export of raw materials and nonferrous metals in exchange for food shipments that never arrived.

Paddock traced the footsteps of Putin as he moved from East Germany, where he served for ten years as a KGB spy, to Leningrad where he became a member of the city government. He soon rose to the position of deputy mayor. Following the accusation of abuse of power, he was spirited off to Moscow in 1996, where he fell in with members of The Family. Apparently, his benefactor of that time was Anatoly Chubais, a longtime Yeltsin advisor, who brought Putin into the Kremlin and placed him as deputy to Pavel Borodin, the head of the Kremlin's property department. Together, the pair oversaw the Kremlin's huge real-estate holdings.

Simultaneously with Putin's arrival in 1996, Yeltsin was re-elected, and rewarded Berezovsky for his campaign support with a post as deputy secretary of the Security Council. Paddock opined that this was the time when the paths of Putin and Berezovsky most likely crossed. The next year, Yeltsin rewarded Putin by appointing him as head of the Audits Directorate and naming him as a deputy chief of staff.[34]

Shortly thereafter, as interim president, Putin sent troops to regain control of Chechnya. Why this brutal massacre of Muslim Checnyans? Oil of course – the second largest reserve among the Caspian Sea neighbors (Azerbijan being the first).

The Russian electorate loved it and Putin's popularity soared.

THEFT BY PRIVATIZATION

As an indicator of the gigantic privatization grab then underway by the financial oligarchs, the Onexim Bank Group picked up Svyazinvest (major state telecom) and Norilsk Nickel. Yeltsin then invited the six top bankers to the Kremlin, promising them that to avoid infighting, he, Yeltsin, personally would oversee the rest of the slated privatization to take place.

The "lucky" winners include Vladimir Gusinsky, head of Media-Most group, Vladimir Potanin, head of Oneximbank, Vladimir Vinogradov of Inkombank, Mikhail Fridman of Alfa Bank, Mikhail Khodorkovsky of the Rosprom-Menetep Group, and Aleksandr Smolensky of SBS-Agro Bank Group. An article by Anton Surikov appeared in *Zavtra* (#33-194) Aug 1997. *Zavtra* is the leading opposition newspaper in Russia and is supported by most nationalist elements, including the Communists. The major print and electronic media in Russia came increasingly under the control of a very few super-rich oligarchs, such as Berezovsky and Gusinsky.

The title of Surikov's article is "The Disintegration of Russia and the Jews." He led off:

> Under the leadership of Anatoli Chubais, the radical faction of the Moscow financial elite is today undertaking desperate measures to usurp the entire economic and political power in the country. The recent revelation of the privatization of Svyazinvest demonstrated that the actions of our first deputy premier were sanctioned by and in complete

accord with the wishes of the United States. This is attested to by the participation in this scandalous affair of the international financial speculator George Soros together with the speculative office 'Deutsche Morgan Grenfell' which has close ties with the British Special Services and a series of articles in the Western press that revealed the billions in wealth possessed by Chernomydin, Berezovsky, Gusinsky and accused them of engaging in 'criminal activities'.[35]

He stressed in his article that the final objective of the Americans is the complete deindustrialization of Russia, the reduction of its population by 25 - 30% and the conversion of the country into a raw-materials colony of the United States, which would be governed to serve US interests by people like Chubais.

"The regional leaders are becoming much more active in taking over control of impoverished enforcement agencies in the various regions and are closely associated with the governors and heads of the Republics by ties far more binding than with the Moscow directorates," Surikov reported. "If the military districts and the governors agree among themselves not to accept Moscow's control, the disintegration process will inevitably assume avalanche proportions. The hatred of the Russian provinces for the 'democrats' in the capital, for Chubais personally, and for the super-rich middleman Moscow in general, has been at the critical point for some time now."[36]

Surikov recently returned from a visit to Jerusalem where he met persons in official establishments. "The Israelis believe that Moscow's loss of control over events in the provinces will become increasingly irreversible." He further stated:

> If you can believe them, real power in our country (Russia) is in the hands of the largest number of Jews since 1937, including Chubais, Nemtsov, Urinson, Berezovsky, and many others. Representatives of the Jewish community completely control the financial world and the mass media, which is to say that the Jewish community actually controls Russia.
>
> There is a real danger that events will go uncontrolled, that there will be a destructive social upheaval, and that the country will sink into chaos. Concurrently with the growth of anti-Chubais, anti-democratic, anti-Moscow sentiments among Russians living in the provinces is a growing enmity toward the Jews who are seen constantly on TV and who

are viewed as tied in with the current power structure and the Moscow ruling elite. All of this threatens to spill over into ethnic clashes and then into a banal 'cleansing' of Moscow, St. Petersburg, Novgorod, Ekaterinburg and other major cities with large numbers of Jews.[37]

Surikov concluded:

> In the words of the Israelis, they are now – in the event of *force majeure* – preparing to evacuate quickly up to one million Jews and relocate them in the 'historical homeland'.[38]

REFORM BY LOOTING

A Russian economist, Sergei Glazyev, a member of the government until 1993 when he resigned from his exalted position as Minister of Foreign Economics following Yeltsin's abolition of the constitution, functioned as an advisor to the upper house of parliament in 1996-97. In an article appearing in *Pravda* (8 Oct 1997), he warned that Russia is fast becoming a colony of the "world oligarchy," made up of international financial banks and corporations who, together with their legal advisors and theoreticians, constitute a "new world order." Glazyev asserted:

These financial looters are controlling the second stage of "reform" after devoting five years to disorganizing the economy, appropriating state property and natural resources, and criminal transfer of control of all wealth to foreign owners. To cover interest to foreign creditors, this criminal oligarchy joined to the power elite presently governing Russia, have usurped the state budget into a tax-collection agency.[39]

According to Glazyev, the only salvation from transnational capital oligarchs is to develop a "resistance and recovery" strategy, which would work only if "state policy proceeds exclusively from the national interest."[40]

Because what he outlines may also be happening here in the United States, there is a possibility that either country could attempt to extricate itself from the steady and increasingly brutal subjugation by the international criminal oligarchy. The tools of the trade are there and have been used many times since World

War II. One is the classic *coup d'état*; another, bloody revolution; still another, civil war.

RUSSIAN ECONOMY "LIKELY TO FAIL"

Washington Post writer, Thomas W. Lippman, wrote a lengthy but informative piece in the 7 Nov 1998 issue on "Russian Economic Recovery Plan Likely to Fail, US Diplomat Says."

The diplomat is none other than Strobe Talbott, Deputy Secretary of State, at one time Bill Clinton's roommate at Oxford University and, since 1993, Clinton's chief Russian strategist. Lippman caught his speech to Stanford University students in November 1998. Lippman tells us that Talbott "offered Washington's strongest criticism so far of the economic plan announced a week ago by Prime Minister Yevegeny Primakov."[41]

Talbott warns that the Russian government's economic recovery program will almost certainly fail, and if it does, "we may be in for some heightened tensions over security and diplomatic issues."[42]

Lippman points out that since Russia devalued the ruble and defaulted on part of its debt, igniting a financial crisis that has paralyzed the country, the Clinton administration has put increasing distance between itself and Moscow.

Talbott, in his speech, offered a limited range of narrowly focused endeavors, such as food aid. This largesse was designed "to help see Russia through the winter." The Japanese are kicking in as well, with Prime Minister Keizo Obuchi informing Primakov that Tokyo will provide an $800 million loan.

The US loan is for 20 years at 2% interest and a five-year grace period. So much for Talbott's "limited range of narrowly focused endeavors." In fact, we are seeing yet another US handout in a series of handouts to the Bolsheviks never-ending since 1933, when FDR rushed to recognize the Soviet Union, at the very time when Stalin was starving, collectivizing and murdering 8-10 million Kulak peasant farmers.

In *Modern Times*, Johnson tells us that the famine of 1932, the worst in Russian history, was virtually unreported. At the height of it, George Bernard Shaw and his traveling companion, Lady Astor, visited Stalin in Moscow. Her ladyship asked Stalin, "How long are you going to go on killing people?" When he replied "As long as necessary," she changed the subject and asked him to find her a Russian nurserymaid for her children.[43]

Referencing Lippman's excellent article wherein Talbott singles out "nuclear materials safety" as another way to help the Russians, a program "in which the United States is about to pump millions of dollars into finding new missions to keep scientists employed in the formerly closed 'nuclear cities' of the Soviet Union."[44]

This is a subject Clinton had planned to raise with Primakov when they were to meet in Kuala Lumpur, Malaysia (called off because of Clinton's pending impeachment), particularly as it relates to "the flow of ballistic missile technology to Iran."[45]

Why Iran? To fully comprehend the game plan for that Mideast country, check Chapter 10, *Israeli Acts of Terror an 'Open Secret',* wherein Israel Shahak, a distinguished professor at Jerusalem University, lets us in on the "open secret" that Israel is poised to sling a few barbs (nukes) in Iran's direction in order to maintain its hegemony in the Mideast.

Talbott sees Russia – without all this external help – faced with "three disagreeable choices: one, crank the printing presses even faster; two, plunge deeper into default; or, three, stop paying wages and pensions and conducting basic government functions."

"Whatever combination of these measures the government adopts, Russia's economic situation is likely to deteriorate further," Talbott concludes.[46]

RISE OF JEWISH FINANCIAL POWER IN USSR

We get a view of this enigma from a book, *Russia's Secret Rulers,* by another Russian, Lev Timofeyev (translated by

Catherine Fitzpatrick). Timofeyev, an economist, was thrown in prison in 1985 for "anti-Soviet" activities, served two years of an 11-year sentence, and became a journalist promptly upon his release. The thrust of his book has to do with the Soviet system as one gigantic black market in goods, services, position and privilege where a very few (a chosen few) at the very top – the *nomenklatura* – lead a life of royal splendor and absolute power.

In this land of absolutes, where the State owns everything, the only marketable commodity is power. It is here in the USSR where the factories and the goods they produce, as well as such tangibles as gold, silver, diamonds, paintings, can be bought and sold through the underground market economy. It has survived and thrived for over 70 years! He describes the power over the work force and other humans as "the sweetest form of power there is."[47]

And what we now see emerging, as a result of *perestroika* and *glasnost,* is the exact parallel of an earlier age in Canada and the United States after the bootleg era...the rise, through a strange metamorphosis, from rags to rackets to riches to respectability.

From the time of the initial takeover of Russia by the Bolshevists (*cum* Zionists) in 1917, there has been a thriving underground criminal class which sprang up spontaneously in the major cities and rapidly spread throughout all the republics. We could call it a mafia, but there were no Italians as such; a few Georgians, Letts and Uzbeks, but just as in the United States and Canada, the leadership, the brains and the business acumen was (and is) Jewish. This particular group in what became the USSR had one advantage over their counterparts in America; there were no inhibiting rules and regulations, no written laws and no morality. The criminal class shared a heritage which could be classed as law – the Babylonian Talmud – with the ruling class, the secret police and the Red army; and, of course, that law does not recognize as criminal any "taking advantage" of the goyim or gentiles.

Timofeyev can be considered an expert in the role of the black market in Soviet affairs, having lived with it and studied it face to face, so to speak, although from a slightly different perspective. Simis was a lawyer, Timofeyev a journalist *cum* economist. From both accounts, an identical picture emerges which can hardly be refuted. That view is one of close and continuous liaison between the *nomenklatura* and the criminal underworld, with the KGB acting as a catalyst (appropriately bribed and "taken care of") in order for the racketeers to pass from "criminal" to "entrepreneur."

Of course, under Lenin and his cohorts, a harsh code of laws emerged which, coupled with terror and repression and mass murder, established totalitarianism as never seen or practiced in modern times. One would have to revert back 2,500 years to the basic source model for such repression, to the return of the tribes of Judah and Benjamin from Babylonian captivity. They brought with them the Babylonian Talmud and the "oral tradition of the elders," both based on hate and vengeance, and calling for utter destruction of their enemies.

A curious kind of camaraderie has always existed in the USSR, uniting various *apparaturas* with the ruling *nomenklatura* and their "enforcers," whether Cheka, NKVD, KGB or GRU, so that even though this underground "entrepreneurship" was both informal and illegal, it survived and thrived and became most recently the very basis for privatization and the setting up of a "free market" system.

This in fact was and is a very important part of the international game plan for world control, which must start in the economic sphere and then spread into the political and sociological.

What we should find particularly engrossing about these fairly recent revelations emanating out of the former USSR is that they are being revealed by erudite Jews who either never were Communists or Zionists, or have turned their backs on this inherently evil and totalitarian system.

The most frightening aspect of these revelations is that the two systems of "entrepreneurship," with roots in *Babylonian*

Talmudism, flourished under two ostensibly opposite economic systems, "Communism" in the USSR and "Capitalism" in the US.

And now, every political indication points toward uniting these two disparate systems under the banner of one-world "Socialism." That same group – what Churchill called "the most formidable sect in the world" – have risen to riches and respectability here in the United States. They have come the route from pushcarts and loansharking to prostitution, bootlegging and extortion, to chain stores and shopping malls, to stock and commodity manipulation, to banking and investment.

On the other hand the United States of America are still not ripe for the slaughter, because they are needed as the base for operations during the Capitalistic phase of the overall plan. But should the time come when Socialistic World Government will be imposed on us all, then, because Americans would offer tough resistance, America, like Russia, may be forcibly subjected to extreme Socialism. Let none say 'it cannot happen here'; it has happened in too many places already. Be warned, and be prepared.

George Knupffer, *The Struggle for World Power: Revolution and Counter-Revolution*

CHAPTER IV
FDR'S BLOODY ROAD TO BOLSHEVISM
(Destroying the Republic)

For among my people are found wicked men: they lay wait, as he that setteth snares; they set a trap, they catch men.

Jeremiah 5:26

PART ONE
BEGINNING THE IMPERIUM

THE Bolshevization of America commenced in 1933 with the coming of Franklin Delano Roosevelt to the highest office of the land. His 12-year reign saw the transition of our form of government from a Republic to a Democracy, and thence to an Imperium.

In fact, one could look at the paternal FDR as the first Caesar of the American Century. President Clinton fancies himself as the second, and therein lies the danger. In order to comprehend what is happening to us as a distinct people who had pioneered and developed this once-great nation as a Christian society from about 1620 until 1901, one must look more closely at the man whom we cherish as FDR, and particularly examine the cunning cabal who expertly collaborated with him before, during and after his 12-year reign.

To understand FDR, one must understand his New Deal. For a good source, look to a book published in 1995, *Burden of Empire,* by Garet Garrett, which is a collection of his revealing essays, especially "The Revolution Was," published in 1938. Here is a startling quote:

> There are those who still think that they are holding the pass against a revolution that may be coming up the road. But they are gazing in the wrong direction. The revolution is behind them. It went by in the Night of Depression singing songs to freedom.
>
> There are those who have never ceased to say very earnestly, 'Something is going to happen to the American form of government if we don't watch out.' These were the innocent disarmers. Their trust was in words. They had forgotten their Aristotle. More than 2,000 years ago he wrote of what can happen within the form, when 'one thing takes the place of another so that ancient laws will remain, while the power will be in the hands of those who have brought about the revolution in the state'.[1]

Well, friends, it happened – in 1933. And those of us who still hope to hold the pass (or the gate, or the bridge) are still gazing in the wrong direction, for the enemy is inside the gates, and while we valiantly stand guard "at the ready," our patrimony is being plundered.

In Garrett's work, we see – finally, and perhaps too late – that he accurately and aptly characterizes the New Deal as the "revolution within the form."

My friends, ask not whence comes the revolution; it has passed us by. Garrett knew it and expounded upon it in 1938; and yet, we wait...why? Garrett tells us that it was a "silent revolution" and implemented by a "scientific technique" which was intentionally prepared from the outset to bring about domestic socialism as a result of, and a solution to, the planned and manipulated "Great Depression."

And each carefully calculated step along the way, FDR and his court handlers (the "administrators" of the New Deal) scientifically selected the next step in order to "ramify the authority and power of the executive."

FDR engineered the New Deal that brought about a massive transfer of power from the citizens to the central state. Garrett informs us that the next step taken by the "administrators" was designed to "strengthen its hold upon the economic life of the nation...extend its power over the individual...degrade the parliamentary principle...impair the great American tradition of an independent, constitutional judicial power...weaken all other powers, and exalt the leadership principle."[2]

Garrett concludes:

> The revolutionaries were on the inside, the defenders were on the outside. A government that had been supported by the people and was so controlled by the people became one that supported the people and so controlled them. Much of it is irreversible.[3]

WHO WERE THE "REVOLUTIONARIES"?

A glaring and unemotional fact of the Rooseveltian reign as president of the United States from 1933 to his death in 1945 is that he was totally helpless physically, in that he could neither dress himself nor even go to the bathroom unassisted. Struck down by polio in 1924, he not only never walked again, but could not even stand alone. He was in fact the superb puppet of which the Elders of Zion speak so eloquently in their Protocols.

Could a man who could not even minister to his bodily needs run a normal household, much less a country in the throes of financial disintegration? Ponder that a moment as we look at a partial listing of those who really ran the country, and then to Whittaker Chambers in his testimony *Witness*.

Bernard Baruch, unofficial President of the US; Judge Samuel Rosenman, Head of the Brain Trust, advisor and speech writer; Prof. Raymond Moley; Prof. Felix Frankfurter; Henry Morgenthau, Sr. and Henry Morgenthau, Jr.; Harry Dexter White; Alger Hiss; Judge Benjamin Cardozo; Charles Taussig; Nathan Margold; Charles Wyzanski; Prof. Leo Wolman; Rose Schneiderman; Isador Lubin, Jr.; Sol Rosenblatt; Jerome Frank; Mordechai Ezekile; Herbert Feis; David Lilienthal; Sidney Hillman; Prof. Albert Taussig; Alexander Sachs; Maurice Karp; Robert Freshner; Robert Strauss; Donald Richberg; Ferdinand Pecora; Samuel Untermayer; Prof. James Landis; Samuel Dickstein; Herbert Lehman; James Warburg; David Stern; Henry Horner; Louis Kerstein; Ben Cohen; Walter Lippman; William Bullitt; Adolf Berle.[4]

Here is an unalterable fact: of the 75 close advisors and high government officials with whom FDR surrounded himself, upon assuming the office of the Presidency, 52 were Jewish. Add to that number their "lesser brethren" who had been surreptitiously slipped into policy-making positions in all the governmental departments. Recognize too that of these interconnected groupings, most, if not all, were either card-carrying Communists or fellow travelers.

Professor Howard Sachar, in his *History of the Jews in America* (1992), boasts the following:

> Following Roosevelt's election to the presidency, Brandeis prepared a detailed blueprint for a major segment of the New Deal reform program. He discussed it at length with Frankfurter. Both agreed that much would depend on Frankfurter's ability to secure key assignments for his protégés. Gradually, those prospects materialized, as professor found important slots in Washington for his ablest former students and disciples. There were scores of these young people, so many that the press began dubbing them 'Frankfurter's Happy Hot Dogs.'
>
> Four or five thousand Jews operated at various echelons of government during the 1930s. If their numerical presence was less than spectacular, their influence was more than noteworthy. So was their visibility. [5]

Whittaker Chambers gives us a plentitude of names in his revelation *Witness:*

> Lee Pressman, Nathan Witt, John Abt, Dr. Philip Rosenbleitt, Marian Bacharach, Philip Reno, Schlomer Adler, Alexander Trachtenberg, Morris Karp (brother-in-law of Molotov), Heda Gompertz, Walter Krivitsky, Charles Kraemer, Victor Perlo, Harold Ware, Sam Kreiger, Eve Dorf, Abraham Silverman. [6]

These were the direct and totally treasonous links to the Soviets. Consider this passage from *Witness*:

> In the persons of Alger Hiss and Harry Dexter White, the Soviet Military Intelligence sat close to the heart of the United States Government. It was not yet in the Cabinet room, but was not far outside the door. In the years following my break with the Communist Party, the apparatus became much more formidable. Then Hiss became director of the State Department's office of Special Political Affairs and White became the Assistant Secretary of the Treasury.[7]

Chambers continues:

> In a situation with few parallels in history, the agents of an enemy power were in a position to do much more than purloin documents. They were in a position to influence the nation's foreign policy in the interests of the nation's chief enemy, and not only on exceptional occasions, like Yalta or through the Morgenthau Plan for the destruction of Germany, but in what must have been the staggering sum of day-to-day decisions. That power to influence policy had always been the ultimate purpose of the Communist Party's infiltration. It was much more dangerous, and, as events have proved, much more difficult to detect, than espionage, which beside it is trivial, though the two go hand-in-hand.[8]

Chambers reveals the depths of penetration of the government under FDR by a curious mix of International Zionists and Fabian Socialists linked directly to Soviet Bolshevism (Communism; earlier, Social Democracy; now, once more, Social Democracy). And FDR had not only encouraged it, but reveled in what he was doing, for he saw himself ultimately as the First President of the World Government under a United Nations.

One other quote from Chambers is highly pertinent as regards to Socialism and its companion, terrorism, for those who have made deep penetrations of our government in such areas as Justice, FBI, BATF, and the CIA. Here is Chambers:

> It was perfectly clear, too, that if socialism was to stem the crisis and remake the world, socialism involved a violent struggle to get and keep political power. At some point, socialism would have to consolidate its power by force.... Here was no dodging of the problem of getting and keeping power. Here was the simple statement that terror and dictatorship are justified to defend the socialist revolution if socialism is justified. Terrorism is an instrument of socialist policy if the crisis was to be overcome. It was months before I could accept even in principle the idea of terror. Once I had done so, I faced the necessity to act.[9]

A world-renowned author, playwright and poet, the Hungarian patriot, Louis Marschalko, in his 1958 masterpiece *The World Conquerors*, speaks eloquently of the role of International Zionism since its formation in Basel, Switzerland in 1897, and its continuing goal of world domination under a "United Nations":

Christian resistance should have followed at the moment when Bolshevism broke out in Russia and when the work of Jewry became visible through the Versailles Treaty. The message of Christendom should have been the restoration of unity in disorganized Europe, and the elevation of the Christian concept of hierarchy that would guard against the individual being reduced to herd level.

Bolshevism as well as the soulless liberal capitalism should have been effectively mastered by their only real adversary – by Christian resistance.... Perhaps Christ himself might have come with his scourge to drive the money-changers out of the House of God, thus restoring justice, goodwill and social peace, and once more address his Christian peoples with Peter's forthright words: 'Save yourselves from this untoward generation!' [10]

But Christianity was reluctant to adopt revolutionary methods in order to wrench world power out of the hands of those whom Christ assailed on Maundy Thursday. The spirit of Christianity should have impressed itself upon public life, upon governments, upon the press and the trade unions, but it failed miserably to fulfill its mission.

ZIONISTS DECLARE WAR

International Zionism declared war on Germany's National Socialism in 1933, for they saw in it the seeds which would elevate the German people from the total degradation into which they had plunged following the Talmudic revenge of the Versailles Treaty. They thus set the scene for the savage carnage of World War II. Here are some quotes:

"The US has entered the first phase of a second war." (Henry Morgenthau, Jr., just appointed Secretary of the Treasury by FDR; *Portland Journal,* 12 Feb 1933).[11]

As reported by Forest Davis (author of "What Really Happened in Teheran?" in the *Saturday Evening Post,* 20 May 1944:

Morgenthau was preparing for the resumption of American-Soviet relations which became a fact shortly after FDR assumed the Presidency. The first Soviet ambassador to the US was Litvinov [real name: Finkelstein].[12]

"I am for war!" (Rabbi Stephen Wise, 8 May 1933)[13]

Coupled with these bellicose statements was the earlier declaration of war on Germany and Christianity by International Zionists. Jewish groups combined to publish a full-page ad in the *New York Times* on 16 Sep 1932, stating *inter alia:* "Let us boycott anti-Semitic Germany!"[14]

This theme was enlarged by radio broadcasts and newspaper advertisements in 1933 by Samuel Untermyer of the World Jewish Congress, who proclaimed *inter alia* (*New York Times,* 7 Aug 1933) that Zionists were "the aristocrats of the World" and were declaring a "holy" war against Germany and its people.[15]

Continuing to beat the kettle drums of war, Vladimir Jabotinsky, perhaps the world's leading Marxist terrorist, stated (25 Jan 1934) "We shall let loose a spiritual and material war of the whole world against Germany."[16]

A revealing article published in the London *Sunday Chronicle* (2 Jan 1938) under the heading "500,000,000 Pound Fighting Fund for the Jews," included this threat and promise:

> The Jew is facing one of the biggest crises in his troubled history. In Poland, Rumania, Germany, Austria, his back is to the wall. But now he is going to hit back hard.... The great international Jewish financiers are to contribute approximately 500,000,000 Pounds [$2 billion, 500 million]. The sum will be used to fight the persecuting states. The battle will be fought on the world's stock exchanges. Since the majority of the antisemitic states are burdened with heavy international debts, they will find their very existence threatened."[17]

Rabbi Maurice Perlsweig, head of the World Jewish Congress, told a Canadian audience (Toronto *Evening Telegram,* 26 Feb 1940): "The World Jewish Congress has been at war with Germany for seven years."[18]

Ludwig Lewisohn, Zionist Organization of America, stated in an article carried in the September 1942 *Jewish Mirror* (NY) *inter alia:*

> The Jewish people is the symbol of the nature of this war. Nothing else.... On this central point, on this very heart and core of the

whole matter the West is still recalcitrant.... Yes, the Jews are the chief enemies of National Socialism.... This is the Alpha and Omega, the beginning and the end of the whole matter. [19]

WILL THE REAL FDR PLEASE STAND UP?

Social reform in America during the height of the 1930s Depression was called the New Deal, which means the new distribution. Marschalko again: "This will be the year for sounding the trumpets in America [1933]...our bankers, our socialists and our journalists will be blowing the trumpets and our Brain Trust will execute the New Deal at the expense of the American pioneer-population...the only remaining question: Whom are we going to put in the Presidential Chair in Washington?"[20]

The rest is recent history, for his name was Franklin Delano Roosevelt...but, who was he, really, and who was Eleanor?

Robert Edward Edmondson in his famous book *I Testify* refers to the Roosevelt family tree compiled by the Carnegie Institute (1934) from which it is evident that the President of the United States from 1933 to 1945 was of Jewish descent:

> These people came to America in 1682, led by the patriarch Claes Martenzen van Rosenvelt and on the distaff side Janette Samuel. Originally of Spanish Sephardim Jews who had escaped from Spain to England in 1492, their tree is studded with Jacobs, Isaacs and Samuels. Franklin and Eleanor were cousins.[21]

The *New York Times,* 14 Mar 1935, quotes the President:

> In the distant past my ancestors may have been Jews. All I know about the origin of the Roosevelt family is that they are apparently descendants of Claes Martenzen van Roosevelt who came from Holland.[22]

The *Washington Star* on 20 Feb 1936 published a genealogical chart prepared by the Carnegie Institution, under the direction of Dr. H. H. Laughlin (7 Mar 1934), "Famous Sons of Famous Fathers – The Roosevelts," which depicted the family lineage of both Franklin and his cousin, Theodore, running back through Isaac, Jacobus, Johannes, Nicholas to Claes Martenzen van Rosenvelt. *The Times* of St. Petersburg, Florida ran an article (14 Apr 1934) regarding the nationality of the Roosevelt family, based on an interview with the former governor of Michigan, Chase S. Osborn:

> Although a Republican, the former governor has a sincere regard for President Roosevelt and his policies. He referred to the 'Jewish ancestry' of the President, explaining how he is a descendant of the Rosocampo family expelled from Spain in 1620. Seeking safety in Holland and other countries, members of the family, he said, changed their name to Rosenberg, Rosenbaum, Rosenblum, Rosenvelt and Rosenthal.[23]

The *New York Herald-Tribune* (8 May 1937) featured an article, later carried coast-to-coast by the Associated Press, stating that "President Roosevelt will receive the tenth award of the Gottheil Medal for distinguished service to Jewry." The medal featured the head of Roosevelt on one side and the six-point Solomon Star, synagogue symbol of possession and world power, on the other, with a mystical "good luck" idiom in the center of the star. The awarding of the medal included a card bearing the following inscription:

> Good Luck and Wisdom to Franklin D. Roosevelt, our modern Moses, leading Jewry in 'The Promised Land' under the 'Seal of Solomon.'[24]

A US Genealogist, B. Schmalix, writing about the genealogy of the Roosevelt family (14 May 1939), stated:

> In the seventh generation we see the mother of Franklin Delano Roosevelt (Sarah) as being of Jewish descent. The Delanos are descendants of an Italian or Spanish Jewish family – Dilano or Dillano – one of whom had drafted an agreement with the West Indian Company in 1657 regarding the colonization of the island of Caracao.[25]

As we entered the stage of Bolshevism here in America in 1933 under FDR, Bernard Baruch controlled the 351 most important branches of American industry during WW II, while Alger Hiss conducted the talks with Stalin. It was Einstein, Oppenheimer and David Lilienthal who produced the atomic bomb, while Fiorello La Guardia and Herbert Lehman managed UNRRA. Henry Morgenthau, Jr., along with his chief protégé, Harry Dexter White (Dexter Weiss), controlled the US Treasury for the entire twelve years of the Roosevelt reign and prepared a splendid plan for the extermination of the German people.

Bernard Baruch, a Sephardic Jew whose family came from Europe via Brazil to North America in the early 1700s, has become legendary. Mrs. Noma Aguilar, as of 2000 is living in California, recalls that her father, Benjamin Booker Linton, was, with such luminaries as Joseph P. Kennedy, a member of the War Production Board. Upon the closing of World War I, Baruch, whose salary as chairman was one million dollars a year, boasted to the other members, "We made you all millionaires, now we will get the next war started and you can all become billionaires."

FDR – OUR PREMIER DICTATOR

One who saw clearly in the 1930s what FDR and his "Reds" in government were doing toward destroying US sovereignty and aligning our country with the Soviets in order to set up a world socialist power was Ralph Townsend. Perhaps his best work was *There Is No Halfway Neutrality*, published in March 1938, more than three years before Pearl Harbor. Townsend exposed the machinations in the establishment media to bring America into a war with Japan:

> Efforts to involve America abroad are now more elaborately organized than in 1898 or 1917. Alien aims are plain. Only our strictest neutrality toward all – with favors to none – can hold urgently needed trade and provide a basis for America's continued peace.
>
> Of course the agitators aren't calling for war outright – not yet. Their first step is to build the state of mind which leads to war. Once they generate sufficient hate, the rest is easier.... That is similar to the path by which a shrewd minority launched the United States into needless wars in 1898 and 1917. Only later were the many crooked deals which engineered our entry revealed. Only after the World War was it disclosed that dominant forces had agreed to get America into it in return for political concessions. The success of a few scheming scoundrels in that feat was called 'America's great moral choice'.
>
> Most leaders in the campaign for trouble with Japan are on record as ardent friends of the Soviet Union. Communist party members agitate everywhere in the effort to boycott Japan.... Red aims are plain: (1) Generating the notion that Japan is an enemy, thus paving the way for

US aid to the Soviets as an ally against Japan; (2) Tension in which an incident may be fanned into serious trouble; (3) Sympathy for Chinese Reds now fighting Japan and on the edge of controlling China's tottering government; (4) Promoting unemployment among US workers by halting silk imports and cotton exports, with resulting distress which could be blamed on the Japanese.

If war with Japan can be arranged Reds will gain enormously in political power here. Just as in 1917 the government will declare America under special wartime emergency rule. This will again put the country under a complete dictatorship as it was under Woodrow Wilson in wartime. But there will be an important difference. Many high officials in our government now are known to favor Soviet theories and methods.

These alien-minded officials will become dictators in their departments if war can be arranged. Thus far Americans have successfully objected to their Bolshevik schemes. But under special war powers opposition will be called treason. Objectors will be jailed. This is not imaginary. We know what certain schemers in our government have been trying to do. We know that with wartime powers they would be able to do it.

After 'peace' came this increased power of Reds in America might be broken only by severe civil war. Well-meaning Americans stirred by talk of needless trouble with Japan in the name of Chinese freedom are thus playing into the hands of a minority eager to destroy all remaining freedom here at home.

Any movement seeking followers by falsification must be viewed with distrust by thinking and honest people. The movement to make trouble with Japan is almost wholly of this kind. Agitators call the conflict in China a war on democracy. Democracy never existed in China....

Knowing that average Americans do not fancy a dictatorship, agitators call Japan one.... No single individual in Japan exercises as much power as our own president of the United States. Within modern times no person in Japan has had the supreme financial authority now enjoyed by Secretary of the Treasury Henry Morgenthau in America, nor has any Japanese exercised the supreme power over his nation's industries such as was enjoyed by Bernard Baruch in America during the World War

Our choice is plain. If complaints against Japan were bona fide, the agitators would not need to resort to so much misrepresentation. Dangerous undercurrents of alien politics are obvious.... This is our country – your country –. If foreign trouble comes it will be your trouble.

Only a fixed policy of no partisanism is insurance against it. In this aim each good citizen can put personal influence to public service. But the choice for peace must be definite – with no meddling, no boycotts, no war loans.

There is no halfway neutrality.[26]

RENDEZVOUS AT CASABLANCA

FDR's "terrible secret in the closet" was revealed in *Roosevelt's Road to Russia* by George N. Crocker. He has interwoven it into FDR's travels about the world to meet with, first Churchill, then Churchill and Stalin, in such exotic places as Casablanca (January 1943).

Josef Stalin could hardly have done better for his cause if he had attended the Casablanca Conference in person. There, FDR did him two favors. One was tentative, but the other was final and of historic importance. For the first time he threw cold water on the incipient British plan to strike at Germany through the Balkans and thus frustrate the postwar domination of central and Eastern Europe by the Soviet Union.

Roosevelt pronounced "unconditional surrender" as the only condition which could bring the wars in Europe and Asia to a close. This meant that Germany and Japan, the two nations whose geographical position and historic roles made them the only bulwarks against Communist expansion, were not only to be defeated but were also to be made prostrate. This, in the words of Lord Hankey, 'removed the barriers against communism in Europe and the Far East and greatly decreased the security of the whole world.' Hanson W. Baldwin has said that it was 'perhaps the biggest political mistake of the war.' For the United States and many other nations, it was a calamity. [27]

It was here at Casablanca that FDR was at the high pitch of his wartime ebullience. John Gunther recalls:

He behaved in some ways like a conqueror and lord of the earth when he reached Africa, giving out decorations almost as a monarch does; he talked about the French empire as if it were his personal possession and would say things like, 'I haven't quite decided what to do about Tunis.'[28]

As for "unconditional surrender," renowned military historian Gen. J.F.C. Fuller put it thus:

First, that because no great power could with dignity or honour to itself, its history, its people and their posterity comply with them, the war must be fought to the point of annihilation.... Secondly, once victory had been won, the balance of power within Europe and between European nations would be irrevocably smashed. Russia would be left the greatest military power in Europe, and, therefore, would dominate Europe. Consequently, the peace these words predicted was the replacement of Nazi tyranny by an even more barbaric despotism.[29]

And so, for more than two years longer, the Germans fought on, with the courage of despair. On the other side of the world, Roosevelt's words hung like a putrefying albatross around the neck of America and Britain. They led, in the words of Lord Hankey, to "the culminating tragedy of the two atomic bombs in Japan." By mid-1943, the Japanese knew they would lose the war and prayed for any face-saving way to accept defeat. But no; the carnage had to continue, even after Emperor Hirohito informed the Supreme War Direction Council that the war should be ended on any terms short of unconditional surrender. The horrors of Hiroshima and Nagasaki followed.

PLOTTING POISONOUS PERFIDY

George Fowler, writing in *The Barnes Review* (Jan 1995), exposed "The Price We Paid for Roosevelt's 'Unconditional Surrender.'" The time: mid-January 1943, the place: Casablanca, the plotters: President Roosevelt and Prime Minister Churchill. Fowler cites a recounting of British intelligence activities by a former top MI6 operator in *Through the Looking Glass,* which made this crucial point:

> By early 1943 even Josef Goebbels' propaganda efforts could not mask the precariousness of Germany's situation. Had the American and British governments been so disposed, this period marked the first major time frame (save for mid-1940 when Churchill refused to entertain Germany's honorable peace overtures) when an initiative for peace could have succeeded.[30]

Fowler tells us that British intelligence considered the surrender of Germany's Sixth Army at Stalingrad to be the start of the cold war. "From that point, top MI6 figures concluded, Soviet expansion aims should have been a primary consideration in Western Allied war planning. Instead, FDR, meeting with British Prime Minister Winston Churchill at Casablanca, slammed the door on what many would consider not only an option but a paramount responsibility to avert further bloodshed and destruction."

Fowler further quotes former Ambassador Charles P. "Chip" Bohlen: "Responsibility for this unconditional surrender doctrine rests almost exclusively with President Roosevelt...."

FDR's son, Elliott, present at Casablanca as an aide to his father, quoted the President as saying: "Of course, it's just the thing for the Russians. 'Unconditional surrender'. Uncle Joe might have made it up himself."

Fowler emphasizes that "there is solid body of evidence spelling out how President Roosevelt rejected a prime opportunity to end the European war in 1943. Had Roosevelt seized the moment, he would have strengthened the West's hand immeasurably and cut the legs from under a murderous despot named Josef Stalin." He further states that the abject failure of the 1943 German peace attempts indicates that the British and American warlords would "parley" with no one, not even those who risked everything, their families included, in opposing Hitler. "Many have concluded that they had always looked beyond Hitler to the destruction of Germany itself."[31]

Fowler concluded his brilliant essay by stating that Roosevelt, who came in with Hitler in 1933, went out with him in 1945. Churchill lasted two decades longer:

> He saw his beloved empire crumble, Britain enter succeeding stages of economic and social rot, and Germany re-emerge as Europe's leading nation.
>
> Ironically, one must conclude that those who placed their heads on the block to kill Hitler might have heeded his words and saved themselves the trouble.[32]

SURRENDER "UNCONDITIONALLY"

And now, those same shadowy forces who manipulated both FDR and Churchill seem bent on destroying – or at least bolshevizing – America.

Just who were these "shadowy forces" who convinced the ailing FDR to push for "unconditional surrender"? We get a clue from *Unexplained Mysteries of World War II* by William B Breuer (1997). FDR and Churchill convened at the Hotel Anfa, Casablanca, 13 January 1943. Before departing for home, FDR and Churchill held a press conference. Breuer informs us that "[W]ith scores of journalists avidly taking notes, the American President casually observed: 'Prime Minister Churchill and I have determined that we will accept nothing less than unconditional surrender of Germany, Italy and Japan.'

Seated beside the president and drawing on a large black cigar, Winston Churchill was stunned. That was the first time that the prime minister had heard the phrase 'unconditional surrender' used with regard to the current war.[33]

Later, a high official of the British government told Churchill: "Unless these terms are softened, the German army will fight with the ferocity of cornered rats." Churchill, already on public record, merely shrugged.

Breuer asks some cogent questions: "Had Franklin Roosevelt, a cerebral politician long accustomed to speaking in the global spotlight, truly been so muddleheaded as to make the seemingly offhanded 'unconditional surrender' ultimatum? Or had this unrehearsed press conference been a carefully calculated scenario, cooked up by the president and a few key advisers in the White House to trap Winston Churchill into a situation wherein he could not disagree?"[34]

Churchill, time and again, proved a willing accomplice to the Bolshevist plan for the total destruction of Germany and the establishment of a one-world government. In the process, he betrayed his country – just as did his naval chum, FDR. In the words of the noted British historian, Col. J.F.C. Fuller, "the peace these words predicted was the replacement of Nazi tyranny by an even more barbaric despotism."

QUEBEC I – HELPING "UNCLE JOE"

Then came Quebec I (August 1943). It was another Big Two conference. It was here that FDR and Churchill decided on an Anglo-American invasion of France in the spring of 1944. Churchill continued to argue here and later at the Teheran Conference, that the invasion of Europe should be through the Balkans, the "soft underbelly" of Europe. He wanted to "prevent a Soviet rush into the area which would permanently establish the authority of the Soviet Union there, to the detriment of Britain, and incidentally to the United States."[35]

Of course, FDR wanted that which came to pass, the invasion of Europe through France. According to Crocker, "Churchill understood perfectly that what was involved was not the winning of the war but the geopolitics of postwar Europe. At stake was the heartland of the Continent."

It was part and parcel of "the terrible secret in the closet" which FDR shared with Harry Hopkins, Samuel Rosenmann, Bernard Baruch and other "great" Americans. Were they also traitors?

What Churchill was really talking about was not the war with Germany, but the other one – the hush-hush one – of militant Bolshevism, incarnate as the New Russian dictatorship which had risen from the grave of the last Czar, against the capitalist West, which, by the basic assumption and written words of both Leninism and Stalinism, it was pledged to annihilate.[36]

Crocker states:

> The busiest beaver at Quebec was Harry Hopkins. He had in his pocket an extraordinary top-secret document, headed 'Russia's Position.'" It was an arrogant pronouncement of political policy of far-reaching consequences for the nation's future. The contents were not revealed to the American public until after Roosevelt's and Hopkin's deaths. Its precise authorship has never been disclosed. It was claimed that it was extracted from 'a very high level' United States military strategic estimate.[37]

What "high level"? The office of the Chief of Staff? Or from the Commander-in-Chief? It was a model of what a "military strategic estimate" should not be. Consider a couple of key paragraphs:

> Russia's post-war position in Europe will be a dominant one. With Germany crushed, there is no power in Europe to oppose her tremendous military forces....
>
> The conclusions from the foregoing are obvious. Since Russia is the decisive factor in the war, she must be given every assistance and every effort must be made to obtain her friendship. Likewise, since without question she will dominate Europe on the defeat of the Axis, it is even more essential to develop and maintain the most friendly relations with Russia.[38]

CAIRO - SELLING OUT CHINA

Then came the Cairo Conference in November of 1943.

Crocker writes that it was here that FDR's self-conceit took on a new dimension. For, beginning with the Cairo meeting with Churchill and Chiang Kai-shek of China, Roosevelt began to fall victim to the messianic complex that had destroyed President Wilson in 1919. "He began to envisage himself as the Master Builder of the shiny new postwar world. It was a role he was pathetically unsuited to attempt."[39]

China had two enemies; first, the Japanese, which she could have handled. Unfortunately, China faced a second enemy more terrible than the first – internal Communist rebellion. It ultimately destroyed the Chinese government and bolshevized the mainland, helped along the way by such as General George Catlett Marshall and his 1945-46 "Mission" to China, and ably assisted by such Left-Wing "advisers" as Owen Lattimore, Lauchlin Currie and John Carter Vincent.

Currie was, as the spy disclosures of 1948 reveal, very much a working part of the Silvermaster espionage cell in Washington DC. (See *Witness* for details.)

It was at Cairo that FDR notified the beleaguered Chiang Kai-shek that he must take the Communists into his cabinet: it was done clandestinely, as part of an under-the-table deal. It was also here at Cairo that FDR, egged on constantly by Harry Hopkins, prepared to invite, entice and even bribe the Soviets to come into the war against Japan.

It was also at Cairo that FDR made one historic decision, which is generally believed to have pleased Churchill. He selected Gen. Dwight David Eisenhower to command Overlord, the proposed invasion of Europe through France.

TEHERAN – MORE "TERRIBLE SECRETS"

Then came the fateful meeting in Teheran in December 1943. It was here that Czechoslovakia was betrayed. It was here that Churchill and Roosevelt secretly consented to Red Army "liberation" of Czechoslovakia.

Dr. Eduard Benes, the last and tragic president of the First Republic of Czechoslovakia, voiced the postwar bitterness of his tortured people: "General Patton was stopped from liberating Czechoslovakia by General Eisenhower acting on instructions from Washington as a result of Teheran and Yalta. Patton had to stand by while the Nazis were shooting Czechs until three days later when the Reds came in...."[40]

And it was here at Tehran where Stalin discovered that he had the President of the United States *dans sa poche* (in his pocket) . So closely guarded were some of the Teheran decisions during the last months of the war that even Vice President Harry Truman (a Senator from Missouri at the time of the conference) was unaware of them and of their Yalta sequels. He was hurriedly briefed by Hopkins, Rosenmann and Marshall when he was projected into the Presidency in April 1945. By then he was already a prisoner of Roosevelt's folly.[41]

Significantly, it was the Bolsheviks in the United States who were never in doubt about the decisive impact of what had taken place. Getting their newest line through their international grapevine, they quickly announced that Teheran had changed the world. It had generated, they said, a new atmosphere in which Communists (Bolsheviks) could work unreservedly in Washington. Earl Browder, then chief boss of the American Communist party, held a rally in Madison Square Garden (25 May 1944) where he bellowed to 15,000 collected commies that Teheran had supplied the pattern for the postwar world. Later, he celebrated that theme in a book *Teheran and After.*[42]

FDR maintained a secret alliance with Browder throughout the war. It was an artist, Josephine Adams, who acted as courier. She met with FDR "38 and 40 times during the three-year period preceding his death; meetings held in the White House or in FDR's Hyde Park home." (Miss Adams testified under oath before a subcommittee of the US Senate.) This was confirmed by Browder, taking obvious pride in the fact that he had presented his "views on world events" to the President by this device and adding that FDR "appreciated the service I gave to him."[43]

Was this too a part of the "terrible secret in the closet"?

It was in Teheran that FDR sprang his idea of "The Four Policemen." He conceived a United Nations organization consisting of an Assembly, an Executive Committee, and an enforcing agency, which he termed "The Four Policemen." The Soviet Union, the United States, Britain and China were to comprise the constabulary.

Here is the gist of that conception, implemented with a vengeance under Imperial Majesty, William Jefferson Clinton. FDR outlined his plan at Teheran. It was enlarged and put in place at Yalta:

> Little nations threatening the peace would be handled by blockades and embargoes. A major threat to world peace would arise if a large power made a gesture of aggression; in this case, the Four Policemen would send an ultimatum to the threatening nation, and, if the demands were not immediately met, they would bomb and, if necessary, invade that nation.[44]

And so it was that under another *Imperium*, ostensibly headed by George Bush, Iraq was bombed back to the Stone Age in 1991 (Operation Desert Storm). Later, King William (Clinton) would dispatch "smart bombs" and cruise missiles onto the pockmarked soil of Iraq; and still later, hit Afghanistan and Sudan with 79 Tomahawk missiles "to combat terrorism." This was followed by a supreme act of arrogance – and desperation – when, as commander-in-chief, he ordered our military to strike Iraq with bombs and missiles for "noncompliance" with a UN dictum.

On that fateful day (16 Dec 1998), Gen Henry "Hugh" Shelton, as chairman of the Joint Chiefs, had two choices: he could comply (which he did, under the banner of bravado…Desert Fox); or, he could resign (by calling his four Service chiefs together, along with the commander of the Central Command, and instructing them to "stand down," i.e., not carry out the unjust and illegal order from their commander-in-chief).

In a front-page article, under the banner "Shelton calls air strikes timing 'incredible' but just," Bill Gertz of the *Washington Times* (9 Jan 1999) led off:

> The chairman of the Joint Chiefs of Staff said yesterday the timing of recent military attacks on Iraq was 'absolutely incredible' because they took place so close to key events in the Monica Lewinsky impeachment scandal.
>
> But Army Gen Henry H. Shelton insisted the strikes were based on military advice and were not moves by President Clinton to deflect political heat.[45]

The roots of this despotic destruction were formed at Teheran. They were well-watered and pruned at Yalta where they would later bear a bitter fruit. To our degradation, our body politic still eats from that poisoned plant today, as our military, under the fig leaf of NATO, wages a bloody non-war against the Serbian nation.

Crocker writes of the farewell banquet hosted by Stalin who proposed a blood-curdling toast. The strength of the German army depended, he said, upon fifty thousand high officers and technicians. His toast was a salute to shooting them "as fast as we capture them, all of them."

Churchill was horrified. Quick as a flash, he was on his feet. His face and neck were red, says Elliott Roosevelt, who was present. He announced that the British conceptions of law and justice would never tolerate such butchery. Into this breach stepped Roosevelt. He had a compromise to suggest. Instead of fifty thousand, perhaps "we should settle on a smaller number. Shall we say 49,500?"[46]

Here we see the implementation of the top-secret document Harry Hopkins carried about at Quebec. Not only was Russia to dominate Europe, but was also to be assisted and propitiated by the United States in every possible way.

And it was here that FDR went into a private talk with Stalin and Molotov about their plans to carve up both Germany and Poland.

ANOTHER "TERRIBLE SECRET"

A prelude to the sell-out at Teheran and Yalta was contained in another secret paper, referred to as the *Zabrousky Document*. It was in fact a personal letter, dated 20 Feb 1943, from FDR to his friend and emissary to Stalin, Lev Zabrousky. Here is the crux of that letter. For the entire text, see Count Leon de Poncins' amazing book, *State Secrets*:

Dear Mr. Zabrousky:

As I have already had the pleasure of telling you, together with Mr. Weiss, I am deeply moved to hear that the National Council of Young Israel has been so extremely kind as to propose me as mediator with our common friend Stalin in these difficult moments, when any menace of friction among the United Nations – in spite of the many, self-denying declarations which have been obtained – would have fatal consequences for all, but principally for the USSR itself....

The United States and Great Britain are ready, without any reservations, to give the USSR absolute parity and voting rights in the future reorganization of the post-war world. She will therefore take part in the directing group in the heart of the Councils of Europe and of Asia; she has a right to this, not only through her vast intercontinental situation, but above all because of her magnificent struggle against Nazism which will win the praise of History and Civilization.

It is our intention – I speak on behalf of our great country and of the mighty British Empire – that these continental councils be constituted by the whole of the independent States in each case, with equitable proportional representation.

And you can, my dear Mr. Zabrousky, assure Stalin that the USSR will find herself on a footing of complete equality, having an equal voice with the United States and England in the direction of the said Councils. Equally with England and the United States, she will be a member of the High Tribunal which will be created to resolve differences between the nations, and she will take part similarly and identically in the selection, preparation, armament and command of the international forces which under the orders of the Continental Council, will keep watch within each State to see that peace is maintained in the spirit worthy of the League of Nations. Thus these inter-state entities and their associated armies will be able to impose their decisions and to make themselves obeyed....

We will grant the USSR an access to the Mediterranean; we will accede to her wishes concerning Finland and the Baltic, and we shall require Poland to show a judicious attitude of comprehension and compromise; Stalin will still have a wide field for expansion in the little unenlightened countries of Eastern Europe...he will completely recover the territories which have temporarily been snatched from Great Russia.

Most important of all: after the partition of the Third Reich and the incorporation of its fragments with other territories to form new nationalities which will have no link to the past, the German threat will conclusively disappear in so far as being any danger to the USSR, to Europe, and the entire world....

As I told you at the time, I was very pleased at the gracious terms of the letter informing me of your decision and of the desire you expressed to offer me in the name of the National Council of Young Israel a copy of the greatest treasure of Israel, the scroll of the Torah. This letter will convey the confirmation of my acceptance; to those who are so frank with me, I respond with the greatest confidence. Be so good, I beg of you, to transmit my gratitude to the distinguished body over which you preside, recalling the happy occasion of the banquet on its 31st anniversary ... very sincerely yours, (signed) Franklin Roosevelt[47]

QUEBEC II - BLESSING MORGENTHAU PLAN

Nine months after the Teheran Conference, FDR and Churchill met once more at Quebec. Overlord had been a stupendous success and the Anglo-American armies were poised at the Siegfried Line. The Soviets had pushed the Germans from their soil and were now at the Vistula in Poland.

It was here in Quebec that both Churchill and Roosevelt initialed the infamous Morgenthau Plan. Henry Morgenthau had looked upon World War II as a punitive expedition against the

Germans for persecuting the Jews. Powerful circles centered in New York City "induced" FDR to invite the Secretary of the Treasury to Quebec, along with his able assistant, Harry Dexter White (his parents were Jacob and Sarah Weiss who had emigrated from Russia to America).

In brief, the Morgenthau Plan called for stripping, pillaging and so destroying Germany that it would be permanently converted into "a country primarily agricultural and pastoral in character." But that was not all. Even more diabolical punishment was prescribed for the German people and their children and grandchildren – Talmudic justice with a vengeance.

First, a list was to be made of Germans who were to be shot at once upon apprehension and identification (still being carried out by the Weisenthal group). Similar lists are also in existence here in America – the "Red List," the "Blue List" and the "Green List," each categorizing selected individuals as "dangerous to government order and tranquillity."

Second, the entire German population was to be held down to a standard of living no higher than bare subsistence. Secretary Hull called it "blind vengeance." It was "blind," as it was "striking at all of Europe... The Treasury recommendation that the German mines be ruined was almost breath-taking in its implications for all of Europe, because various other countries relied upon German coal for their industries." As for turning Germany into a goat pasture, Hull argued: "Seventy million Germans could not live on the land within Germany. They would either starve or become a charge upon other nations. This was a scheme that would arouse the eternal resentment of the Germans. It would punish all of them and future generations too for the many crimes of a portion of them. It would punish not only Germans but also most of Europe."[48]

Secretary of War Stimson was horrified at the idea of turning "the center of one of the most industrialized continents in the world" into a nonproductive "ghost territory." He told the President, "I cannot conceive of turning such a gift of nature into a dust heap."[49]

And so, to Yalta...FDR's last bloody footprint.

The 'house of world order' will have to be built from the bottom up rather than from the top down...but an end run around national sovereignty, eroding it piece by piece, will accomplish much more than the old-fashioned frontal assault.

Richard Gardner, Former U.S.
Deputy Assistant Secretary of State

CHAPTER V

WHAT *REALLY* HAPPENED AT YALTA?

(Forging the Instrument for Peace)

We have seen the best of our time: machinations, hollowness, treachery, and all ruinous disorders, follow us disquietly to our graves.

Shakespeare, *King Lear,* 1605

PART ONE
STEAMROLLING FDR

THE first plenary meeting was held on 5 Feb 1945 at the Livadia Palace, where the seriously-ill Roosevelt and his entourage were quartered. Bear in mind that Roosevelt had not been in charge of the government for months. Churchill writes that, "With Stalin and Molotov were Vyshinsky, Maisky, Gousev (USSR ambassador to Britain), and Gromyko (USSR ambassador to US – real name, Katz). Pavlov acted as interpreter."[1]

All except Stalin were Zionists, and he was married to Jewess Rosa Kaganovich, sister of the "butcher of the Ukraine," Lazar Kaganovich.

Yalta dealt primarily with how Germany was to be dismembered, what lands of Poland the Soviets would take, and what part of Germany would become Poland.

At Stalin's request Maisky then expounded a Russian scheme for making Germany pay reparations and for dismantling her munitions industries. Churchill warned that "it would not be possible to extract from Germany anything like the amount which Maisky had suggested should be paid to Russia alone. Britain too had suffered greatly."[2]

Churchill next discussed the world instrument for peace. He stated that there was a large measure of support in the United States for such a World Organization. They discussed voting rights in the Security Council "...each member of the Council should have one vote."

The meeting the next day led to a curve ball being thrown by Vyacheslav Mikhaylovich Molotov (Benjamin Skryabin). Both Churchill and Roosevelt suckered for it; both struck out. Molotov announced that they were now satisfied with the new voting procedure with the provision that the three Great Powers must be unanimous. There was only one thing to be settled. Should the Soviet Republics be members of the World Organization with votes in the Assembly?

"We fully agree," Molotov ended, "with the President's proposal about voting, and we ask that three, or at any rate, two, of our Republics should be founder members of the World Organization."[3]

Churchill writes, "This was a great relief to us all, and Mr. Roosevelt was quick to congratulate Molotov.... My heart went out to mighty Russia, bleeding from her wounds but beating down the tyrants in her path."[4]

Late that night, Churchill sent a dispatch to his Deputy Prime Minister, Clement Attlee (who, even then, was under the influence of Harold Laski and Judge Samuel Rosenmann) in which he said, in part:

> They also cut down their demand for 16 membership votes of the Assembly to two, making the plea that White Russia and the Ukraine had suffered so much and fought so well that they should be considered for inclusion among the founder members of the new World Organization. [5]

Stalin would sucker them again over the issue of whether the Soviet-sponsored Lublin Government of Poland would tolerate representation from the London Polish Government: Stalin's views won out in the end. He would later violate the border agreements by advancing his forces deep into Poland and thereby displacing over eight million Germans.

We had a situation at Yalta which probably existed earlier at Dumbarton Oaks, and certainly later at Potsdam, where Churchill and Stalin, representing Fabian Socialism and International Bolshevism (Zionism), steamrollered the sickly Roosevelt and sandbagged the pliable Truman. One only has to look at the President's staff at these meetings to know that they too were in on the sellout which related directly to the San Francisco World Organization meeting – May-June 1945. The seeds for that meeting were planted at an estate in the District of Columbia, known as Dumbarton Oaks, where "conversations" were held in October 1944 among representatives of the major powers (US, UK, USSR and China). The result of these discussions, commonly known as the Dumbarton Oaks Proposals, was a blueprint for a world organization to be known as the United Nations.

Regarding Russian involvement in the war in the Pacific, Churchill states in *Triumph and Tragedy* that, "The Far East played no part in our formal discussions at Yalta. I was aware that the Americans intended to raise with the Russians the question of Soviet participation in the Pacific War...."[6]

Roosevelt, Harriman and Bohlen met with Stalin on 8 Feb 1945 to discuss his demands. Two days later the Russian terms were accepted (with certain exceptions, which Harriman mentioned in his testimony before the US Senate in 1951). "In return Russia agreed to enter the war against Japan within two or three months after the surrender of Germany."[7]

Churchill added: "I must make it clear that though on behalf of Great Britain I joined in the agreement, neither I nor Eden took any part in making it. It was regarded as an American affair.... In the United States there have been many reproaches about the concessions made to Soviet Russia. The responsibility rests with their own representatives."[8]

At the final dinner on 10 February, the President, who seemed very tired, responded to a toast by recalling a visit Eleanor had made to a school in the US. "In one of the classrooms she saw a large map with a large blank space on it," Roosevelt said. "She asked what was the blank space and was told they were not allowed to mention the place – it was the Soviet Union. That incident was one of the reasons why I wrote President Kalinin asking him to send a representative to Washington to discuss the opening of diplomatic relations. That is the history of our recognition of Russia."[9]

Here, one begins to understand why Eleanor became a strong voice in support of such Communist spies as Hiss, Currie, White et al; and later, a member and staunch supporter of the Zionist front organization, Americans for Democratic Action (ADA).

Whether the story about a map in a classroom was true or not doesn't really matter. It was the final act in a sorry series of world-altering events that took place at Yalta.

Hitler's unsavory mouthpiece, Herr Josef Goebbels, perhaps said it best in an article printed in the 23 Feb 1945 edition of *Das Reich:*

> If the German people should lay down their arms, the agreement between Roosevelt, Churchill and Stalin would allow the Soviets to occupy all of Eastern and Southeastern Europe, together with the major part of the Reich. An iron curtain would at once descend on this territory, which, including the Soviet Union, would be of tremendous dimensions. Behind this curtain there would begin a mass slaughter of peoples.... All that would remain would be a type of human being in the raw, a dull, fermenting mass of millions of proletarian and despairing beasts of burden who would know nothing of the rest of the world except what the Kremlin considered useful to its own purposes....
>
> The rest of Europe would be engulfed in chaotic political and social confusion which would only represent a preparatory stage for the coming Bolshevization.[10]

So, what really happened at Yalta? FDR never presented the Yalta agreement to Congress as a treaty. Did he consider it an "Executive Act"? Crocker says that he probably never gave it much thought. "In essence, it was a personal agreement by Roosevelt with the prime minister of Great Britain and Stalin of Russia changing boundaries of Poland and other countries and determining the nationality of some millions of unconsulted human beings."[11]

Arthur Bliss Lane, US Ambassador to Poland, branded the agreement "a capitulation on the part of the United States." Horrified and saddened, he resigned and wrote a book entitled *I Saw Poland Betrayed.*[12]

Former Ambassador to Russia and France, William C. Bullit, later wrote of the infamous agreement: "No more unnecessary, disgraceful and potentially dangerous document has ever been signed by a President of the United States."[13]

When Joseph C. Grew, the prewar Ambassador to Japan, learned about the secret Yalta deal, he wrote a grave memo that the State Department promptly locked up.   Once Russia is in the Japanese war, he predicted, "Mongolia, Manchuria and Korea will gradually slip into Russia's orbit, to be followed in due course by China and eventually Japan."[14]

Joseph Grew, as Acting Secretary of State in 1945, along with several high-ranking military officers, fought courageously to prevent the dropping of the atomic bombs on Japan.   They were overruled by such stalwart Americans as Judge Samuel Rosenmann, Bernard Baruch and J. Robert Oppenheimer.

In his classic work *Advance to Barbarism: The Development of Total Warfare,* F.J.P. Veale states:

> The motivation behind the dropping of the atomic bomb on Hiroshima may be said to be still a subject of dispute.   It is certain that Truman did not give the order for it to be dropped on the insistence of his military advisers.   Some of the scientists concerned in its construction opposed this step on humanitarian grounds; others, including the famous Jewish physicist Dr. Robert Oppenheimer were in favour because, they urged, only by a test in war conditions could it be demonstrated that their long and costly efforts had succeeded in creating a weapon of unique power for taking human life.   In short the Japanese people were to be enlisted as human guinea-pigs for a scientific experiment.

> At the inquiry before the US Atomic Energy Commission in the spring of 1954 to investigate his alleged communist associations, Dr. Oppenheimer explained: "When you see something that is technically sweet, you go ahead and do it.... We always assumed that if the bombs were needed, they would be used.... We wanted to have it done before the war was over and nothing more could be done."[15]

Which brings us back to our presidential potentate FDR: what did he know (about the atomic bomb) and when did he know it? Crocker explains:

> The prime minister induced President Roosevelt to sign one agreement at Quebec (August 1943) which was so secret that it lay hidden for almost eleven years. It gave Britain an equal voice in the use of the atom bomb, which the United States was soon to possess. In the first week of April 1954, Sir Winston Churchill brought it to light in a debate in the House of Commons, causing an uproar on both sides of the Atlantic. It was at once apparent that the McMahan Act of 1946, which restricted exchange of American atomic information with foreign powers, had canceled the agreement, which few men knew anything about. Congress had abrogated a secret agreement made by the deceased President while having no inkling of it.

> The secret agreement pledged that neither the United States nor Britain would ever use the bomb against the other, that neither would divulge any information to third parties without mutual consent, and that neither country would use the bomb against a third nation without the consent of the other. Actually, Roosevelt had made an unwarranted gift of power to a foreign country, however friendly at the time. It is unthinkable that the Senate of the United States would ever have ratified a treaty conferring this veto power over weapons, strategy, and, in the dawning nuclear age, American foreign policy itself.

> On this too, the Secretary of State was kept in the dark. "I was not told about the atomic bomb," Cordell Hull's memoirs reveal. "I did not know about it until it was dropped." But Klaus Fuchs and Harry Gold and David Greenglass and the Rosenbergs knew about it. People of alien and hostile backgrounds were being welcomed into installations where the newest weapons were being developed and into governmental positions....

> The Communist party knew about the development of the atomic bomb before the FBI, which learned about it not from the Roosevelt administration but from undercover informants in Bolshevik circles on the West Coast. FBI men got their first information in 1943 from the Bolsheviks who had friendly contacts with some of the scientists at a secret project at the University of California from which it was known to be leaking, and the FBI was promptly requested to discontinue its investigation of one of the scientists.[16]

Just before he left for the Yalta conference in February 1945, FDR received the momentous news at the White House that the atomic bomb had a "99% certainty" of success. In a meeting with Secretary of War Stimson and Gen Leslie R. Groves, director of the Manhattan Project, Groves informed FDR that "it would probably be ready in August," and that it would be "extremely powerful."

Even as he was told of this "sweet technical success," FDR knew that it would not be needed to end the war in the Pacific. In July 1944 in Honolulu he discussed the war in the Pacific with Gen. Douglas MacArthur and Adm. Chester W. Nimitz. He was told that "Japan could be forced to accept our terms of surrender by the use of sea and air power without an invasion of the Japanese homeland."[17]

Crocker explains about the relationship of the atomic bomb development to FDR's decision to allow Russia to enter the war against Japan when that tiny insular country had already been defeated.

> When Roosevelt went to Yalta, he kept MacArthur and Nimitz far away. He asked them nothing, told them nothing. In view of what he did at Yalta, this would seem an incomprehensible neglect on his part to avail himself of the counsel of the two men most qualified to give it. The only explanation that makes any sense is that he already knew what their advice would be, that it was not compatible with his plans, and that he would not welcome having their opinions – overwhelmingly authoritative as they would be – presented.
>
> At this stage, elementary statesmanship for the security of American interests in the Far East required that the Soviet Union be, at almost any cost, dissuaded, discouraged, and forestalled from entering the war with Japan. Roosevelt went to Yalta and secretly did just the opposite.[18]

All of this has a bearing on what Crocker calls FDR's terrible secret in the closet.

FDR'S "THIRD WAR"

"The secret which FDR guarded so obstinately could not, from his point of view, be allowed to come out. He had too much at stake. And public suspicion of it had to be stifled. It was not a small secret, like those, which often burden politicians, such as departmental scandal or some shady vote-trading deal or petty personal graft. Roosevelt's robust genius far transcended these lesser stratagems. This man did everything in a big way; even his secrets were gigantic. This one was as big as a war. In fact, it was a war."[19]

But it was not the war with Germany and Italy, nor was it the clash with Japan.

There was also a third war, one which FDR was determined should be hidden from the masses of the American people by a camouflage which was to be his *chef-d'oeuvre*. That war involved Soviet Russia, the fount of Communism (Bolshevism). In it, Russia was the aggressor...on the march, both literally and figuratively, waging offensives with a perseverance and cunning never before equaled in the annals of warfare. Crocker explains:

> This secret war must not be confused with the others mentioned, although they overlapped...the war which was dearest to his heart [Stalin] and which was implicit in his ideological credo had started long before Hitler's Panzers rolled into the Ukraine and was to continue long after *der Fuhrer* was a charred corpse under the rubble of Berlin and his Third Reich but a memory. It was destined to prevent the return of peace and security to the world... World War II was really three wars. Two of them ended in 1945. The third one did not....
>
> The more immediate victims were Russia's territorial neighbors. On a broader scale, but with equal intensity of purpose, the war was being waged against all of the capitalist countries of the world, by military attack or threats of attack, subversive conspiracy and infiltration, economic debilitation, or by a combination of these means.... The United States and Great Britain, as the major bulwarks of democratic capitalism, were, of course, archenemies whose ultimate downfall was essential.... Germany and Japan, the two great buffers against Bolshevik expansion in Europe and Asia, were first to be removed from the path in two simultaneous wars. England, France and the United States would help Russia crush Germany. The United States could vanquish Japan singlehandedly; there was no doubt about that. The Soviet Union would not have to dissipate its strength fighting Japan, but only manage to swoop in at the surrender. A new chaos would be precipitated in China and into the power vacuums thus created in both Europe and Asia, Soviet Russia would then step.
>
> Through his sources of information in the United States, some of whom were in high places, Stalin knew that FDR could be relied upon to see at least this phase of the program through. He was not mistaken.[20]

PART TWO
THE SECRET POWER STRUCTURE

YALTA, however, was only another step along the way to a one-world Zionist government that actually began with the Barbarians' (Jews who are not Jews) invasion of Russia in 1917. It could not have happened without the collusion of Fabian Socialist factions in Britain and the United States.

It was also at that final dinner during the Yalta conference that Stalin revealed his intense hatred for monarchies. Insofar as a united socialist Europe is concerned, the chief stumbling block is the British Royal Family and the adulation of it by not only the British, but by the various Commonwealths about the world, especially Canada. Churchill relates:

> At the Yusupov dinner Stalin had proposed the King's health in a manner which, though meant to be friendly and respectful, was not to my liking. He had said that in general he had always been against kings, and that he was on the side of the people and not that of any king, but that in this war he had learnt to honour and esteem the British people, who honoured and respected their king, so he would propose the health of the king of England.[21]

This bears on current events in England where the Royal Family has become an object of ridicule and scorn, due, on the surface to the sexual romps of Fergie and of Di, who was murdered in Paris in 1997. This makes for good tabloid journalism, but the intent and purpose goes much deeper. The British Royal Family must go, just as the Czar and his family had to go in 1917...not for what it is, but for what it represents, a unifying nation state.

And, like Christianity in the annals of International Zionism – Fabian Socialism, it is a no-no.

The Communists (Bolshevists/Zionists/Fabian Socialists) have proven time and again that these centripetal forces must be destroyed before a peaceful and beneficent one-world socialist government can be set up. Royalty must go. Christianity must go.

One only has to look to what the Bolsheviks did to France early on, and then to Spain. Franco prevented its happening by establishing a dictatorship that lasted 36 years. We may eventually have to do likewise here in the United States.

And then came the heating up of something called the "cold war," artfully designed to follow up the sellout to the Soviets at Yalta; i.e., to turn eastern Europe (including Poland and East Germany) over to Stalin and his fellow Bolsheviks.

The leaders of the West – occasionally referred to as the Free World – appeared to make some really stupid moves during those years; however, we now know they were smart moves by the Barbarians within. Looking back at the various high-level conferences... Dumbarton Oaks, Quebec, Teheran, Yalta, Potsdam ... each was a calculated sellout to the Soviets, and done by design.

And the chief instrument for carrying it out was an Imperium set up here in the United States in 1933 under Franklin Delano Roosevelt.

The forces behind these sellouts are brought out in living color in Whittaker Chambers' book *Witness*. He was indeed witness to the near-total sellout on the part of those incredibly evil men, whose intent throughout this century has been either to destroy or to enslave the rest of mankind.

Another witness to this facet of history was the renowned British author and World War II London *Times* journalist, Douglas Reed, who stressed:

> The money-power and the revolutionary-power have been set up and given sham but symbolic shapes ("capitalism" or "communism") and sharply defined citadels ("America" or "Russia"). Suitably to alarm the mass-mind, the picture offered is that of a bleak and hopeless enmity and confrontation.... But what if similar men with a common aim secretly rule in both camps? ...I believe any diligent student of our times will discover that this is the case.[22]

Professor Carroll Quigley emphasized in *Tragedy and Hope:*

> Jerome Greene is a symbol of much more than the Wall Street influence in the IPR (Institute of Pacific Relations). He is also a symbol

of the relationship between the financial circles of London and those of the eastern United States which reflects one of the most powerful influences in twentieth-century American and world history. The two ends of this English-speaking axis have sometimes been called, perhaps facetiously, the English and American establishments.

There is, however, a considerable degree of truth behind the joke, a truth which reflects a very real power structure. It is this power structure which the radical right in the United States has been attacking for years in the belief that they were attacking the communists.[23]

Reed, in his prolific writings, aptly identified a segment of this power bloc, especially in the financial and pseudo-intellectual circles, in *The Controversy of Zion*. However, Quigley was reluctant to tie the Jewish "nation" and/or international Zionism directly into the English and American Establishments.

So later was Jean-Francois Revel, a remarkably prescient writer; and yet, it is there in his works for any diligent student of our times to discover.

Revel, once editor and director of *L'Express,* France's leading news magazine, wrote a string of best-sellers, most of them translated from the French by William Byron, including *How Democracies Perish, The Totalitarian Temptation, Without Marx or Jesus.* He gives the diligent student another view of the ongoing "struggle" between the two power blocs of "East" and "West" (America vs. Russia... capitalism vs. Communism). Revel is astute in his perceptions of the dissimulation, disinformation, propaganda, hoaxes and outright lies that have characterized the relationships between these two ostensibly opposing forces – the Soviet Union and the United States.[24]

And it is here he misses an important point, whether intentionally or on purpose. Repeating Reed: "What if men with a common aim secretly rule in both camps?"[25]

Revel singles out the great con game perpetrated on the West... that the world was supposed to have been "divided up" between the two superpowers at Yalta in Feb 1945.

And here, to perpetuate the myth of Yalta (as well as such other hoaxes as the Holocaust's death of six million), we see the vital need of those who secretly rule in both camps to monopolize the media, even as Lenin, Stalin and other Bolsheviks stressed.

Revel further shreds the Yalta myth by pointing to a more recent, more exemplary and better-documented capitulation, the surrender at Helsinki, "It was there in 1975, and not at Yalta in 1945, that the West formally recognized the legitimacy of the Soviet Union's postwar annexations and colonizations."[26]

What Revel reveals throughout his work is that time and again the West caved in to the Soviets, beginning especially at Yalta which "represented a bonanza of unilateral concessions.... It displayed the West's inability to understand Communism and thus to negotiate with the Communists.... Yalta, with its sister conferences at Teheran and Potsdam, simply delivered Eastern and Central Europe over to Stalin without sharing in anything."[27]

FDR SOLD US OUT AT YALTA

Yalta was a watermark, of course, but there were events long before Yalta which should have flashed signals to the more astute that the Barbarians within the gates – firmly ensconced at the highest levels in the Roosevelt administration – was selling our country and the republic down the river to international Bolshevism.

In the book, *Mission to Moscow*, written by our then ambassador, Joseph E. Davies, covering the years 1936-38, he said, "all the facts supported his personal opinion that the Soviet Government's word of honor was as good as the Bible." (This was the time of Stalin's purges and show trials and mass executions, of which Davies had to be aware.)[28]

There are current historians who assume that during the conferences at Yalta and Teheran, the West – meaning the US and the UK – were convinced that Moscow really desired peace. They make both FDR and "Winnie" appear naive, if not stupid. We should understand they were neither; that, in fact, they were carrying on a continuation of their game plan which had begun during World War I when Churchill as Lord of the Admiralty and

Roosevelt as an assistant Secretary of the Navy colluded (with others) to bring about the sinking of the *Lusitania* as a trigger to get America into that war.

These gentlemen – together with their Bolshevik handlers – had a front-row seat, if not a direct hand, in such other joint British-American exercises as the Versailles Treaty, the League of Nations, the Bolshevist invasion of Russia, and the Balfour Declaration (the trigger for the Zionist takeover of Palestine). All of these ventures flowed naturally from the wellhead of the "Great War."[29]

In later years, when they headed their respective governments during the second war to make the world safe for democracy, they colluded once more to bring the United States into yet another European conflagration.

Naïve? Hardly. More likely, part of a grand design to strengthen "Communism" which was a transitional name for totalitarian Fabian Socialist-International Zionist one-world government.

If we look at it all in the light of men with a common aim secretly ruling in both camps, the picture that emerges is one of diabolical cunning.

We get an indication of that cunning from the official publication, *The Conference at Malta and Yalta, 1945,* which the State Department released on 16 Mar 1955. It revealed for the first time that FDR had a private man-to-man chat with Stalin at the end of the Yalta Conference and on the eve of the President's departure to visit King Ibn Saud of Saudi Arabia. There came up the subject of a Jewish homeland, which Stalin acknowledged "was a very difficult one." He stated that the USSR had tried to establish a national home for the Jews in Birobidzhan, but that they had only stayed two or three years and then scattered to the cities.

Roosevelt then stated that he was a Zionist and asked Stalin whether he was one. Stalin replied that he was one in principle, but he recognized the difficulty.[30]

Reed, in his 1956 book, *The Controversy of Zion*, explains this phraseology:

> In this passage, again, the Georgian bank robber sounds more like a statesman and speaks more prudently than any Western leader of the last forty years, none of whom have admitted any 'difficulty' (Churchill was wont to denounce any 'difficulty' as anti-Jewish and antisemitic).[31]

Stalin later asked Roosevelt if he meant to make any concessions to King Saud, to which the President replied that there was only one concession he thought he might offer and that was to give Ibn Saud "the six million Jews in the United States."[51] That final statement was expunged from the official record; however, the morning after the report was released in 1955, newspapers across the land broke out in headlines. Reed cites the *Montreal Star* as bannering: "World Capitals Dismayed, Shocked over Disclosures of Yalta Secrets."[32]

"FOREIGN GROUP" CONTROLS POWER

Reed says, "nonsense" indicating that by 1955 the masses were apathetic about such things, "having been brought by control of the press to the condition of impotent confusion foretold in the Protocols of 1905." He indicates that the history of the Yalta papers shows that ten years after the war, power was still in the hands of the essentially "foreign group" which during the war had been able to divert supplies, military operations, and State policy to the purpose of "extending" the revolution.

> They were still able to override the public undertakings of Presidents and to frustrate the will of Congress; they still held the reins. This meant that the infestation of the American government and its departments by agents of the revolution, which began with Mr. Roosevelt's first presidency in 1933, had not been remedied in 1955, despite many exposures; and that, as this was the case, American energies in any third war could in the same way be diverted to promote the overriding plan for a communized world-society (Lenin's third stage in the process).

> This undermining of the West was not confined to the United States; it was general throughout the Western world.... A similar condition was shown to exist in Britain, from which the great overseas

nations originally sprang, and in the two greatest of these, Canada and Australia.[33]

Exposure of Bolsheviks at the highest levels of government began in Canada. Reed clarifies this infestation in his book, pointing out that it was a Russian who, at the risk of his life, disclosed to the Canadian prime minister of that time, Mackenzie King, that a network of espionage had been set up in Ottawa and had burrowed deep within the Canadian Government. The center of this group was the Russian embassy. Reed reports that when King became convinced of the truth of Igor Gouzenko's statements he saw that they revealed "as serious a situation as ever existed in Canada at any time."[34]

King flew to the United States to alert President Truman, and then to Britain to inform Prime Minister Clement Attlee. King later revealed that the situation was shown by them to be "even more serious in the United States and England."[35]

Reed reports that Whitaker Chambers' documentary proof showed that Alger Hiss had been the center of a Soviet network in the State Department, and that this proof had been available to, but ignored by, two American presidents for six years.

Reed gives credit to "individual patriots," including a new Representative from California, Richard M. Nixon, who compelled disclosure on the part of a reluctant government:

> In the sequence to the Hiss affair a mass of disclosures followed, which showed American government departments to have been riddled with Soviet agents at all levels.[36]

England chose to do nothing for another six years, when their hand was forced by the sudden disappearance of two senior Foreign Office officials, Burgess and Maclean. Belatedly, the British Foreign Office announced in 1955 that the two had been under suspicion of conveying secret information to the Soviet Government from 1949.

It was at this time that another Russian, Vladimir Petrov, of the Soviet Embassy in Canberra, defected. The Australians quickly formed a Royal Commission of three judges who were as thorough as the Canadians. Their report revealed that the Soviet Embassy in Canberra from 1943 on had "controlled and operated an espionage ring" and gave warning that Soviet intelligence agents were still operating in Australia through undercover agents entering the country as immigrants.

Reed points out that all four of the governments misinformed the public by concentrating on the issue of "espionage," which was relatively minor compared to the truly grave condition which was exposed. "This was not the mere theft of documents, but the control of state policy at the highest level." (Chambers says essentially the same in *Witness*.) Reed writes:

> It was this that enabled arms, supplies, wealth, military operations and the conduct of Western politicians at top-level conferences all to be guided into a channel where they would produce the maximum gain, in territory and armed strength, for the revolutionary State. Exposure of this condition came only in the Hiss trial and its numerous attendant investigations and disclosures. These showed that the revolution had its agents at the top levels of political power, where they could direct State policy and the entire energies of nations.[37]

He singles out Alger Hiss and Harry Dexter White as the chief traitors of that time, emphasizing Hiss's predominant role at the Yalta Conference.

COMING: NATIONAL EMERGENCY

Shortly after assuming office in 1933, FDR issued the following decree:

> By virtue of the authority vested in me by Section 5 (b) of the act of October 6, 1917 (War Powers Act), as amended by Section 2 of the act of March 9, 1933...I Franklin Delano Roosevelt, President of the United States of America, do declare that a period of national emergency still continues to exist and pursuant to said section do hereby prohibit the hoarding of gold coin, gold bullion and gold certificates within the continental United States by individuals, partnerships, associations and corporations... [38]

In that famous speech he ordered all persons to turn in to the Federal Reserve System (a private corporation run by arch-criminals) all gold holdings in their possession by 1 May 1933. The current president may use the identical ploy by declaring a national emergency as a result of "calculated acts of terror." Coupled to a horrendous financial implosion, plus the distinct possibility of massive power grid failures, these criminal acts could trigger anarchy, not only in the inner cities, but also in the countryside of Middle America.

Declaration of martial law would be the logical result, followed by implementation of a global despotic government under the UN. It has been long on the drawing board. We were almost there at the end of World War II in 1945. It has since been a bloody road to global despotism.

The spring of 1933 also witnessed the beginning of a period of private cooperation between Zionism and the German fascist regime to increase the inflow of German Jewish immigrants and capital to Palestine. The Zionist authorities succeeded in keeping this cooperation a secret.

Klaus Polkehn, Journalist, East Germany

CHAPTER VI
NAZI – ZIONIST SECRET ALLIANCE
(Was there a "Final Solution"?)

In working for Palestine, I would even ally myself with the devil.
Vladimir Jabotinsky, 12th Zionist Congress, 1921

PART ONE
ADOLF HITLER: CO-FOUNDER OF ISRAEL

A quick review of several pertinent facts which we have covered in earlier chapters is in order. We saw the founding of International Zionism in 1897 as a potent political force to unite what its founders styled "the Jewish Nation."

The two leaders of Zionism were Theodor Herzl and Chaim Weizmann; however, they had a falling-out over where the new Jewish homeland should be located. Herzl was ready to settle for the British offer of Uganda. Never mind that Uganda was not Britain's to give: of course, neither was Palestine. We also discovered that as a result of the infamous Versailles Treaty, Britain received "mandated control" over Palestine from the newly formed and equally infamous League of Nations.

Long prior to that event, the Sixth Zionist Congress convened at Basle, Switzerland in 1903. The main speaker was Dr. Max Nordau, who put the question of Palestine in its proper context. He said, *inter alia*:

> That great progressive power, England, in sympathy for our people, offered the Jewish Nation, through the Zionist Congress an autonomous colony in Uganda. While it was not Palestine, nothing is so valuable as amicable relations with such a power as England. Thus, accept the offer to create a precedent in our favor. Sooner or later, the Oriental question – where England's interests are – will have to be

solved, and the Oriental question means, naturally, also the question of Palestine.

Herzl knows that we stand before a tremendous upheaval of the whole world. Soon, perhaps, some kind of a world-Congress will have to be called and England – the great, free and powerful England – will then continue the work it has begun with the generous offer to the Sixth Congress.

And if you ask me now what has Israel to do with Uganda, let me tell you the following words as if I were showing you the rungs of a ladder leading upward and upward: Herzl, the Zionist Congress, the English Uganda proposition, the future world war, the peace conference, where, with the help of England. a free and Jewish Palestine will be created.[1]

One of the many "American" citizens who attended the Jewish Congress at Basle in 1903 was Litman Rosenthal. He published Dr. Nordau's speech in the *American Jewish News* (19 Sep 1919) and called it the "ladder revelation."[2]

There were further rungs in the ladder that continued to lead "upward and upward" before a "free and Jewish Palestine" was actually created. Of prime importance was the secret alliance between the top echelons of International Zionism and National Socialism (Nazism).

Why was this natural alliance kept secret for so long a time?

Perhaps because its factual reportage would interfere with the greatest propaganda coup of the 20th century, "the Holocaust of six million," the so-called "final solution."

For one of the most meticulously detailed reports on this astounding alliance, one must read *The Secret Contacts: Zionism and Nazi Germany – 1933-1941* by Klaus Polkehn, a prominent East German journalist in the German Democratic Republic. It appeared in the *Journal of Palestine Studies*.

The Jewish nation, in Palestine, represented by its international governing body, the Zionists; and the German nation, represented by Hitler and his National Socialists, had common cause in that both groups wanted the Jews out of Germany (and eventually out of Europe). This factor is highlighted by certain visits to Berlin on the part of Zionist leaders from Palestine; e.g., Feivel Polkes, a general staff officer of the underground Jewish militia, the Haganah, to his counterpart in the Reich, Herbert Hagen, director of the Office of Jewish Affairs (*Judenreferat*) and SS-head, Adolf Eichmann.[3]

Polkes told Eichmann (28 Feb 1937) that he was interested above all in "accelerating Jewish immigration to Palestine, so that the Jews would obtain a majority over the Arabs in his country."

Eichmann and Hagen, on the invitation of the Haganah commander, traveled to Haifa, Palestine on the ship *Romania*, docking on 2 Oct 1937; however, the British authorities would not let the two SS emissaries disembark (because of the ongoing Arab revolt over the Jewish settlement in Palestine). They then went on to Egypt, where they rendezvoused with Polkes in Cairo's Cafe Groppi (10-11 Oct 1937). The Haganah officer told them:

> The Zionist State must be established by all means and as soon as possible so that it attracts a stream of Jewish immigrants to Palestine. When the Jewish state is established according to the current proposals laid down in the *Peel Papers*, and in line with England's partial promises, then the borders may be pushed further outwards according to one's wishes.[4]

In his statement, the Haganah commander referred to a Royal Commission set up under Lord Peel to examine the situation in Palestine in 1937, after the outbreak of the Arab revolt. It laid out a plan to divide Palestine into a Jewish and an Arab state. The Peel Papers also throttled Jewish immigration to Palestine, resulting in bitter enmity on the part of the Haganah underground army towards the British. It led to a series of acts of terror and assassination against the British military forces in Palestine.

Polkehn reveals that collaboration between the Zionists and the German Reich was cemented by the *Mossad Aliyah Beth* which had been created by the Haganah as an illegal immigration organization. Emissaries of the Mossad (Pina Ginsburg and Moshe Auerbach), with the blessings of the Reich authorities, set up quarters in Berlin to carry out their immigration activities in 1938.

According to Jon and David Kimche, in their book *Secret Roads,* the Mossad special mission "converged with the intentions of the Nazi government.... Only with the support of the Nazi leaders could the project be carried through on a large scale." The Gestapo had discussed with Ginsburg "how to promote and expand illegal Jewish immigration into Palestine against the will of the British mandate government."[5]

In the summer of 1938 Eichmann met in Vienna with another Mossad emissary, Bar-Gilead, who requested permission to set up training camps for emigrants so they could be prepared for their work in Palestine. Eichmann, after coordinating with Berlin, granted permission, and supplied all requirements for the training camps. Ginsburg, in Berlin, working with Nazi authorities, also set up training camps.

In a revealing footnote, Polkehn states that Mussolini in Italy had supported the right wing of Zionism, the Revisionist party (forerunner of the terrorist *Irgun Zvai Leumi*) and permitted them to establish a school for training navy soldiers. Vladimir Jabotinsky, Revisionist party leader, had in 1932 made the proposal that the mandate over Palestine should go to Italy, because Mussolini would be more amenable than Britain to furthering the cause of the Jewish State.[6]

Polkehn refers to economic agreements between the Zionists and the German government even before Hitler's rise to power in 1933. "The Foreign Office had already taken up a pro-Zionist attitude on many occasions," including meetings between Chaim Weizmann and State Secretaries von Schubert and von Bulow. He also mentions the Zionist official Gerhart Holdheim, who wrote:

> The Zionist programme encompasses the conception of a homogeneous, indivisible Jewry on a national basis. The criterion for Jewry is hence not a confession of religion, but the all-embracing sense of belonging to a racial community that is bound together by ties of blood and history and which is determined to keep its national individuality."[7]

Polkehn flags the similarities between these ideas and those of the Fascists. He quotes Alfred Rosenberg, the chief ideologue of the Nazi party, who wrote:

> Zionism must be vigorously supported so that a certain number of Jews is transported annually to Palestine or at least made to leave the country.[8]

During those critical years of which Klaus Polkehn writes – 1933-1941 – the so-called Haavara agreement was in effect, which allowed for the transfer of immense amounts of money from German Jewish accounts to Palestine. Two companies were established: the Haavara company in Tel Aviv and a sister company named Paltreu in Berlin.

Polkehn describes the transaction:

> The Jewish emigrant would pay his money into the German account of Haavara, either at the Wassermann Bank in Berlin or the Warburg Bank in Hamburg. With this money the Jewish importers could purchase German goods for export to Palestine, while paying the equivalent value in Palestinian pounds into the Haavara account at the Anglo-Palestine Bank in Palestine. When the emigrant arrived in Palestine he received from this account the equivalent value of the sum he paid in Germany.[9]

What was Hitler's view regarding this magnanimous transfer of wealth to Palestine? All the indications are that he approved. Polkehn points out that Herr Hitler decided on 27 Jan 1938 that the Haavara procedure should continue.

GENOCIDE IN THE EYES OF THE BEHOLDER

Just as President George Bush saw the psychological need in 1990 to demonize Saddam Huessein of Iraq, FDR also recognized the value of portraying Adolf Hitler as the devil incarnate in 1940. The similarities between Hitler and Hussein are striking in that both were financed and supported by identical universalist moneychangers.

And for identical reasons, namely to protect the continued existence and survival of what Chaim Weizmann called *Eretz*

Israel. In his *Speeches and Essays*, published in Berlin in 1937, this noted leader of the Zionist forces stated:

> The only dignified answer to all that has been done to the Jews of Germany is a large and a beautiful and a just home in *Eretz Israel* – a strong home.[10]

The question arises; just what was done to the Jews of Germany which necessitated transplanting these people to the Land called Palestine? For a partial answer, we can turn to the writings of an author, editor and historian, Andrew Gray, who reviewed a book by the German author, Udo Walendy, *Truth for Germany: The Guilt Question of WW II* in the December 1997 edition of "The Barnes Review." Gray writes:

> When we refer to the bar of history, we are not thinking of Jack Daniels – at least not immediately. Adolf Hitler and the government of the Third Reich stand accused of provoking and commencing World War II. By consensus of establishment historians, and by media propagandists of virtually every stripe, they have been pronounced guilty.
>
> Is the verdict just? A similar charge was leveled at the Kaiser and his government for the outbreak of World War I and written into the Versailles Treaty as supposedly incontestable truth. Thanks in a large part to Harry Elmer Barnes, this contention was in due course overthrown, and today, despite the continuing emphasis of anti-German bias in academia, few serious historians assign the preponderance of war guilt to the Germans.[11]

Gray explains that a close examination of the evidence presented by Walendy "does not convict Hitler of willfully fomenting the war. In contrast, it demonstrates that the men who actually wanted war were elsewhere – mainly in London (Lord Halifax) but also in Washington and represented there by Franklin Roosevelt himself."

Gray emphasizes Walendy's conclusion "which delivers his strongest indictments of the establishment historians, all of whom have relied quite heavily on documents that turn out to be either doctored or entirely fabricated."[12]

In an earlier edition of *The Barnes Review* (May 1997), best-selling author Gregory Douglas homed in on two of these establishment historians. Super-sleuth that he is, Douglas went to the source of the document cited by one of the authors, Dr Christopher Browning, for his claim in *The Path to Genocide,* (1992):

> In the summer of 1941, probably in July, Hitler indicated his approval for the preparation of a plan for the mass murder of all European Jews under Nazi control, though just how and when this was communicated to Himmler and Heydrich cannot be established.[13]

Douglas wanted to establish the facts behind such a statement and contacted Dr. Browning, who replied (23 Nov 1994) that the speech in question was taken from Nuremberg Document 221-L. He explained further that the reference he made to a speech was not really to a speech but a monologue to a limited audience.

Well! What's a factual historian to do? Douglas obtained a copy of Nuremberg Document 221-L and discovered that it was "neither a speech nor a monologue, but a précis of a high level conference concerning primarily the administration of newly-acquired territory in the USSR."[14]

Douglas states, "There is not one word in the text of this conference that refers to Jews or any theoretical plan for their mass extermination in former Soviet territory or anywhere else."

Mentioned further by Douglas, was an article in the *German Studies Review* by Richard Breitman, in which he refers to various meetings of top Third Reich leaders with such comments as: "There is no record of who else (besides Hitler) was present or exactly what was discussed." And, "The content of these meetings of the key authorities on the Final Solution went unrecorded – or at least no notes of them have survived."

Breitman states, "To my knowledge, neither Heydrich or Himmler referred directly to the date of the plans for the Final Solution or of Hitler's authorization of it in a form that has reached posterity."[15]

Douglas states, "In short, both Browning and Breitman make the same points, namely that no written proof is extant and that which appears to be a possible proof is neither conclusive nor convincing unless enhanced by tenuous support systems that must be maintained more by wishful thinking than fact."

Douglas cites the Soviet archives, which contain the complete file of the German concentration camp system. "These are not fragmentary records," Douglas states, "but complete, and from these, it is apparent that the death toll in all the camps from their beginnings to the end of the war was approximately 400,000."[16]

Douglas cites the *New York Times* (3 Mar 91):

> An article on former Soviet archival material addresses the total figure of 400,000 dead in the camps 'under the Third Reich'. It specifically refers to the 70,000 dead in Auschwitz. The actual figures found on Soviet archival microfilms show a slightly higher figure for Auschwitz *vis* 73,000. A response to these totals, astonishing in their nature, is that no allowance has been made for 'secret lists' which, since they are secret, cannot be found.

It all depends on where you look. Klaus Polkehn, in his diligent and scholarly search, did find such a secret document. But it did not specifically mention the "Final Solution" – perhaps because there has never been a document unearthed to reflect that any individual, whether a part of the Third Reich or any other such grouping, ever used the phrase.

The still-classified document that follows uses the phrase "radical solution of the Jewish question through evacuation."[17]

WAS THIS THE "FINAL SOLUTION"?

Perhaps the most revealing datum of Polkehn's research is that the *Irgun* faction made an "incredible offer of collaboration" to Hitler's Reich a year and a half after the outbreak of WW II. This Top Secret document, according to the author, is still kept in a locked archive in Britain. The document (11 Jan 1941) speaks of "Fundamental Features of the Proposal" by the *Irgun Zvai Leumi* (National Military Organization-NMO) "concerning the solution of the Jewish Question in Europe and the active participation of the NMO on the side of Germany."[18]

Here is the text of that incredible note:

It is often stated in the speeches and utterances of the leading statesmen of National Socialist Germany that a New Order in Europe requires as a prerequisite the radical solution of the Jewish question through evacuation (*Judenreines Europa*).

The solving of the Jewish problem and thus the liberation of the Jewish people once and for all is the objective of the political activity and the years long struggle of the Jewish freedom movement: the National Military Organization (*Irgun Zvai Leumi*) in Palestine.

The NMO, which is well acquainted with the goodwill of the German Reich government and its authorities towards Zionist activity inside Germany and towards Zionist emigration plans is of the opinion that:

1. Common interests could exist between the establishment of a new order in Europe in conformity with the German concept, and the true national aspirations of the Jewish people as they are embodied by the NMO.

2. Cooperation between the new Germany and a renewed Hebrew nation (*volkisch-nationalen-Hebraertum*) would be possible.

3. The establishment of the historical Jewish state on a national and totalitarian basis and bound by a treaty with the German Reich would be in the interest of maintaining and strengthening the future German position of power in the Near East.

The indirect participation of the Israeli freedom movement in the drawing up of the New Order in Europe, already in its preparatory stage, would be connected with a positively radical solution of the European Jewish problem in conformity with the above-mentioned national aspirations of the Jewish people. This would strengthen to an uncommon degree the moral basis of the New Order in the eyes of the entire world.

Proceeding from these considerations, the NMO in Palestine offers to take an active part in the war on Germany's side, provided the above-mentioned national aspirations of the Jewish liberation movement are recognized by the German Reich government.

This offer by the NMO, whose validity extends over the military, political and information levels, inside and also according to certain organizational preparations outside Palestine, would be bound to the military training and organizing of Jewish manpower in Europe, under the leadership and command of the NMO. These military units would take part in the fighting to conquer Palestine, in case such a front is formed.

> The cooperation of the Israeli freedom movement would also be in line with one of the recent speeches of the German Reich Chancellor in which Herr Hitler stressed that any combination and any alliance would be entered into in order to isolate England and defeat it.[19]

And the rest, as they say, is history. We witnessed in earlier chapters what these incredibly gifted people did to the Russians under Bolshevism and what they did to the Germans during and after World War II, especially in the conduct of the Lindemann Plan which called for the destruction by saturation bombing of German cities and their entire populace; then, immediately after the war, in the conduct of the fraudulent Nuremberg Trials – an orgy of murder and endless revenge. We will analyze this legal fraud in Chapter 7.

Add to those mindless atrocities what we, the victorious Allies, did in 1945 to the refugees; and to the German soldiers – over a million of them – that General of the Army Dwight David Eisenhower kept exposed to the elements in concentration camps, after the war ended, leaving them to die of pneumonia, dysentery and hunger. Afterward, they were buried with huge mechanical shovels. Canada and the Red Cross endeavored to help them, but Eisenhower said that they were not prisoners of war, but were "disarmed enemy personnel," a classification he had created.

As to the Soviets, Ilya Ehrenburg exhorted them officially:

> Better than one dead German, are two. Kill them all, men, old men, children and the women, after you have amused yourselves with them![20]

In his profound book, T*he Psychology of War and the New Era in 2000*, Salvador Borrego reveals startling similarities between the apparent hatred and utterly evil forces the Allies unleashed and certain passages from the Old Testament. Borrego asks some gut-wrenching questions: Was there, in fact, some likeness to the Old Testament? Was there something of those watchwords the ancient Jews believed were received from Jehovah?[21]

> With this knife thou shalt kill all the males. All their booty thou shalt take for thyself, and thou shalt eat of the leavings of thine enemies.

The men-servants and the maid-servants thou mayest need shall be of the nations around you. You shall leave them in heritage to your children after you, in hereditary possession.

And they killed all the males...the sons of Israel took captive the women with their children.... Now you shall kill every male among the children, kill also every woman who may have known a man, but keep for yourselves all the girl children who have not known a man.[22]

PART TWO
THE TRANSFER AGREEMENT

*The fight against Germany has now been waged for months by
every Jewish community and by every single Jew in the world. We
shall start a spiritual and material war of the whole world against
Germany... our Jewish interests call for the complete destruction of
Germany.*

Vladimir Jabotinsky, Zionist leader, 15 Jan 1934

TO understand fully this secret alliance between the Zionists and
the Nazis, we must read two startling, yet factual, books. One is by
an erudite scholar of Jewish heritage, Edwin Black, who spent five
years on three continents researching and writing *The Transfer
Agreement: The Untold Story of the Secret Pact Between the Third
Reich & Jewish Palestine* (1984). Dr. Sybil Milton of the Simon
Wiesenthal Center calls it "a spellbinding, exciting book. This
subject has not been previously explored. It adds a significant new
dimension to our understanding of this critical era."

And so it does. As Yoav Gelber of the Yad Vashem, Israel
Holocaust Memorial, states: "Edwin Black's research is striking in
its dimension and scope. The vast uncovering of source material
and its extensive use are almost overwhelming. He penetrates deep
into the political and economic processes of inter-Jewish relations
and into gentile attitudes involving the rescue of Jews from Nazi
rule for the benefit of the Zionist enterprise in Eretz Yisrael."[23]

The thrust of Black's voluminous work has to do with the
decision on the part of elements of the Jewish nation to declare war
against Germany in 1933 by a worldwide boycott of all German
goods. The terms of the Transfer Agreement were that the boycott
would cease in return for the transfer of German Jews to the
Palestine. Black reveals the cliffhanger negotiations of the
controversial pact and fleshes out the main characters on both
sides. He also stresses "the anguish of world Jewry over their
choice [to carry out the pact]."[24]

The chief go-between was Sam Cohen; the chief problem was the barrier of currency restrictions that seemed to preclude an orderly transfer of the wealth and the citizens of Germany's middle class. These restrictions, which were put in place under Chancellor Heinrich Bruning, prohibited anyone – Jew or Christian, German or foreigner – from taking currency out of Germany without permission. Black states that the restriction was not aimed at Jews, but at speculators and hoarders.

According to Klaus Polkehn, at the same time, the British, who controlled Palestine under mandate, limited Jewish entry into Palestine only to those in possession of at least a thousand pounds (about $5,000).

Enter, the "facilitator," one Sam Cohen. Born in Poland in 1890, Cohen traveled to Germany in 1907 to study finance and economics at the University of Marburg in Germany. During the Great War, Cohen made a fortune in real estate in Berlin. He developed a reputation for "philanthropy." Some looked upon him as "an evil rogue, interested in no more than his own greed at the expense of his people; to them, he was a traitor, a collaborator, a wealthy manipulator, a liar and a fraud."

Black tells us that others looked upon him as "a munificent man of the Jewish cultural movement, a man who worked tirelessly, often selflessly, to help the Jewish people... a committed Zionist, a rescuer...."[25]

In the final analysis, Cohen, although playing a pivotal role in bringing the agreement to fruition, appeared to be in it for personal enrichment. Another role-player – Chaim Arlosoroff – was brought into the small circle of Zionists working to implement the Transfer Agreement in March 1933. According to Black, "Arlosoroff was a member of the Jewish Agency Executive Committee and one of Zionism's most respected personalities."

Much of Black's work is devoted to the almost implacable struggle between two factions within the Zionist organization. "The Mapai, or Labor Zionism, considered Palestine as a home for a Jewish elite that would toil in the noble vocations of manual work and farming. Their orientation was communal, socialist. They wanted collective farms and villages. Moreover, Labor Zionism desired the many, but not the multitudes. Mapai's Israel would not be for every Jew – at least not in the beginning...."[26]

In opposition were the Revisionist Zionists wanting a nation of ordinary Jews in a mixed urban-rural society. It would be based on free enterprise rather than socialism. While the Mapai envisioned gradual "constructive programs" to build a new Jewish Homeland, the Revisionists pushed for a rapid transfer of the largest number of Jews in the shortest time in order to achieve a quick majority in Palestine and then declare the State. Black says that Revisionism was very much an updated version of Max Nordau's catastrophic Zionism.

Black stresses that Mapai's battle tactic was "political warfare," while the Revisionists "were heavily Fascist and profoundly influenced by Mussolini." Vladimir Jabotinsky, the Revisionist leader, called for a rigid worldwide boycott of German goods, while the Mapai condemned both the boycott and acts of terrorism as main planks of the Revisionist platform.

The Transfer Agreement degenerated into a personal feud between two strong characters, both Zionists; Arlosoroff, who advocated a bi-national community, and Sam Cohen, who had masterminded an international economic and political coup, wherein he would control millions of dollars, thousands of people and large tracts of land. "One man, working alone could, if allowed, deliver the Jewish nation to the Jewish homeland. Cohen could be this private messiah."

He decided that Arlosoroff was robbing him of his promise and his profit. Arlosoroff would have to be stopped.

Other factions were after Arlosoroff as well. He was looked on as an enemy by several factions, not the least Jabotinsky's Revisionist Union, several of whose members had called for Arlosoroff's assassination as early as 1931. Arab extremists considered Arlosoroff the most dangerous man in

Palestine. "Not because he sought to conquer. But because he sought to combine."

He had created enemies also in Britain. The Mandate Government saw that the transfer, which they had originally envisioned as a boon for the British economy leading to extending their economic sphere of influence over the entire Mideast, would now lead to that prize going to Germany.

Black does a masterful bit of writing in building up this story to its ultimate tragedy, the shooting of Arlosoroff on the night of 16 Jun 1933 as he walked along the beach north of Tel Aviv with his wife, Sima. He was rushed to hospital where, according to Black, "the doctors were ill-prepared and indecisive. This being *shabbat*, there was no surgeon on duty. Arlosoroff reached the emergency room at eleven-thirty – about an hour after being shot. The first surgeon arrived before midnight, but would not operate until joined by three other specialists still *en route*. It was too late. Arlosoroff died in the hospital bed. He was 34."[27]

As we saw in Part One, the Transfer Agreement was put into effect. As Black points out, a nation was waiting. A small group of men foresaw it all:

> That's why nothing would stop them; no force was too great to overcome. These men were the creators of Israel. And in order to do so, each had to touch his hand to the most controversial undertaking in Jewish history – the Transfer Agreement. It made a state. Was it madness, or was it genius? [28]

He gives us a partial answer in his Afterword, wherein he asks three questions that have haunted the readers of his manuscript:

> First: Could the boycott really have overturned the Hitler regime?

> The second question: By undermining the boycott, are the Zionists responsible for the Hitler regime's not being toppled, and by extension are they responsible for the Holocaust?

> The third haunting question is: Was the continuing economic relationship with Germany an indispensable factor in the creation of the State of Israel? The answer to that is yes.[29]

PART THREE
A NEW TRANSFER AGREEMENT

FLASH - New York – "While Russian President Boris Yeltsin and President Clinton went through the motions of their halting, hollow and hangdog summit met in Aug 1998 – dubbed the "Boozer and Abuser Show" by press wags – more important and ominous talks were going on in the hidden recesses of the Kremlin."[30]

This was the lead to a front-page story by Warren Hough (*Spotlight*, 21 Sep 1998) which stressed that the outcome of these super secret negotiations would be the emergency evacuation of up to a million Jews from Russia to the United States in the event the former Soviet Union "heartland" is hit by economic collapse and political turmoil.

Dennis Braham, chairman of the US National Conference for Soviet Jewry, expects that Russia will be engulfed by a tide of nationalism, populism and anti-Semitism. "There is tremendous apprehension that [these] bad things can happen, and we have to be prepared," he said.[31]

Braham was a key member of the visiting delegation to Moscow, which was headed by the whisky king, Edgar Bronfman, president of the World Jewish Congress. It included top executives from nearly all the Zionist groups in the US, as well as high Israeli officials, such as Nathan Sharansky, the mini-state's Russian-born trade and industry minister.

Hough informs us that the home team was headed by Yevegeny Primakov, the former Soviet secret police chief, who was selected by Yeltsin as prime minister early in September. Vladimir Gushinsky, a billionaire Moscow financier, who chairs the Russian Jewish Congress, was his co-host.

Hough points out that Primakov learned how to deal with international crises in a lifetime spent mostly as a Communist secret agent, and that he had cast off his Jewish name (Pincas

Finkelstein) and upbringing early in his career in order to rise to the top of the old Soviet secret service.

"It is the ethnic identity of the men at the top who have plundered Russia and plunged it into disarray," Hough reports. The most urgent question has to do with the growing rage of the Russian people at this Jewish community in their midst who are blamed for the nation's political chaos, endemic corruption and economic breakdown.

A most unusual story substantiates this; unusual in that the Moscow correspondent for the *Washington Post,* David Hoffman, reports that the Russians are not looking for the principal culprits of the country's misfortunes among their national leaders, but that the real masters of the former Soviet heartland are the members of the *semibankirshchina* – that is, "the regime of the seven banker oligarchs."[32]

Hoffman discovered that these seven oligarchs are in reality unscrupulous financial speculators, newly minted billionaire tycoons, united by their ethnic and emotional ties to Israel, who are the real rulers of post-communist Russia.

Hoffman related that "after staging rigged elections in Russia in the mid-1990s, the seven tycoons met and decided to insert one of their own into government. They debated who, and chose [financier] Vladimir Potanin, who became deputy prime minister."

Hoffman boldly states that, "One reason they chose Potanin was that he is not Jewish and most of the rest of them are [and they] feared a backlash against the Jewish bankers."[33]

According to Hoffman, the pressures behind the gathering storm are not hard to understand. These seven bankers corrupted and manipulated post-communist Russia's elected government, "They used their newly found powers to plunder the nation's wealth and its natural resources."[34]

The seven oligarchs immediately began to undermine Russia's national economy by "speculating against the dollar-ruble exchange rate – often using the government's own money." When they needed hard currency financing, they turned to Wall Street, where they found a confederate with some of the deepest pockets in the world's money markets, billionaire currency speculator George Soros.

Warren Hough also reports in his twin articles (*Spotlight* 21 Sep 1998) that these seven oligarchs, threatened by the revolt of Russia's defrauded and plundered masses, are being rescued by such US Zionist leaders as World Jewish Congress president Bronfman, who is behind the emergency exodus from Russia to the US.

Such an exodus may take on the trappings of the 1948 Berlin Airlift, but larger and faster, to fly hundreds of thousands of Russian Jews to safety if law and order break down in the former Soviet heartland, Hough reports.

The US government will defray the costs of this gigantic jet-propelled exodus, according to Hough, and will grant "'political asylum" to all Russian Jews who choose to go to America rather than Israel.

"With regard to the Russian government, the Zionist negotiators presented four core demands," Hough writes:

- Instant collective, unrestricted exit permits for all Jewish emigrants cleared to board Bronfman's emergency airlift;

- Open landing and departure clearances, refueling and related airport services "as needed" for US aircraft participating in the operation;

- Open access roads and unhindered passage to and from Russian airports for the buses, trucks, and vehicles participating in the emergency evacuation of Jewish refugees; and

- Blanket permission for Jewish emigrants to take abroad with them "as substantial a portion of their assets and savings as may prove compatible with their departure by air."[35]

Hough concludes his lead article with a critical statement that "no one seems to have thought of asking the opinion – much less the consent – of ordinary Americans regarding such a sudden and massive influx of aliens, most of whom will require, beyond the steep cost of their hasty aerial exodus, billions of dollars in long-term public assistance."

A ONE-STATE SOLUTION

In a startling article under the banner "The One-State Solution" (*The New York Times* magazine, 10 Jan 1999), Professor Edward Said, professor of literature at Columbia University, outlines why the only answer to Middle East peace is Palestinians and Israelis living as equal citizens under one flag.[36] The thought is – you know – beautiful. Is it practicable... is it possible?

The key word is "reconciliation"; yet, he states that the Zionist-Israeli official narrative and the Palestinian one are irreconcilable. So, it becomes a question of which side will give?

He points to a recent book by the distinguished Israeli historian Zeev Sternhell, *The Founding Myths of Israel*, in which he states:

> Even Zionist figures who had never visited the country knew that it was not devoid of inhabitants.... The real reason for this was not a lack of understanding of the problem, but a clear recognition of the insurmountable contradiction between the basic objectives of the two sides....[37]

Said quotes David Ben-Gurion, the first Israeli prime minister, who stated in 1944:

> There is no example in history of a people saying we agree to renounce our country, let another people come and settle here and outnumber us.[38]

Yet we saw in previous chapters of *Barbarians* that the Palestinians after 1944 were eventually outnumbered and were driven from their homes and lands by systematic acts of sheer terror, murder and mayhem. Did they indeed agree to renounce their country?

Prof. Said answers that question, and provides a wealth of detail in his article and in his book, *Peace and Its Discontents*. In the *New York Times* article he stresses that following the 1917 Balfour declaration the Palestinian Arabs vastly outnumbered the

Jews, and that they always refused anything that would compromise their dominance. Even at the time in 1948 when the Zionists exultantly proclaimed "The state of Israel exists!" (and it was immediately recognized by Harry S. Truman), the Jews held only 7% of the land. Prof. Said declares:

> The conflict appears intractable because it is a contest over the same land by two peoples who always believed they had valid title to it and who hoped that the other side would in time give up or go away. One side won the war, the other lost, but the contest is alive as ever. We Palestinians ask why a Jew born in Warsaw or New York has the right to settle here (according to Israel's Law of return), whereas we, the people who lived here for centuries, cannot.[39]

Prof. Said points to the fact that Israel's *raison d'être* as a state has always been that there should be a separate country, a refuge, exclusively for Jews. "The effort to separate has occurred simultaneously and paradoxically with the effort to take more and more land, which has in turn meant that Israel has acquired more and more Palestinians. In Israel proper, Palestinians number about one million, almost 20% of the population...."

He emphasizes that Zionists in and outside Israel will not give up on their wish for a separate Jewish state:

> The more that current patterns of Israeli settlement and Palestinian confinement and resistance persist, the less likely it is that there will be real security for either side.... My generation of Palestinians, still reeling from the shock of losing everything in 1948, find it nearly impossible to accept that their homes and farms were taken over by another people. I see no way of evading the fact that in 1948 one people displaced another, thereby committing a grave injustice....[40]

The good professor emphasizes that "There can be no reconciliation unless both peoples, two communities of suffering, resolve that their existence is a secular fact, and that it has to be dealt with as such."[41]

My friends, it will never happen. So the question becomes, what will happen – not only to the land once called Palestine, but to the once-Republic of the United States? Both countries were invaded over time by an alien force.

NAZIS AS FERVENT ZIONISTS

Two books have emerged from obscurity; one was by a German Jewish schoolteacher, Dietrich Bronder, *Before Hitler Came*; and the other, *Adolf Hitler: Founder of Israel*, by Henneke Kardel. Bronder's book was published in 1964 in Germany. It was promptly suppressed and is now out of print. Kardel, an Austrian Jew, who moved to Israel after World War II, published his book in 1974 in Switzerland.

Both works reflect the fact that Adolf Hitler, as well as the majority of his top officers and associates, were Jewish. Bronder includes such notables as Hitler's deputy, Rudolf Hess, *Reichmarshall* Hermann Goering, Dr. Josef Goebbels, Gregor Strasser, Alfred Rosenberg, Hans Frank, Heinrich Himmler, *Reichminister* von Ribbentrop, SS leader Reinhard Heydrich, and Hitler's bankers Ritter von Strauss and von Stein.[42]

According to Kardel, writing in *Adolf Hitler: Founder of Israel*:

> The cooperation which existed between Heydrich's Gestapo and the Jewish self-defense league in Palestine, the militant Haganah, would not have been closer if it was not for Eichmann who made it public...the commander of Haganah was Feivel Polkes, born in Poland, with whom in February 1937 the SD troop leader Adolf Eichmann met in Berlin in a wine restaurant Traube (Grape) near the zoo. These two Jews made a brotherly agreement. Polkes, the underground fighter, got in writing this assurance from Eichmann: 'A body representing Jews in Germany, will exert pressure on those leaving Germany to emigrate only to Palestine. Such a policy is in the interest of Germany and will be executed by the Gestapo.'[43]

Polkes invited his "brother" Eichmann to their ancestors' land (Palestine). When Eichmann returned to Germany, he reported:

> People of Jewish national circles are very excited about the radical German politics toward the Jews, as this has increased Jewish population in Palestine many-fold. In a short time they will become the majority among the Arabs.[44]

A LOOK AT JEWISH FUNDAMENTALISM

Most fundamentalists, whether they be Christian, Muslim or Jewish, look upon God, the Almighty, Allah, Jehovah as a revengeful deity and one to be feared. The noted Israeli author and scholar, Israel Shahak, in his most recent work, *Jewish Fundamentalism in Israel*, provides startling and rare insights into the history and practices of fundamentalism, and how it has come to dominate the politics of that tiny but supremely powerful country once called Palestine.

We referred to Shahak's previous works, *Jewish History, Jewish Religion* and *Open Secrets,* earlier. Now, in the capstone of his jarring trilogy, Shahak has teamed up with an American scholar, Prof. Norton Mezvinsky of Connecticut State University, to examine the most dangerous strains of Jewish fundamentalism. They place the assassination of Prime Minister Rabin in the context of what the authors see as a tradition of historical punishments and killings of those Jews perceived to be heretics.

Shahak refers to Rabbi Yitzhak Ginsburgh, who originally came to Israel from the United States, and has often expressed his views in American Jewish publications. In the New York *Jewish Week* (26 Apr 1996), Rabbi Ginsburgh spoke freely (during an interview) of Jews' genetic-based spiritual superiority over non-Jews. In the eyes of the Torah, he asserted, it is a superiority that invests Jewish life with greater value. "If every simple cell in a Jewish body entails divinity, is a part of God, then every strand of DNA is part of God. Therefore, something is special about Jewish DNA," the learned rabbi declares.[45]

According to Shahak, if one were to change the words "Jewish" to "German" or "Aryan" and "non-Jewish" to "Jewish," this would turn the Ginsburgh ideology into the doctrine that made Auschwitz possible.

In discussing the status of non-Jews in the *Cabbala* (Jewish mysticism) as compared to that of the Talmud, Shahak points out that certain Jewish authors "have employed the trick of using words such as 'men', 'human beings' and 'cosmic' in order to imply incorrectly that the *Cabbala* presents a path leading toward salvation for all human beings." Shahak states that cabbalistic texts emphasize salvation only for Jews.[46]

Shahak singles out a passage from the *Halacha* (the entire body of Jewish religious law), taken from the Talmud, which clearly shows that a non-Jew should be put to death if he kills an embryo, even if the embryo is non-Jewish, while the Jew should not be put to death, even if the embryo is Jewish. He stresses that the above-stated difference in the punishment of a Jew and a non-Jew for the same crime is common in the Talmud and Halacha.[47]

Especially revealing is the consideration of differences between a Jew and a non-Jew as described in Rabbi Yehuda Amital's article, "On the Significance of the Yom Kippur War." Israeli Prof. Uriel Tal interpreted Amital's views: the Yom Kippur War had to be comprehended in its messianic dimension – a struggle against civilization in its entirety.[48]

According to Tal, the war was – as are all the Jewish wars – directed against the "impurity of Western culture."

Tal stated:

> We thus learn that there is only one explanation of the wars; they refine and purify the soul. As impurity is removed, the soul of Israel – by virtue of the war – will be refined. We have already conquered the lands; all that now remains is to conquer impurity.[49]

Tal also describes the 1967 war as a "metaphysical transformation" and that the Israeli conquests transferred land from the power of Satan to the divine sphere. Shahak says that such transformation supposedly proved that the "messianic era" had arrived. Prof. Tal emphasized that any Israeli withdrawal from conquered areas would have "metaphysical consequences which would restore Satanic sovereignty over the land."[50]

During the invasion of Lebanon in 1982, for example, Shahak explains that the military rabbinate issued a map which designated Lebanon as land once belonging to the ancient northern tribes of Israel. The rabbis exhorted the Israeli soldiers to follow in the footsteps of Joshua and to re-establish his divinely ordained conquest of the land of Israel, to include extermination of all non-Jewish inhabitants.[51]

To illustrate the purity of Israeli conquest of other lands as "divinely ordained," Prof. Tal stressed that Israel's presence in Lebanon confirmed the validity of the Biblical promise in Deuteronomy 11:24: "Every place on which the sole of your foot treads shall be yours; our border shall be from the wilderness, from the River Euphrates, to the western sea."[52]

In this regard, Shahak and Mizvinsky reveal an absolutely startling fact, based on their in-depth research:

> The similarities between the Jewish political messianic trend and German Nazism are glaring. The gentiles are for the messianists what the Jews were for the Nazis. The hatred for Western culture with its rational and democratic elements is common to both movements. Finally, the extreme chauvinism of the messianists is directed towards all non-Jews. The 1973 Yom Kippur War, for instance, was in Amital's view not directed against Egyptians, Syrians and/or all Arabs but against all non-Jews. The war was thus directed against the great majority of citizens of the United States, even though the United States aided Israel in that war. This hatred of non-Jews is not new but, as already discussed, is derived from a continuous Jewish cabbalistic tradition. Those Jewish scholars who have attempted to hide this fact from non-Jews and even from many Jews have not only done a disservice to scholarship, they have aided the growth of this Jewish analogue to German Nazism.... This ideology assumes the imminent coming of the Messiah and asserts that the Jews, aided by God, will thereafter triumph over the non-Jews and rule over them forever.[53]

Shahak also stresses that the idea of redemption through contact with a spiritually potent personality has been a major theme common to all strands of Jewish mysticism. The messianic movement stresses that everything can be redeemed, not only by following the collective Messiah, but also such material objects as battle tanks and money if touched or possessed by Jews. This movement argues that what appears to be confiscation of Arab-owned land for subsequent settlement by Jews is in reality not an act of stealing but one of sanctification; that is, redeeming the land by transfer from the Satanic to the divine sphere.

Further, Dr. Shahak states that the messianic rabbis, politicians and ideological populizers compare Palestinians to the ancient Canaanites, whose extermination or expulsion by the ancient Israelites was, according to the Bible, predestined by a divine design. He sees this factor as creating great sympathy for the Israelis among many Christian fundamentalists who anticipate that the end of the world will be marked by slaughters and devastation. This led them willingly to support with funds the Jewish collective messianic takeover of the Middle East. Shahak writes, "As Jewish fundamentalists who abominate non-Jews, they forged a spiritual alliance with Christians who believe that supporting Jewish fundamentalism is necessary to support the second coming of Jesus."[54]

Continuing, Shahak quotes Rabbi Zalman Melamed, chairman of the Committee of the Rabbis of Judea, Samaria and Gaza: "No rabbinical authority disputes that it would be ideal if the land of Israel were inhabited by only Jews." This argument was extended to Muslims and Christians by Rabbi Shlomo Min-Hahar, who claimed: "The entire Muslim world is money-grubbing, despicable and capable of anything. All Christians without exception hate the Jews and look forward to their deaths."[55]

In contrast, Shahak singles out a book, *Intifada Responses,* written by Rabbi Shlomo Aviner in 1990, which provides plain Hebrew *halachic* answers to the questions of what pious Jews should do to Palestinians during situations that arise at times similar to the *Intifada*. The book cautions those not conversant with the *Halacha* not to compare Jewish and gentile under-age minors. "As is known, no *halachic* punishments can be inflicted upon Jewish boys below the age of thirteen and Jewish girls below the age of twelve.... Maimonides (the greatest medieval Jewish philosopher) wrote that this rule applied to Jews alone... not to any non-Jews. Therefore, any non-Jews, no matter what their age, will have to pay for any crime committed.

Aviner explained that if a non-Jewish child intended to commit murder, for example, by throwing a stone at a passing car, that the non-Jewish child should be considered a 'persecutor of the

Jews' and should be killed. He asks the question: "Does the Halacha permit inflicting the death penalty upon Arabs who throw stones?" His answer was that inflicting such a punishment is not only permitted but mandatory.[56]

What Israel Shahak reveals so clearly in all of his erudite works is that the leaders of this tiny Jewish principality, transplanted by conquest and terror into the midst of a sea of Arabs and other "foreigners," use the diobolical teachings of the Talmud and the Halacha so to control its fundamentalist followers that they will willingly go forth to slaughter other peoples and steal their lands in the belief that they are doing God's divinely ordained will. By removing those lands from the control of Satan and placing them under the protection of Jewish benevolence, they "sanctify Israel."[57]

Shahak states that during the time of the state's creation, the number of non-Ashkenazi Jews in Israel was relatively small. "The Israeli government induced Jewish immigration from Iraq by bribing the government of Iraq to strip most Iraqi Jews of their citizenship and to confiscate their property."[58]

As we saw earlier, in order to obtain the necessary "refugees" from other lands to populate Palestine, secret deals were struck with Hitler's minions, and the sympathy factor was cunningly manipulated to obtain tacit financial and moral support of the gullible goyim.

How can we escape from the death grip of the "clammy hand of communism," as Churchill phrased it? How can we defeat this barbarian horde of Bolshevists who have swept onto our shores and have infiltrated and subverted our government, our courts, our financial institutions, and monetary system, as well as our very way of life? How can we stop this mad march to global despotism? Consider the protocol delivered by Henry Kissenger as the grand finale address at the Bilderberger meeting at Evian, France, 21 May 1992:

> Today Americans would be outraged if UN troops entered Los Angeles to restore order; tomorrow they will be grateful! This is especially true if they were told there was an outside threat from beyond,

whether real or promulgated, that threatened our very existence. It is then that all peoples of the world will pledge with world leaders to deliver them from this evil. The one thing every man fears is the unknown. When presented with this scenario, individual rights will be willingly relinquished for the guarantee of their well-being granted to them by their world government.[59]

Before we address these highly pertinent questions, we must consider the distinct possibility of a *coup d'etat* being carried out here in the United States. Is it possible for a tyrant occupying the office of the president to declare martial law, thus pulling a *defacto* coup? Or, conversely, is it possible for a dedicated military force, under a modern-day Gideon, to rise up and pry the critical levers of power loose from those clammy hands of our modern-day Bolshevists, the Barbarians Within the Gates.

It is true that there were no extermination camps on German soil...A gas chamber was in the process of being built at Dachau, but it was never completed.

Simon Wiesenthal, *Stars and Stripes,* 1993

CHAPTER VII

NUREMBERG TRIALS AS FRAUD
(Creating ex-post-facto Law)

The Nuremberg trial constitutes a real threat to the basic conceptions of justice which it has taken mankind thousands of years to establish.
Prof. Milton R. Konvitz, NYU, Jan 1946

PART ONE
MAJOR ADVANCE TO BARBARISM

THERE were several momentous gatherings toward the end of World War II and immediately thereafter...Yalta, Potsdam, San Francisco, Bretton Woods, Nuremberg. Each of them was a staged and manipulated "event," each related to the others, much like acts or scenes in a play. Each of them separately and all of them collectively had the ultimate goal of establishing a one-world despotic dictatorship under a United Nations.

Let's look more closely at the Nuremberg Trials, especially at the main event which extended from 20 November 1945 until the Purim Fest of 16 October 1946... the Grand Finale.

Let's first consider the setting for these trials, that of Nuremberg, once a proud and historic city of 450,000 residents. In his highly readable book, *Nuremberg: Infamy on Trial* (1994), Joseph E Persico sets the scene by describing the transformation of the "treasure chest of the kingdom" that "chilled Justice Jackson" (chief US prosecutor, Robert Jackson) when he first arrived in July 1945. He and "Wild Bill" Donovan, head of the OSS, traveled in a C-47 Dakota aircraft over the rubble that had once been Germany. They met with General Lucius Clay, Ike's deputy. Donovan noted that the Russians would insist on Berlin for the trial, but Clay said

that the army could not find housing for the trial staff in that
shattered city. Clay had a better alternative. They reboarded the
Dakota transport. Persico reports:

> Jackson dozed off briefly, only to be awakened by Clay pointing
> earthward.   That was it, the general said.   Jackson gazed out the
> starboard window. He had seen the bomb damage in London, the ruins
> of Frankfurt and Munich. But nothing had prepared him for the urban
> corpse below. Where were they? He asked. Where Jackson would
> likely find his courthouse, Clay said. That was Nuremberg.[1]

In two days of saturation bombing by over 2,000 Flying
Fortresses on 18-19 February 1945, over 20,000 high explosives
and incendiaries were rained down on the hapless city. This was
the culmination of the top secret Lindemann Plan, which was
implemented by Churchill in 1942. Between October 1943 and the
February 1945 raid, Nuremberg had been bombed 11 times, mostly
by the Royal Air Force at night.

As in the case of the Dresden destruction, also in February
1945, Nuremberg was 90% destroyed, and of the original
population of 450,000, only 130,000 were still alive at war's end.
Persico informs us that the Americans declared Nuremberg
"among the dead cities of the European continent." Yet, Persico
writes, "there survived on its western edge, a huge frowning
structure, the *Justigehaude,* the Palace of Justice: the courthouse of
the government of Bavaria."

It was here in that very Palace of Justice that "victor's
justice" would prevail, leading to the sentencing of 11 Germans to
death by hanging for "crimes against humanity."

For still another view of "victor's justice," let's turn to
another great historian – called "America's intellectual giant" by
his peers – Harry Elmer Barnes. Writing in *Barnes Against the
Blackout*, he quotes a highly literate World War II veteran, Edgar L
Jones, writing in the *Atlantic Monthly* (Feb 1946):

> We topped off our saturation bombing and burning of enemy
> civilians by dropping atomic bombs on two nearly defenseless cities,
> thereby setting an all-time record for instantaneous mass slaughter.[2]

According to Barnes:

Two great wrongs don't make a right. Hitler's evil deeds have been told and retold, beginning long before 1939. After the Cold War started the Western World began to learn something about the monstrous and nefarious doings of Stalin – that 'man of massive outstanding personality, and deep and cool wisdom,' as Churchill described him – which far exceeded those of Hitler. But we have heard little of the horrors which were due to the acts and policies of Churchill and Roosevelt, such as the saturation bombing of civilians, the atom bombing of the Japanese cities (planned by Roosevelt), the expulsion of about 15 million Germans from their former homes and the death of four to six million in the process, and the cruel and barbarous treatment of Germany from 1945 to 1948. The greatest horror that could be fairly traced to their doings is still held in reserve for us – the nuclear extermination of mankind.[3]

NUREMBERG: WOE TO THE VANQUISHED

Nuremberg: The Last Battle by the British writer, David Irving (1998) sheds new light and insight on many of the aspects of the Nuremberg Trial. Irving uncovered long-suppressed facts from private diaries and letters from prosecutors and judges, defendants and witnesses. He shows that the Allies who sat in judgment were themselves guilty of many of the crimes for which the German defendants were tried and hanged. He also exposes the Tribunal's double standard, with the Allies acting as judge, prosecution, jury and executioner. He also reveals how Aushwitz commandant Hoes and other Germans were tortured to produce phony "evidence" that is still widely accepted as fact. He details the invention of the oft-repeated hoax of "six million" victims of the "holocaust."

Irving reveals particularly the views of the chief American prosecutor, Robert H Jackson. Initially enthusiastic about his role as an architect of international law, his enthusiasm waned even before the opening session of the International Military Tribunal (IMT). Irving reports that Jackson told his superiors back in Washington DC:

> If we want to shoot Germans as a matter of policy, let it be done as such, but don't hide the deed behind a court. If you are determined to execute a man in any case, there is no occasion for a trial; the world yields no respect to courts that are merely organized to convict.[4]

We should also consider the Nuremberg Trials in light of the views of learned judges, high-ranking military officers and university professors. Irving reports that it was US Supreme Court Chief Justice Harlan Fiske Stone who in 1945 called the Nuremberg trials a fraud:

> [Chief US Prosecutor Robert] Jackson is away conducting his high-grade lynching party in Nuremberg. I don't mind what he does to the Nazis, but I hate to see the pretense that he is running a court and proceeding according to common law. This is a little too sanctimonious a fraud to meet my old-fashioned ideas. [5]

Supreme Court Associate Justice William O. Douglas charged that the Allies were guilty of "substituting power for principle" at Nuremberg. He later wrote:

> I thought at the time and still think that the Nuremberg Trials were unprincipled. Law was created *ex post facto* to suit the passion and clamor of the time."[6]

As the first trial – the main show – dragged on interminably, Justice Hugo Black ridiculed the IMT, calling it a "serious failure," and placed the blame for that failure on his colleague, Robert Jackson.[7]

Actually, it was in all respects a political show trial fashioned after those of Soviet Russia, as explained by Professor Richard Pipes of Harvard in his outstanding book *Russia Under the Bolshevik Regime*. Pipes states that:

> [T]he Bolsheviks established the original show trial – carefully staged proceedings in which the verdict was preordained and whose objective it was to humiliate the defendants, and, by their example, to intimidate those who sympathized with their cause.[8]

These elaborate show trials were later mimicked by the IMT at Nuremberg, and still later by the Communists in Red China. And all were designed to further the cause of the Universalists to set up a despotic one-world socialist government. Today, that sanctimonious fraud continues at the international court in The Hague under the aegis of the United Nations.

CREATING A GLOBAL MONSTER

Patrick J. Buchanan, in a syndicated column (2 Jul 1998) considers that in Rome delegates from 156 nations are creating an International Criminal Court (ICC) to prosecute the soldiers and leaders of any nation it finds guilty of "crimes against humanity," including our own. "Like the monster of the Frankenstein films, the United Nations has begun to assert a power and authority above that of its creators."[9]

Buchanan writes, "Sensing victory, UN Secretary General Kofi Annan is exploiting our isolation at Rome to coerce us to accept his enlarged vision of an ICC or feel the lash of world opinion. 'No one country,' he says, 'will want to be responsible for the failure of the conference.'

"We want a 'court with teeth'," he writes in London's *Financial Times*, "where acting under orders is no defense and... all individuals in a government hierarchy or military chain of command, without exception, from rulers to private soldiers, must answer for their actions... our own century has seen the invention and use of weapons of mass destruction...."

"Now," Buchanan writes, "since the greatest such weapon of mass destruction ever invented and used was the atomic bomb at Hiroshima, one wonders if Annan believes that General George Marshall and President Harry Truman should have been put in an ICC dock."

Buchanan stresses that "the goal is power – the transfer of power from this republic to international bureaucrats." Buchanan points out that "without an army of its own, the ICC is going to have to rely on the most powerful UN nation to arrest the war criminals it alone decides to prosecute. And guess who that is."

Buchanan winds up his sharp rebuke of the Global Monster taking shape in Rome by stating that Congress should pass a joint resolution that the United States will not assist an ICC created against our wishes, will not fund it, will not permit it to operate on US territory, and will work for its early dissolution.

"We do not need any more institutions that trample on our national sovereignty."[10]

DEFENDANTS ALREADY CONVICTED

The presiding chief judge for the USSR, I. T. Nikitchenko, explained the Soviet view before the Tribunal convened:

> We are dealing here with the chief war criminals who have already been convicted and whose conviction has already been announced by both Moscow and Crimea (Yalta) declarations by the heads of the (Allied) governments... The whole idea is to secure quick and just punishment for the crime.[11]

Both the chief Soviet prosecutor, Lt Gen Roman Rudenko, and Nikitchenko, were Soviet Bolsheviks. Rudenko would later prosecute the US pilot of the U-2 spy plane, Gary Powers.[12]

The greatest problem they faced, according to Jackson, was to overcome criticism that they were creating *ex post facto* law. *Nullum crimen et nulla poena sine lege,* the ancient Romans had said: "no crime and no punishment without law." Related to that problem was another, as explained by the British prosecutor, Sir David Maxwell-Fyfe. Irving reveals that he brought up another Latin expression, *tu quoque,* the "so-did-you" defense.

If the crimes they were defining applied only to Germans, how would they escape history's verdict that the trial was not justice but merely victors' vengeance? Atrocities had been committed on all sides. Further, they were planning to prosecute aggression as a war crime. Yet sitting in judgment would be Russians, whose nation had invaded Finland in 1940 and grabbed a chunk of Poland under its 1939 pact with the Nazis.[13]

In sharp contrast to his public utterances, the Chief US prosecutor, Robert Jackson, privately acknowledged in a letter to President Truman:

> [The Allies] have done or are doing some of the very things we are prosecuting the Germans for. The French are so violating the Geneva Convention in the treatment of [German] prisoners of war that our command is taking back prisoners sent to them [for forced labor in France]. We are prosecuting plunder and our Allies are practicing it. We

say aggressive war is a crime and one of our allies asserts sovereignty over the Baltic States based on no title except conquest.[14]

PREPARING THE SCRIPT FOR A DOCUDRAMA

Historian David Irving highlights this fact in *Nuremberg: The Last Battle*. He relates that in June 1945, Jackson met in New York with representatives of "several powerful Jewish organizations." One of them told Jackson that six million Jews had been "lost" during the war and that he had arrived at this figure by extrapolation. Irving states that "in other words his figure was somewhere between a hopeful estimate and an educated guess." Irving further noted that the six-million figure had been cited 26 years earlier in a leading Jewish-American periodical. Irving reveals:

> In a 1919 essay by a former governor of New York (Martin Glynn), readers were told that '6 million Jews are dying in a threatened holocaust of human life' as victims of 'the awful tyranny of war and a bigoted lust for Jewish blood'.[15]

Such blatant propaganda was designed to excite the sympathy factor, and as a cover for the ongoing rape of Russia 1917-1924 by eastern European émigrés. Coupled with such intent was the implementation of the Balfour Declaration concerning a Jewish homeland in Palestine.

Such deception became the driving force for a future drama staged by the US, Britain, France and the USSR (the United Nations) before the Nuremberg Military Tribunal which played for five years (1945-49) and was written by a great "playwright," lawyer and avowed Zionist, Murray Bernays. We will shortly discover how this attorney from New York capitalized on this bit of artful deception to create the fraud known as the Nuremberg Trials during World War II.

In October 1944 the Joint Chiefs of Staff approved a program dealing with war crimes. It had been drawn up by the Judge Advocate General of the US Army. At the same time, a War Crimes Branch was established in the office of the Judge Advocate General (JAG). Gen John Ware, assisted by Colonel Melvin

Purvis, was to handle all matters related to war crimes for the Departments of War, Navy and State. The approved program was traditional in nature, in that war crimes were based on the accepted laws of war in the field; i.e., a belligerent may try enemy soldiers for the same offenses for which he would try his own troops.

Alas, somebody else was in charge.

It was Samuel Rosenmann, speechwriter and confidant of FDR, who lined up Associate Justice of the Supreme Court, Robert H. Jackson, for the top job of presiding over the Nuremberg Trials. Rosenmann had just returned from an unofficial meeting in England with the British prime minister when FDR died. Because both Rosenmann and Baruch had been wired into the White House loop early on, and because the hapless Harry Truman, as V.P., had been definitely out of the loop, it was a cinch for Rosenmann to convince the new President that Bob Jackson was the man for the job.

In January 1945, Rosenmann met with Secretary of War Henry L. Stimson and Attorney General Francis Biddle. The thrust of the meeting had to do with meting out proper punishment for the "war criminals" already convicted. It was a stacked deck from the beginning. Attorney General Biddle, who later served as a judge at the Trials, gave FDR the following advice for use at the coming Yalta confab: "The German leaders are well known and the proof of their guilt will not offer great difficulties."[16]

WHO WAS MURRAY BERNAYS?

Bernays, an avowed Zionist, graduated from Harvard in 1915 and became a New York lawyer. He was granted a commission in the Army in 1942 and spent the war in a small office on the third floor of the War Department Building on Pennsylvania Avenue (near the White House). He devoted his entire time to preparing plans for the trials of German "war criminals." He joined Jackson in London in June 1945. From his prior work of nearly three years emerged the final plan for the conduct of the trials. The key to this staged docu-drama was the earlier propaganda ploy emerging from World War One, having to do with the "holocaust of the six million." Bernays enlarged on this aspect, as well as on the Biblical *Book of Esther.*

Murray Bernays came to America with his Lithuanian Jewish parents in 1900, when he was six years old. He graduated from Harvard and the Columbia Law School, then joined the New York law firm of Morris Ernst. Along the way, he married Hertha Bernays, a niece of Sigmund Freud, and changed his name from Morris Lipstitch to Murray Bernays – certainly a compliment to his lovely wife.

Perhaps more important than his heritage was the detail of Bernays' plan and how the judges of the four countries involved in the IMT carried it out to the letter... even to the point of sentencing 11 – and only 11 – to be executed by hanging.

One of the first to view Bernays's "top secret" handiwork was Herbert Wechsler, who worked for Attorney General Francis Biddle.

"What was this conspiracy nonsense?" Wechsler asked. "And defining acts as criminal after they had been committed? That was *ex post facto* law, bastard law. And declaring that whole organizations – some of whose members numbered in the hundreds of thousands, some in millions – were criminal? This meat-ax approach was fraught with potential for injustices."[17]

Wechsler would serve as Biddle's legal advisor at the Trials. Jackson was so impressed by Bernays and his plan for the conduct of the trials that he hired him as his executive officer – "his right arm," Persico tells us. He also explains in his chapter, "Prelude to Judgment," how the delegates from the four allied countries who would try the German "war criminals" got around the business of *ex post facto* law.

"On August 8, roughly six weeks after the allied representatives had first assembled at Church House (London), they were ready to sign an agreement to try war criminals in an international court. The document defined the crimes, the structure of the court, the procedures and punishments. But what to name the new instrument? Nomenclature had been tricky. To call it a law, a statute, a code, would brand it, at the outset, as *ex post facto*. And so a neutral term, charter, was settled on: the Charter of the International Military Tribunal."[18]

Murray Bernays authored the Nuremberg Trial's charter which defined four crimes: 1) conspiracy to carry out aggressive war, 2) the actual launching of aggression; 3) killing, destroying, and plundering during a war not justified by military necessity; and 4) crimes against humanity, including atrocities against civilians, most flagrantly the attempt to exterminate the Jews.

CELEBRATING PURIM FEST

Most haunting regarding the main event of the farcical Nuremberg Trials was the scheduled hanging of 11 "war criminals" on the Jewish Purim Fest. This was the grand finale of the script prepared by the great playwright and Biblical scholar, Murray Bernays.

The first scenario dragged on from March 1946 until that fated day – Purim Fest on 16 October – when just after the stroke of midnight, 11 (mark well the number) already sentenced by the four "impartial" judges of the IMT for execution by hanging, were unceremoniously dragged from their beds and escorted to the gymnasium, where Master Sergeant John Woods, Third US Army's official hangman, had constructed three gallows.

Why 11?   Because that number was preordained in Bernays' grand design as the frosting on the cake, so to speak. One must read the *Book of Esther* to understand the implications fully, as many did when Dr. Baruch Goldstein went on a killing rampage in Hebron, Israel, murdering over 30 Arabs as they knelt in prayer. Only by going back to the basics of this philosophy of utter destruction (to be followed by "a day of feasting and gladness" which came to be called Purim) will we begin to understand the rationality of the massacre in the mosque. It was but one more act of endless revenge, carried out in accordance with Talmudic law and justice.   Carried out with appropriate celebrations on Purim Fest.

In the *Book of Esther,* King Ahasuerus, urged on by his favorite concubine, Esther, and her uncle, Mordecai, hanged Haman and his ten sons:

> The Jews gathered themselves together in the cities throughout all the provinces of the King Ahasuerus, to lay hand on such as sought their hurt: and no man could withstand them; for the fear of them fell upon all the people... and slew of their foes seventy and five thousand.[19]

Related to the dissimulations emerging from World War One and the effort, especially on the part of Britain, to discredit the Germans was the business of "gassing innocents." Bernays would twist an earlier and cruder propaganda ploy – to prove that all Germans were barbarians – concerning the supposed gassing of innocents. (See the London *Times* for 8 March 1917, which asserted that the Germans had gassed 700,000 Serbian civilians.) This hoax was resurrected 25 years later and appeared in the underground Bund report (25 May 1942) from the Warsaw Ghetto that "the Nazis have already exterminated 700,000 Polish Jews."[20]

This lie became the trigger for the "extermination of six million Jews" by the Nazis, first by burning in fiery pits, then by steaming to death in showers and finally by "gassing." Such is the nature of propaganda, especially when one controls a complicit press, that even today, two-thirds of the people polled still accept the "holocaust of six million" as fact.

Meaning that a third do not.

Jean-Francois Revel explains just how such dissimulation works in *How Democracies Perish:*

> It is an occupational habit for actors on the political stage to distort the truth, for reasons and in ways that vary with the nature of the power they hold. Autocrats, in direct control of all means of communication and expression, disguise the present and rewrite the past... in free societies the past is sometimes misrepresented, not as in slave societies, by crude state censorship and lies, but suavely, through legitimate persuasion and the free propagation of an adulterated or entirely bogus version of an event. With repetition, this version joins the body of accepted ideas, those the masses believe; it acquires the status of truth, so firmly that hardly anyone thinks of checking the original facts for confirmation.[21]

PART TWO
THE BIG SHOW IN THE MAIN TENT

The Nuremberg Trials have made the waging of unsuccessful war a crime: the generals on the defeated side are tried and then hanged.

Field Marshal B. L. Montgomery, 9 Jun 1948

THE trial opened at Nuremberg on 20 Nov 1945. It was a done deal before it started. The Judge Advocate General (JAG), Maj Gen Myron Kramer, was in league with Justice Jackson from the start. The JAG's War Crimes Branch took over the screening and selection of prosecution and defense lawyers.

The "big trial" conducted by the International Military Tribunal at Nuremberg ran from March until October 1946. It resulted in three acquittals (one of them, Hjalmar Schacht), seven prison sentences and 11 death sentences, which were immediately carried out by hanging (with the exception of Goering, who swallowed a potassium cyanide capsule).

The strangest prison sentence was meted out to Rudolph Hess by the tribunal in absentia. Hess, who had flown a fighter to Scotland early in the war, had surrendered to the British, and had proposed a plan whereby the Germans and the British would team up to defeat Josef Stalin and prevent the spread of Communism throughout Europe. Because the spread of socialism worldwide was one of the reasons for fighting World War II, one can understand in retrospect why Hess was placed in isolation and solitary confinement – the only prisoner in Spandau – for the rest of his natural life.

And Hjalmar Schacht (Hajim Schachtl), the man behind Hitler, the man behind the international financial chaos of the 1920s and '30s, went free.

Bear in mind that of the 21 men in the dock at Nuremberg, only 11 were preordained to be sentenced to death by hanging.

This in fact was known ahead of time by the four judges of the IMT and their alternates, as well as by others, particularly by the US military officers in attendance.

They too had read Murray Bernays's top secret script.

A THREE-RING CIRCUS

From 1946 to 1949, a series of twelve less important trials were staged by the US before the Nuremberg Military Tribunal. These trials in the main were politically instigated. There have been many books printed regarding them, one being Professor Arthur Butz's *Hoax of the Twentieth Century*. However, the statement by one of the American presiding judges, Charles F. Wennerstrum, sums it up:

> If I had known seven months ago what I know today, I would never have come here.... The high ideals announced as the motives for creating these tribunals has not been evident.... The entire atmosphere here is unwholesome.... The trials were to have convinced the Germans of the guilt of their leaders. They convinced the Germans merely that their leaders lost the war to tough conquerors... abhorrent to the American sense of justice is the prosecution's reliance on self-incriminating statements made by the defendants while prisoners for more than $2^1/_2$ years, and repeated interrogation without presence of counsel...the lack of appeal leaves me with a feeling that justice has been denied....[22]

Professor Butz reports:

> These trials were supervised by the War Crimes Branch. They were perhaps the most shameful episodes in US history.[23]

He explains that the entire repertoire of third degree methods was employed, with beatings and brutal kicking, to the point of ruining testicles in 137 cases, knocking out teeth, starvation, solitary confinement, torture with burning splinters, and impersonation of priests in order to encourage prisoners to "confess."

One notable incident occurred when investigator Joseph Kirschbaum brought a certain Einstein into court to testify that the accused Menzel had murdered Einstein's brother. When the accused was able to point out that the brother was not only alive and well, but was sitting in the court, Kirschbaum was deeply embarrassed and scolded Einstein: "How can we bring this pig to the gallows, if you are so stupid as to bring your brother into court?"[24]

The US Army authorities admitted to some of the charges. When the chief of the Dachau War Crimes Branch, Colonel A. H. Rosenfeld, quit his post in 1948, he was asked by reporters if there was any truth to the stories of mock trials at which sham death sentences had been passed, he replied, "Yes, of course. We couldn't have made these birds talk otherwise.... It was a trick and it worked like a charm."

The makeup of the War Crimes Branch was essentially Jewish. It was headed by Colonel David "Mickey" Marcus after Judge Samuel Rosenmann had been picked by Truman to oversee the trials of German war criminals. Marcus remained the chief of the War Crimes Branch until April 1947, when he left the Army and went into private law practice.

There is an interesting sequel to Mickey Marcus. It emerges from an AP story, 12 Jun 1948, that a "Mickey Stone" had been killed in action while serving as supreme commander in the Jerusalem sector in the Jewish-Arab war for the control of Palestine. He was adulated in the *New York Times*, with all of his accomplishments listed, not as Mickey Stone, but as David Marcus. Strangely, his service as head of the War Crimes Branch during the Nuremberg trials was omitted. So was the fact that he was not killed in action in some bloody engagement in Palestine, but was shot by one of his sentries as he made a late-night foray to the latrine.[25]

VICTORS' JUSTICE

In 1946 Capt B. H. Liddell Hart's book *The Evolution of Warfare* was published in London. He stated that victory had been achieved by "practicing the most uncivilized means of warfare that the world had known since the Mongol devastations." He included not only the terror bombings of German civilians, but the deliberate murder of hundreds of thousands of Japanese citizens by nuclear extermination at Hiroshima and Nagasaki in August 1945, as well as the setting up of the system of "war-crimes trials."[26]

In his classic *Advance to Barbarism* (1948), Frederick J. P. Veale detailed "the development of Total Warfare from Sarajevo to Hiroshima":

> It cannot be denied that this particular reversion to Barbarism was accepted by the public with astonishingly few misgivings.[27]

Another book outstanding for what it portrays, viz. "justice," or the lack thereof, was *Epitaph at Nuremberg* by Montgomery Belgion, first published in 1946, then updated and republished in 1949 by the Henry Regnery Company in the United States under the title *Victors' Justice*.

By examining the novel method of disposing of war prisoners agreed upon at Yalta, Belgion determined that "the Nuremberg Trials were not inspired by any overwhelming passion for justice and by a righteous determination that crime should not escape punishment." In essence, he pointed out, "a trial is a means by which an existing law is enforced, and that at Nuremberg there was no existing law to enforce... the Hands may have been the hands of Justice, but the Voice was Propaganda's voice."

Further, he traces it back to World War I and to Article 231 of the Treaty of Versailles, which declared Germany solely guilty for the First World War, but had neither moral weight nor judicial validity. And so the victors of the Second World War decided to hold trials of the vanquished that would, they hoped, conclusively establish for all time Germany's guilt.

That, he submitted, was the real object of the Nuremberg Trial: "It was a gigantic 'put up show,' a gigantic piece of 'propaganda.'"[28]

STAGE-MANAGING THE TRIAL

The Trial was decked out to look like an authentic judicial process; the victors showed a really astonishing contempt for justice and a really pathetic faith in sophistry. Veale singles out, in addition to the mass murders committed under the saturation bombing of German cities, the mass-deportations of populations totaling over 14 million and entailing indescribable misery. It was sanctioned by Gen Eisenhower under "Operation Keel Haul."[29]

In most cases these deportations followed wholesale mass-murder carried out in the homelands of the populations condemned to deportation. Not only had Ike had a hand in this, but Gen. Bill Donovan as well. Donovan headed the Office of Strategic Services (OSS) which would later become the CIA. Irving reveals their role:

> It soon became clear that the OSS had intended all along to manage the whole trial along the lines of the NKVD [Soviet] show-trial... they proposed to run a pre-trial propaganda campaign in the US, with 'increasing emphasis on the publication of atrocity stories to keep the public in the proper frame of mind.[30]

As regards the Nuremberg Trials, Veale states that: "It is perhaps hardly necessary to comment on the fundamental injustice of inventing *ad hoc* law and then bringing charges alleging acts in breach of this law committed before the law existed."

In the United States this injustice was widely recognized. Irving brings this out clearly in his book; he quotes US Secretary of War Henry Stimson:

> I found around me, particularly in Morgenthau [Secretary of the Treasury], a very bitter atmosphere of personal resentment against the entire German people without regard to individual guilt, and I am very much afraid that it will result in our taking mass vengeance on the part of our people.... I cannot believe that he [Roosevelt] will follow Morgenthau's views. If he does, it will certainly be a disaster.... The President appoints a committee and then goes off to Quebec with the man [Morgenthau] who really represents the minority and is so biased by his Semitic grievances that he is really a very dangerous advisor....[31]

As the leading Republican Senator, Robert A. Taft, a politician respected by all parties, pointed out:

> It is completely alien to the American tradition of law to prosecute men for criminal acts which were not declared to be so until long after the fact. The Nuremberg Trials will forever remain a blot on the escutcheon of American jurisprudence.[32]

UNDERSTANDING "THE LONDON AGREEMENT"

Veale is at his very best describing not only the fundamental injustice of the Trials, but the actual stupidity of the major participants in the prosecution of what came to be called "Crimes against peace" and "Crimes against humanity."

Of course, it was a sort of stupidity clever in its cunning. It trickled out, over an inordinate time, in the wellspring of regurgitation flowing forth from "The London Agreement," which in fact was the formulation of *ex post facto* or bastard law.

The London Agreement was a pact drawn up, in London of course, between and among the British, French, Russian and American Governments in 1945 for the trial of "the major war criminals whose offenses have no particular geographical location."[33]

No definition of "major war criminals" was ever given, except that each participant in the farce reserved the right to try, according to its own laws, any war criminal in its hands for offenses committed on its own territory.

Veale explains that attached to the Agreement was a sort of schedule "grandiloquently labeled 'the Charter,' which purported to define the powers of the Tribunal and the procedure which it was to adopt."[34]

Unsaid by Veale is that the common thread throughout the London Agreement and subsequent trial of "war criminals" was the law of the Babylonian Talmud as interpreted by that great legal scholar, Murray Bernays. The setting up of the London Agreement coincides with his arrival on the scene from his War Department office in Washington, DC, at the behest of that great criminologist, Robert J. Jackson.

An important part of the Agreement is contained in Article 6 of the Charter (actually composed by Bernays). It is as much a fraud as the United Nations Charter, and cunningly concocted by the same group of Zionists and their pawns. As Veale explains, it purports to create two new crimes against international law:

"Crimes against peace" are defined as "planning or waging a war of aggression or a war in violation of international treaties. Crimes against humanity" are defined as "inhuman acts against any civilian population before or during the war and persecutions on political, racial or religious grounds."

Veale further states:

> With regard to the first of these novel creations, the framers of the Charter had abandoned in despair a desperate attempt to define 'a war of aggression' without implicitly condemning Russia for her numerous unprovoked attacks on her neighbors. The chiefs of state at the Yalta Conference had cheerfully convicted their captured enemies of having plotted and waged a war of aggression, and set the framers of the Charter the utterly impossible task of defining this alleged offense. Of course, they failed.[35]

As we saw earlier, it was equally impossible to define the second novel crime at the same time as the victors were engaged in mass deportations of 14 million people, coupled with mass murder in their homelands. Add to this the saturation and terror bombing of German cities under the Lindemann Plan, and the scheme to convert Germany to a goat pasture – the Morgenthau Plan – which, if carried out, would have destroyed another 14 million Germans.

Considering the fire-bombing of Japanese cities, along with the *finale* of dropping the two atomic bombs on Hiroshima and Nagasaki, one can begin to understand that such crimes as defined under Article 6 applied only to the losers and therefore needed no definition, as it was the victors who not only created these new laws (after the fact), but interpreted them in a fraudulent court of law and meted out unjust punishment in direct violation of the Geneva Convention.

This is truly victors' justice writ large. In fact, it is Talmudic revenge. It is being practiced assiduously today under UN auspices, and controlled by the coterie of modern-day Bolsheviks who are bent on establishing international law as the Law of the Land. By using US forces to capture alleged war criminals (already convicted) in Bosnia and carting them off to a UN tribunal of "justice" in The Hague, they are following once more the script of Murray Bernays and the perfidious London Agreement.

MILITARY VIEWS OF REVENGE FOREVER

Lastly, a personal reflection as we close our inspection of the fraudulent Nuremberg Trials and prepare to examine current and ongoing frauds of a similar nature in the tiny theocratic state of Israel.

This author recently renewed his acquaintance with a former boss in the military. He was a lawyer by education and profession, and would become a federal judge: he is now retired. We met for dinner, which extended into the wee hours in a discussion of the Nuremberg Trials, for he was there and participated as a young captain seconded from his Civil Affairs and Military Government unit to serve in the War Crimes Branch.

His studied opinion, based on 50 years of reflection, was that the Nuremberg Trials were fraudulent, were based on hate and vengefulness; and perhaps most important, are continuing today under the aegis of the Office of Special Investigations (OSI) of the Justice Department. In answer to the question, was there justice at Nuremberg, he said, "no, only revenge, for the war crimes trials of the '40s, as well as the ongoing witchhunt for 'hidden Nazis' are based on hate and revenge ... forever."

Was this learned judge and former military officer perhaps prejudiced, or mistaken in his belief, his views but an aberration?

The 25th Infantry Division commander in Korea was a tough old soldier, later a three-star general, Samuel T. Williams. We called him (behind his back) "Hangin' Sam." He was brave and gruff and demanding; we feared and respected him, but admired him too. Later, after he retired, he and I became good friends.

"Hangin' Sam" earned his sobriquet at the Nuremberg Trials. He was one of the judges, and his response when the judges debated the sentencing was invariably "hang 'em." There was nothing personal about it, he reminisced. He knew what was expected of him, as "the Jews were in charge of the trials and it was the blood libel of the Jews.... They were getting even for 2,000 years of persecution."

One of General Williams' last tours before retirement had been as the senior military advisor for the US Army in Saigon after the fall of Dien Ben Phu and the defeat of the French in 1954. He had warned President Eisenhower not to get involved "in another rice paddy war" in the Far East and apparently Ike had heeded his advice, for we didn't venture into that "shit pit," as Williams called it, until after the John F. Kennedy assassination and the advent of LBJ's Great Society.

Following the October 1973 Yom Kippur War in the Middle East, we shared a dinner and conversation with the hero of the Battle of St. Vith in World War II, General Bruce C. Clarke, friend and neighbor in Arlington, Virginia, who had been our Corps commander in Korea, 1952-53. Gen Clarke considered the conduct of the Nuremberg Trials a black mark on the otherwise unblemished "Crusade in Europe." He also scoffed at the obviously fabricated yarn that the Israelis had been "surprised at prayer on this, their holiest day" when the Arabs launched a major offensive on Yom Kippur (1973). "Since 1948, Israel has been our surrogate in the Middle East," he said. "Now, we have become the surrogates of Israel and international Zionism.... Personally, I fear for my Country."[36]

These three officers reflect a knowledge and belief held by most of us who served in combat in some of the bloodiest wars of this century; not only officers, but the countless enlisted men who went forth to defend their country against an ill-defined enemy from without while a well-defined "fox," hiding under our cloak, was busily gnawing at our guts.

Consider the decisions made at the end of the war by another of our colleagues in uniform who wore five stars on the epaulets of his jacket – one Dwight David Eisenhower. As recorded by James Bacque in *Other Losses* (1989), Ike issued an order that German prisoners in our custody would no longer be treated in accordance with the Geneva Convention (on treatment of

Prisoners of War). This one act condemned hundreds of thousands of POWs to death by starvation and disease.[37]

We can look back to a revealing issue of the British weekly *The Economist* (5 Oct 1946) wherein an editorial stated in part:

> Among crimes against humanity stands the offence of the indiscriminate bombing of civilian populations. Can the Americans who dropped the atom bomb and the British who destroyed the cities of western Germany plead 'not guilty' on this count? Crimes against humanity also include the mass expulsion of populations. Can the Anglo-Saxon leaders who at Potsdam condoned the expulsion of millions of Germans from their homes hold themselves completely innocent?... The nations sitting in judgment [at Nuremberg] have so clearly proclaimed themselves exempt from the law which they have administered.[38]

In looking back at the fraudulent Nuremberg trials, one must ask the question: who was really in charge? We get a clue (or an admission) from one Nahum Goldmann among others, then the president of the World Jewish Congress, who stated in his autobiography (1969) *inter alia*:

> It [the Nuremberg Tribunal] was the brain-child of World Jewish Congress officials.... Only after persistent effort were WJC officials able to persuade Allied leaders to accept the idea.[39]

Today, we can ask the identical question: who is really in charge? For another clue (or admission), let's venture a little farther down that bloody and rocky road which leads, however circuitously, to the final goal of our fearful masters – establishment of a global government of absolute despotism.

The money-power and the revolutionary-power have been set up and given sham but symbolic shapes ('Capitalism' and 'Communism') and sharply defined citadels ('America' and 'Russia'). Suitably to alarm the mass mind, the picture offered is that of bleak and hopeless enmity and confrontation...But what if similar men, with a common aim, secretly rule in both camps and propose to achieve their ambition through the clash between these masses? I believe that any diligent student of our times will discover that this is the case.

Douglas Reed, *Far and Wide*

CHAPTER VIII
ROCKY ROAD TO GLOBAL DESPOTISM
(Using the Absolute Weapon)

MacArthur thought it a tragedy that the Bomb was ever exploded. [He] believed... that the military objective should always be limited damage to noncombatants.... MacArthur, you see, was a soldier. He believed in using force only against military targets, and that is why the nuclear thing turned him off.

Former President Richard M. Nixon, 1985

PART ONE
BETRAYING THE NATION

WHY did we drop the two atomic bombs on Hiroshima and Nagasaki in August of 1945 although, at the time, every major US military commander (except George Catlett Marshall) opposed it – some violently so?

Who actually made the fateful decision and for what overriding reason?

Three publications provide some startling revelations which help to clarify what I consider to be an intentionally-obscured picture of the events leading up to the destruction of two major Japanese cities and virtually all of their civilian populace.

The Soviet wartime cables (Venona Intercepts) remove all doubt about the American Communist Party's role as the linchpin of a Russian spy network, which was pervasive throughout our government at the highest levels before, during and after World War II. Writing in the *Washington Times* (1 Jan 1998), Evan Gahr stated: "That revelation, of course, directly contradicts the notion that Communist Party members were simply idealists or 'liberals in a hurry.'"

The deciphering of nearly 3,000 secret Soviet cables transmitted between the US and the USSR – what came to be known as the Venona Intercepts – was accomplished by the US Army Signals Security Agency, then located in Northern Virginia. A leading military historian, Ulick Steadman, stresses the importance of these secret messages:

> The de-mystified Moscow cable traffic revealed that there were hundreds of Soviet spies burrowed into key positions in various branches of the American government. They were US citizens, but for the most part were foreign born or from recent immigrant stock. Adherence to political Zionism apparently attenuated their allegiance to America and made them willing recruits for Soviet espionage....

> Gen Omar Bradley, chairman of the Joint Chiefs of Staff in 1947, respected and liked Truman, but he knew – as did other top national-security officials in Washington – that Truman's entourage had been penetrated by Zionist agents. Concerned that anything known to the White House would soon become known to the Zionist insiders, and subsequently to the Soviets, Gen Bradley ordered the Venona intercepts withheld from Truman, his commander-in-chief. [1]

Martin Mann, writing in a special report in the weekly newspaper *Spotlight* (14 Dec 1998), states that the Venona transcripts released by the CIA, and now accessible to such researchers as those at Harvard University, prove that Sen. Joseph McCarthy was right when he warned the nation on 9 Feb 1950 that 205 Communist agents had infiltrated the US government. "That was almost exactly the number of Soviet spies who were identified from the nearly 3,000 intercepted Venona messages decoded by the US Army," says retired Pentagon cryptographer, H. Deter Gamage.

Is there in fact a connection between these revelations and the decision made at the highest levels of the three "Allied" governments in 1945 to totally devastate two major Japanese cities and all of the civilian populace living therein? Was America betrayed at Yalta – at Potsdam? If so, by whom? For a partial answer, let's look to a syndicated column (16 May 1994) by

Patrick J. Buchanan, one of our Country's most erudite political commentators and writers.

"Who betrayed the nation? Who was a fellow traveler? Who was a dupe? Who was wrongly accused or falsely smeared?" Buchanan asks these pointed questions regarding Soviet spy Sudoplatov's revelation that J. Robert Oppenheimer periodically supplied the USSR with data on the construction of the first atomic bomb. His stated guess is "that there is more, much more, to come out."[2]

And now, after Buchanan's pressing questions, the truth of these conspiratorial crimes against humanity – perpetrated by the Boshevist Communists – is almost literally gushing out. *The Secret World of American Communism,* by Harvey Klehr, John Earl Haynes and Fridrikh Igorovich Firsove, not only confirms the thesis in this paper, but leaves no doubt that by 1919 American Communist party members had set up an underground spy network, complete with Soviet controllers, and financed by both Russian and Wall Street sources.[3]

The book also details the transfer of atomic data by a host of Communist Bolsheviks, among them the Rosenberg couple and the infamous Alger Hiss, whose espionage has been surpassed only by Henry Kissinger's. It is interesting to note that Hiss got his start in 1936 in the State Department, which Kissinger eventually took over.... Today the latest crop of Communist Bolshevists is pervasive throughout the government. Declassified documents taken from the archives of the Communist International (Comintern) reveal irrefutable first-hand accounts of base treachery against the United States of America and its Constitution. The goals have not changed over the entire time span from 1919 to date.

"McCarthy was right that there were Communists in government," according to the book reviewer Philip Terzian, "but William Blake was wiser, 'A truth that's told with bad intent/Beats all the lies you can invent.'"[4]

As for the business of inventing lies, first prize must go to FDR. When one reads the official statements of FDR leading up to the critical election of 1940, following the outbreak of the European war in 1939, one is struck by his seemingly overriding thought: how to keep the United States at peace.

By artful use of this subterfuge and at the same time working assiduously with such as Winston Churchill, First Lord of the Admiralty and later Prime Minister, "FDR lied us into war " according to former Representative Clare Booth Luce.

NO NEED TO DROP "THE BOMB"

Several high-ranking US military officers were well aware as early as 1942 that both secret data and material components of the atomic bomb were being provided surreptitiously to the Soviets. For any number of reasons, most chose – and still choose – to remain silent about the clandestine and treasonous transfer. Why?

That same group of military officers also knew in 1945 that there was absolutely no military requirement to drop the atomic bombs on Japan.

Emperor Hirohito, negotiating with the US through the good offices of the Vatican in April/May 1945, was willing to surrender on exactly the same terms later effected in August.

This was the considered view of Harry Elmer Barnes, an American intellectual giant and noted historian. In a series of essays against interventionism, collectively titled, *Barnes Against the Blackout*, he states that the Japanese "had been trying to surrender on the same terms finally accepted in August 1945 – terms submitted to President Roosevelt through General MacArthur, who vainly urged Roosevelt to consider them." Barnes quotes the British Colonel J.F.C. Fuller, who described the needless bombing as something "which would have disgraced Genghis Khan and Tamerlane."[5]

The questions remain: Why was it done? Who were the high-level perpetrators? Who benefited? Keep in mind that since

1954 both the US and the USSR have exchanged detailed atomic research and test results through the Pugwash Conferences (named after the hideaway of their host, Cyrus Eaton, in Canada, and started by a most curious pair indeed – Albert Einstein and Bertrand Russell).

Earlier, it was Bernard Baruch who called the atomic bomb the "absolute weapon." He set himself up as the head of an international organization, which he called "the United Nations Atomic Energy Commission." This was in 1944, some 16 months before most of the cabinet – including the then vice president, Harry S Truman – knew of the bomb's existence and before the initial meeting of a United Nations founding group. Truman, when he became president, appointed Baruch to just such a position.[6]

Baruch knew of both coming events, for he was in on the planning (present at the creation), as was his good friend, Albert Einstein. Both men were avowed "internationalists," both were touted by a slavish and controlled press as being "great men"; Bernard Baruch, financier, philanthropist, "elder statesman" and "patriot"; Albert Einstein the "genius" and "pacifist." And both played a major role in setting up a one-world government based on fear, as viewed by the founders of the United Nations, and so succinctly stated by Einstein in 1945:

> Since I do not foresee that atomic energy is to be a great boon for a long time, I have to say that for the present it is a menace. Perhaps it is well that it should be. It may intimidate the human race into bringing order into its international affairs, which, without the pressure of fear, it would not do.[7]

EINSTEIN'S WORLD DESPOTIC GOVERNMENT

Einstein reveals himself in his two books, *Why War?* (an exchange of letters with Sigmund Freud) and *The World as I See It.* In the previously mentioned article in *The Atlantic Monthly* (Nov 1945) "Einstein on the Atomic Bomb," the professor spoke of the "secret of the bomb," which he felt should not be given to the United Nations, nor shared with the Soviet Union.

Now comes the dichotomy.

Einstein proposes instead that "The secret of the bomb should be committed to a World Government and the United States should immediately announce its readiness to give it to a World Government."[8]

Next, this "genius" proposes that such a World Government should be founded by the United States, the Soviet Union, and Great Britain – "the only three powers with great military strength." He adds that each of these three Great Powers should "commit to the World Government all of their military strength."

Does this idea trouble you just a little?

How would such a World Government be formed? Dr. Einstein enlightens us (and the world as he saw it): "Since the United States and Great Britain have the secret of the atomic bomb and the Soviet Union does not, they should invite the Soviet Union to prepare and present the first draft of a Constitution for the proposed World Government."

Here is Einstein's convoluted reasoning:

> That action should help to dispel the distrust which the Russians already feel because the bomb is being kept secret, chiefly to prevent their having it. Obviously the first draft would not be the final one, but the Russians should be made to feel that the World Government would assure them their security.[9]

Dr. Einstein then proposes that smaller nations should be invited to join the World Government, but would be free to stay out. "The World Government would have power over all military matters and need have only one further power: the power to intervene in countries where a minority is oppressing a majority and creating the kind of instability that leads to war."

Einstein stresses that: "There must be an end to the concept of non-intervention, for to end it is part of keeping the peace."

Einstein continues: "[A] World Government is preferable to the far greater evil of wars, particularly with their intensified destructiveness."[10]

Here we see the eternal Talmudic threat and promise embodied in the French Revolution and again in the Russian Revolution. It hung as a dark shadow over FDR and his New Deal, over Yalta and Potsdam, involving those three great powers of which Einstein speaks so eloquently. It contains both the threat and the promise and is embodied in its myriad statutes and judgments. Einstein, that noble American import from Germany, gives us threat and promise in spades.

Toward the end of his lucid article, *Time's* Man of the Century, Einstein states:

> Now that we have the atomic secret, we must not lose it, and that is what we should risk doing if we should give it to the United Nations organization or to the Soviet Union.
>
> But we must make it clear, as quickly as possible, that we are not keeping the bomb a secret for the sake of our power, but in the hope of establishing peace in a World Government, and that we will do our utmost to bring the World Government into being.[11]

So we see throughout that strange article not only the dichotomies, but the promise of glorious world peace by way of world government coupled with the threat of destruction – via UN league to enforce peace – by nuclear means.

UNIVERSAL FEAR OF NUCLEAR POWER

It was Einstein's British friend, Bertrand Russell, who stated boldly (*Bulletin of Atomic Scientists*, Oct 1946) that it was necessary to "interject fear of nuclear weapons in order to force all nations to give up their sovereignty and submit to the dictatorship of a United Nations."[12]

And it was this kind of thinking that prevailed at the second Pugwash Conference in 1958, which produced the policy that came to be known as Mutual Assured Destruction (MAD).

How did this concept of fear of nuclear power evolve?

In May of that fateful year (1945), this author was with a US military force driving the remnants of the defeated Japanese out of North Burma. Our headquarters was in Namhkam, Burma and we would shortly head for Kunming, China. Simultaneously, our B-29s, flying from Pacific atolls, devastated Tokyo with a series of raids (27 May 1945).

Two days after the raids, the acting Secretary of State, Joseph C. Grew, called on President Truman. He recommended that the President enlarge his previous statement – "unconditional surrender of Japan would mean neither annihilation nor enslavement" – to include the statement that "surrender would not mean the elimination of the present dynasty if the Japanese people desired its retention." Truman favored this approach: he asked Grew to get a consensus from Secretary of War Henry L. Stimson and other advisors. Grew met with Stimson, James Forrestal, Gen. Marshall, John McCloy, Elmer Davis and Judge Samuel Rosenmann on 29 May 1945.[13]

The gist of Grew's memo following the meeting reflected that he, Stimson, Forrestal and Marshall favored the proposal, while the others "for certain military reasons" considered it "inadvisable" for the President to make such a statement. Grew said:

> The question of timing was the nub of the whole matter. I reported this to the President and the proposal for action was, for the time being, dropped.[14]

Of course, this "question of timing" had to do with the coming Potsdam Conference, its ultimatum issued to Japan from the three great powers, and the belated entry of Soviet Russia into the war against Japan just days before the dropping of the atomic bombs and the surrender.

As Grew would later write: "If surrender could have been brought about in May 1945, or even in June or July, before the entrance of Soviet Russia into the war and the use of the atomic bomb, the world would have been the gainer."

Why did Rosenmann, McCloy and Davis hold out at the meeting with Secretary of State Grew? What did they know and when did they know it? For a clue, turn once more to a statement made by Grew to Stimson in a personal letter dated 12 Feb 1947:

"If only it (had been) made clear that surrender would not involve the downfall of the dynasty."[15]

This point was clearly implied in Article 12 of the Potsdam Proclamation, to wit:

> The occupying forces of the Allies shall be withdrawn from Japan as soon as there has been established in accordance with the freely expressed will of the Japanese people a peacefully inclined and responsible government.[16]

The psychological spin behind exploding the bombs was to create such a worldwide fear of the power of nuclear energy that countries would give up their sovereignty, turn all their weapons and armed forces over to a world government, and surrender their freedom.

Which takes us right back to Einstein and his belief that "A world government is preferable to the far greater evil of wars." What he was saying in fact – and if we are to give any credence at all to his "brilliance," we must agree – that we can submit to absolute global despotism of the league to enforce peace or be annihilated by the absolute weapon.

DROPPING THE BOMB: THE MILITARY VIEW

Perhaps the premier work on the decision to drop the atomic bombs on the Japanese cities of Hiroshima and Nagasaki is *The Decision to Use the Atomic Bomb and the Architecture of an American Myth* by Gar Alperovitz (1995). It is an exhaustive and impeccably documented treatise of the events of that fateful summer of 1945. Its conclusion, corroborated by nearly all the military leaders and many of the political advisers to President Truman, is that there was absolutely no need to drop the bombs.

Alperovitz reveals that Japan was on the verge of surrendering as early as April 1945, and that virtually every member of the military high command was opposed to their use. Truman's final decision was later (and still is) justified by a gigantic "deception" (say lie) – the claim that upwards of a million soldiers' lives were saved which might otherwise have been lost in an invasion of the Japanese home islands.

That myth has become the second greatest exaggeration of the twentieth century.

Here are a few expressed views of some of the key military officers involved in the dropping of the two atomic bombs on Hiroshima and Nagasaki in August of 1945:

> It always appeared to us that, atomic bomb or no atomic bomb, the Japanese were already on the verge of collapse. (Gen Henry "Hap" Arnold, CG, US Army Air Force)

> The Air view was that the Japanese were finished. That they had had it.... Arnold's view was that it [the dropping of the bomb] was unnecessary. He said that he knew the Japanese wanted peace. There were political implications in the decision and Arnold did not feel that it was the military's job to question it. (Gen Ira Eaker, Dep CG, US Army Air Force)

> The use of this barbarous weapon at Hiroshima and Nagasaki was of no material assistance in our war against Japan... [I]n being the first to use it, we had adopted an ethical standard common to the barbarians of the Dark Ages. I was not taught to make war in that fashion, and wars cannot be won by destroying women and children. (Adm William Leahy, Flt Adm US Navy and Chief of Staff to both FDR and Harry Truman)

> When the atomic bomb was first discussed with me in Washington I was not in favor of it just as I have never favored the destruction of cities as such with all inhabitants killed... (Gen Carl "Tooey" Spaatz, CG, US Army Strategic AF)

> Well, Tooey Spaatz came in... he said, 'they tell me I am supposed to go out there and blow off the whole south end of the Japanese islands. I've heard a lot about this thing, but my God, I haven't had a piece of paper yet and I think I need a piece of paper....' (Gen Thomas Handy, Dep C of S US Army)

> I had been conscious of a feeling of depression and so I voiced to (Sec War Henry Stimson) my grave misgivings, first on the basis of my belief that Japan was already defeated and that dropping the bomb was completely unnecessary, and secondly because I thought that our country should avoid shocking world opinion by the use of a weapon whose employment was, I thought, no longer mandatory as a measure to save American lives. (Gen Dwight D. Eisenhower)

> By the spring of 1945 most of Japan's shipping had been sunk, her Navy had been all but totally destroyed, and her Air Force had been driven from the skies.... Our intelligence reports should have told us not

> to use the atom bomb and not to give Russia an opportunity to enter the struggle. (Gen Albert C. Wedemeyer, CG Chinese Theater of Operations, in his book *Wedemeyer Reports!*)
>
> The war would have been over in two weeks without the Russians entering and without the atomic bomb.... The atomic bomb had nothing to do with the end of the war at all. (Gen Curtis LeMay, 20 Sep 1945)
>
> LeMay felt, as did the Navy, that an invasion of Japan wasn't necessary. He saw that we had the Japanese licked. (Gen Roscoe Wilson, C of S, 316th Bomb Wing at Okinawa) [17]

To understand the political implications, we get a clue from Gen Laurence Kuter in 1974: "Numerous accounts made it clear that given the position of the air force in 1945, Arnold regularly supported Marshall in meetings of the Joint Staff. Arnold was Marshall's subordinate and there was never a minute's doubt about it on King's part.... Arnold never differed with Marshall at the Joint table...."

While Arnold didn't believe the use of atomic weapons was necessary, he instructed Eaker to support the position taken by Marshall. We get a clue of the political aspect from Deputy Secretary of Defense Paul Nitze as well, who stated that Arnold had made an agreement with Marshall that if Marshall backed an independent strategic air command during the war, then after the war he, Marshall, would support a separate air force. This came to pass in 1947 under the Defense Reorganization Act.

Gen "Tooey" Spaatz emphasized: "The dropping of the atomic bomb was done by a military man under military orders. We're supposed to carry out orders and not question them." He told Ambassador Harriman that even he did not know why a second bomb had been used against Nagasaki.

> I thought if we are going to drop the atomic bomb, drop it on the outskirts – say in Tokyo Bay – so that the effects would not be as devastating to the city and the people. I made this suggestion over the phone between the Hiroshima and Nagasaki bombings and I was told to go ahead with our targets.

The succinct comment by Gen Spaatz about carrying out orders has been echoed over the ensuing years by many of our military leaders. Not all of our military endeavors were successful; we were often sent out on ill-starred missions, such as the great adventures in Korea and Vietnam. We were soldiers once... and young; therefore, when our superiors defined the enemy, we saluted smartly and went off to fight him.

Unfortunately, totally corrupt politicos at the very highest levels of the government were defining that enemy. We soldiers didn't realize we were expendable until many of us were expended; and we came home from Korea and Vietnam in defeat...as was planned all along, for the Barbarians were already inside the gates and issuing the orders for the ultimate destruction of our own forces.

And subversion under a United Nations command.

The Nuremberg Trials proved nothing about following orders. We, the military, followed the orders of our superiors in executing such missions as the terror-bombing of Germany, the fire-bombing of Japan; and finally, the use of the two atomic bombs on Hiroshima and Nagasaki and the devastation of their populations.

To close with the enemy and destroy him was always our stated mission. But we, the military, were never allowed to define the enemy. It was FDR and his Barbarian (Bolshevist) advisers who in 1943 came up with the term "unconditional surrender." For the first time in the history of modern warfare, that term called for the total subjugation of the enemy, to include his sheep, cattle, goats, women, children and suckling babes.

We see explicit evidence of this concept in the message sent to Japan on 24 Jul 1945 from the Potsdam Conference which warned the Japanese that they would suffer the same fate as Germany. That message ends: "We call upon the Government of Japan to proclaim now the unconditional surrender of all the Japanese armed forces, and to provide proper and adequate assurances of their good faith in such action." [18]

The alternative for Japan is complete obliteration.

PART TWO
CRIMES AGAINST HUMANITY

WE are led to believe that, in the mad scramble to come up with what Bernard Baruch called "the absolute weapon," the Soviets trailed behind the combined efforts of Britain and the US, working the Manhattan Project, and the separate effort by the Germans, to produce an atomic bomb. We are further led to believe that the USSR, on its own, ultimately developed a weapon.

Now, as we begin to grasp just who the Bolsheviks were, we can better understand what many of us have recognized for years, that the development of nuclear weapons of mass destruction came from a single source and that work was shared by a group of admittedly brilliant scientists of a common persuasion, no matter in which country they temporarily resided and to which they gave no allegiance.

There is a recent book which provides some valuable missing links as to how atomic data were smuggled into the Soviet Union in order for the Bolsheviks to develop their own weaponry: *Stalin and the Bomb: The Soviet Union and Atomic Energy 1939-1956*, by David Holloway.

A Soviet physicist, Igor Kurchatov, built a cyclotron in Leningrad (1933) and began reproducing experiments in nuclear physics. The Nazi invasion of 1941 interrupted his work, except that Giorgi Flerov, a colleague of Kurchatov's, actually designed an atomic bomb in December 1941.[19]

We learned from other sources, including *Witness* by Whittaker Chambers, that the physicist, Klaus Fuchs, ensconced in the Manhattan Project at Los Alamos, joined forces with David Greenglass and the Rosenbergs, and thus a steady stream of top secret data was fed to Kurchatov. We will shortly see how Harry Hopkins, a close FDR adviser, mightily assisted this effort, including the passing of uranium. (In *Controversy of Zion*, Douglas Reed provides a comprehensive account taken from Maj

Racey Jordan's diary exposing Harry Hopkins and Alger Hiss' clandestine transfer of US atomic bomb secrets and uranium to the Soviet Union.)

Holloway appears to be proud of their achievements, seeing them as being "on the way up from the Platonic cave toward the sun." They are in fact a cohesive band of brilliant Jewish scientists, whether in the Soviet Union, the United States or Britain, dedicated to the setting up of a one-world despotic government with their Bolshevik Masters in charge. Just as Albert Einstein and Lord Bertrand Russell did, they promised blessed peace or fearful destruction.

Witness their cunning, their patience and, above all, their absolute evil in such evidence as the Versailles Treaty following the Great War, which paved the way for the second war to make the world safe for democracy – and to totally devastate Germany by such calculated acts of terror as the Morgenthau Plan, the Lindemann Plan, and the farcical Nuremberg Trials.

TERROR-BOMBING GERMANY

"With regard to the bombing of the enemy civilian population, everyone [in England] knew that civilians in Germany were being slaughtered wholesale but it was believed that this was an unavoidable by-product of an air-offensive against military objectives. The comforting reflection was accepted that the German civilian population could at any moment bring its suffering to an end by surrendering unconditionally." (F. J. P. Veale, author of *Advance to Barbarism: The Development of Total Warfare*.)[20]

At this moment in the United States, the American people are suffering from related and ongoing calculated acts of terror potentially every bit as destructive to us and our way of life as was the saturation bombing of German civilians from March 1942, culminating in the vast destruction of the city of Dresden toward the war's end in February 1945. It is a continuing chapter taken from the Babylonian Talmud.

Such despicable acts as the shooting down of Korean Air Flight 007, the blowing up of Pan Am 103 over Scotland, the bombing of the Trade Center in New York, the Waco incineration, the blowing up of the federal building in Oklahoma City by explosive charges placed against pillars at the third floor level are calculated acts of terror cunningly designed to cause dissension and distrust amongst the governed.

The downing of TWA 800 passenger line by an errant US Naval missile immediately prior to the 1996 Olympics, was a coverup of the highest order.

Just as Henry Morgenthau, Jr., and his capable assistant the KGB agent Harry Dexter White (Dexter Weiss) served FDR (and Soviet Bolshevism) in the Treasury Department for 12 years, and hatched the infamous Morgenthau Plan calling for the conversion of Germany to a goat pasture; and just as Albert Einstein, J. Robert Oppenheimer and other Talmudic scholars worked overtime in that same time frame (1942-45) to develop the atomic bomb – what Bernie Baruch called "the absolute weapon" – the Lindemann Plan proposed the terror bombing of the German civilian populace.

Who was Karl Lindemann? He was a Jewish physicist, a refugee from continental Europe, who came to London in the mid-1930s. He became an advisor to and confidant of Churchill.

In 1961, a book, *Science and Government* by Sir Charles Snow, revealed a closely guarded secret kept from the public for 20 years...the Lindemann Plan:

> Early in March 1942 Professor Lindemann, by this time Lord Cherwell and a member of the Cabinet, laid a top secret paper before the Cabinet on the strategic bombing of Germany. It described in quantitative terms the effect on Germany of a British bombing offensive in the next 18 months (Mar 42-Sep 43). The paper laid down a strategic policy. The bombing must be directed essentially against German working-class homes. Middle-class houses have too much space round them and so are bound to waste bombs; factories and 'military objectives' had long since been forgotten, except in official bulletins, since they were much too difficult to find and hit.

The paper claimed that, given a total concentration of effort on the production and use of aircraft, it would be possible, in all the larger towns of Germany (that is, those with more than 50,000 inhabitants), to destroy 50% of all homes."[21]

The Lindemann Plan was eagerly accepted by the War Cabinet, with full realization of its enormity in the commission of mass murder of non-combatants. Over the next three years, systematic terror bombing was put into effect by the Royal Air Force Bomber Command. Following the absolutely devastating pounding into rubble of the city of Dresden in a series of raids involving thousands of bombers – both British and US, and night and day – beginning on the night of 13 Feb 1945, a major debate on the subject of terror-bombing took place in the House of Commons on 6 Mar 1945. The debate followed an Associated Press report authorized from Supreme Allied Headquarters in Paris, which declared in part that "the long-awaited decision had been taken to adopt deliberate terror bombing of German populated centers as a ruthless expedient to hasten Hitler's doom."[22]

The British Government finally, in 1961, issued four volumes entitled *The Strategic Air Offensive*, containing a wealth of detail regarding the official policy of terror bombing against Germany from March 1942 through May 1945 "in accordance with the Lindemann Plan."[23]

One might rightfully ask: When and where were the seeds of this base criminality planted? What led us up to committing such heinous acts as the terror-bombing of German civilians, the fire-bombing of Japanese cities, the mass deportations of millions from their homelands in Eastern Europe, the devastation of two Japanese cities by "the absolute weapon"?

The planting of the seeds of this scene of hatred and destruction took place at the First Zionist Conference, held in Basel, Switzerland in 1897. It called for a continuing round of political assassinations, acts of outright terror, and bloody revolutions. Russia became the first major target. Mexico became the second, as it too entered the twentieth century fomenting bloody revolution.

In the late 1930s, President Roosevelt ordered US Catholic bishops to withdraw the book, *No God Next Door* by Reverend Michael Kenny, SJ, which exposed the Communist/Zionist takeover of Mexico, threatening to take away the tax exemption of the Roman Catholic Church.

TALMUDIC TAKEOVER

Half a century ago, Fulton Oursler, in the popular *Readers' Digest*, forecast the political environment of today:

> Today's curse upon political life is not so much what is unlawful as what is unscrupulous. At the root of our decay is a sickness of conscience.... The American people are finding it increasingly difficult to be shocked, no matter what happens. Instead of resisting breaches of public morality, we tend more and more to condone them, and dishonesty along with them....
>
> Moral lassitude seems constantly to deepen in a world situation of the greatest seriousness. One has only to watch the headlines to realize that Democrats and Republicans alike have led us into a twilight of dishonor.
>
> We shall be lucky if it is not also the doom-time of democracy.[24]

This then is the ultimate betrayal. We come back to that very basic question asked by ancient Romans who survived under another Caesar: *Cui bono?* That is, who profits?

The unalterable fact is that FDR during World War II joined Stalin and international Zionism. Consider the following ecerepts from *Roosevelt and Stalin* by Professor Robert Nisbet:

> During WW II Churchill voiced his views to Anthony Eden concerning the postwar relationship between Russia and the rest of Europe. Churchill wrote: "It would be a measureless disaster if Russian barbarism overlaid the ancient states of Europe."[25]

FDR, in a talk with Francis, Cardinal Spellman (1944), said that the European people (not just the eastern European, note, but the European people) would simply have to "endure Russian domination in the hope that in ten or twenty years the European influence would bring the Russians to become less barbarous."

Nisbet's book is filled with factual incidents of not only sell-out, but outright treason, by FDR. He and Harry Hopkins, for example, colluded secretly with the likes of Julius and Armand Hammer, Bernard Baruch, and the Russian ambassador to have "as much direct control of Russian aid, and just as little oversight from the established congressional and executive agencies, as was humanly possible."[26]

Hopkins "was seeking to organize the Soviet aid program in such a manner as to insure its control from the White House, thereby circumventing the countervailing policy approaches entrenched in other Washington quarters."

While "Harry the Hop" and Henry Morgenthau, along with Harry Dexter White, were providing the Soviets with the latest nuclear bomb data from the Manhattan Project (as well as with Treasury plates so that the Communists could print American money for use in Eastern Europe), Senator Robert Taft warned the American people:

> The victory of communism would be far more dangerous than the victory of fascism...communism masquerades, often successfully, under the guise of democracy, though it is just as alien to our principles as nazism itself.
>
> It is a greater danger to the United States because it is a false philosophy which appeals to many. Fascism is a false philosophy which appeals to a very few indeed. [27]

Nisbet also records Rooseveltian duplicity in attempting to swing religious America into supporting Soviet Communism. This blatant appeal to "Christian morality" is doubly important to recognize today. Clinton used the same kind of propaganda (lies) to swing the voting public (still mainly, if only nominally, Christian) behind his false appeals to "sacrifice" and to "humanitarianism."

Nisbet points out that, in 1941, the White House, in an effort to capture Protestant sympathies (for Stalin and against Hitler), easily prepared a list of a thousand Protestant well-wishers of the Soviets.

The liberal Catholic Church had not yet come into being in America; but the liberal-progressive Protestant faith was already significant.[28]

In fact, in November 1941 (when FDR was well aware of the impending attack by the Japanese), he spoke as follows at what Nisbet calls "a notorious press conference."

Roosevelt referred to Article 124 of the Russian Constitution and even quoted bits of it... freedom of conscience... freedom of religion... as well as "freedom equally to use propaganda against religion, which is essentially what is the rule in this country...."

Nisbet quotes the historian Robert Dallek:

Roosevelt knew full well there was no religious freedom in the Soviet Union. Nor was he blind to the fact that he could extend lend-lease help to Russia without demonstrating her devotion to religious freedom. But his concern to associate the Soviets with this democratic principle extended beyond the question of aid to the problem of American involvement in the war. Convinced that only a stark contrast between freedom and totalitarianism would provide the emotional wherewithal for Americans to fight, Roosevelt wished to identify the Russians regardless of Soviet realities, with Anglo-American ideals as fully as he could.[29]

Even then, patriotic Americans inveighed against this artful propagandist whose major goals of getting the United States embroiled in another European conflict were twofold: (1) Bolshevize the entire European continent; (2) Establish a Zionist nation in Palestine.

Our circuitous and rocky road will take us to that Zionist nation in the following chapters.

The Communist soul is the soul of Judaism. Hence it follows, that just as in the Russian revolution the triumph of Communism was the triumph of Judaism, so also in the triumph of Fascism will triumph Judaism.

Rabbi Harry Waton, *A Program for the Jews and Answer to All Anti-Semites*, New York, 1939

CHAPTER IX
FASCISM'S FRIENDLY FACE
(A Calculated Strategy of Tension)

*Communism teaches and seeks two objectives: unrelenting class
warfare and the complete eradication of private ownership. Not
secretly or by hidden methods does it do this, but publicly openly and
by employing any means possible, even the most violent.*

Pope Pius XI in the encyclical *Quadragesimo Anno*, 1931

PART ONE
COVENANT OF RACE SUPERIORITY

ONE of the most interesting facets of 20th century history,
although little known, was the marriage of convenience
between the Jewish Zionists and the National Socialists (Nazis) of
Germany. We saw in Chapter 6 how a calculated strategy of
tension was created by the leaders of these two groups in order to
bring about the emigration from Germany (and eventually much of
Europe) of Jewish people for resettlement in Palestine.

We also discovered early on in this work how such Marxist
followers as Lenin and Trotsky established Bolshevism, also
known as Communism or Social Democracy, in Russia. It was the
natural outcome of another marriage of convenience, between the
political arm of the Jewish Nation, called Zionism, with Britain's
Fabian Socialism.

Bolshevism led to the setting up of dictatorial forms of
government, first Fascism in Italy (1922) under Mussolini, and
then National Socialism in Germany (1933). The roots of National
Socialism go back to the National Socialist German Workers Party
(NSDAP) founded in 1919. Just as in the taking-over of Russia

under Bolshevism, both Fascism and Nazism were directly financed by the Universalist bankers located in Berlin and Frankfurt, as well as in the City of London and in New York City.

There was an important difference in the setting up of these various dictatorships. Let's first consider the dictionary definition of what we call *Fascism*: "a rigid one-party dictatorship, forcible suppression of the opposition, the retention of private ownership of the means of production under centralized governmental control, belligerent nationalism and racism, glorification of war, internal suppression of the citizens by a brutal and secret police force."

We find Fascism alive and well in many countries of the world, most often under other names. The important difference is that such names as "democracy," "socialism," "social democracy," and even "Communism" are meant to convey to the unwary ear a kinder, gentler form of tyranny. As Dr. John Coleman so aptly describes in his hard-hitting book *Socialism: The Road to Slavery,* all of these forms of totalitarianism, regardless of whether they are deemed to be "benevolent" or "brutal," lead to a repressive one-world socialist government, with a very few of the superior or chosen ones in total charge and the vast balance of mankind leveled out at the bottom as helots, slaves and/or "worker bees."[1]

We see this idea reflected in *The Traditions of the Jews* by that renowned 19th century Talmudic scholar, J. P. Stehelin. He quotes from *Baba Bathra* (in the Talmud*)*:

> Let us see a little after what manner the Jews are to live in their ancient Country under the Administration of the Messiah. In the First Place, the strange Nations, which they shall suffer to live, shall build them houses and cities, till their ground, and plant their vineyards; and all this without so much as looking for any reward of their labor. These surviving Nations will likewise offer them all their wealth and furniture; and Princes and Nobles shall attend them; and be ready at their nod to pay them all manner of obedience; while they themselves shall be surrounded with grandeur and pleasure, appearing abroad in apparel glittering with jewels like Priests of the Unction, consecrated to G-d....[2]

Wilhelm Marr, who played a key role in fomenting the revolution of 1848, wrote of the coming Jewish conquest of the world. "The epitome of the degradation of humanity," he declared, "is the so-called religion called Christianity."

In 1879 his *Conquest of Germanism by Judaism* was published. He wrote:

> The advent of Jewish imperialism, I am firmly convinced is only a question of time.... The Empire of the World belongs to the Jews... *Val Victus!* Woe to the conquered! I do not pretend to be a prophet, but I am quite certain that before four generations have passed, there will not be a single function in the State, the highest included, which will not be in the hands of the Jews.... To judge by the course of events, the capitulation of Russia is only a question of time.... In that vast Empire, Judaism will find the fulcrum of Archimedes which will enable it to drag the whole of Western Europe off its hinges once for all. The wily Jewish spirit of intrigue will bring about a revolution in Russia such as the world has never seen.... When the Jews shall get control of the Russian State...they will set about the destruction of the social organization of Western Europe. This last hour of Europe will arrive at least in a hundred or a hundred and fifty years.... What Russia has to expect from the Jews is quite clear.[3]

In *Beasts of the Apocalypse* Olivia Maria O'Grady reveals that, following WW II, such organizations as the United World Federalists (UWF) had invaded the teachers' unions in the United States and were striving to inculcate into the minds of impressionable students the idea of a one-world of peace and brotherhood, including "warm milk" for the school children of central Africa, which, freely given, would be a generous gesture, but so typical of the Communists who are past-masters in the art of window-dressing.

She asks the question: Is the United World Federalists subversive? Defining the term subversive as having a tendency to overthrow, upset or destroy, the answer must be a resounding "yes." She then asked if the UWF advocated the overthrow of the sovereignty of the United States? It does, she said, but added that its activities are perfectly legal and within the provisions of the Constitution of the United States itself.

> It advocates an amendment to the Constitution by constitutional methods, which, if adopted, would of course destroy the Constitution and all that it stands for. In a sense the movement is in the category of

national suicide by legitimate means, and there is not much that anyone can do about it.[4]

O'Grady declares that "the faith of the Jews that they, as the Chosen People, will ultimately rule the world, while based on their misconception of the covenant between Jehovah and Abraham, is a manifestation of a race-superiority concept that towers a hundred times over any idea ever advanced by Hitler. It is an amazing concept that divides the world into two classes: the Chosen People and 'cattle' (goyim)."[5]

She cites the history of "One People; One Nation; a Chosen People, destined to rule the world," and traces their educational process, always under the rigid control and guidance of the rabbis:

> Every minute of the day and every day of the year had its precise regulation. Every act was molded to fit the tortured interpretation of the Scriptures, while the most trivial incident of existence was decided by the dialectic mental gymnastics of the men of the Talmud...the mind of the Jewish child developed in the ever-present strait-jacket of race-superiority.[6]

Upon this Millennium we witness the culmination of that Covenant between Jehovah and Abraham – "One People; One Nation... a Chosen People, destined to rule the world," especially in the tiny theocratic state of Israel where, after 50 years of brutally subjugating the Arab peoples who had lived there for 2,000 years, the Zionists in 1996 relocated their capital from Tel Aviv to Jerusalem. O'Grady explains the import of that particular city:

> Each Jewish community throughout the world turned its thoughts toward Jerusalem and, as the centuries rolled by, the ancient seat of Jewish power came to symbolize the central theme of Judaism – the ultimate fulfillment of the Covenant Jehovah had made with Abraham. Certainly, before the Gentile world lay at their feet, the Chosen People must re-establish the seat of world government in its ancient place – Jerusalem.[7]

O'Grady points out that the dream of a renewed national existence and a return to Palestine, with Israel dominant over all the Gentile nations of the world, has been the most persistent obsession of the Jews through the centuries. While some of the moderate Jews, particularly those who came to the United States in the 19th century, attempted to blot out this sinister doctrine, the rise of political Zionism through the zealous and energetic support of the Khazar Jews of Eastern Europe (who comprised 90% of the Jews gathered at the momentous conference in Basle, Switzerland in 1897) completely smothered the good sense of the Reformed Jews.

The descendants of the captive tribes of Babylon (Judah and Benjamin) continually looked forward to re-establishment of their kingdom. O'Grady says they have always looked to the day when Israel would rule the world from Jerusalem.

BARBARIANS TAKE OVER PALESTINE

Following is synopsis of Palestine history. Following the partition of the Roman Empire (AD 395), Palestine fell to the Empire of the East. For more than 200 years the country enjoyed a pastoral peace. Palestine was then a part of Syria.

In AD 611 the peace of the Holy Land was broken by the thunder of war as the armies of Persia invaded Syria, destroying everything in their path. Jerusalem was taken. The Church of the Holy Sepulcher was razed to the ground, its treasures carted off; not a church or cross was left standing. In 628 Emperor Heraclius reconquered the lost territory and returned it to the Byzantine Empire.

Abu Bekr, who succeeded Mohammed, carried the crescent into Syria, defeating Heraclius. City after city fell under the onslaught. A major battle was joined in 636, and Heraclius was defeated. Jerusalem capitulated.

Then came the Crusades, then the Mongolians of Central Asia. Palestine eventually came under the Mameluke sultans of Egypt; then came the Tatar tribes – and finally the Turks. O'Grady writes:

> This is the land the Jews claim as their own. Four thousand years ago Jehovah said: "Unto thy seed will I give this land...." Jewry contends that Jehovah promised that the Jews would return to Palestine and that this promise will be fulfilled because of its divine origin. The

Jews well know that this prophecy was fulfilled over two thousand years ago. Only the Christians seem to have forgotten it.[8]

In his epic work *Zionists and the Bible*, Professor Alfred Guillaume of the University of London points out that the Jews did return to Judea, they did rebuild the walls of Jerusalem, and they did rebuild the temple (under the Maccabees). "Thus the prophecies of the Return have been fulfilled, and they cannot be fulfilled again. Within the canonical literature of the Old Testament there is no prophecy of a second return from the Babylonian Exile."[9]

The very basis of the 63 books of the Talmud (the Law) is the promise of the re-establishment of the power of Israel and its ultimate control over the affairs of all mankind. The destruction of the Temple (70 AD) in Jerusalem by Titus and Vespasian "only served to rekindle the burning fever for the great day of retribution and revenge," reports O'Grady.

She further states that this doctrine is expressed in numerous Jewish prayers. "The *Cabala* gives particular emphasis to the Judaic dream of world-domination. The *Zohar* treats the event as having taken place. *Toldoth Noah* explains that 'the Feast of the Tabernacles is the period when Israel triumphs over the other people of the world.'"[10]

Throughout the centuries, Cabalistic doctrines spread about the Jewish communities, reawakening hopes of the coming of the "true" Messiah who would establish the Covenant and bring the entire Gentile world under Jewish domination. This doctrine is nurtured by the Sons of the Covenant which, we saw earlier, was created in 1843 in Charleston, South Carolina by a small group of land- and slave-owning Jews who established the Independent Order B'nai B'rith. By 1930, O'Grady informs us, there were seven Grand Lodges in the United States and eight abroad. By 1990 there were 267 lodges throughout the world.

Their ultimate creation was the Anti-Defamation League (ADL), a sub-lodge established in 1913 as an "enforcer" arm of their Cabalistic doctrine. By this time, the Khazars – Jews who were not Jews, but descendants of the fierce and warlike tribes of Turko-Asiatic who had been converted to Judaism in the seventh century – had pervaded the United States. Between 1881 and 1920, two million Khazars entered our portals. During that time, the increase in population of the United States as a whole was 112 percent, while the Jewish increase was 1300 percent.[11]

And during that time we witnessed the complete destruction of Russia, as foretold by Wilhelm Marr (among others) in 1879.

Simultaneously with the subjugation of the Russian peoples by the Bolsheviks, a document in the form of a handbill was discovered in wide circulation among the Jews of the Czech Republic, in Budapest, in Belgrade, and in Estonia, as well as in Russia, during the period 1919-21. It was written in Hebrew, but was translated and read in a speech before the Czech Parliament by a deputy named Masanac. A translation also appeared in *The Rulers of Russia* by Dr. Hans Eisele. The text follows:

> Sons of Israel! The hour of victory is at hand. We are on the eve of becoming masters of the world. What seemed to be merely a dream is on the point of being realized. Formerly weak and feeble we can now proudly lift up our heads, thanks to the disorder and confusion of the world. By clever propaganda we have held up to criticism and ridicule the authority and practice of a religion which is foreign to us. We have plundered the sanctuary of that foreign cult, and we have shaken the hold of their traditional culture upon nations, finding among them more helpers than we needed in our task. We have succeeded in bringing the Russian Nation under Jewish sway and we have compelled it, at last, to fall on its knees before us. Russia, mortally wounded, is now at our mercy.
>
> The fear of the danger in which we stand will not allow us either to exercise compassion or to feel mercy. At last it has been given us to behold the tears of the Russian people. By taking away from them wealth and their gold, we have turned the Russians into wretched slaves. But we must be prudent and circumspect. We have to eliminate all the best elements of Russian society, in order that the enslaved Russians may have no leaders. Thus we shall forestall every possibility of resisting our might. Wars and civil strife will destroy all the treasures of culture created by the Christian peoples.

Be prudent, Sons of Israel. Do not confide in treacherous and mysterious forces. Bronstein, Rosenfeld, Steinberg, Apfelbaum, and many other faithful sons of Israel are in the ranks of the commissars and play the leading roles, but do not lose your heads over the victory. Be prudent, for you can rely only on yourselves to safeguard you and defend you. Sons, of Israel, close up your ranks and combat for your eternal ideal.[12]

FASCISM'S TRIPLE PLAY - 1917

The Arabs, believing they were fighting for independence, fought and died in England's war – the Great War. At the same time, A. J. Balfour had promised Palestine as a home for the Jews. In addition to this base treachery, England and France agreed (by the Sykes-Picot Treaty) to divide the Arab lands between them after the war. Ramsay MacDonald, British statesman, summed up this triple dealing:

We encouraged an Arab revolt in Turkey by promising to create an Arab kingdom from the Arab provinces of the Ottoman Empire, including Palestine. At the same time, we were encouraging the Jews to help us by promising them that Palestine would be placed at their disposal for settlement and government; and also at the same time we were making with France the Sykes-Picot agreement partitioning the territory which we had instructed our governor general of Egypt to promise the Arabs. The story is one of crude duplicity and we cannot escape the reprobation which is its sequel.[13]

Thirty years later, Arnold Toynbee in *A Study of History* stated virtually the same:

While the direct responsibility for the calamity that overtook the Palestinian Arabs in AD 1948 was on the heads of the Zionist Jews who seized a *lebensraum* for themselves in Palestine by force of arms in that year, a heavy load of indirect yet irrefutable responsibility was on the heads of the people of the United Kingdom; for the Jews would not have had in AD 1948 the opportunity to conquer an Arab country in which they had what amounted to no more than an inconsiderable minority in AD 1918 if, during the intervening thirty years, the power of the United Kingdom had not been exerted continuously to make possible the entry of Jewish immigrants into Palestine contrary to the will, despite the protests and without regard to the foreboding of Arab inhabitants of the country who in AD 1948 were duly to become the victims of this long pursued British policy.[14]

CONTROLLING THE TREATY OF VERSAILLES

Beasts of the Apocalypse records that on June 10, 1917 American Jews cast 350,000 ballots for delegates to the first American Jewish Congress, which opened in Philadelphia December 15, 1918.

The Congress demanded that the forthcoming Peace Conference establish "equal civil, political, religious and national rights for all citizens of a territory without distinction as to race, nationality, or creed." It also demanded "recognition of the historic claims of the Jewish people with regard to Palestine, and establishment of such political, administrative, and economic conditions in that country as would assure its development into a Jewish Commonwealth."[15]

O'Grady points to the obvious paradox:

> Having won full citizenship rights in the United States they now boldly proclaim that they are a single separate nation...they brazenly demanded a special status for themselves.... In particular they demanded recognition of their historic claim to the land of another people, and called upon the world powers to assist them in their proposed conquest of that land....
>
> The World Jewish Congress was actually the creation of the American Jewish Congress. World War I forever destroyed the fiction that Jews were citizens of the countries of their birth or naturalization.... As the war developed and Allied victory became certain, American Jewry prepared to join with the international Jews of the world for participation as a nation in the inevitable Peace Conference.[16]

The dawn of the so-called "peace" conference in 1919 found Paris literally flooded with Jews from all over the world. As O'Grady relates:

> Whatever their status in the lands that harbored them, they remained merely the sons of the covenant; one people, one nation. Each felt he was playing a historic part in the destiny of Israel. Not one of them was concerned with 'making the world safe for democracy'.
>
> They shared a single thought and purpose – the capture of Palestine and a world government to make the world over for their domination. They went to work, forming the *Comite des Delegations Juives aupres de la Conference de la Pai* (Committee of Jewish

Delegations at the Peace Conference). In addition to delegates from various countries, representatives of the World Zionist Organization and the B'nai B'rith were included in the Committee's membership. It purported to speak for ten million Jews....

Laying the groundwork for another world war, the 'new and enlarged states' were compelled 'to assume an obligation to embody in a treaty with the principal Allied and Associated powers such provisions as might be deemed necessary by the said Powers to protect the inhabitants who differed from the majority of the population in race, language or religion'.[17]

WHO WERE THE KHAZARS?

One of the Jewish Americans attending the Peace Conference in Paris was Benjamin H. Freedman. The young and impressionable New Yorker was an aide to the banker, Henry Morgenthau, Sr. The proceedings at the Conference and its aftermath led Freedman eventually to reject the teachings of the Talmud and its doctrine of a superior race chosen by Jehovah to rule the world. An avowed Zionist at the time of the Peace Conference, he became a vocal anti-Zionist and then eventually "joined mankind" by becoming a Christian.

In 1954 Dr. Benjamin H. Freedman published his work *Facts are Facts*, stating on the frontispiece that "The historic facts revealed here for the first time provide incontestable evidence that their continued suppression will prove inimical to the security of the nation, the peace of the world, the welfare of humanity, and the progress of civilization."

He singles out the rise and fall of the Kingdom of the Chazars (Khazars) as defined in the *Jewish Encyclopedia* – whom he calls "the so-called or self-styled Jews" (the Jews who are not Jews) – as being the key to the understanding of the 20th-century world's international problems inimical to the nation's security.

He states that "the divine and sacred mission of the Christian faith is in jeopardy today to a degree never witnessed before in its long history of almost two thousand years." He warns of a diabolical group intent on destroying that faith, "while Christians appear to be sound asleep. The Christian clergy appear to be more ignorant or more indifferent about this than other Christians" (the Christians who are not Christian).[18]

"The confusion in the minds of Christians concerning fundamentals of the Christian faith is unwarranted and unjustified," he states. "It need not exist. It would not exist if the Christian clergy did not aid and abet the deceptions responsible for it."

Freedman refers to the official *Soncino* edition of the Talmud published in 1935, stating that "there have never been recorded more vicious and vile libelous blasphemies of Jesus, of Christians and the Christian faith than you will find between the covers of the infamous 63 books of the Talmud which "forms the basis of Jewish religious law, as well as being the textbook used in the training of rabbis."[19]

Freedman outlines the history of the Khazars, stating that they were not Semites, but in fact were an Asiatic Mongoloid nation, classified by modern anthropologists as Turko-Asiatics racially. A warlike nation, they were driven from Asia and invaded Eastern Europe to escape further defeats by the Asians.

> The Khazars were a pagan nation when they invaded eastern Europe," Dr. Freedman writes. "Their religious worship was a mixture of phallic worship and other forms of idolatry." In the 7th century, their King Bulkan selected as the future state religion, "Talmudism," now known as "Judaism."[20]

From the 10th through the 13th centuries the rapidly-expanding Russian nation gradually swallowed up the Khazar kingdom. This accounts for the large number of so-called or self-styled Jews in Russia, Dr Freedman explains. They were no longer known as Khazar but as the "Yiddish" populations. According to Dr. Freedman:

> Approximately 90% of the world's so-called or self-styled Jews, living in 42 different countries of the world today are either emigrants from eastern Europe, or their parents emigrated from eastern Europe. 'Yiddish' is a language common to all of them as their first or second language.

Freedman singles out the word "antisemitism" as one that should be eliminated from the English language. "Antisemitism serves only one purpose today," he states. "It is used as a smear word." He continues: "I can speak with great authority on that subject. Because so-called or self-styled Jews were unable to disprove my public statements in 1946 with regard to the situation in Palestine, they spent millions to smear me as an antisemite, hoping thereby to discredit me in the eyes of the public who were very much interested in what I had to say. Until 1946 I was a little saint to all the so-called or self-styled Jews. When I disagreed with them publicly on the Zionist intentions in Palestine I became Antisemite No. 1."[21]

PART TWO
"DEMOCRACY IN ACTION"

DATE: August 1945; place: London; event: a special gathering of the World Jewish Congress, whose delegates resolved that the Congress:

Fully endorses the demand that the Palestine White Paper of 1939 should be immediately abrogated and that the gates of Palestine should be opened to unrestricted immigration and urges that the United Nations should without delay give their approval for the establishment of a Jewish democratic State in Palestine.[22]

Notice the choice of words...demand...immediately abrogated...without delay...democratic State.... This, of course, is not "democracy" as we were taught its meaning, but Fascism, pure and simple. Nevertheless, it was an effective choice of words, which the founding members of the United Nations (convened in San Francisco that very month under Alger Hiss) understood, principally because they spoke the same language.

Ernest Bevin, British Secretary of State for Foreign Affairs (13 Nov 1945), declared that "Jewry as a whole" must be distinguished from the Zionist Jews who were demanding the ancient home of the Arabs.[23]

The WJC quickly replied:

> The World Jewish Congress, speaking for Jewish communities and organizations in 32 countries, and expressing what is without question the attitude of the great majority of the world, completely repudiates the existence of any such distinction. The World Jewish Congress and Jews everywhere will continue to give the Jewish Agency for Palestine... their fullest support in its battle for the rights of the Jewish people with regard to Palestine.[24]

What the WJC was addressing was "democracy in action"... a concept come to full flower in the United States, especially in our august body known as the Congress, whose members purport to "represent" the majority of their constituents. This is Fascism in full flower. That cluster of pretty posies – its petals labeled socialism, democracy, Communism, Bolshevism, Nazism, Zionism – emits the same mesmerizing odor, the smell of offal we call Fascism... but with a pretty face.

O'Grady gives us statistics of the time; call it a body count. She states that in 1944 there were 1,062,277 Arabs in Palestine. The Christian population numbered 135,547. By steady "colonization" the Jewish population had increased to 528,702.

In 1946, came the terror. During that year, the Palestinian Jews embarked on a sustained campaign of terror against the British administration. O'Grady says, "assassinations, bombings and other criminal activities were carried out systematically."

The Palestine Zionist *Irgun Zvai Leumi,* encouraged by Jewish support from abroad – particularly from the United States – stepped up its treacherous terrorist activities. Elements attacked air-fields, radars, rail lines, armories and military posts on a daily basis; roads were mined and ships blown up in Haifa harbor. Banks were held up in a fashion startlingly reminiscent of the activities of that great Georgian Bolshevist and bank robber, Joseph Vissarionovich Djugashvili, aka Stalin, prior to the Russian Revolution of 1917.

On 22 Jul 1946, the Irgun gangster-statesmen, under the leadership of Manachem Begin – later to become prime minister – blew up the King David Hotel in Jerusalem, containing the British military headquarters and the civil secretariat. Ninety-one persons were killed outright and 45 injured, among them a then major of the Royal Signal Corps, Thomas Foster (who, along with his wife, Doreen, would become dear friends of mine when we were stationed in the Pentagon in the 1960s). Colonel Foster, with typical British stoicism, held no animosity toward either the Zionist gangsters or the Jewish people in general, but laid much of the blame on the "utter stupidities" of the British governing elite – including Winnie, whose reign ended rather suddenly in August, 1945.

An Anglo-American Committee of Inquiry on Palestine was set up in January 1946. Influenced by a statement on the part of the British section of the World Jewish Congress, the Committee published a report (29 Mar 1946) calling for issuance of 100,000 immigration certificates for European Jews, "to be used as far as possible in 1946." It also called for continuance of the British mandate, pending trusteeship under the United Nations.

Typical of the fast-fading British Raj was Prime Minister Clement Attlee, who stated on 1 May 1946 that the implementation of the (Jewish) report by Britain would depend first on "the extent to which the US Government would be prepared to share the resulting military and financial responsibilities."[25]

Harry Truman cabled Attlee on 4 October, urging immediate issue of the 100,000 certificates to create "a visible Jewish state in control of its own immigration and economic policies in an adequate area of Palestine instead of the whole of Palestine." (Words taken from the counter-proposal of the Jewish Agency for Palestine.)[26]

The Holy Land became an armed camp. The Stern Gang and *Irgun Zvai Leumi* terrorists intensified their attacks on the British troops and police. Lord Moyne, the British executive, was assassinated. The secret Jewish army, *Haganah*, vigorously organized Jewish emigration from Europe to Palestine, in spite of British action in turning back Jews illegally entering the country.

The United Nations Special Committee on Palestine (UNSCOP) was appointed on 15 May 1947 to render a report to the General Assembly. On 6 Aug 1947, the World Jewish Congress sent a memo demanding a Jewish state in Palestine. Affiliates of the Congress from several European countries bombarded the Special Committee with demands to dispossess the Arabs and give the Jews "their" country.

The Arabs, in turn, warned the United Nations that partitioning Palestine into two states would bring perpetual war into the area. The Arabs demanded a "democratic, independent Palestine with equal rights for all its inhabitants."[27]

The Jews were horrified to learn that their new State, as designated by the United Nations, now contained approximately an equal number of Arab inhabitants. How would it be possible to have a "democratic" Jewish State if half the state was Arab?

The terrorists set out to "equalize." They blew up the Semiramus Hotel in Jerusalem (5 Jan 1948), burying 22 Arabs beneath the rubble. A terrific explosion in the public square of the city of Jaffa killed 30 Arabs and injured 98 others.

The main Jewish attack was against the numerous isolated villages. At Dair Yasin the Zionists massacred the entire population of 250 men, women and children. The assassins boasted of the exploit as "a masterpiece of military tactics." Menachem Begin, *Irgun* leader, declared:

> All the Jewish forces proceeded to advance through Haifa like a knife through butter. The Arabs fled in panic shouting 'Dair Yasin' [28]

Historian, Arnold Toynbee, referring to the many Jewish atrocities, declared:

> In AD 1948, the Jews knew from personal experience what they were doing; and it was their supreme tragedy that the lesson learned by them from their encounter with Nazi gentiles should have been not to eschew but to imitate some of the evil deeds that the Nazis committed against the Jews. [29]

O'Grady states that as the date for termination of the British Mandate grew closer, the Zionists intensified their attacks, occupying most of the towns of Palestine and driving Arabs and Christians from their homes.... Tiberias and Samakh, attacked and occupied, 19 Apr 1948; Haifa, 22 Apr; Jaffa, 29 Apr; the Arab Quarter of Katamon in Jerusalem, 30 Apr; Safed, 10 May; Beisan, 11 May; and Acre, 14 May.

O'Grady makes the telling point that all of these "military" operations of the Zionist armies "were against a peaceful, unarmed, defenseless people. And all of these conquests and occupations took place before the British withdrawal on 15 May 48 – at a time when there was not a single soldier from any Arab State on the soil of Palestine." [30]

The Jews, not content with the territory allotted them by the United Nations, attacked the Arab populations in other districts.

Galilee was occupied, as was Lydda, Ramleh, Majdal and Beersheba. As a result of this expansionist maneuver, the Zionists grabbed most of the fertile land out of which the Arabs were to have carved their "state" under the partition plan of the United Nations.

On 15 May 1948, the date of the creation of the State of Israel, the Zionists owned less than 6% of the land of Palestine. By 1958 they owned over 80%.[31]

Another quote from Toynbee is highly revealing:

> The evil deeds committed by the Zionist Jews against the Palestinian Arabs that were comparable to crimes committed against the Jews by the Nazis, were the massacre of men, women and children at Dair Yasin on the 9th of April 1948, which precipitated a flight of the Arab population in large numbers from districts within range of the Jewish armed forces and the subsequent deliberate expulsion of the Arab populations from districts conquered by the Jewish forces.... The Arab blood on the 9th of April 1948 at Dair Yasin was on the head of Irgun; the expulsions after the 15th of May 1948 were on the heads of all Israel.[32]

Following proclamation of the new Jewish state of Israel, the five great powers of the Security Council of the United Nations named Count Folke Bernadotte to act as mediator between the Jews and Arabs, the latter rejecting the UN partition of their country and refusing to recognize the Jewish state.

O'Grady writes that Count Bernadotte possessed courage and a high sense of fairness, and believed in doing justice. He called for Jerusalem to be placed under UN control and called upon the UN to affirm the right of the Arab refugees to return to their homes in Jewish-controlled territory. O'Grady reports that he submitted his recommendations to the UN on September 16, 1948, and the Zionists murdered him and his aide, Colonel Serot, the very next day. His proposals for peace were not acted upon by the United Nations.

Perhaps the most telling – certainly the most tragic – note to be found in Olivia Maria O'Grady's epic work is her quote of

Rabbi Elmer Berger's views regarding the Arab refugees. She comments:

> It must not be believed that all Jews share the Nazi-like characters of the Israelis – and no doubt there are Jews of Israel who are completely disillusioned by the reality as they look back on the dream. The American Council for Judaism is a group of American Jews who are not ashamed to be American and who adhere to the finest principles, ideals and morality of their religion. Rabbi Elmer Berger is a member of that organization. His voice, like the voice of so many others, is silenced by the overpowering influence of the Zionist Jewish organizations.[33]

Rabbi Berger visited the Holy Land in 1955; his impressions have been published under the title *Who Knows Better Must Say So.* He speaks of the Arab refugees, "but the condition of the refugees," he writes, "is not the whole tragedy."

> No less appalling and depressing is the frame of mind of those charged with 'solving' or 'alleviating' this problem. It is difficult to suppress the overpowering surge of moral outrage one feels as he looks at the refugees... and sees in his mind Mr. Eban's [Prime Minister Abba Eban's] glib advice that the Arab states have a lot of land and let them absorb these people.

> It is another thing to look at a fraction of 'these people' and see them – and their children – as living human beings offered Mr Eban's glib solution. And I could not stand in these places – remember that I am a Jew – and not cringe with shame and disgrace and – I do not hesitate to say it – a hatred of 'Jewish' racism that created a state which now says that these people cannot live in it because they are not Jews.[34]

ISRAELIS CONFRONT THE MYTHS

Is criticism of what the Zionist Bolsheviks did to the land once called Palestine confined to such Jewish writers and historians as Israel Shahak, Rabbi Berger, Dr. Freedman and Jack Bernstein? No indeed!

A 22-part television series entitled *Tkuma* (Rebirth) has stirred widespread controversy in Israel," reports Allan C. Brownfeld, editor of *Issues*, the quarterly journal of the American Council for Judaism.[35]

He cites Joel Greenberg, who writes in the *New York Times* that the series challenges "the traditional Zionist tale of heroic return and nation-building in an empty, desolate homeland," and has evoked reactions from outrage to quiet approval.

"The widely watched program," writes Greenberg, "is an unvarnished historical Zionist story with a variety of narratives, including the voices of Palestinians, Israeli Arabs and Sephardic Jewish immigrants resentful of their treatment by Israel's European-born establishment."[36]

The re-examination of Israel's beginnings, Greenberg points out, "reflects a process that began more than ten years ago, when a few Israeli scholars began challenging conventional accounts of their country's history."[37]

Among the events highlighted by these "new historians" are the expulsion and flight of the Palestinians, "the killing of Arab civilians in border skirmishes and retaliatory raids and terrorist attacks in the 1950s, and what the scholars described as missed opportunities to negotiate with Arabs."

Critics on the right charged that the series questioned the justice of the Zionist enterprise. Cabinet member Aerial Sharon urged Education Minister Yitshak Levi "to ban the series from the schools."

Aryeh Caspi, writing in the Israeli paper *Ha'aretz*, declares:

> The anger at 'Tkuma' is because we don't want to know and we can't bear the sense of guilt. The establishment of the state of Israel was justice for the Jews, but it was accompanied by a terrible injustice to the Palestinians.[38]

Leonard Fein, writing in the Jewish weekly *The Forward*, points out that Israel's 50th anniversary produced far more celebration in the US than in Israel itself. There, he notes:

> Disenchantment, quite literally, was in the air. The Founding Fathers were unveiled as having feet of clay. Revisionist historians, controversial in the groves of the academy, had successfully altered the public consciousness, hence, much cynicism, little trust, low morale.[39]

Brownfeld states that Israeli intellectuals are beginning to question the basic tenets of Zionism. He singles out as having particular interest the book *The Founding Myths of Israel* by Zeev

Sternhell, professor of political science at Hebrew University of Jerusalem.   He advances a radical new interpretation of the founding of modern Israel.   The founders claimed that they intended to create both a landed state for the Jewish people and a socialist society.   However, according to Sternhell, socialism served the leaders of the influential labor movement more as a rhetorical resource for the legitimation of the national project of establishing a Jewish state than as a blueprint for a just society. He argues that socialist principles were subverted in practice by the nationalist goals to which socialist Zionism was committed.[40]

Modern Zionism is more rooted in the 19th-century nationalism of Eastern Europe, in Sternhell's view, than it is in anything in Jewish religious history.

What grew in Palestine, Sternhell writes, was a "tribal view of the world.... What fell victim to national objectives was not only the rights of workers but the very aims of socialism as a comprehensive vision of a changed system of relationships between human beings.... Ben-Gurion knew that a national movement does not function in a void and that Palestine was not an uninhabited territory.... From the beginning he was convinced that settling Jews on the soil of *Eretz Israel* would mean a conquest of land and a rivalry with Arabs."

The ideology which dominates Israeli life today, Sternhell argues, is precisely the same nationalist ideology which gave birth to the state.   He says that denial of the legitimacy of the Arab national movement was not a form of blindness that afflicted only Golda Meir.   The prime minister at the time of the Yom Kippur War (1973) was chosen as a successor to Levi Eshkol to ensure the perpetuation of a worldview.   Meir appealed to history as proof of the legitimacy, morality and exclusivity of the Jewish people's right to the country – to the entire country.   For her, there was room for only one national movement in Palestine, i.e., Zionist Bolshevism.

There was never any intention of allowing a 'Palestinian national movement' or 'Palestinian state'.[41]

CHAPTER X

ISRAELI ACTS OF TERROR AN "OPEN SECRET"

(Backed by Nuclear Power)

We came and turned the native Arabs into tragic refugees. And still we dare to slander and malign them, to besmirch their names. Instead of being deeply ashamed of what we did and trying to undo some of the evil we committed... we justify our terrible acts and even attempt to glorify them.

Natyhan Chofshi, *The Spectator*, 12 May 1961

PART ONE
ISRAELI NUCLEAR/FOREIGN POLICY

ONE should read a startling book, *Open Secrets: Israeli Nuclear and Foreign Policies* (1997) by Israel Shahak.

Shahak, a Jewish anti-Zionist and Israeli citizen, is a prolific and hard-hitting writer who has incurred the wrath of those he calls "the Israeli Jewish elite." He stresses in his Introduction that the aims of the State of Israel (and its predecessor the Zionist Movement) at any given period of time have to be understood according to what the Israeli leaders say to their followers, and now especially to what they say to the Israeli Jewish elite. "They cannot be understood according to what they say to the outside world."[1]

He warns his readers that the "wish for peace," so often assumed as the Israeli aim, "is not in my view a principle of Israeli policy, while the wish to extend Israeli domination and influence is." His key word is "hegemony," or dominance over all states of the Middle East.

The confirmation of these assertions will be found in the book. In simple terms, Israeli policy is based on the Talmudic threat and promise; that is, glorious peace or nuclear holocaust... and other acts of terror, the latter not necessarily confined to the Middle East.

In defining certain principles, Shahak stresses that Israeli policies are based, first, on regional aspects – that is, the entire Middle East from Morocco to Pakistan – and in addition they have an important global aspect, especially prominent in the 1990s. Shahak states that "in this book you will find much evidence that Israel is quite involved in Kenya, South Korea and Estonia, countries which are surely not a part of the Middle East! However, I consider that Israeli policies outside the Middle East are subordinated to Israeli regional aims."[2]

ISRAELI PLAN TO CRUSH IRAN

He defines these two intertwined aims as (1) hegemony-seeking and (2) support of the "stability" of most of the now existing regimes in the Middle East, *with the notable exception of Iran.* (Emphasis added.) Iran is the next targeted country to be devastated in the Middle East; Iraq was first.

He regards the overthrow of the Iranian regime, "now a chief Israeli aim," as being justified, especially in the US, "with claptrap about 'fighting Islamic fundamentalism' for the supposed benefit of the West. This explanation, tamely accepted by many US 'experts' is, in my view, obviously incorrect."[3]

Shahak states that: "Israel has for years supported Hamas and other Islamic fundamentalist groups against the PLO, when it thought that such support would serve its interests."

He flags the real reason for Israeli enmity to Iran – which may yet lead to an Israeli assault on it – as "Israel's hegemonic aspirations." He explains that a state aspiring to hegemony in an area cannot tolerate other strong states in that area. If such a war is waged against Iran, Shahak avers, it will undoubtedly be represented for the benefit of the Western media as "War for the

Peace of the Middle East," just as the invasion of Lebanon in 1982 was officially called by Israel "War for the Peace of Galilee."

Although Palestinians are the first victims of Israeli policies, and the people who have most suffered from them, Shahak writes, the most important part of Israeli policies is not concerned with the Palestinians. "Even a real peace between Israel and the Palestinians will not lead to peace in the Middle East."[4]

Shahak states that, on the contrary, although there is an Israeli wish to keep the Palestinians quiet under a form of Israeli control, this control is intended to promote its real policies... its wish to topple the Iranian regime.

DESIRE FOR ISRAELI NUCLEAR UMBRELLA

In its desire to establish hegemony over the Middle East, he points to the distinct possibility of "an Israeli nuclear umbrella for the Gulf" which is indeed supported by some strategists of Kuwait, Quatar and Oman. Shahak refers to the prestigious Hebrew paper, *Haaretz*, which carried an interview with Sammy Faraj, a Kuwaiti strategy expert, who told the reporter that "provided Israel makes peace with Syria, it should be included in an alliance which would secure the peace in the Gulf by its [Israel's] nuclear weapons."[5]

In Shahak's view, the establishment of Israel as the nuclear power in the Gulf – supposedly to secure the Gulf states – is in reality intended to acquire hegemony over them.

Shahak's warning is clear: "[S]uch Israeli intervention in the Gulf may lead to war against Iran - even a war in which nuclear weapons will be used – from which untold calamities will ensue."[6]

Finally, Shahak points to the key for carrying out Israeli hegemonic policies, namely the Israeli influence over US policies carried out through what is called the "Jewish lobby" in the US. He says that: "especially under Clinton [that is] surely correct." (Clinton was called the 'real Israeli ambassador in Washington' by an important Hebrew press commentator.) Shahak says that: "Israel can influence the US not only because of the influence of the 'Jewish lobby' (helped by Christian fundamentalists), but also because Israel is, in itself, a strong state."

Shahak gives us a chilling analysis of "Israeli official ideology," namely discrimination, amounting to a form of apartheid. "Israel discriminates not only against Arabs, or only against Palestinians... but against all non-Jews, including its best non-Jewish friends," he writes. "It follows from that official attitude which Israel tries to inculcate among all its Jewish citizens that Israel must regard even its best non-Jewish friends as its potential enemies."

> A political conclusion follows from that ideological attitude: there exists in Israeli policies a latent (and often a not-so-latent) hostility toward its present allies. Thus, the Israeli claim that its hegemony is intended to be exercised for the benefit of the West (by itself an absurd claim if one considers the 'normal' behavior of states) cannot possibly be true in the case of a state which officially defines itself as a 'Jewish state' and, as a point of principle, discriminates against all non-Jews.[7]

Shahak leaves us with a Francis Bacon quote: "Knowledge is power." The only way of avoiding Israeli hegemony, according to the author of this exceptionally revealing book, is a detailed knowledge of Israeli policies and the way they are presented to the Israeli Jews. He warns us that "lack of knowledge is weakness." He also stresses that increased Israeli hegemony in the Middle East will also be a disaster for Israeli Jews.

WAGING TALMUDIC WARFARE

For a greater understanding of this bloody trail of destruction and revenge, refer again to Shahak's *Jewish History, Jewish Religion*. Dr Noam Chomsky regards Shahak as "an outstanding scholar, with remarkable insight and depth of knowledge. His work is informed and penetrating, a contribution of great value."[8]

Shahak speaks of a "closed Utopia" called the Jewish state which will strive to achieve its "Biblical borders" over the near time frame. To the initiated, those borders encompass not only the tiny theocratic kingdom of Israel, but the Sinai and part of northern

Egypt, all of Jordan, a large chunk of Saudi Arabia, all of Kuwait (which until 1931 was part of Iraq), a part of Iraq south of the Euphrates, all of Lebanon, all of Syria, a part of Turkey (up to Lake Van), and the island of Cyprus.

Despite all the talks of peace between Israel and the Palestinians, there will be no peace. Through what Shahak calls "prejudice and prevarication" and a totalitarian history, the Talmudic terrorists of Eastern Europe, now very much in charge, not only in Israel, but in the twin fortresses of democracy in the Western Hemisphere, namely the United States and Canada, will slowly enclose much if not all of the Biblical borders.

These gangster-statesmen, similarly to their heroes who conquered all of Russia earlier, want it all. David Ben-Gurion, whom Shahak admired as a youth while living in a kibbutz back in the 1950s, announced to the Knesset that the real reason for the Suez War of 1956 was to restore the kingdom of David and Solomon to its Biblical borders.[9]

And Prime Minster Benyamin Natanyahu had the identical goal; however, he was badly defeated in a special election held on 17 May 1999 by Labor party challenger, Ehud Barak. In a news analysis, the *Washington Times* (17 May 1999) indicated that Barak, Israel's leading "war hero," would probably resume peace talks with the Palestinians, and might even give up the territory captured by Israel in the Six Day war. The prime minister (Natanyahu) repeatedly warned that Jerusalem may be redivided into Jewish and Arab sovereignties if Mr. Barak is elected.

According to the *Times* story, growing tribalism has made Israel something far different from the unified nation that Zionist founder, Theodor Herzl, and the first prime minister, David Ben-Gurion, set out to build earlier this century.

> Today, nearly 1 million Russian Jews, who emigrated after the collapse of the Soviet Union in 1991, hold the key to power in Israel and possibly to stability in the volatile Middle East – a tinderbox of passions that have fired disputes over land.... Sephardic Jews from Morocco, many of whom swarmed into Israel in the early 1950s, resented the

economic and political clout of earlier arrivals from Poland and Russia, who held the reins of power in Israel for decades.

Mr. Barak made a shrewd move by dropping the Labor Party label – a name that many Jewish voters from Arab countries equate with Israel's Ashkenazi European elite.[10]

In a breakdown of "Israel's political tribes," the *Washington Times* displayed the major divisions of Israel's 6 million people. The Sephardim (the true Jews) make up 35% of the electorate, while the Ashkenazim (the Jews who are not Jews, but descendants of the fierce non-Semitic Khazars) – including those of the former Soviet Union arriving since 1989 – comprise 44%. Of the balance, 11% are the native Sabras, born in Israel; and the Israeli Arabs, mainly living in Galilee in Northern Israel, are 11% of the electorate.

ISRAEL GRABS MORE ARAB LAND

Dateline, Jerusalem – 12 Nov 1998: In a *Washington Post* story (13 Nov 1998), Lee Hockstader writes that: "Less than 24 hours after it ratified the latest US sponsored Middle East Peace Plan, the Israeli government today took a decisive step toward building a huge new Jewish neighborhood in the traditionally Arab part of Jerusalem despite strong objections by the Palestinians and the United States."[11]

Prime Minister Benyamin Natanyahu had solicited bids calling for the first thousand homes to be built in the project, which will eventually be the new home of 30,000 Jews. Hockstader points out that although the Palestinians are strongly opposed to the development, it is unlikely to derail the land-for-security peace plan, under which the Palestinians would gain control of chunks of new territory in the Israeli-occupied West Bank, as well as the right to use an airport in the Gaza Strip and other economic and political benefits.

The Oslo Accord of 1993 left the ultimate status of Jerusalem, which Arabs and Jews alike regard as their rightful capital, to be negotiated in a final round of talks between the two sides. But Natanyahu has insisted that Jerusalem is Israel's eternal and indivisible capital, and that construction decisions here are Israel's exclusive prerogative.

"I've said it for the last two years. Har Homa will be built by the year 2000," Natanyahu told a group of foreign journalists. "It's an issue not only of community needs but of sovereignty."[12]

Palestinian negotiator Hassan Asfour said, "If the Israeli side continues in this way it means they want to lead the relationship with Palestinians to confrontation."[13]

Haim Ramon, a liberal Jewish member of the Labor Party, said, "Netanyahu will try to sabotage the peace in any way that he will find, because basically if you don't believe in the process and you don't believe in your partner you cannot make peace."[14]

Meanwhile, as reported in the same issue of the *Post* in an article headlined "Support for US Stance on Iraq Grows," Thomas W. Lippman and Bradley Graham write:

> The United States began deploying 139 heavy bombers and other warplanes to the Persian Gulf region yesterday [12 Nov 1998], beefing up its forces for possible air strikes against Iraq as administration officials cited growing international support for its position that Baghdad must resume cooperation with UN weapons inspectors....
>
> Clinton called the leaders of Germany, Sweden and Belgium yesterday to discuss the situation. "What we hear in these calls is a united international community," said White House spokesman Joe Lockhart....
>
> At a news conference in Norfolk ... [Sec Def William S.] Cohen reiterated that the aim of US military action would be to 'degrade' Saddam Hussein's ability to threaten his neighbors or produce chemical, biological and nuclear weapons.[15]

TALMUD FORBIDS OUTRIGHT MURDER

Israel Shahak describes in grisly terms how the harsh doctrine of the Halakhah was followed to the letter by the Israeli soldiers as they advanced through enemy territory in southern Lebanon in 1982. According to the Halakhah, the duty to save the life of a fellow Jew is paramount, while, toward the Gentiles, the basic Talmudic principle is that their lives must not be saved,

although it is forbidden to murder them outright. This exhortation
was included in a booklet of the Central Region Command of the
Israeli Army (1973). In it, the Chief Chaplain writes:

> When our forces come across civilians during a war or in hot
> pursuit or in a raid, so long as there is no certainty that those civilians are
> incapable of harming our forces, then according to the Halakhah they
> may and even should be killed.... Under no circumstances should an
> Arab be trusted, even if he makes an impression of being civilized.... In a
> war, when our forces storm the enemy, they are allowed, and even
> enjoined by the Halakhah to kill even good civilians, that is, civilians
> who are ostensibly good.[16]

Why would a chaplain exhort the troops to murder?
Consider the original instructions as explained by Olivia Maria
O'Grady in *Beasts of the Apocalypse*. She transports us back in
time to Jehovah's promise to Abram (Abraham) – a covenant that
was to be everlasting between Jehovah and Abraham's seed:

> And I will give unto thee, and to thy seed after thee, the land
> wherein thou art a stranger, all of the Land of Canaan for an everlasting
> possession; and I will be their God.[17]

These then are our chosen allies for the coming war in the
Middle East. Surely, if they are carrying out the commands of the
mighty Jehovah as elucidated in the sacred writings of the Talmud,
we must be on the winning side... for... are we not as civilized?

RISE OF JEWISH POWER IN US

Following one of his frequent visits from Israel to the
United States, Avinoam Bar-Yosef published an article in the 2
Sep 1994 edition of *Ma'ariv*, an influential Hebrew-language
newspaper published in Tel Aviv. The thrust of his article was that
Jewish political power in Washington had markedly increased
under the Clinton administration. "Indeed," he wrote, "as far as the
Jews are concerned, President Bill Clinton has contributed toward
a real change in administration outlook, having concluded a series
of changes which enhance Jewish power, a process that began
under Reagan and his Secretary of State, George Schultz."[18]

Bar-Yosef concedes that while Jewish influence was
evident in America for decades, citing Kissinger under Nixon, as

well as several cabinet members under Carter, they were exceptions. "Especially, pious Jews were seldom appointed to participate in political work concerning the Middle East." [19]

He informs his Israeli readers that "[T]he picture now has totally changed, and not only about the Middle East.... In the National Security Council seven out of 11 top staffers are Jews. Clinton has especially placed them in the most sensitive junctions in the US security and foreign policy slots. Samuel Berger is the deputy chairman of the Council [since elevated to top slot]; Martin Indyk (an Australian), the intended ambassador to Israel, is a senior director in charge of the Middle East and South Asia; Dan Schifter, senior director and adviser to the President, is in charge of Western Europe; Don Steinberg, senior director and adviser to the President, is in charge of Africa; Richard Feinberg, senior director and adviser to the President, is in charge of Latin America; Stanley Ross, senior director and adviser to the President, is in charge of Asia." [20]

Bar-Yosef continues to drop names of important personages in charge of the US government. "The situation is not much different in the President's office," he reports, "which is full of warm Jews; the new White House counsel, Abner Mikva; the president's program director, Ricki Seldman; deputy chief of staff, Phil Leida; economic adviser, Robert Rubin; Ely Segal in charge of volunteers; Ira Magaziner, in charge of the health program; Labor Secretary Robert Reich and Mickey Kantor, in charge of international trade agreements. They are joined by a long list of senior Jewish officials in the State Department, headed by the chief of the Middle East team, Dennis Ross, followed by many deputy secretaries and senior chiefs of staff." [21]

He stresses that the "enormous Jewish influence in Washington" is not limited to the government, but includes "a very significant part of the most important personages on the TV and the senior media correspondents, newspaper editors and analysts (who) are warm Jews too."

Toward the end of his lengthy and informative article, Bar-Yosef points to the Jewish predominance in academic institutions, the National Institute of Health, in the fields of security and science, in the film industry, in art and literature.

"The Jewish influence can only be described as immense, with a corresponding enhancement of Jewish power," Bar-Yosef concludes.[22]

JEWISH POWER DIRECTS IRAQI DESTRUCTION

In its insatiable desire to establish absolute hegemony over the Middle East, Israel (and the Zionist movement before 1948) occasionally calls on its allies for assistance. It is an "open secret" that its allies include Britain, United States, Russia, and to a lesser degree, France.

In order to grasp the force and persuasiveness of what both Israel Shahak and Avinoam Bar-Yosef called "Jewish power" and/or the "Israeli Jewish elite," let's now examine certain related facts which were contained in an article published by Eric D. Butler in the February 1990 issue of the Australian monthly *The New Times,* as well as in the prestigious journal of the Council on Foreign Relations (CFR), "Foreign Affairs."

Butler singles out President George Bush, backed by the likes of Henry Kissinger and other such "advisers," who sought to solve the problems of the Middle East inside the framework of what they called "a New World Order." Butler emphasizes that all the available evidence is progressively reinforcing the view of those who believe that war (Desert Storm) was deliberately sought by the top echelons of the Zionist movement.[23]

In his *New York Times* article, Butler stresses the growing close relationship between Moscow and Washington (Bush and Gorbachev), "The Soviet wanted military war in the Middle East," Butler says. "If they were genuinely opposed, they had the power to prevent it by using their veto in the UN Security Council."

> Not only did the Soviet fail to use the veto, it also failed to warn Saddam Hussein about the consequences of annexing Kuwait, even though it had a strong contingent of military advisers in Iraq. Simultaneously, it was fulfilling its agreement with the Zionist leaders to permit the massive emigration of hundreds of thousands of Soviet Jews to

Israel, a policy calculated to intensify the fears of the Arab world concerning Israeli expansion.[24]

Former terrorist leader and Israeli Prime Minister, Yitzhak Shamir (Yezernitzki), planned to annex all of the Palestinian territories occupied during the 1967 war, which had been deliberately triggered by the Soviet strategists. To aid him in this plan, he brought former army general Rehavm Ze'evi into his cabinet. Ze'evi favored the "transfer" of the entire Palestinian population out of Israel. The oppression of the Palestinians became more severe, resulting in their becoming increasingly bitter and desperate.

Victor Ostrovsky, a former Mossad officer, addressed this factor in his chilling revelations about Mossad operations, *By Way of Deception*:

> The intifada and resultant breakdown of moral order and humanity are a direct result of the kind of megalomania that characterizes the operations of the Mossad. That's where it all begins. This feeling that you can do anything you want to whomever you want because you have the power.

> Israel is facing its biggest threat ever. This thing is uncontrollable. In Israel, they're still beating Palestinians, and Shamir says 'They're making us become cruel. They're forcing us to hit children. Aren't they terrible?'

> That is what happens after years and years of secrecy, of 'we're right, let's be right, no matter what....' It is a disease that began with the Mossad and has spread through government and down through much of Israeli society. There are large elements inside Israel who are protesting this slide, but their voices are not being heard. And with every step down, it gets easier to repeat, and more difficult to stop.[25]

"THE ROAD TO WAR"

"The Road To War" was the title of a lengthy editorial carried in the journal *Foreign Affairs*, published by the Council on Foreign Relations, in the Spring of 1991. Here is an excerpt which reveals in startling clarity the obvious intent of that organization to subvert the Constitution of the United States and bring about a one-world government under the United Nations:

Never before in American history was there a period quite like it. For 48 days the United States moved inexorably toward war, acting on authority granted by an international organization. On November 29, 1990, in an unprecedented step, the United Nations Security Council authorized the use after January 15, 1991 of "all necessary means" to achieve the withdrawal of Iraqi forces from the territory of Kuwait. On January 12 the Congress of the United States authorized President Bush to use American armed forces to implement that resolution. This too was unprecedented. [26]

What actions did the then President Bush take prior to such a decision? Why did an equally culpable Congress put holy water on his treasonous decision?

There is no question that George Bush, a Yale University Skull and Bones initiate in 1947, has been under the thumb of the CFR. Let's examine some of his public utterances just prior to, during and after the so-called Gulf War.

Out of these troubled times, our fifth objective – a new world order – can emerge.... We are now in sight of a United Nations that performs as envisioned by its founders.[27]

Let me give you this final message. If we use the military we can make the United Nations a really meaningful, effective voice for peace and stability in the future.[28]

I think that what's at stake here is the new world order. What's at stake here is whether we can have disputes peacefully resolved in the future by a reinvigorated United Nations.[29]

And that world order is only going to be enhanced if this newly-activated peace-keeping function of the United Nations proves to be effective. That is the only way the new world order will be enhanced.[30]

In the Gulf, we saw the United Nations playing the role dreamed of by its founders.... I hope history will record that the Gulf crisis was the crucible of the New World Order.[31]

The crowning glory (for Bush) came on 23 Sep 1991 when he delivered his *"pax universalis"* speech at the UN. As John McManus, president of the John Birch Society, reported, "He placed our Nation on record as favoring UN military action to settle 'nationalist passions' within the borders of any nation. He even sanctioned the use of UN power to remove a nation's leader."[32]

PART TWO
DEFINING ISRAEL'S SACRED TERRORISM

TO comprehend the term "sacred terrorism," one must go to the personal diary of a fervent but principled Zionist, Moshe Sharett (Shertok) who was Israel's first foreign minister and who, for two years, replaced David Ben-Gurion as prime minister. Born in Harsson, Russia in 1894, he emigrated with his family to Palestine in 1904. During World War I, he served as an officer in the army of the Ottoman Turks who then controlled Palestine. He would later rise to a position of power as head of the Jewish Agency's political department under David Ben-Gurion, who was head of the Agency.

In her revealing work on the subject of *Israel's Sacred Terrorism*, Livia Rokach concentrates on Sharett's entries in his intimate personal diary which he wrote from October 1953 to November 1956. The diary is a 2,400-page document in eight volumes. It reflects the fundamental difference between Ben-Gurion's preference for the use of force, versus Sharett's preference for diplomacy. This conflict characterizes 25 years of close collaboration at the very summit of the Zionist movement and the state of Israel.

Popular support for the tiny state of Israel by such Western countries as France, Britain, the United States, and, indirectly, by the Soviet Union, has been based on a series of untruths, sometimes referred to as myths, chief among them the myth of Israel's "security." This has been the driving force behind the huge amounts of public funds poured annually into the coffers of this fascistic country to sustain it militarily and economically.

Such blatant propaganda, which reflects the Zionist "sacred" right to a vast area of the Middle East, called "Greater Israel," has led from roughly 1917 until now to murderous and continuous "sacred acts of terror," revenge and retribution on the part of the controlling element of Israeli society, to which Israel

Shahak and other Jewish writers refer as the ruling oligarchy of the Israeli elite. In fact, as such other writers as Alfred Lilienthal and Benjamin Freedman point out, this select group of terrorists, murderers and thugs is comprised of "Jews who are not Jews," that is, not a Semitic people, but descendants of a Turko-Asiatic tribe, the Khazars whom we earlier described in some detail. Their profound and awe-inspiring abilities to use all imaginable (and some unimaginable) terror tactics, coupled to a total disregard for the morals and mores of the western peoples with whom they dwelt (albeit as "a people apart") was no passing fancy or exigency of the moment, but a permanent and diabolical plan to rule the earth in its entirety.[33]

A CLOSER LOOK AT "SACRED TERRORISM"

Let's concentrate for a moment on the contents of Moshe Sharett's diary, which was published in Hebrew in 1979, and is now sealed to public exposure in the Israeli archives. While portions leaked out before the Israeli government conviscated and sealed the documents, the only source for the analysis of his innermost thoughts (and abhorrence of the terror tactics of some of his fellow Zionists) is Livia Rokach's seminal work *Israel's Sacred Terrorism* in which she stresses the following points made by the Israeli prime minister in his diary:

> The Israeli political/military establishment never seriously believed in an Arab threat to the existence of Israel. On the contrary, it sought and applied every means to exacerbate the dilemma of the Arab regimes after the 1948 war.

> The Israeli political/military establishment aimed at pushing the Arab states into military confrontations which the Israeli leaders were invariably certain of winning. Its goal was radical transformation of regional balance of power in order to transform the Zionist state into the *major Middle East power.*[34]

In order to achieve their strategic purposes the following tactics were used:

a) Large and small scale military operations aimed at civilian populations across the armistice lines, especially in the Palestinian territories of the West Bank and Gaza, then respectively under the control of Jordan and Egypt. The double purpose was to terrorize the civilians and to create permanent destabilization.

b) Military operations against Arab military installations in border areas to undermine the morale of their armies and intensify the regimes' destabilization from inside the military.

c) Covert terrorist operations in depth inside the Arab world, used both for espionage and to create fear, tension and instability.

Further, Ms. Rokach stresses the following, garnered from Sharett's personal diary:

a) New territorial conquests through war, "a vital factor in Israel's transformation into the major regional power."

b) Liquidate all Arab and Palestinian claims to Palestine through the dispersion of the Palestinian refugees of the 1947-49 war to faraway parts of the Arab world.

c) Subversive operations designed to dismember the Arab world, defeat Arab national movement, and create puppet regimes which would gravitate to the regional Israeli power. [35]

Ms. Rokach reveals that the diary "deals a deadly blow to a number of important interpretations which are still being presented as historical truths. Among them:

> Most scholars and analysts cite nationalization of the Suez Canal as chief motivation for the October 1956 war; however, Sharett tells us that a major war against Egypt aimed at the territorial conquest of Gaza and the Sinai was planned as early as 1953. It was agreed then by the Israeli leaders that "international conditions for such a war would mature in about three years."

> Later occupation of the West Bank and Gaza in 1967 was touted as an Israeli defensive measure against Arab threats; however, Sharett's diary gives unequivocal evidence that occupation of Gaza and the West Bank was part of Israel's expansion plans since the early fifties.

> Continuing violent Israeli aggressions against Lebanon is still attributed, shamelessly, to Israel's security needs. Israeli spokesmen, echoed by the major western media, try to explain this massive intervention and destruction in Lebanon with the following historical arguments:

a) In the "inevitable" struggle between Muslims and Christians, the struggle would have broken out regardless of outside interference. Israel was motivated by a desire to help "defend the Christian minority."

b)The presence of Palestinian resistance, or in Israeli terminology, of Palestinian terrorism, in that country required Israeli intervention.[36]

Striking in candor was Sharett's documentation of how in 1954 Ben-Gurion developed the diabolical plan to "Christianize" Lebanon, i.e., to invent and create from scratch the inter-Lebanese conflict, and how a detailed "blueprint for the partition and subordination of that country to Israel was elaborated by Israel more than 15 years before the Palestinian presence became a political factor in Lebanon."[37]

Israeli Prime Minister Moshe Sharett summed up his personal feelings regarding the use of terror and aggression to provoke or create the appearance of an Arab threat to Israel's existence:

I have been meditating on the long chain of false incidents and hostilities we have invented and on the many clashes we have provoked which cost us so much blood, and the violations of the law by our men – all of which brought grave disasters and determined the whole course of events and contributed to the security crisis.[38]

A week earlier, Moshe Dyan, then Israel's chief of staff, explained why Israel needed to reject any border security arrangements offered by the neighboring Arab states, or by the UN, as well as the formal security guarantees suggested by the United States. Such guarantees, he predicted, might "tie Israel's hands."[39]

The attacks and incursions across armistice lines by the Israeli armed forces in the 1950s went under the euphemistic name of "reprisal actions." According to Dyan, these actions "help us to maintain a high tension among our population and in the army… in order to have young men go to the Negev we have to cry out that it is in danger."[40]

Livia Rokach's fascinating prose is interspersed with excerpts from Sharett's diary and statements by his cohorts, all of which provide incontrovertible proof of Zionist and Israeli base treachery and inhuman brutality against its Arab neighbors, and especially against the Palestinians who once lived a peaceful and quiet and uneventful life in the land now called Israel. Her book proves beyond any doubt that the faction made up of "Jews who are not Jews" and "Christians who are not Christian" expects to conquer and establish suzerainty over not only the lands that once constituted Biblical Israel, but over the entire Middle East from Morocco to Pakistan; i.e., the old Phoenician Empire. This fact is corroborated by Israel Shahak in his voluminous writings.

To sum up her remarkable treatment of *Israel's Sacred Terrorism*, Rokach writes that "a strategic goal such as the transformation of Israel into a regional power inevitably presupposed the use of large-scale, open violence, and could not pretend even mythically to be achieved on the basis of the earlier moral-superiority doctrine which, therefore, had to be replaced with a new one." Terrorism and revenge were now to be glorified as the new "'moral...and even sacred' values of Israeli society."

> In a historical perspective Sharett's self-portrait as it emerges from his personal diary, thus also explains why no so-called moderate Zionist proposal is possible, and how any attempt to liberalize Zionism from the inside could not but end in defeat.

> In the early fifties the bases were laid for constructing a state imbued with the principles of sacred terrorism against the surrounding Arab societies;

> On the threshold of the eighties the same state is for the first time denounced by its own intellectuals as being tightly in the deadly grip of fascism. [41]

As a so-called moderate Zionist, Moshe Sharett's lifelong assumption has been that Israel's survival would be impossible without the support of the West, but that Western so-called morality, as well as Western objective interests in the Middle East, would never allow the West to support a Jewish state which "behaves according to the laws of the jungle" and raises terrorism to the level of a sacred principle. Rokach concludes her telling work by stating:

> "In the final analysis the West, and particularly the US, let itself be frightened, or blackmailed into supporting Israel's megalomanic

ambitions, because an objective relationship of complicity already existed and because once pushed into the open this complicity proved capable of serving the cause of Western power politics in the region.   Just as Zionism, based on the de-Palestinization and the Judaization of Palestine, was intrinsically racist and immoral, thus the West, in reality, had no use for a Jewish state in the Middle East which did not behave according to the laws of the jungle, and whose terrorism could not be relied on as a major instrument for the oppression of the peoples of the region.   There was a fatal but coherent logic in this newly acquired equation, which would determine the course of future events."[42]

Here is one of Sharett's final entries in his diary, dated 4 Apr 1957:

> I go on repeating to myself: nowadays admit that you are a loser! They showed much more daring and dynamism...they played with fire and they won.... Moral evaluations apart, Israel's political importance in the world has grown enormously....[43]

10 August 1964

Dear Major Grand Pre:

Thank you so much for your very nice note. I am afraid that had I heard Walt Richardson's prediction I would have ridiculed it to no small degree. This appointment came as a complete surprise and I must say was a shock to both of the Johnsons. Nonetheless, we take great pride in the appointment and shall do all in our power to live up to the expectations of our friends.

You obviously are a more recent visitor to North Dakota than I. I hope to get back there one of these days and visit with those of the family that still live there.

Mrs. Johnson joins with me in extending our very best wishes to you and to Mrs. Grand Pre.

Most sincerely,

HAROLD K. JOHNSON
General, United States Army
Chief of Staff

Major Dom R. Grand Pre
2828 24th Street North
Arlington, Virginia

Family friend, Eddie Rickenbacker, with his "Hat in the Ring" Spad - France, 1917

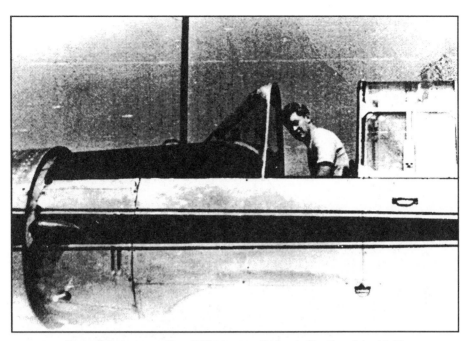

Donn, flying surplus BT-13 over Dakota Badlands - 1947

Captain Ed Agnew, Guadal Canal hero, Dickinson, ND - 1947

General Terry Allen awards Colonel Bob York DSC — Sicily, 1943

FDR pins Lieutenant Colonel Joe Crawford with DSC — Sicily, 1943

General Jim Gavin,
Chief Research &
Development, with
Red Stone Missile
1956

General Bruce Clarke gets 4th Star from his wife, Miss Bessie, and Wilbur
Brucker, Secretary of the Army - 1958

General Trudeau, Chief Research & Development; Donn Grand Pré,
Deputy Chief International Division; Mrs. Yates, Colonel Yates,
Cheif Atomic Division - Ft. Myer, 1962

Colonel Donn Grand Pré,
Commander,
Special Troops
US Army Reserve
Washington DC
July 7, 1971

Donn "Old Blue
Two" of the
Wolfhounds
Korea, 1953

Donn with General Crawford's Chopper - Korea, 1953

Ursella with Bruce, Ft. Rucker, AL - 1951

Donn, 25th Infantry Division - Munsan-ni, Korea 1953

CHAPTER XI

MANIPULATING PUBLIC OPINION
(Mind Control by Propaganda)

*All propaganda has to be popular and has to adapt its spiritual
level to the perception of the least intelligent of those towards whom it
intends to direct itself.*

Adolf Hitler, *Mein Kampf*

PART ONE
REGIMENTING HUMAN THOUGHT

A NY regime in power anywhere in the world recognizes the
necessity to control its population. We will discuss how this is
brought about through the control of the seven M's (Money,
Media, Markets, Mind, Medical, Morals, Muscle), especially –
Money, Media, Muscle (Military). In conjunction with these three
M's, particularly with a media monopoly, our fearful masters
manipulate our little minds. Let's look more closely at this aspect,
for in its nether regions, we find the artful cunning of nearly 3,000
years of expertise in spinning the silky strands of propaganda.

A young computer nerd from London, Nick Leeson,
working for Barings Bank in Singapore, is given credit for racking
up $1.4 billion in derivative losses (which resulted in the collapse
of Barings in Feb 1995). Nick is currently serving time in a
Singapore prison for "the biggest trading disaster in the history of
financial markets." We are to believe that this 28-year-old trader
who broke the bank (which had existed as a solvent institution for
232 years) accomplished its demise all by himself, according to
Stephen Fay, author of *The Collapse of Barings* (1997).

Fay states that because the manipulation of technology has
become so important, there is a huge gap between "computer nerds

and computer illiterates, for whom the future is a closed book." Will it happen again? "Of course it will. Somewhere, it – or something like it – is happening now."[1]

We will discover that there is a direct correlation between financial manipulation and mind control. Both relate to absolute control of the mechanism of deception and distortion in order to indoctrinate the masses systematically and deliberately with particular ideas, doctrines and practices so that a ruling regime can maintain absolute coercive control over these selfsame masses.

Every man, woman and child – some sooner than later – develops a theory of life, an understanding of how the world works. Over time, our ideas coalesce into axioms, which Webster defines as needing no proof because the truth is obvious. Alas, public opinion has the power to twist a maxim or axiom into a belief, which seems to be true or valid, but is in fact the antithesis of truth. We know this technique as propaganda, which is any systematic, widespread, deliberate indoctrination or plan for the spread of ideas or customs from person to person or generation to generation. Propaganda is generally used in a derogatory sense, connoting deception or distortion.

Consider first our Constitution, which is a set of resolutions hammered out in 1787 to govern our new union. It was then, and could be today, our maxim for daily living; our code of honor, if you will. It has over time been cleverly subverted to suit the aims and principles and goals of an alien force within, who have used the technique of propaganda to convince the masses to subscribe to a contrived set of axioms – each of them false and most in direct opposition to those truths embodied in our Constitution. We need only examine the decisions of that august body, the Supreme Court, over the past 40 years to grasp how blatantly the "supreme law of the land" has been subverted.

Such manipulation of the public mind has brought us today to a crisis of epic proportions so vast and all-pervasive that by the end of this millennium most of us could be caught up in abject slavery. This has been the goal of the Barbarians within since the founding of our union in 1789, but was put on fast-forward at the turn of the twentieth century to bring about in the year 2000 total despotism over all the people of this once-Christian nation known as the United States of America.

We saw in earlier chapters how such Christian countries as Germany, Russia and Mexico were targeted for destruction by war and revolution at the turn of this century, brought about by the two world wars, both of which would have ended much earlier had it not been for the manipulation of information, which caused the purposeful entry of the United States into the fray, resulting in the prolongation and extension of those wars.   Here is Winston Churchill addressing the subject in 1936:

> America should have minded her own business and stayed out of the World War. If you hadn't entered the war, the Allies would have made peace with Germany in the spring of 1917. Had we made peace then there would have been no collapse in Russia followed by Communism, no breakdown in Italy followed by Fascism, and Germany would not have signed the Versailles Treaty which has enthroned Nazism in Germany. If America had stayed out of the war, all of these 'isms' wouldn't today be sweeping the continent of Europe and breaking down parliamentary government, and if England had made peace early in 1917, it would have saved over one million British, French, American and other lives. [2]

Why didn't we, the United States of America "mind our own business" and stay out of what was just another European squabble for commercial control of their continent, as well as the high seas surrounding it?

We get an important clue from the *New York Times* for 24 Mar 1917. The blaring headlines alone of that edition tells us much as to the political persuasion of those who wanted the United States to get into the war:

> "Pacifists Pester Till Mayor Calls Them Traitors"

> "Socialists at Carnegie Hall Fail to Make Russian Celebration a Peace Meeting"

> "Rabbi Wise Ready for War"

> "Kennan Retells History"

> "How Jacob Schiff Financed Revolution Propaganda" [3]

The occasion was the celebration of the Russian Revolution at Carnegie Hall on the evening of 23 Mar 1917 (eight months before the Bolshevik Revolution.) The mayor of New York City, Marvin Mitchel, was the featured speaker. He was introduced by the president of the Society of Friends for Russian Freedom, Herbert Parsons, who informed the packed Hall that Mayor Mitchel was a "man of a race that has also struggled for freedom." According to the *New York Times*, "The galleries were largely filled with Socialists."[4]

"We are gathered here," the Mayor began, "to celebrate the greatest triumph of democracy since the fall of the Bastille." The *Times* reports that there were some cheers. "America rejoices," the Mayor said. "How could she do otherwise when she sees power in Russia transferred from the few to the many, and in the country where there seemed the least hope of the cause of democracy triumphing. America, the great democracy, is proud tonight because democracy in Russia has supplanted the greatest oligarchy that remained on the face of the earth."

Then the Mayor stepped back and said: "But I submit we have another reason to be proud. It is now inevitable, so far as human foresight can make a prediction, that the United States is to be projected into this world war and – "

"No! No!" rolled the chorus from the galleries.

There was quiet for an instant. Then the audience downstairs and in the boxes began to rise and a shout of 'Yes! Yes!' answered the galleries.

"And when America does enter the contest," shouted the Mayor, "it will be to vindicate certain ideas as fundamental as those on which the Republic was builded (*sic*), and among them will be the cause of democracy throughout the world. Let us be glad that, instead of fighting side by side with autocratic Russia, we shall be fighting side by side with democratic Russia."[5]

It was at this point that the galleries became so demonstrative that Mitchel told them they must be Americans or traitors. He then left the hall, followed by shouts of condemnation and of praise.

The Mayor was followed at the podium by Rabbi Stephen Wise, "a worker for world peace, but not an extreme pacifist," according to the *New York Times* article.

> The Mayor is right when he says we are on the verge of war. I pray God it will not come, but if it does the blame will not rest upon us, but upon that German militarism which may it be given to the German people to overthrow as the Romanoffs have been forever overthrown. I cannot forget that I am a member and a teacher of a race of which half has lived in the dominion of the Czar and as a Jew, I believe that of all of the achievements of my people, none has been nobler than that part the sons and daughters of Israel have taken in the great movement which has culminated in the free Russia.[6]

George F Kennan, a sometime diplomat and future ambassador to Russia, followed Rabbi Wise. He praised the work of the Friends of Russian Freedom and pointed out that the revolutionary movement "was financed by a New York banker you all know and love," referring to Jacob Schiff.[7]

Mr. Parsons then arose and said: "I will now read a message from White Sulfur Springs sent by the gentleman to whom Mr. Kennan referred." Here is that message:

> Will you say for me to those present at tonight's meeting how deeply I regret my inability to celebrate with the Friends of Russian Freedom the actual reward of what we had hoped and striven for these long years! I do not for a moment feel that if the Russian people have under their present leaders shown such commendable moderation in this moment of crisis they will fail to give Russia proper government and a constitution which shall permanently assure to the Russian people the happiness and prosperity of which a financial autocracy has so long deprived them. Signed: Jacob H Schiff.[8]

This message from President Woodrow Wilson was then read:

> The American ambassador in Petrograd, acting under instructions from this government formally recognized the new government of Russia. By this act the United States has expressed its confidence in the success of and its natural sympathy with popular government. Signed: Woodrow Wilson.[9]

And the rest, as they say, is history.

Thus is "public opinion" (propaganda) formed. Thus was America subverted, not only when the above story appeared in the *New York Times* in 1917, but throughout the rest of the century. It is ongoing today.

SCIENTIFIC MIND-MANIPULATION

Three members of the Royal Institute for International Affairs in London led the way in the initial manipulation of public opinion; Lord Northcliffe, Lord Rothermere and Arnold Toynbee. They were aided by two Americans, Edward Bernays and Walter Lippmann, dispatched to London in 1914 to work out the techniques to bring about the support of the unthinking masses in both Britain and the United States, which would cause the young men especially to want to throw their bodies on the bayonets of the "fearful Hun," as the Germans were called by the propagandists during World War I.

From this talented group of specialists emerged an astounding revelation: only a very small group – something on the order of 13% of any given population – will make use of a rational thought process when confronting a problem, as opposed to 87% who will merely pass an opinion on it. This applies to such grave matters as waging war, as well as to any other problem facing humanity.

It is based on the fact that the human mind has a limited capacity of thought; only so many problems and matters of personal concern can occupy one person's conscious thought. As a new concern enters, an existing one must leave. What is true for the individual is also true for a society. John Naisbitt outlines this process in his methodology "Trend Report" which was developed for a string of clients, such as General Motors, Chase Manhattan Bank, the White House and the Harris polls.[10]

One can spot a trend in doing a content analysis of any daily newspaper or periodical. Advertising is the driving force, taking up most of the space in any periodical, leaving a limited area for what the media call "news holes." The space for "news" is limited, and when some new event is introduced, others are omitted. By controlling what goes into the "news holes," one can control public opinion, sometimes called popular opinion. The end goal is not just the gamesmanship involved in manipulating opinion, but in the creation of a mass of unthinking helots here in America...like 87% of them.

POLLING BY "PEOPLEMETER"

Nielsen Media Research is the new name for an old watchdog, A. C. Nielsen Co. It's sort of a Big Brother, watching what you watch on the idiot box. It provides audience estimates and demographics on which most advertising agencies say they have based their decisions for decades, according to a revealing writeup in the *Spotlight* newspaper.[11]

Here is the anomaly. A 1997 *TV Guide* poll found that more than half the viewers desire more moral and religious themes on TV; yet, Nielsen Media Research, as well as other pollsters, either ignore this factor, or by deliberate distortion and outright rigging of ratings reach research data reflecting different preferences.

Their principal tool is the "peoplemeter" which Nielsen has used for decades. This is a device the viewer turns on and then codes with a record of who is "in the room" at the time of viewing. Panel members, supposedly picked randomly, receive a one-time compensation of $50 for having the device installed. Nielsen currently has 5,000 such "panel members," whose viewing choice reflects the entire population of 200 million. Its list of panelists and the formula it uses to determine ratings are secret.

How advertisers interpret these ratings is certainly subjective at best. The *Spotlight* staff, in their accompanying article, shows that the commercial media are under the economic thumb of dictatorial ad agencies. Advertising is the lifeblood of all media forms. As we will discover in the chapter on media monopoly, to disregard the ad agencies and their political masters is to court disaster.

Stephen Fox, author of *The Mirror Makers* (1984) brags that Albert Lasker "flexed his advertising muscle on behalf of Jewish interests" after the *Saturday Evening Post* ran an article that criticized Jews. His powerful Madison Avenue ad agency pulled all of its clients' ads from the *Saturday Evening Post,* which led to the financial collapse of what had been one of America's most successful magazines.[12]

The trend toward political correctness in media content really took off after World War II, where advertisers seemed to decide that such content as Western cowboy serials, family type "humor pages" and uplifting articles were outdated and artificial. Influenced by the ad agencies, the advertisers pulled large accounts from popular media which did not reflect the political ideas desired by the agencies.   Blacklisted media went bankrupt, and the remainder learned quickly to toe the line or be destroyed.

Due to mergers and globalization, there are now only two huge umbrella advertising groups in America – Omnicom Group and Interpublic Group. Both rank high in Standard and Poor's 500, each with assets over $4 billion. The *Spotlight* staff points out that these umbrella groups use their expertise to maneuver public opinion as a power tool and cultural apparatus in order to reshape the world to their desired image.

David Acker and John Myers, in *Advertising Management,* state that "advertisers using subconscious motives uncovered by motivation research can manipulate an unwilling consumer." Whether in politics or in business, truth is no longer relevant, winning is everything.[13]

PAINTING PRETTY PICTURES IN THE MIND

There are two books still available which were published in the 1920s, but whose subject matter is more than pertinent currently. They deal with mass manipulation, and were written by erudite and scholarly experts in their fields. Both evolved from the wellspring of Babylonian Talmudism and the covenants contained therein.

Walter Lippmann's book *Public Opinion*, published in 1922, detailed the study in which he and Edward Bernays were involved while in London during the First World War. It had to do with creating pictures inside people's heads, which were cunningly and deliberately designed by expert craftsmen to mislead not only individuals but entire societies. Lippmann describes the basics as "PUBLIC OPINION with capital letters." He wrote that "Public opinion deals with indirect, unseen and puzzling facts, and there is nothing obvious about them." He also stressed that: "The picture inside the head often misleads men in their dealings with the world outside of their heads."[14]

His colleague of those stimulating days in London, Edward Bernays (whose relative by marriage, Murray Bernays, prepared the scenario for the fraudulent Nuremberg Trials), also produced a book, *Crystallizing Public Opinion,* and in 1928 published another dealing with a continuation of the subject, appropriately titled *Propaganda.* His helpmate in this endeavor was the master manipulator and historian, H. G. Wells. It was the latter's contention that nations could be defeated, not by overt warfare, but by the thought processes, e.g. propaganda and public opinion formation, i.e., the manipulation of minds on a mass scale.[15]

Both Bernays and Wells believed in regimenting human thought to the degree that an "invisible government" could take over an increasingly complex civilization. Bernays revealed in *Propaganda* that the conscious and intelligent manipulation of organized habits and opinions of the masses is an important technique in a democratic society.

"Those who manipulate this unseen mechanism of society constitute an invisible government, which is the true ruling power in our country," Bernays wrote in 1928. "It remains a fact that in almost every act of our daily lives, whether in the sphere of politics or business, in our social conduct or our ethical thinking, we are dominated by the relatively small number of persons (who) pull the wires which control the public mind, who harness old social forces and contrive new ways to bind and guide the world...."[16]

For his epic work, Bernays was handed CBS by his controllers, most of them centered in the newly-formed Council of Foreign Relations, an offshoot of the Royal Institute for International Affairs (RIIA) which sprang from the fertile loins of the Round Table in Britain. Bernays was replaced by his understudy, William Paley, who has carried that media firm to new heights of popular-opinion formulation.

PHILOSOPHY OF DESTRUCTION

In a broad philosophic sense, in order to get a grasp of what is happening to us individually and as a nation, we must understand the terms "existentialism" and "nihilism." They are the antithesis of Christianity.

"Existentialism" springs from the French *exister*, to be, or actual being. The notorious and prolific writer Jean-Paul Sartre popularized this literary-philosophic cult of nihilism and pessimism in France after World War II. It holds that each man exists as an individual in a purposeless universe, and that he must oppose the hostile environment through the exercise of his free will.

"Nihilism" is the denial of the existence of any basis for knowledge or truth, and thus rejects customary beliefs in religion or morality. Politically, it holds that all social, political and economic institutions must be completely destroyed in order to pave the way for new institutions (a New World Order). It advocates revolutionary reform such as took place in Russia and Mexico during the first 20 years of this century. It was the prevailing philosophy of the Bolsheviks who set out to destroy the world in order to rebuild it according to their satanic blueprint, as embodied in the 63 books of the Babylonian Talmud; and, more recently, in their "Blueprint for Conquest," circa 1897, better known as *The Protocols of the Learned Elders of Zion*.

Nihilism as a political movement relies on a combination of brutal assassinations and calculated acts of terror to foment violent and bloody revolution.

Such acts as the terror-bombing of the World Trade Center in New York followed by the Federal Building in Oklahoma City in 1995, have been integral parts of this psychological ploy to condition peoples' dependency on government and its law enforcement agencies (gestapo). Question: Will a national police force constitute a KGB operative? You bet it will.

Included and very much a part of this overall strategy is the Talmudic terror tactic of the assassinations and attempted assassinations of Pope John Paul II, Indira Ghandi of India by her son, Rajiv; and in the 1960s, of President Kennedy and Charles de Gaulle, as well as Bobby Kennedy and Malcolm X.

The driving force behind all of these acts of terror and brutal assassinations is nihilism and existentialism, as embodied in various secret societies, global in scope, and subordinate to International Zionism and Fabian Socialism joined together in the unholy writ of French Grand Orient/Scottish Rite Freemasonry. Its communications net worldwide comprises the 267 Freemasonic Lodges of B'nai B'rith, which relies on its sub-agency, the Anti-Defamation League for closely monitoring the activities of all possible elements in the United States which might rise up against its grand design for world conquest.

This then becomes the *raison d'être* for the media barrage against such organizations as citizens' militias, patriot groups, Christians and Muslims. By the adroit use of *agents provocateur* and by burrowing within any and all patriotic groups, attention can be directed immediately toward various patriot and Christian or Moslem groups as the perpetrators of acts of terror and assassination.

PART TWO
CONTROLLING THE UNIVERSE

IN 1843, in Charleston, SC, a group of Jewish land-owners and slave-owners, working closely with British businessmen and bankers, as well as with US citizens still loyal to the Crown of Britain, formed a separate lodge of Scottish Rite Freemasonry which they called B'nai B'rith.

Another "invisible" society, *L'Alliance Israelite Universelle*, was founded in 1860. Its president for nearly 20 years was a French citizen and businessman, Adolph Cremieux. Its stated purpose was to be the political government of the Jewish "nation," comprised of all Jews from wherever they resided, and coming under the authority of the secret *kahal* or community rule. Cremieux was the link between the Alliance and the Grand Orient Masonic organization. Its avowed aim of bringing a super-government of the world under Jewish control was inculcated into the world Zionist movement of 1897 and is today being pursued by the Jewish World Congress (headed by Edgar Bronfman in the 1990s).

In 1857, a Jewish rabbi, Jacob Brafmann, became a Christian. He produced two books, *The Book of the Kahal* (1869) and *The Jewish Brotherhoods* (1868). Brafmann, who professed Judaism until the age of 34, was asked by Czar Alexander II in 1860 to develop a means of overcoming the obstacles to the conversion of Jews to Christianity. He was joined by other "enlightened Jews." Together, they researched both the *Kahal* (civil administration) and the *Beth-Dins* (Talmudic law courts). They reveal that these documents show that Jews must abide by the *Kahal* and *Beth-Din*, even in contradistinction to the public law and their own conscience.[17]

The *Kahal*, for example, states that the Jews have the right (*Hasaka*) to the real estate and appurtenances of any gentile. This led to suppression of the Jewish *Kahal* by a circular of 1867, the formation of the "nihilists," and to the assassination of Czar Alexander II in March 1881 by a Jewish nihilist. President Garfield would be assassinated in September of that same year by a like-minded person.

As depicted in Robert Wilton's 1920 suppressed volume, *The Last Days of the Romanovs*, Czar Nicholas II, his wife and children, would also be assassinated by a Jewish cabalistic group in 1918. These murderers were followers of the cabala, an occult religious philosophy developed by Jewish rabbis, based on mystical interpretation of the Scriptures. (See *Dogme et Rituel de la Haute Magie* by Eliphas Levy.)[18]

The assassins left behind an inscription of the letter "L"; one called *lamed* in the cursive handwriting of ancient Hebrew, followed by the letter *lamed* in Samaritan script; and the third letter, the Greek *lambda*. The use of the letter "L" symbolizes the heart (*lamed*) which is located between the liver (*kaph*) and the brain (*mem*). According to the ancients, the heart is king of the body (*melek*-king). We find symbolically the first letter of each, "m," "l," and "k."

The cabalistic meaning of the inscriptions on the wall: "Here the King was sacrificed to bring about the destruction of his Kingdom."[19]

Then, as now, we are dealing with a cabalistic group operating under the command of occult forces who resort to ancient cabalistic power in order to bring about the destruction of existing power structures. We saw it most clearly in the assassination of Premier Yitzhak Rabin in Israel (4 Nov 1995) which had been ordered by a New York Jewish rabbi and carried out by a young so-called extremist, Yigal Amir, but with the blessings of the *Likud* party and such stalwarts as the "Butcher of Lebanon," Gen Ariel Sharon. Such machinations led to placing a pseudo-American, albeit with close ties to the ADL, one Benyamin Netanyahu (aka Barry Sullivan in the US), on the exalted throne of Israeli Prime Minister. Call him *melek* (king).

We also saw it (or heard it) on the night of 2 May 1934 in a radio address by Representative Louis T. McFadden when he spoke of "The Organization of British Slavery or Fabian Socialism." He tied in the "political and economic planning" (PEP) of the Fabian Socialists in England with the "new policy" of FDR under the National Recovery Act (NRA). He referred to a tract published in 1918 by Adolf Berle, "The Significance of a Jewish State" (dedicated to his friend Justice Louis Brandeis). Berle, who became a confidant and advisor to FDR, regarded the Jew as "the barometer of civilization at all times." He pointed to the inability of Christianity to avert war, and seemed to think that the Jews were the only power who could do anything about it. He discussed the "new policy" as being part and parcel of the Fabian Society of England, drawn up by Israel Moses Seiff (director of the Marks & Spencer chain stores in England) who relied almost exclusively on slave-labor imports from Soviet Russia in order to undersell his competitors. Representative McFadden emphasized:

> It would be a monstrous mistake for any intelligent citizen of whatever nation to close his eyes to the evident fact that for nigh sixty years, the Jews have surely and rapidly though almost invisibly climbed to the heights of government wherefrom the masses are ruled. Politically, financially and economically they have seized the reins of the governments of all nations and their invasion in the realms of social, educational and religious fields is not less important.[20]

OUR BOLSHEVIST BORDER

Two revealing books dealing with the Bolshevization of Mexico were published in 1935. One of them, *No God Next Door* by Rev Michael Kenny, SJ, has recently been republished by GSG & Associates.

"Russia on the Rio Grande" and "Our Bolshevist Border" were frank descriptions of the Mexican government when the book first came out, and still hold true over 70 years later. Father Kenny states that the administrative system was more ruthlessly planned and executed, and more destructive of law and liberty and every elemental right, human and divine, than the reddest and rawest *gulag* that Lenin and Stalin inflicted on humanity.[21]

In a chapter on "The Calles Plan to Capture Consciences," Kenny details the psychological spin and diabolical tactics used by Plutarco Elias Calles, a Jewish émigré from Poland who "Latinized" his name and reigned supreme south of the border for ten years (1924-34) as *"El Jefe Maximo de la Revolucion"* – the Supreme Chief of the Revolution.[22]

We see how Calles used the techniques of forming public opinion by propaganda and mind manipulation, applying Moscow's atheizing methods in his Bolshevist plan to destroy Christianity and the educational system in Mexico.

He addressed the entire people of Mexico from the Governor's Palace on 20 Jun 1925:

> The Revolution had been realized," he said, "in the definite ideology of President Rodreguez and his similarly ideological successor Cardenas, but has yet to be completed and made permanent in the psychological period which the Revolution has now entered. We must enter into consciences and take possession of them; the conscience of the children and the conscience of the youth; for youth and child must belong to the Revolution.[23]

In another book, *Blood-Drenched Altars* by Msgr. Francis Clement Kelley (1935), was a Catholic commentary on the history of Mexico. Kelley was well versed in the 19th-century repression of Christianity in that country. The conquest of Montezuma and the Aztec Indians by the Spanish ended a reign of terror by the Aztecs over other Indian tribes, highlighted by cannibalism and human sacrifice. Spain ruled Mexico for 300 years (1521-1821) and raised that country to equality with European countries, producing a flourishing and prosperous Catholic civilization, complete with universities, hospitals, orphanages and institutions for the care of the poor.

All this practicing Christianity was swept away in the wanton devastation planned and carried out by Scottish Rite Freemasonry, centered in the United States, extending from 1810 to 1928, with but one peaceful interlude of 35 years (1876-1911) during the rule of Porfirio Diaz, who stopped the Masonic-instigated revolutions and established order and tranquillity.[24]

The result of the series of revolutions has been that Mexico, despite her former prosperity and resources at least equal to those of the United States, became abjectly poor; and despite her population being almost entirely Catholic, was forced to suffer bitter and virulently anti-Catholic governments; and that Mexico, despite proclaiming itself a democratic republic, is governed by one party, which alone possesses the "right" to rule.

That same clique set out to destroy both sovereignty and Christianity in France, Spain, Germany, Russia and the United States, following our revolution of 1776-83. We saw earlier how the Babylonian Talmud was the source for Weisshaupt's *Illuminati* which invaded many of the Masonic lodges of Europe and worked its tentacles into the United States. The results of such massive destruction are embodied in what the *Christian Science Monitor*, in a front-page editorial (19 Jun 1920) called "The Jewish Peril," also known as *The Protocols of Zion*, which surfaced in 1905.[25]

There was an earlier *Protocol* which appeared in a French newspaper about the same time as the editorial in the *Christian Science Monitor*. "The Fatal Discourse of Rabbi Reichhorn" appeared in the French newspaper *La Vielle France* (21 Oct 1920 and 10 Mar 1921). "There is a striking analogy between the *Protocols of the Learned Elders of Zion* and the discourse of the Rabbi Reichhorn, pronounced in Prague in 1869 over the tomb of the Grand Rabbi Simeon-ben-Ihuda... the general ideas formulated by the Rabbi are found fully developed in the *Protocols*." Key details follow (emphases in original):

> Every hundred years, We the Sages of Israel, have been accustomed to meet in *Sanhedrin* in order to examine our progress toward the domination of the world which *Jehovah* has promised us, and our conquest over the enemy – *Christianity.*

> *Gold* always has been and always will be the irresistible power. Handled by expert hands it will always be the most useful lever for those who possess it, and the object of envy for those who do not. With gold we can buy the most rebellious consciences, can fix the rate of all values, the current price of all products, can subsidize all State loans, and thereafter hold the states at our mercy.

The other great power is *The Press.* By repeating without cessation certain ideas, the Press succeeds in the end in having them accepted as actualities. *The Theatre* renders us analogous services. Everywhere the Press and the Theatre obey our orders.

By the ceaseless praise of *Democratic Rule* we shall divide the Christians into political parties, we shall destroy the unity of Nations, we shall sow discord everywhere. Reduced to impotence, they will bow before the *Law of our Bank,* always united and always devoted to our Cause.

We shall force the Christians into wars by exploiting their pride and their stupidity. They will massacre each other and will clear the ground for us to put our own people into.

The possession of the land has always brought influence and power. In the name of *Social Justice* and *Equality* we shall parcel out the great estates; we shall give fragments to the peasants who covet them with all their powers, and who will soon be in debt to us by the expense of cultivating them. *Our Capital* will make us their masters. We in our turn shall become the proprietors, and the possession of the land will assure the power to us.

Let us try to replace the circulation of gold with paper money; our chests will absorb the gold, and we shall regulate the value of the paper which will make us masters of all positions.

By gold and by flattery we shall gain the proletariat which will charge itself with annihilating Christian capitalism. We shall promise the workmen salaries of which they never dared to dream, but we shall raise the price of necessities so that our profits will be greater still.

In this manner we shall prepare *Revolutions* which the Christians will make themselves and of which we shall reap the fruit.

By our mockeries and our attacks upon them we shall make their priests ridiculous, then odious, and their religion as ridiculous and as odious as their clergy. Then we shall be *masters of their souls.*

We have already established our own men in all important positions. We must endeavor to provide the *goyim* with lawyers and doctors; the lawyers are *au courant* with all our interests; doctors, once in the house, become confessors and directors of consciences.

But above all, let us monopolize *Education.* By this means we spread ideas that are useful to us, and shape the children's brains as suits us.

Let us take care not to hinder the marriage of our men with Christian girls, for through them we shall get our foot into the most closely locked circles.

For ages past, the sons of Israel, despised and persecuted, have been working to open up a path to power. They are hitting the mark. They control the economic life of the accursed Christians; their influence preponderates over politics and over manners.

At the wished-for hour, fixed in advance, we shall *let loose the Revolution*, which by ruining all classes of Christianity will definitely enslave the Christians to us. Thus will be accomplished the promise Jehovah made to his People.[26]

PART THREE
PSYCHOPOLITICS OF FORCE AND BRUTALITY

A Soviet textbook on mass mind-control called *Psychopolitics* has a direct bearing on our subject of take-over by an enemy within, for two basic reasons:

(1) Psychopolitics is being practiced on a concerted and daily basis here in the United States;

(2) Its techniques and tactics dovetail perfectly with what Douglas Reed calls "the Blueprint for Conquest" in his seminal work *The Controversy of Zion*.

Our soldiers captured by the North Koreans and the Chinese in their attack against the South in 1950-53 were subjected to the process called "brainwashing" by their captors. This in fact was nothing more nor less than the use of the Soviet Bolshevik tactics of mind-control or psychopolitics. The pattern used against the individual prisoners included the triad of degradation, shock and endurance. Important to recognize – it works! In fact, as stated in Chapter VIII of the Soviet textbook, *"Degradation and conquest are companions."*

Let's consider a synthesis of the 14 chapters of this amazing and chilling work by a cabal of evil men whose current and ongoing goal is total subjugation of all peoples throughout this planet. Their goal is stated in the summation:

> The end of war is the control of a conquered people. If a people can be conquered in the absence of war, the end of war will have been achieved without the destruction of war. A worthy goal.[27]

Each year during the 1930s a handpicked group of American students traveled to Moscow to attend an indoctrination course at Lenin University in Moscow. Stalin's chief thug, one Lavrenti Beria, chief of the secret police, welcomed the students in 1936:

> American students at the Lenin University, I welcome your attendance at these classes in Psychopolitics.

Psychopolitics is an important if less known division of Geopolitics. It is less known because it must necessarily deal with highly educated personnel, the very top strata of 'mental healing'

By Psychopolitics our chief goals are effectively carried forward. To produce a maximum of chaos in the culture of the enemy is our first most important step. Our fruits are grown in chaos, distrust, economic depression and scientific turmoil. At last a weary populace can seek peace only in our offered Communist state....

You must labor until we have dominion over the minds and bodies of every important person in your nation. You must achieve such disrepute for the state of insanity and such authority over its pronouncement that not one statesman so labeled could again be given credence by his people. You must work until suicide arising from mental imbalance is common and calls forth no general investigation or remark.

You must dominate as respected men the fields of psychiatry and psychology. You must dominate the hospitals and universities....

Psychopolitics is a solemn charge. With it you can erase our enemies as insects. You can cripple the efficiency of leaders by striking insanity into their families through the use of drugs...you can change their loyalties by Psychopolitics....

Use the Courts, use the judges, use the Constitution of the country, use its medical societies and its laws to further our ends....

By Psychopolitics create chaos. Leave a nation leaderless. Kill our enemies. And bring to Earth, through Communism, the greatest peace man has ever known....

MIND CONTROL IN THE US

The returning students found fertile ground in which to sow their seeds of psychopolitics and mass mind control in the hallowed halls of academe, in the not-so-hallowed halls of the diverse governmental bureaucracies flourishing in Washington, DC under the benevolent imperium of FDR and his New Deal, and throughout the media, especially in the propaganda mills of Hollywood during and after WW II.

There are two highly important documents recently made available by former government agents involved in creating "Manchurian Candidates," also known as "sleepers," who are mind-controlled and programmed individuals, some at the highest levels of government. Others are created for a single special mission, such as the assassination of a key personality, or the takeout of a particularly strong presidential candidate who might be a threat to the chosen candidate of the power brokers. That technique is referred to as "neutralization." It can involve coercion, intimidation, or actual killing.

One report, "Mind Control in America: Five Easy Steps to Create a Manchurian Candidate," details the CIA "Operation Open Eyes," which locates and selects personnel to be used as "sleepers." The procedure begins at Level One to determine, under heavy hypnosis, the future value of the candidate. A recall command and a trigger word is written into the personality. Level 2 hypnosis is used on those who pass certain tests, at which time specific instructions are written into the personality.[28]

Advancing to Level 3 hypnosis for a few with higher IQs, a new identity, called an "overwrite," is created, and the original personality is repressed or hidden under the overwrite. This is the technique used on field operatives to prepare them for a deadly covert mission.

For those with still higher IQs (130-140), a subject will be brought to "The Farm," or one of the numerous facilities throughout the US and Canada, where the subject undergoes Level 4 hypnosis. At this stage, the subject is told that he is superhuman; he no longer differentiates between right and wrong. His moral code, respect for the law, and fear of dying are replaced with new superhuman feelings; i.e., he is now a mortal god, who is beyond all human laws. In the CIA vernacular, he is now a "Clear Eyes."[29]

The report states that many politicians and government officials on a world-wide level have been brought in to the "Clear Eyes" level, where their own beliefs are replaced with the agenda of the programmers.

President Clinton is an example of a world leader who has been programmed with this technique. Senator John McCain and Secretary of State Madeleine Albright are two other examples of an 'agenda overlay' being 'overwritten' onto the subject's own personality. Their own personalities and memories are still present, although childhood and early adolescent memories are sometimes erased.[30]

A few subjects, who have been so chosen, then advance to Level 5, a "programmed sleeper assassin." At this level, a code word, sequence of numbers, or a voice imprint is etched into the subject's brain. This is the trigger which will activate the subject at the critical time a murder or assassination is to be committed. Because of the programming, the subject will not be able to associate with the crime. In most cases of programmed "Clear Eyes" who commit murders or assassinations, the agent is killed on the spot, or self destructs.[31]

The other report is on Project Mirror, still classified above top secret. It was formulated at the National Security Agency (NSA), the electronic spook facility located at Fort Meade, Maryland. It was (and probably still is) a covert operation involving up to 30 special operatives who would work together to liquidate certain foreign leaders about the world. The mind-control techniques in this project were similar to those of other code-named operations, such as Project Blue, which was the Johnstown, Guyana massacre of the entire cult of James Warren Jones.[32]

Yet another report, named after the attorney, Paul Wilcher, who prepared it, details the mass murder at Ranch Apocalypse out of Waco, Texas in 1993. Paul Wilcher later disappeared. His body was discovered in his Washington, DC apartment. The 100-page report which he prepared, and planned to present to Attorney General Janet Reno, also disappeared, along with his records and computer hard drive; however, the report surfaced through the good offices of a well-known Washington, DC reporter (purposely unnamed), who held a duplicate copy of the document.[33]

WHAT POWER DIRECTS MIND CONTROL?

Here, as tersely as possible, are the ongoing implementations of that *Blueprint for Conquest,* which in fact constitute crimes of the most heinous magnitude against this nation, its Constitution and its peoples:

In order to put public opinion into our hands we must bring it into a state of bewilderment... to multiply national failings so that it will be impossible for anyone to know where he is in the resulting chaos...

If any state raise a protest against us, it is only *pro forma* at our discretion and by our direction, for their anti-Semitism is indispensable to us for management of our lesser brethren...

It is from us that the all-engulfing terror proceeds. We have in our service persons of all opinions... each one of them is boring away at the last remnants of authority...

Then it was that we replaced the ruler by a caricature of a government, by a president, taken from the mob, from the midst of our puppet creatures, from our slaves...

We shall establish the responsibility of presidents... to prepare unification under our sovereign rule...

The chamber of deputies will provide cover for, will elect presidents, but we shall take from it the right to propose new laws, for this right will be given by us to the responsible president, a puppet in our hands...

The key of the shrine shall be in our hands... no one outside ourselves will any longer direct the force of legislation...

We shall emasculate the universities...

The complete wrecking of the Christian religion will not be long delayed...

The recognition of our despot will come when the peoples, utterly wearied by the irregularities and incompetence of their rulers, will clamor: 'Away with them and give us one king over all the earth who will unite us and annihilate the causes of discords...'

We will discover in the following chapter just how a covenant of race superiority is leading us down the slippery slope to a repressive one-world socialist government, with a very few of the superior or chosen ones in total charge, and the vast balance of mankind leveled out at the bottom as helots, slaves and/or "worker bees."

The next century can be and should be the humanistic century...we stand at the dawn of a new age...a secular society on a planetary scale.... As non-theists we begin with humans not God, nature not deity... we deplore the division of humankind on nationalistic grounds.... Thus we look to the development of a system of world law and a world order based upon transnational federal government.... The true revolution is occurring.

The Humanist Manifesto II, 1973

CHAPTER XII

DEFINING THE NEW COVENANT

(The Coming Kingdom of Darkness)

*And he (Moses) was there with the Lord forty days and forty nights;
he did neither eat bread, nor drink water. And he wrote upon the
tables the words of the covenant, the ten commandments.*

Exodus XXXIV, 28

PART ONE
COVENANT BUILDING BLOCKS

A T critical times throughout history the original Covenant
between Moses and Jehovah, forged eons ago on a
mountaintop in the Sinai Desert, has been systematically attacked,
eroded, neglected and purposely forgotten and/or altered to suit the
needs of some political faction   attempting to seize power from
another.

We saw evidence of that in 1638 when the Presbyterians of
Scotland agreed to a National Covenant that opposed episcopacy.
This led to the First Bishops' War in Scotland, wherein Charles I,
king of both England and Scotland, accused the Scots of seeking to
overthrow royal power.   The Covenanters launched an attack,
taking Edinburgh, Dumbarton and Stirling.   The war quickly
ended, with Charles signing the "Pacification of Berwick," which
abolished episcopacy in Scotland.   In 1643, at the height of the
English Civil War, the Parliaments of England and Scotland agreed
to the Solemn League and Covenant that extended and preserved
Presbyterianism in England.[1]

The Second Bishops' War in 1640 saw the Covenanters of
Scotland crossing into England and defeating Charles' forces,
leading to the Treaty of Ripon. Two years later, Charles attempted

to arrest five members of The Commons and failed. He fled with
his family to Hampton Court.

The English Civil War began in 1642. Charles' supporters,
the Cavaliers, took Marlborough; his opponents, the Roundheads
under Oliver Cromwell, seized Winchester. The Roundheads
(Covenanters) consistently defeated the Royalist forces until the
Civil War ended in 1646. Charles I was imprisoned but escaped.
The Scots began a Second Civil War in 1648, and were defeated.
Parliament voted to bring the King to trial, which opened 19 Jan
1649. The following day, Charles I was beheaded. This led to
Oliver Cromwell's becoming Lord Protector. In 1655, Cromwell
dissolved Parliament and divided England into 11 districts, each
with a major general as governor. He also prohibited Anglican
services.[2]

Let's now shift the scene and the time to France, 1789: the
beginning of the French Revolution; the script remains the same,
i.e., murder the monarch and mortally wound the Church.
Mirabeau emerged as a national figure; the Paris mob stormed the
Bastille, freed seven prisoners; the National Assembly took over
all Church property, issued *assignats* (paper money) against it. In
1790, King Louis XVI accepted a new constitution. The following
year, Mirabeau was elected president of the French Assembly.
King Louis tried to escape, was caught and returned to Paris. In
1792, the royal family was imprisoned and a French Republic
proclaimed (22 Sep): Jacobins under Danton seized power; trial of
Louis XVI; France declared war on Austria, Prussia and Sardinia.
In 1793, Louis was beheaded; Committee of Public Safety
established with Danton at its head; Reign of Terror began; Roman
Catholicism banned in France; Queen Marie Antoinette
guillotined; Holy Roman Empire declared war on France, US
proclaims its neutrality; French troops driven out of Germany.
Danton and Robespierre were executed, followed by mass killings;
"Feast of the Supreme Being" celebrated in Paris. These
momentous events of both joy and murder were followed in 1795
by bread riots and the "White Terror" in Paris; Napoleon appointed

commander-in-chief; married Josephine de Beauharnais in 1796. They lived unhappily ever after.

COVENANT OF THE LEAGUE OF NATIONS

Another shift both in time and place.... Russia, 1917: the beginning of the Russian Revolution; the script remains the same, i.e., murder the monarch, mortally wound the Church – these events were discussed at length in previous chapters.

At the height of this Bolshevik massacre, the infamous Versailles Treaty (1919) formally ended the Great War. The first section of the Treaty of Versailles was called "The Covenant of the League of Nations." It was in fact the constitution of the League of Nations. It insured that two, and only two, dissident elements – the Bolsheviks of Soviet Russia and the Zionist movement planning the seizure of Palestine – would benefit. For clarification of the latter element, again refer to *Facts are Facts* by Benjamin Freedman, who was a liaison between Henry Morgenthau, Sr., and the Wilson administration.[3]

Could it be possible that these revolutionary historical events may be played again in Russia; and even here in the United States, with perhaps the dissolution of Congress and establishment of ten (or 11, again) districts under FEMA control? Could Clinton's New Covenant lead to such a repetition? Before answering, let's examine further some of the weak links in the corroded chain leading back to Moses on the Mount and the "eternal" Covenant.

REVOLUTION AND NATURAL LAW

"To what extent (if at all) does natural law entail religious liberty?" This was the lead question of a most thoughtful and provocative article by Robert D. Hickson in *Chronicles* magazine (Dec 1998). Hickson is an instructor at the United States Military Academy. Another of his thought-provoking questions: "at the heart of the concept and reality of religious liberty.... What is freedom and what is freedom for?"[4]

He referred to an article by Tom Wolfe (author of *Bonfire of the Vanities*), entitled "The Meaning of Freedom." Appropriately, the essay appeared as the lead article in *Parameters* (Mar 1988), published by the Army War College.

Wolfe's article looked at the four phases of American freedom. We are now, he wrote, in the fourth phase, which is highly pertinent especially to all military personnel. Wolf writes:

> The fourth phase is freedom from religion. It is not freedom of religion; it is freedom from religion....[5]

Gone is the conception so aptly described by Alexis de Tocqueville in 1835, in which he described American democracy as "the freest form of government in the world." He attributed this to the internal discipline of the American people, rooted in their profound devotion to religion.

Wolfe says, "What we are now seeing is the earnest rejection of the constraints of religion... not just the rules of morality but even simple rules of conduct and ethics...."[6]

What we are now seeing is the total rejection of the "eternal" covenant, and its replacement by a "new" man-made and man-centered covenant. Wolfe homes in on his military audience:

> You (the American military) are going to find yourselves required to be sentinels at the bacchanal. You are going to find yourself required to stand guard at the Lucullan feast against the Huns approaching from outside. You will have to be armed monks at the orgy.[7]

"If I use religious terminology," Wolfe writes, "I use it on purpose. One of the most famous addresses ever delivered in this century by an American was the address of 12 May 1962 by Douglas MacArthur at West Point, in which he enunciated the watchwords of Duty – Honor – Country."

> . . . He said that the soldier, above all other men, is expected to practice the greatest act of religion: sacrifice.[8]

And it is here that Hickson makes his most cogent point: "But these Huns, 'approaching from outside' are also approaching from 'within.'" He quotes Whittaker Chambers (*Cold Friday,* 1964):

> It (communism) seeks a molecular re-arrangement of the human mind. It promotes not only a new world. It promotes a new kind of man [i.e., the 'revolutionary, democratic personality', not the 'authoritarian personality']. The physical revolutions which it once incited and now imposes, and which largely distract our attention, are secondary to this internal revolution which challenges each man in his mind and spirit.[9]

Hickson concludes his exceptionally fine article with a quote from Augusto del Noce's interview with a Madrid newspaper (1976) on Euro-Communism and other indirect variants of cultural subversion:

> The conquest of power can no longer be achieved by traditional revolutionary means. Civil society must first be conquered, and then the state will collapse.... In Italy, all the essentials are under control; the publishing houses, the schools, quite a few universities, the judiciary. The confrontation in the fight to dominate the sources of culture is not between the proletariat and the bourgeoisie but between tradition and modernity.[10]

Hickson explains that a new culture and a new system of values are created precisely so that the freedom of ideas may be redefined. Gramsci (Italian Communist leader) also understood that the only hope of eliminating the Catholic Church was to undermine her and destroy her from within.

This unceasing effort to destroy Christianity from within has passed through several "covenants," none more damaging than what has transpired in this century from the results of two major wars and the Bolshevik Revolution in Russia.

And in the subsequent "quiet Bolshevik revolution" here in the United States, commencing in deadly earnest under FDR's imperium (1933-45) and continuing without let-up through the reigns of such imperial notables as Dwight David Eisenhower, Lyndon Baines Johnson, George Herbert Walker Bush, and William Jefferson Clinton, the latter two concentrating their talents and personalities on establishing a new covenant with the Soviet Union (now Bolshevik Russia) as our "partner for peace."

RUSSIA – A FIT "PARTNER FOR PEACE"?

Ivor Benson, in *The Zionist Factor,* provided further pertinent background for this "New Covenant" which is slowly but assuredly bolshevizing our entire society. He explained that one of the keys to the Revolution riddle was the conference of Russia's Social Democrats in Stockholm in 1908, where the word "Bolshevik" first came into use.

All of the delegates were agreed in their attachment to the teachings of Karl Marx (Mordecai), but seemed to be divided on the ways and means for putting them into effect. Lenin's group pushed for radical bloody conflict, and were called the Bolsheviki because they were the majority. The other group argued for elimination of capitalism by propaganda and organization, and were called the Mensheviki (the lesser).

Nearly all Bolsheviks were atheists, called "pseudo-Jews," as opposed to "religious Jews." They could also be called "pseudo-Russians," concealing their identity as Jews behind Russian names. This practice survives today at the highest levels of Soviet power.[11]

However, within the ranks of "Social Democrats" were two radically different groups: those who believed in socialism as a philosophy and as a program for political change; and those who did not believe in it, but recognized it as a valuable device to be used in the conduct of political warfare.

It was at this stage that the Jewish faction fell back on their age-old technique of dissimulation, and as "pseudo-Russians" (Jewish nationalists), gained control of the socialist and progressive parties set up to oppose the Bolsheveki, Benson reports.

Here is another view, taken from Lloyd Wright's foreword to Rose L. Martin's 1968 epic *Fabian Freeway*:

> Because some of the Jews were traditionally small merchants in Russia as elsewhere, and were at sword's point with the czars, a percentage originally became interested in socialism. They joined Jewish intellectuals and students in supporting revolutionary activities, and thus

many were in the vanguard of the two Russian revolutions of 1917. The majority, however, accepted only the logical aspects of Marxism and leaned toward Zionism (i.e., the creation of a homeland with laws and customs to suit themselves). Zionists are survivalists. On the other hand, Jewish Communists are assimilationists; and promptly after the Revolution, they ordered all Jewish organizations disbanded and Jewish customs suppressed. A homogenized population would produce the desired environment.[12]

The fact is that Zionism/Bolshevism and Communism/Socialism are bicephalous – two heads attached to the same monster. As we will shortly discover, the same situation prevails here in the US, with the identical practices of name-changing and dissimulation.

JEWISH WAR OF AGGRESSION

...there was no such thing as a Bolshevik Revolution. There was a Jewish war of national agression carried out under cover of a Russian socialist revolution. [13]

As Ivor Benson relates (*The Zionist Factor*), after World War II, the terrorism and tyranny of Jewish nationalism spread like colonies of cancer cells all over Eastern Europe. In Communist Poland, Ambassador Bliss Lane recorded the predominance of Jews in the key posts of population control. In Hungary, Matyas Rakosi (Roth) was installed as prime minister with Red Army support, his cabinet being predominantly Jewish (as reported by the London *Times*). In Czechoslovakia, both the party intellectuals and the key men in the secret police were Jewish (*New Statesman* magazine).

The *New York Times* reported in 1953, "Romania, together with Hungary, has probably the greatest number of Jews in the administration." There, the terror raged under Anna Pauker, the daughter of a rabbi. In East Germany the Communist reign of terror was presided over by Hilde Benjamin, first as vice-president of the Supreme Court, then as Minister of Justice.

Everywhere, the same revolutionary pattern has been seen: population control as a means of creating disorder and of undermining the status quo, the creation of chaos and its reformulation as order by an

alliance of Money and Jewish nationalism to meet the requirements of a
planned New World Order.[14]

These factors were certainly well known among the ruling
elite of most European countries, as well as in the US and Canada.

Winston Churchill, writing an article in the London
Illustrated Sunday Herald, stressed that this movement among the
Jews is not new:

> From the days of Spartacus-Weishaupt to those of Karl Marx,
> down to Trotsky (Russia), Bela Kuhn (Hungary), Rosa Luxembourg
> (Germany), and Emma Goldman (US) this worldwide conspiracy for the
> overthrow of civilization and for the reconstruction of society on the
> basis of arrested development, of envious malevolence and impossible
> equality, has been steadily growing.[15]

Churchill was neither that naïve nor unknowing. He had
already forged workable links among such British establishments
as the Round Table group, British intelligence, the Fabians; and
through such links as Professor Harold Laski of the London School
of Economics and Justice Felix Frankfurter, directly with FDR in
the US; and with Harold "Kim" Philby to Josef Stalin in the USSR.

He was also locked in with Sir William Wiseman and
William "Intrepid" Stephenson to the Zionists, not only in Britain,
but in New York and Washington, as well as in Palestine, paving
the way for the creation of "a homeland for the Jews."

Nowhere are these unbroken links more in evidence than
the daisy chain draped about the twin banners of New World Order
and "inter-dependence" as described by Rose L. Martin in *Fabian
Freeway*. By a careful reading of this outstanding work, as well as
Witness by Whittaker Chambers, one sees clearly the unholy
matrimony between Fabian Socialism and International Zionism.

FORGING THE CHAIN OF DESTINY

This linkage runs unbroken through key organizations and
individuals down to the present. One doesn't have to be that
discerning to see a pattern in the names and activities of a group
totally dedicated to setting up a New World Order of Zionist
totalitarian socialist world government, with themselves in charge

and everyone else relegated to the position of worker bees or warrior bees, presided over by the Queen Bee and the Lords of the World. This in fact would become the New Covenant under President Bill Clinton. It is much more dangerous than FDR's New Deal and LBJ's Great Society.

Looking back on the farcical election campaigns of 1992 and 1996, we see that the main candidates were, in effect, backed by the same powerful groups; however, the CFR and its masters concentrated both money and media on a Clinton win. Here indeed was a reincarnated Leviathan – if not a Messiah – who would bring forth the New Covenant!

Look behind Bill and Hillary Clinton and see where their campaign money came from; see the almost invisible faces of their backers and advisors; get a look at those who swooped down on Washington as appointees and cabinet secretaries, as they had under Roosevelt, under Kennedy-Johnson and under Carter. For a time, under Reagan, we kept the barbarians slavering at the gate, but, under Clinton, they again seized America by the throat.

We saw the chain in *Fabian Freeway,* running back to the Fabian International Bureau in London, branching into the American Civil Liberties Union in 1921 (the same year the British Round Table and Colonel Edward Mandell House established the Council on Foreign Relations), the League for Industrial Democracy which spawned the Union for Democratic Action in 1941, which became the Americans for Democratic Action in January 1947.

ADA, called the New Deal-in-exile, included Eleanor Roosevelt, Dave Dubinsky, Walter Reuther, Joseph Rauh, Jr. ("Mr. ADA"), Marquis Childs, James Loeb, Jr., James Wechsler, Dr. Reinhold Niebuhr, Arthur M. Schlesinger, Jr., Senators (and maids-in-waiting) Herbert Lehman, Richard Neuberger, Frank Graham, Hubert Humphrey, and Paul Douglas. The brothers Joseph and Stewart Alsop headed the alphabetical list of ADA charter members.[16]

The chain ran from Wilson-House-Brandeis during WW I years, on to the Paris Peace Conference, where a handful of

Socialist intellectuals and foreign-born radicals were the only "Americans" who wanted any part of International Government. This was the first attempt by Fabian Socialists to penetrate and permeate the executive branch of the US Government and it failed, says Martin. Colonel House was the leader, supported by the likes of the youthful trio, Walter Lippmann, Felix Frankfurter and Franklin Delano Roosevelt.

Other young men of "insider" standing were also present; they would subvert the Constitution at a later date: John Foster and Allen Dulles, Robert Lansing, Christian Herter. House arranged a dinner meeting at the Hotel Majestic on 19 May 1919, with a select group of Britons – notably Arnold Toynbee, R.H. Tawney and John Maynard Keynes. From this small gathering sprang an organization with branches in England and America "to facilitate the scientific study of international questions." Martin reveals:

> Two potent and closely related opinion-making bodies were founded which only began to reach their full growth in the nineteen-forties, coincident with the formation of the Fabian International Bureau. The English branch was called the Royal Institute of International Affairs. The American branch, first known as the Institute of International Affairs, was reorganized in 1921 as the Council on Foreign Relations.[17]

William Yandell Elliott, a young US army artillery officer with Pershing in France in 1918, went to Oxford immediately thereafter as a Rhodes scholar. In 1921, he became a member of the CFR. He went on to head the government department at Harvard, write several books, serve as an advisor to presidents, become a member of the Business Council and be one of three men who are credited with "inventing" Henry Kissinger (Kraemer, Elliott, Rockefeller).

Which brings us rather speedily to the present and to other links of the chain which will bind us to one-world socialism, namely Henry Kissinger and his associates; and the Arkansas Traveler, Governor Bill Clinton, member in good standing of the CFR and of the Trilateral Commission.

The chain remains unbroken.

PART TWO
NEW COVENANT = NEW WORLD ORDER

WHAT were Bill and Hillary Clinton and their many Bolshevik handlers really up to in forging the New Covenant? The answer is, to establish Fascism with a friendly face here in the United States. To bring it off, Clinton and his PR people decided to show the public the "deep inner spirituality" of this man. Let's take a look at this new image and then look behind the image to the real evil design hiding behind that facade.

Time magazine, one of the media empire's many ardent supporters of Bill Clinton and his presidential campaign did some image-building in its 5 Apr 1993 issue. On the cover is (gasp) a cross, which is the symbol of Christianity. A closer inspection shows that the photos inset on that cross are anything but Christian, however; still, they aptly depict what has happened to an entire generation since a conscious program was introduced here in the United States in 1948 to destroy Christianity once and for all.

The bold-face print on the cover, at the side of the cross, proclaims "THE GENERATION THAT FORGOT GOD: The Baby Boom goes back to church, and church will never be the same."

Considering that Easter was fast approaching when the issue came out, the article was certainly timely. Notice the accompanying article (pp 49-51), *Clinton's Spiritual Journey*: "The President's religious life defies both his political temperament and the habits of his generation."

Pricilla Painton did the story. It seems to fit the image of a Jimmy Carter more than a Billy Clinton, and perhaps it was designed to do just that. In her lead, and referring to baby boomers, she asks: "How many of them, if they were about to become President, would leave a black-tie party with Barbara Streisand to attend a midnight church service off-limit to cameras and reporters?"[18]

Good question, eh? It gets better. (We are now informed that Barbara and Bubba went for a roll in the hay in the Lincoln bedroom. They may or may not have indulged in some praying before, during or after the main event.)

> That Bill Clinton has been religious since childhood sets him apart from his peers – the legions who at midlife, are threshing about for spiritual moorings. Clinton from age 8 has possessed a conviction about his Baptist faith so private that he does not even share it with his [Methodist] wife.

Pricilla then includes a parenthetical "(In Little Rock they attended separate churches.)"[19]

She then quotes Clinton speaking on VISN, an inter-faith cable network, while campaigning:

> My faith tells me all of us are sinners, each of us is gone in our own way and fallen short of the glory of God, and that life's struggle is for sinners, not saints, for the weak, not the strong. Religious faith has permitted me to believe in the continuing possibility of becoming a better person every day, to believe in the search for complete integrity in life.[20]

Halleluliah, brothers! And aaaaaamen! To a man that gave us the infanticide of partial-birth abortion.

Look more closely on the image of Clinton, sitting in the pew of a church, elbow resting on an adjacent arm, chin clutched in one hand, the other holding what appears to be a Bible, gazing pensively in the direction of an altar... or perhaps beyond... and in the background, the shadowed image of a cross and the out-of-focus image of his fellow worshippers, mostly blacks.

Here we have the Reverend Billy, a Leviathan; the reincarnation of Oliver Cromwell and the photo image for his "new covenant." A smaller pic is a continuation of the photo opportunity; Bill and Hillary exiting the church, Bill clutching the family Bible, a handsome black minister in the background.

Time magazine puffing another Billy with a Bible. Back in 1948 when Billy Graham was a struggling young tent preacher in the South, it was Henry Luce, owner of Time-Life, who put out the word, "puff up Graham." Without casting aspersions at all on the

Reverend Billy Graham, over time he became the Protestant Pope to a host of American heads of state.

Back to the Reverend Billy Clinton and Pricilla's fine piece of puffery. She concludes:

> He prays with Chelsea at her bedtime on the nights when he is home, and on past occasions, when he and Hillary could not get to church, the family held its own devotional. He has said that in recent years, he and Hillary, a devout Methodist who carried Scriptures on the campaign trail, had increasingly long conversations about how to live an honorable life and the nature of life after death.
>
> On the day after Christmas, at a gathering in Staley's home of Little Rock preachers, Clinton let on that he harbored some pastoral ambitions in the Oval Office. One of the guests handed him a plaque with the verses from Psalms describing how God presented David to his people as their shepherd and 'David cared for them with a true heart and a skillful hand.'
>
> Visibly moved, he replied, 'That's what I want to be.'[21]

Doesn't that kind of grab you?

Here is an appropriate excerpt from a fine editorial in the *Richmond Times-Dispatch* (12 Apr 93) headed simply *Power*. It ends with this weighty thought:

> Consider it just a friendly reminder that regardless of party or ideology or even system, the ultimate political questions have not changed since the ancients first began meditating on the civil society. Politics is about power and who wields it.[22]

NEW COVENANT = NEW PARADIGM

The Clinton Administration was bankrupt, morally, financially and historically. Solzenhenitsyn's words of 1975 ring truer today than at any time in the fleeting history of the 80 years of Bolshevist/Zionist domination:

> ...How will the West be able to withstand the unprecedented force of totalitarianism? That is the problem.... I wouldn't be surprised at the sudden and imminent fall of the West.... One must think of what might happen unexpectedly in the West. The West is on the verge of a collapse created by its own hands.... Nuclear war is not even necessary to the Soviet Union. You can be taken simply with bare hands....[23]

To put a proper handle on what Clinton is designing for us under his special brand of New Age doublespeak; e.g., "microenterprises" and "empowerment" and "new covenant" and "new choices" and "new paradigm," one must have a closer look at an organization set up in 1985 to combat Reagan's rise to popularity and relative success as a leader.

The Democratic Leadership Council had its roots in the South. Its founders included Governor Bill Clinton of Arkansas, Senator Al Gore of Tennessee, Senators Sam Nunn of Georgia, Lloyd Bensen of Texas and Chuck Robb of Virginia, as well as Rep. Dick Gephardt of Missouri and Bruce Babbitt, former Arizona Governor.

Clinton was chairman of this group in 1991, when he declared for the Presidency. A quick check will reveal that he "empowered" many of his colleagues under the "new Paradigm" of his Administration. However, a more detailed check will reveal that most of the real power within the various cabinet offices resides in ADL and Wall Street assets, strategically placed in the Number Two slots and then scattered selectively throughout State, Commerce, Labor, Budget, Justice, IRS, CIA and, in fact, most bureaucracies, especially Defense, once an impenetrable citadel of force, integrity and true patriotism.

There are other ways to beard the lion in his den; hence, the budget cuts for defense, the troop cuts and base closings started by Bush, and increased emphasis on the role of radicfems and queers in the military, designed with but one thought in mind... to weaken the innate strength of a unified (and manly) military force; i.e., to divide and conquer. The farce of the Tailhook fanny grabbers is but one facet in the drama of weakening and belittling the military. Bill Clinton and others of his ilk caused more than a few Flag Officer heads to roll for that convention caper.

James Webb, a former Marine, and Assistant Secretary of the Navy under Reagan, writes knowledgeably about a political witch-hunt: "Spineless Navy Officials Repudiate 'Loyalty Down.'" It's the feminist thing again – outraged female screaming for justice because some drunken pilot patted her fanny in public at their annual brawl. Webb states that the Tailhook scandal has been "spun up," to borrow a service phrase, into a crisis that affects the Navy leadership's credibility on a wide range of issues. He singles out the acting Navy Secretary, Sean O'Keefe, a budgeteer who has never known military service. O'Keefe, after conferring with Defense Secretary Dick Cheney, who likewise had never served, decided he had the moral authority to "discredit the cultural ethos of the entire Navy based on the conduct of a group of drunken aviators in a hotel suite."[24]

Webb's key point is his statement:

> Today at the highest levels of the US military, one searches vainly for a leader who deserves mention along with the giants of the past. Those who might have reached such heights failed the 'political correctness' test and were retired as colonels or junior flag officers.[25]

He points out that to gain a star involves hitching your wagon to a political star. "Our ranking admirals have learned full well to bob and weave when political issues confront them. And few issues are as volatile as those surrounding the assimilation of women into the military – particularly since ardent feminists have focused on the military as an important symbolic battlefield."[26]

Webb's point is that "with the reputations, credibility and even the missions of their people at risk, the senior admirals have either hidden or demurred. In the process, they have abandoned their most sacred fiduciary duty. In military terms it is called "loyalty down."

> Its abrogation has meant doing nothing as civilian officials condemn their subordinates en masse without rebuttal. It has meant allowing a few junior admirals to be 'taken out back and shot', as one Pentagon officer put it to me, while they carefully avoid public comment.[27]

Who will sound the trumpet?

Keep it in mind that Bill Clinton and his new paradigm/new covenant bunch, especially the Wall Street money-changers, hate and fear the military. It is the one force that could undo them. That is perhaps one of the reasons why we have combat forces located in over 120 countries about the world, and have simultaneously allowed within the gates combat forces from eleven UN countries about the world. You don't have to be a military G2 (intelligence officer) to get the picture.

Another larger diversionary task for the military is the extension of brush-fire wars and foreign adventures, so that the patriotic commanders who see the internal danger of our Constitution and our very way of life being eroded on a daily basis will be caught up in "tactical exercises" in the Middle East, in the Balkans and in Africa; and perhaps soon – once more in Korea.

The DLC, through the machinations of its think-tank, the Progressive Policy Institute, has in fact abandoned the so-called middle class and is bringing into the fold an association of financiers, lawyers, accountants, economists, stockbrokers and arbitrageurs who have made vast fortunes under the Reagan business expansion, the Carter deregulations and the Volcker-Greenspan money manipulations.

These parasites and speculators have replaced our once world-class industrial society with a "service" economy which is designed with but one purpose in mind: to destroy the middle class by job destruction, by excessive taxation and debt, and by creation of a closely-held system of monopoly capitalism wherein not only is the federal government all-powerful, but it is in actual partnership with the multi-nationals and the international financiers.

This post-industrial transition to a service-sector economy is in fact Fascism, and it was Bill Clinton himself who tried to mask it with a friendly face. Look back to the DLC convention in 1991, when Clinton was still the chairman. The theme of that gathering was "The New American Choice: Opportunity, Responsibility, Community."

In the statement of their goal, they harked back to the New Dealers of the Rooseveltian era, who were also Fascists:

> Our goal is to make the beliefs, ideas and governing approaches of the New American Choice the dominant political thinking in America before this decade is out.

> Just as the New Deal shaped the political order for the Industrial Age, the New American Choice can define politics in the Information Age.[28]

That program concluded: "the industrial age is over; the old isms and the old ways don't work anymore."[29]

So, what will work?

Call it Fascism, but with a friendly face. If Time and other media can convince the gullible public that Bible-toting Billy really cares about them, and that Hillary really cares about them and their health and diets and recreational pursuits; and then convinces them that for this Big Brotherly caring they in turn must make "sacrifices," we will find ourselves in the Year 2000 in the harshest austerity program ever levied upon the American people.

Looking through back issues of the DLC magazine, *New Democrat,* one is struck by the number of articles pertaining to austerity and the little likelihood that we will experience any economic growth under a Clinton regime. Articles like "Forging a New Social Contract" and "Brave New Economic World" by such Clinton advisers as Robert Shapiro and Al From, or "The Welfare Wars" by Elaine Kamarck, point toward what Thomas Hobbes called "the kingdom of darkness" in his *Leviathan: Defense of Absolute Monarchy.*[30]

We are in for a period of the long, long night and the sharp knives of a peculiar collection of International Zionists, call them Barbarians, that does not bode well at all for middle class Americans.

That group of intense economists whose every waking hour is geared toward the making of money by speculation rather than production, by usury rather than investment, by free trade rather than by protecting what little industry left in the US.

Many of the Clinton crowd attended Oxford University or the London School of Economics. They are well versed in the writings of Hobbes and of John Locke. According to Hobbes, the fundamental law of nature of every man is to seek peace; and when he cannot obtain it, to use all means to defend himself. The second

law of nature is to be content with as much liberty against other
men as he would allow other men against himself, which is the law
of the Gospel; in Latin, *quod tibi fieri non vis, alteri ne feceris*
(What you would not have done to you, do not do to others.)[31]

Hobbes stressed that sovereign power should be absolute,
"whether placed in one man, or in one assembly of men.... And
though of so unlimited a power men may fancy many evil
consequences, yet the consequences of the want of it, which is
perpetual war of every man against his neighbor, are much
worse."[32]

Do you see what is now so plain – the eternal threat and
promise? It came at us (the goyim) as early as the first books of
the Babylonian Talmud; and still later into the agreement between
Rabbi Manasseh-Ben Israel and Oliver Cromwell; and still later,
through Weishaupt's *Illuminati*, to be embodied in the French
Revolution; and again in the Russian Revolution. It was encoded
for posterity (which is us) in Professor Sergei Nilus' "Blueprint for
Conquest." It hung as a dark shadow over FDR and his New Deal,
over Yalta and other manipulated conferences involving those
three despotic powers of which Einstein speaks so eloquently. It
contains both the threat and the promise embodied in its myriad
statutes and judgments.

Thomas Hobbes, the religious conscience behind Oliver
Cromwell, saw this clearly. He wrote in his solemn tome *Leviathan*
the following:

> The school of the Jews was originally a school of the law of
> Moses, who commanded (Deut. 31:10) that at the end of every seventh
> year, at the Feast of the Tabernacles, it should be read to all the people,
> that they might hear and learn it....
>
> It is manifest by the many reprehensions of them by our Savior,
> that they corrupted the text of the law with their false commentaries and
> vain traditions, and so little understood the prophets that they did neither
> acknowledge Christ nor the works that he did, of which the people
> prophesied.
>
> So that by their lectures and disputations in their synagogues
> they turned the doctrine of their law into a fantastical kind of philosophy
> (embodied in the Talmud) concerning the incomprehensible nature of

God and spirits, which they compounded of the vain philosophy and theology of the Grecians, mingled with their own fancies drawn from the obscurer places of the Scripture, and which might easily be wrested to their purpose; and from the fabulous traditions of their ancestors.[33]

A Leviathan is a monster of huge size which might very well be the Bicephalous Monster. Hobbes saw it as an artificial animal and a mortal god constructed by the "covenants of men in the interests of security, justice and peace."

President Bill Clinton carrying out his New Covenant emerged as the "Leviathan" in the 1990s. He and his many Talmudic handlers fast turned "the doctrine of their law into a fantastical kind of philosophy" which gave us brutal Fascism with a friendly face.

Hobbes' work combined the details of psychology with the invective against what he called "the kingdom of darkness." He might well have been writing about the Clinton Administration with its plethora of statutes and judgments and its eternal threat and promise.

Clinton's "new covenant" loomed over us as a black shroud which slowly enveloped and smothered us.... Look, look, up in the sky...is it a bird...is it a plane.... No, it's Hillary's black bloomers emblazoned with "change" and "sacrifice" and "PC."

Friends, there's a pair of knickers we don't want to get into... at any cost, for that's the very gal who displayed on her mantelpiece – in the Oval Office, yet – our collective white, Anglo- Saxon *cojones* in a glass jar of formaldehyde.

The Clinton Crowd let loose the Leviathan in the 1990s. That monster smashed the economy, created a totally oppressive police state, encouraged a drug-induced hedonism and unlimited sexual gratification, and perpetrated obscene acts of terror against its citizens, controlling it all through federal goon squads under their social contract, the New Covenant.

SELECTING A "NEW COVENANT" PREZ

TIME: 17 March 1986

PLACE: Camp Robinson, near Little Rock, Arkansas

EVENT: Taking out a "Second Mortgage"

PLAYERS: Gov. Bill Clinton, William P. Barr (who would be President George Bush's attorney general two years later), Terry Reed, Oliver North, plus two unidentified CIA agents[34]

This sets the scene for treason. Read Terry Reed's explosive exposé, *Compromised,* for greater detail of this and other events leading up to placing an arch-criminal and traitor in the Oval Office – the highest office in the land. A quick scan of the preceding chapters of *Barbarians* will reveal that this was not an unique event in the process of presidential selection; only the nature of the "Second Mortgage" (blackmail) was perhaps unique, in that it involved the wholesale drug-running and money-laundering operation centered at Mena, Arkansas. Both Vice President Bush and Governor Clinton were key players in this illicit and criminal operation, code named "Centaur Rose" and "Jade Bridge" by President Reagan's CIA director, Bill Casey.

The reason for the hush-hush meeting in a musty, poorly-lit World War II ammunition bunker at Camp Robinson was that William Barr had been selected by the fearful masters to break the bad news to Clinton that the illegal drug-smuggling operation was being relocated from Mena, Arkansas to Mexico (under the code name "Operation Screw Worm").[35]

Reed explains that Bill and his friends (including Vince Foster) "just couldn't resist putting Arkansas' hand deeper into the till than they were supposed to." From other sources – including Mossad agent, Mike Harare, Arkansas "businessman" Dan Lasater, and chief smuggling pilot Barry Seal – we learn that Clinton's cut was 10%.

Here are excerpts from the heated exchange in the bunker:

Barr: "The deal we made was to launder our money through your bond business. What we didn't plan on was you... shrinking our laundry.... That's why we're pulling the operation out of

Arkansas. It's become a liability for us. We don't need live liabilities."

Clinton: "What do ya' mean, live liabilities?"

Barr: "There's no such thing as a dead liability. It's an oxymoron, get it? Or didn't you Rhodes Scholars study things like that?"

Clinton: "What! Are you threatenin' us? Because if you are...."

Barr (concluding the exchange): "You and your state have been our greatest asset. The beauty of this, as you know, is that you're a Democrat and with our ability to influence both parties, this country can get beyond partisan gridlock. Mr. Casey wanted me to pass on to you that unless you ---- off and do something stupid, you're No. 1 on the short list for a shot at the job you've always wanted. That's pretty heady stuff, Bill! So why don't you help us keep a lid on this and we'll all be promoted together. You and guys like us are the 'fathers of the new government'. Hell, we're the 'new covenant.'" [36]

By the time of the meeting in the bunker in 1986, the then Governor Bill Clinton was a full-blown "Clear Eyes" operative of his CIA handlers, having passed through Level 4 of the mind control procedures. He no longer differentiated between right and wrong. His moral code, respect for the law, and fear of dying had been replaced with new "superhuman" feelings; he was now beyond all human laws. In the several years of his association with the CIA, an "agenda overlay" had been "overwritten" onto his personality. He was now a "mortal god."

Bill Clinton had a lot going for him – size, good looks, pleasing personality, and an IQ of 136, which helped get him a Rhodes scholarship. This combination helped immensely in elevating him to the governor's mansion in Arkansas. The supreme test for this "Clear Eyes" operative was the business of running drugs and laundering money through Mena. The fact that he and his fellow Arkansas Travelers became excessively greedy was probably a further point in his favor, for his NWO handlers envisioned that when they placed him in the highest office of the land, he would bring about the destruction of the sovereignty of the United States, in order to place it under the total control of the UN.

Bill Clinton had many of the attributes of the youthful John Fitzgerald Kennedy. As President, JFK was also slated to deliver up the sovereignty of the US to the NWO crowd. He had been surrounded by loyal CFR members as advisers and cabinet members, who were programmed to steer him into another no-win war in SE Asia, and then, through a series of deliberate confrontations with the Soviets, to bring about world disarmament.

JFK balked. He went up against the NWO crowd, and was duly terminated in November 1963. He did issue an Executive Order in 1962 that started the wheels of world disarmament turning. This doctrine is known as State Department Publication #7277, which calls for unilateral US disarmament, not only of the US military, but of all its citizens. One only need read the Second Amendment to grasp the importance of this measure, for a global government can only be brought into existence after the shredding of our constitution upon which hangs our national sovereignty. An armed – and suitably outraged – citizenry would prevent this from occurring.

TEMPUS FUGIT
Time Flies

The next overt move to place Bill Clinton in the White House took place in June of 1991. At that time, his quasi-adviser, Vernon Jordan, escorted him to Baden-Baden, Germany where he was presented as the heir-apparent to the Oval Office to the Bilderbergers – the wealthy elite of Europe and the United States – gathered there for their annual top-secret conclave. Bill made his pitch, which was obviously well received, but the price, was the guaranteed surrender of the sovereignty of the United States of America to the UN's New World Order.

At that meeting, David Rockefeller addressed the assembly:

> We are grateful to the *Washington Post*, the *New York Times*, *Times Magazine* and other great publications whose directors have

attended our meetings and respected their promises of discretion for almost forty years.

He went on to explain:

> It would have been impossible for us to develop our plan for the world if we had been subjected to the lights of publicity during those years. But, the world is more sophisticated and prepared to march toward a world government. The supernational sovereignty of an intellectual elite and world bankers is surely preferable to the national autodetermination practiced in past centuries.

President George Herbert Walker Bush had loudly trumpeted the merits of a new world order during his "victorious" war over Saddem Hussein; it wasn't enough. He saw the shadows on the wall and graciously ran a limp-wristed, lackluster campaign for a second term. Helped by a willing third-party candidate, Ross Perot, Bill Clinton won big, with 43% of the votes in the election of November 1992. He and his co-president, Hillary Rodham, launched their sovereignty-destroying program on several fronts in 1993, not the least by a series of enactments to wound the military fatally, in order to destroy its one and only mission of defending the Constitution against all enemies, foreign and domestic.

William Jefferson Clinton, in a manner entirely different from JFK, didn't measure up. Where JFK had balked, Bill Clinton reverted to type and became excessively greedy, to the point of willfully committing acts of treason. The hierarchy decided that he had to go. In August 1996, Sen. Ted Kennedy, along with Robert Strauss and a delegation of top Democrats, paid a social call on the president. They told him to step down.

> In a 'purple fit rage', Clinton told them to 'stick it'. Afterwards, Clinton sent a message to prosecutor, Kenneth Starr, with a clear implication as follows: 'If you indict Hillary or me, you will end up like Vince Foster or Ron Brown'.[37]

It is patently obvious that Clinton knew he could make such a statement and get away with it because of the power elite behind him, those who were directly responsible for getting him elected to the presidency in 1992. He was correct in his surmise, for that same power elite got him elected to a second term three months later.

PART THREE
CLINTON COVENANT – ANTI-CHRISTIAN

THAT very same ethnic group that bolshevized the Slavic Russians brought a slower, more palatable slavery to the peoples of the United States via the New Deal, the Fair Deal, the Great Society and New Covenant; or, as White House special adviser Sidney Blumenthal phrased it in a speech to the John F Kennedy School of Government at Harvard on 23 Apr 1998:

> The goal is to create a new social contract [New Covenant] for a global economy... in which civil society, social harmony, and public safety are restored, and in which multi-cultural people can forge a common identity.[38]

In that same stirring speech, Blumenthal said, "If there is a name for the Clinton approach, it is this: one-nation politics."[41]

What Bill Clinton, Hillary Rodham and their court hangers-on established in the 1990s was in fact Fascism as practiced by several nations in the 1930s.

We seem to forget, perhaps because we would rather not remember, that Mussolini, Hitler and Roosevelt were as much Marxist "socialists" as Lenin and Stalin; they were actually "gentler" in their implementation of it.

In fact, Red is not dead, nor even dormant. It is alive and well and has only, like the chameleon, changed its color and shape somewhat, as well as its name.

We call this strategic deception; and, yes, it is lying, but as Sophocles taught us, if truth might mean tremendous ruin, to lie is pardonable.

BOLSHEVISM IS ALIVE AND WELL

The bloody footprints of the Bolsheviks mark a treacherous path through recent history, from the 1917 invasion of Russia down to the here and now in the United States of America. A very few writers and historians have been able to trace those tracks by way of our closely held intelligence. Much, if not most, of the reach of the clammy hand of communism has been suppressed in our mainline media, simply because the Bolsheviks control 95% of that same media and use it to their own end, which continues to be world despotic dominion with themselves in charge.

Whittaker Chambers finally witnessed the absolute evil of Bolshevism and the designs (and people) behind it, and crossed over to the side of freedom, liberty and Christianity. Others have written in detail about those diabolical evils they witnessed first-hand. In the process, they have corroborated those data and facts known right along by a very few astute readers, and yet, their writings also have been suppressed.

We get a clue to those seeking "world despotic dominion," as opposed to those on the side of "freedom, liberty and Christianity," in a witty and pointed commentary by the editor-in-chief of the *Washington Times,* Wesley Pruden, appropriately headed "The Runaway Bigots in the White House" (8 May 1998). Here it is in part:

> You can find Bill Clinton nearly every Sunday morning on the steps of the church, waiting for the photographers, one hand in Hillary's and the other clutching the biggest Bible he can find.... In his desperation to salvage what's left of his presidency, nothing is off limits, nothing is over the line....
>
> The president's mad dogs, contemptuous as they may be of anyone who wears the military uniform, nevertheless look to old Tecumseh Sherman for their inspiration. 'I can make the march and I can make Georgia howl,' he told an admiring Lincoln in 1864 on the eve of his infamous march from Atlanta to the sea. 'I propose to kill even the puppies, because puppies grow up to be Southern dogs.'
>
> This would become the order of battle for a White House 130 years later: burn everything to the ground and plow up the ashes.
>
> When Sidney Blumenthal and the demented James Carville were loosed on Kenneth Starr and Hick Ewing, proposing to mock and jeer at their evangelical Christianity, the president gave them no caution about observing the decencies and restraint that guide the rest of us....[39]

It was Blumenthal who referred to Hick Ewing (Starr's deputy) as a "religious fanatic" because he admits that he prays for divine guidance.

"RELIGIOUS FANATICS" ATTEND STATE DINNER

"I didn't know there were that many Jews in Washington," a high-level military officer remarked to his colleagues on the morning after a gala state dinner which he and his wife had attended. President Clinton was honoring the president of Hungary, Arpad Goncz. According to the *Washington Times* (9 Jun 1999), the 180 dinner guests were entertained by performances celebrating the folk cultures of Hungary and the United States. Singer Judy Collins, the evening's featured entertainer, sang "Chelsea Morning," a song that inspired the name of the president's daughter. "Actor Tony Curtis, author Kitty Kelley, Nobel laureate Elie Weisel and fashion designer Adrienne Vittadni peppered an eclectic guest list."[40]

One of the general's horse-holders checked out the guest list and verified that over half the attendees were indeed Jewish. "Washington, under Bill Clinton, has become the new Jerusalem," he said. A quick check of the list reveals that the writer who calls herself Kitty Kelley was accompanied by Jonathon Zucker. Susan Sontag was there with another writer, David Rieff; other writers included E. L. and Helen S. Doctorow. To make the evening truly eclectic, the political crowd included such notables as Charlene Barshefsky, with Edward B. Cohen. William S. Cohen was present, with his wife, Janet Longhart Cohen (who is not Jewish). California was well represented by Rep. Tom Lantos and his wife, Annette, as well as Rep. Ellen Touscher and her friend, Sally Bender.

To be sure, many of the guests were Hungarian, not only those who accompanied their president, but several who now reside in the US after fleeing Hungary in 1956.

And therein lies the tragedy, for Hungary, a predominantly Catholic country, has been conquered not once but twice by the Bolsheviks. Perhaps the state dinner, hosted by Bill and Hillary

Clinton, is the prelude for the third time, for Hungary is situated at a most critical crossroads, as regards the destruction and vengeance currently being visited on the Christian Orthodox Serbs.

A very brief history of Hungary is in order. The early settlers, chiefly Slav and Germanic, were overrun by the Magyars from the East in 975, and by the Turks in the 15th-17th centuries. After the defeat of the Turks in 1697, Austria dominated. Defeated with the Central Powers in 1918, Hungary lost territory, including Croatia, to Yugoslavia. A Bolshevist (say Jewish) revolt under Bela Kuhn (Cohen) was routed in 1919, and a monarchy was established in 1920.

Hungary joined Germany in World War II and was overrun by the Soviets in 1945. A republic was declared in 1946, but the Communists forced the elected president out in 1947. Emre Nagy, a moderate, became premier in 1953, but was replaced by another Communist, Erno Gero, who, in turn, was dumped and replaced by Matyas Rakosi.[41]

An astounding fact is that both Gero and Rakosi had originally come with Bela Kuhn from Soviet Russia to introduce the Bolshevik terror to the Hungarians in 1919. Driven out, the two of them returned after World War II as key men in the Communist secret police system in Budapest. Following the Rakosi takeover, *Time* (Nov 1953) wrote of "...the strongly Jewish government of Communist Hungary under Communist Premier Matyas Rakosi, who is himself a Jew." The *New York Herald-Tribune* stated that same month that "Rumania, together with Hungary, probably has the greatest number of Jews in the administration."

Of this time of terror and tribulation, the British author, Douglas Reed, wrote in his seminal work, *The Controversy of Zion,* "The case of Hungary was more significant [than that of Poland], for this country after 1945 endured its second experience of Communist rule. It not only found the terror to be Jewish again, but it was wielded by the same men. This deliberate installment of Jewish terrorists detested by a nation for their deeds of 26 years before is the strongest evidence yet provided of the existence in

Moscow of a power, controlling the revolution, which deliberately gives its savageries the Talmudic signature, not the Soviet, Communist or Russian one."[42]

Emre Nagy was restored as premier in 1956. In October, demonstrations against the Bolsheviks turned into open revolt. On 4 Nov 1956, Khruschev (Perlmutter) launched a massive attack against Budapest, with 200,000 Soviet troops and 2,500 tanks.

More than 200,000 Hungarians fled the country, Nagy was killed, and thousands were arrested, most of them being freed in 1963 by the regime. In 1968, Hungarian troops participated in the Warsaw Pact invasion of Czechoslovakia. In 1989 Parliament passed legislation legalizing freedom of assembly. As Hungary shifted away from communism, the Communist party was formally dissolved, and a parliamentary democracy was established, with Arpad Goncz being appointed president in 1990. The last of the Soviet troops left Hungary in 1991.[43]

That delightful state dinner honoring President Goncz just might be the precursor of another occupation, this time by the peacekeepers of NATO, of which Hungary is now a part, having formally become a member early in 1999. Bear in mind that in each of these historic events – including Bill and Hillary's state dinner – a "hidden hand" has been surreptitiously active, manipulating the tenuous strings from which dangle an assortment of political/ economic/military puppets.

A *Washington Post* article (19 Jun 99) reported, "A flier calling for an end to the North Atlantic Terrorist Organization was uncovered at Knesset Israel (synagogue) by a local television station." In part, the pamphlet read:

> The ugly American and NATO aggressors are the ultimate hypocrites. The fake Albanian refugee crisis was manufactured by the International Jewsmedia to justify the terrorizing, the bestial bombing of our Yugoslavia back into the dark ages. We are Slavs, we will never allow the international Jew World order to take our Land. We fight to keep Serbia free forever.[44]

There is certainly an historic connection between the Christian Slavs of Serbia and Hungary. Could it also be possible that the Bolsheviks continue to play a key role in their ongoing destabilization? Let's focus on the fact that in this chapter, we are addressing a New Covenant of destruction and vengeance on the part of a people who have chosen to live apart – and by their own code of laws – from the rest of mankind. For the past 2,000 years, these people apart have used the psychological techniques of mocking and jeering (and scourging) against those "religious fanatics," the Christians. Generally, the mocking and jeering have been preludes for other, more bloody tactics, often resulting in open warfare, but usually staged in such a way that Christian countries end up fighting and killing each other. Those wars in this century have become unbelievably bloody and destructive.

And so it will continue to be, if the Barbarian within leads us once more into the breach – in essence, World War III.

PART FOUR
ZIONISTS CONTROL CLINTONS/GORE

IPS INFILTRATES AGENCIES

IN September 1993, President Clinton nominated Morton Halperin to be the Assistant Secretary of Defense for Democracy and Peacekeeping. Knowing this man's background as a subversive (as had been his father before him), this author prepared a paper on him and the Institute for Policy Studies (IPS), which he shared with the then national commander of the American Legion, Bruce Thiesen, who sent it to his National Legislative Commission staff in Washington DC. This author joined forces with that powerful group in early January 1994 and personally contacted key Senators of the Senate Armed Services Committee, including the chairman, Sam Nunn. By late February, our combined efforts paid off. Sam Nunn announced on 30 March 1994 that Halperin's nomination was returned to the Executive Branch at the end of the first session of the 103rd Congress and that subsequently Halperin requested that his name not be resubmitted. Clinton was happy to comply, but later that year placed Halperin in a slot within his National Security office in the White House (which needed no Senate confirmation) to function as an assistant for democracy and peacekeeping.

As was mentioned in Chapter 1, John McNaughton, his wife and youngest son were killed in an air accident when their commercial 727 was struck over North Carolina by a private twin-engine aircraft (19 Jul 1967). McNaughton had been the Assistant Secretary of Defense for International Security Affairs (ISA). He was replaced as head of ISA by Paul Warnke, a member of the Marxist/Leninist IPS, who immediately brought on board one of his IPS comrades, Morton Halperin, on a temporary basis. Even then, there were extensive FBI files on, not only Halperin, but other IPS members who had infiltrated into key agencies of the federal government. None could pass a background investigation.

This trend continued and expanded exponentially under the administration of Bill Clinton. (See *Unlimited Access* by Gary Aldrich.)

As we will shortly discover, several of these IPS "comrades" were close personal friends of both Bill and Hillary Clinton, and were not only members of the subversive IPS, but also belonged to the Clintons' exclusive club, the Council on Foreign Relations (CFR), which is dedicated to global government.

We will also discover that Vice President Al Gore (CFR) has had close personal ties to IPS members, and especially to its financial backers.

BACKGROUND: INSTITUTE FOR POLICY STUDIES

Dr. John Coleman, an intelligence officer, issued a warning as early as 1969 that IPS affiliates had penetrated the federal government. He stated in his book, *Conspirator's Hierarchy: The Story of the Committee of 300,* that IPS had shaped and reshaped United States policies, foreign and domestic, since it was founded by James P. Warburg and the Rothschild entities after World War II. They were bolstered by Bertrand Russell and the British Fabian Socialists through its networks in America which included the League for Industrial Democracy in which Leonard Woodcock played a leading behind-the-scenes role. Locals included "conservative" Jeane Kirkpatrick, Irwin Suall of the ADL, Eugene Rostow, Lane Kirkland and Albert Shanker.[45]

For record purposes, IPS was founded in 1963 by Marcus Raskin and Richard J. Barnet. Over the years, it has been financed by the Samuel Rubin Foundation, controlled by Samuel Rubin's daughter, Cora, and her husband, Peter Weiss. Rubin had been a member of Lenin's Comintern, but resided in the United States. With financial help from Armand Hammer, whose father, Julius, founded the Communist Party in the US and had also been a trusted friend of both Lenin and Stalin, Rubin launched a cosmetics business, Faberge, which made him immensely wealthy. In concert with Armand Hammer, they used their wealth to spread Bolshevism throughout the country.

The objectives of IPS came from an agenda laid down for it by the British Round Table, which agenda in turn came from the Tavistock Institute, one of the most notable being to create the "New Left" as a grass-roots movement in the US. The IPS was to engender strife and unrest, and spread chaos like a wildfire out of control, proliferate the "ideals" of left-wing nihilist socialism, support unrestricted use of drugs of all types, and be the "big stick" with which to beat the United States political establishment....

Through its many lobbying groups on Capitol Hill, IPS relentlessly used its "big stick" to beat Congress. IPS has a network of lobbyists, all supposedly operating independently, but in actual fact operating cohesively, so that members of Congress are pummeled from all sides by seemingly different and varied lobbyists. In this way IPS was, and still is, able to successfully sway individual representatives and senators to vote for "the trend – the way things are going." By using key pointmen on Capitol Hill, IPS was able to break into the very infrastructure of our legislative system....[46]

Dr. S. Steven Powell, in his 1987 work, *Covert Cadre: Inside the Institute for Policy Studies,* describes IPS as a "violence-prone group of extremists intent on changing America into a Marxist-socialist society by dismantling the capitalist economic order and reshaping public-sector institutions in ways that give the Left political power thus far denied by the electoral process." In an interview with Dr. Powell in 1983, Robert Borosage, the IPS director, stated that the IPS hoped to move the Democratic Party's debate internally to the left by creating an invisible presence in the party.[47]

LIMBAUGH WARNS OF IPS INFLUENCE

Years before Bill and Hillary Clinton became co-presidents of these United States; they were forming lasting friendships with a varied group of IPS stalwarts. The talk-radio entertainer, Rush Limbaugh, in his newsletter of November 1992, warned his reading public that Clinton had appointed IPS veteran Derek Shearer as his top economic adviser. Limbaugh added that: "Shearer, who is about as leftist as they come, is one of Clinton's closest and cleverest friends."

Derek's second wife, Ruth Yannatta-Goldway, was mayor of Santa Monica, California from 1981-1983. His sister, Brooke, would become Hillary's traveling companion. Their half-brother, Strobe Talbott, who was Bill Clinton's great friend and roommate at Oxford University, would be appointed ambassador to Russia by Clinton and then the Deputy Secretary of State. He can occasionally be glimpsed peeping behind the voluminous skirts of his boss, "Battlin' Madeleine" Albright.

Just prior to Clinton's election in November 1992, Frederick Rose of the *Wall Street Journal* wrote:

> 'Derek is a very old and close friend of Bill Clinton's, and among the advisors he is probably one of the oldest and closest friends,' says Mr. Altman, an investment banker and vice chairman of the Blackstone Group. Gov. Clinton's communications director, George Stephanopolous, calls Mr. Shearer both 'friend and advisor' to the governor, who has hosted the Clintons at his house near the beach.[48]

Shearer best exposed himself as a radical Marxist in his 1980 book, *Economic Democracy: The Challenge of the 1980s.* In it, he stated *inter alia* that "Marxists economic and social philosophy was and is an attempt to humanize economic and social life.... American visitors to China and Cuba... will attest to the austerity of life... yet, they also comment on the spirit of cooperativeness and well-being that pervades Chinese and Cuban life."

Shearer titled his book *Economic Democracy*, he says, because "I am a Socialist. When I speak about socialism people turn their backs to me, but when I substitute the words 'economic democracy' for 'socialism', people listen." Shearer further devulges how he, Clinton, Hillary, Robert Reich, Al Gore and company planned, upon taking the reigns of government, to supplant Ronald Reagan's Reaganomics (Professor Arthur Laffer's supply side economics) with a socialist agenda.

Hillary too has had a lengthy love affair with the IPS crowd, going back to her days as Hillary Rodham (Rodamski), law student at Yale, where she served on the board of editors of the quarterly *Yale Review of Law and Social Action*. The spring edition of 1970, which Hillary edited, featured an article by IPS Director Robert Borosage. A later edition, also edited by Hillary, urged sympathetic understanding of Black Panthers then on trial for murder.

As Director and Chair of the New World Foundation in 1987-88, Hillary praised several far-left organizations and awarded them significant sums of money. Among those notorious groups, which were labeled by the FBI as Communist fronts, was the National Lawyers Guild: Hillary awarded them $15,000. The Committee on Un-American Activities (House Report 3123 on the National Lawyers Guild, 21 Sep 1950) called the NLG "the foremost bulwark of the Communist Party [which] since its inception has never failed to rally to the legal defense of the Communist Party and individual members thereof, including known espionage agents."[49]

The NLG tie-in to IPS was through its chairman Peter Weiss, who served on the NLG's board of trustees. The then director of the NLG, Victor Rabinowitz, awarded sums of money to the IPS through the Rabinowitz Foundation.

These Bolshevik stalwarts were the closest and cleverest friends of both Bill and Hillary going back to at least 1970. They aided and abetted the meteoric rise of that infamous duo to, first, governor of the sovereign state of Arkansas; and then, to the highest office(s) of the land, the co-presidency of the once-sovereign nation, the United States of America. Many of the IPS dignitaries were rewarded with cabinet and advisory positions within the Clinton's inner circle of absolute power, among them, Leon Panetta, Les Aspin, Anthony Lake, Stephen Solarz, Timothy Wirth, Patricia Schroeder, Morton Halperin and Edward Feighan.

All of them – including Bill and Hillary, as well as their esteemed Vice President, Al Gore, Jr. – were also members in good standing of the CFR.

AMERICA – HAMMERED AND GORED

A blistering book about the vice president hit the market in 1999, titled *Gore: A Political Life,* written by Bob Zelnick, former senior ABC News correspondent. His masters at ABC warned him not to publish the book; he did, and was duly fired. Wow! What a book! In his prologue, Bob states in part that "however pure his private habits, Gore like Clinton, was also under investigation for possible crimes committed while in office." In some 250 pages, Zelnick lays out the stark and brutal facts why this man, as well as his immediate superior, Bill Clinton, should have been impeached.

Add to that work a startling monograph published in 1998 by a former AP reporter, Michael A. Hoffman II, "Hammered! The Inside Story of the Top Communist Operative Who Groomed Al Gore to Rule a Soviet America." Double wow!

Edward Jay Epstein in his book, *Dossier: The Secret History of Armand Hammer,* proclaimed Armand Hammer's political ascent was set in motion in 1922, when Lenin wrote a secret letter to Stalin designating Hammer as their official path to the resources of American capitalism. In this role as *homo sovieticus,* which was predicated on the idea that any means, no matter how ruthless or deceptive, was justified if it achieved the desired ends. To these ends, Hammer looked to Senator Alfred Gore of Tennessee. Vice President Al Gore, Bolshevik's designated president, now carries the baton. Al Gore's eldest daughter Karenna has even joined her dad's inner circle by marrying Andrew Schiff, descendant of Jacob Schiff, the Barbarian who, with $20 million of his own funds, financed Levi Braunstein (Trotsky) and Vladimir Ilich Blac Ulanyoff (Lenin) to initiate the 1917 Bolshevik Revolution in Russia.

Yes, Al Gore, Jr., was locked in to the same cabal of globalists that brought Bill and Hillary out of the Ozarks; to identical "Social Democrats" (say Bolsheviks); and to the same high-rolling financiers, namely, Samuel Rubin and Armand Hammer, both Russian émigrés, whose fathers were close associates of Lenin, and elite members of the *nomenklatura* and the *Comintern.*

It is to the latter – Armand Hammer – that Al Gore, Jr. owes his fortunes, both political and monetary. Suave and cunning corruption not only tainted the father – Al Gore, Sr. – as he allowed himself to become Hammer's chief insider in the Senate, but spread to the son like an inherited predisposition to an incurable disease – Spanish flu, aka *alta traicion....* Right, Bill? Right, Hillary? Right, Aaron?

Case in point, as covered by Larry Abraham in his *Insider Report* of Nov 1992 entitled, "How the Gores Got Greased":

> Over the past 20 years, Al Gore, Jr. has collected nearly half-a-million bucks in royalties on a zinc mine which didn't exist for 12 of those years. The Gore benefactor was none other than Lenin's personal bag-man to the US Communist party, Dr. Armand Hammer....
>
> In a deal put together back in 1973, the senior Gore, after losing his Senate seat, was virtually given 88 acres in Carthage, Tennessee, by Hammer, who was then chairman of Occidental Petroleum. The farm, originally purchased by Oxy, was sold to the Gores at well below market prices. Then Hammer arranged for Occidental to pay the Gores annual royalties of $227 an acre, while adjacent farms got $30 per acre. Al Jr. then 'bought' the property from his father, who subsequently went on Hammer's board of directors. The elder Gore was given stock options worth another half-million by Hammer: the senior Gore explains this cozy deal with America's most influential Red as being the result of their mutual interest in Angus cattle.[50]

In his well-documented paper, Hoffman states, "long before he reached the White House, Al Gore, Jr. had become Hammer's partner in subversion, just as his father had, opening doors and arranging contracts from his position as a member of the Senate Armed Services Committee. Congressional investigators have since discovered how well Vice President Al Gore, Jr. learned his lessons taught him by his Communist godfather, Armand Hammer. We now know that in 1996 Gore Jr. peddled White House influence to the Chinese Communists via the Israelis, in return for cash, making contact with Hammer's old allies in the highest echelon of the Chinese Communist Party."[51]

BEHOLD, THE ELDERS OF ZION!

Hoffman aptly describes how, late in life, Hammer launched his last major covert operation, code-named "Elders of Zion":

> This was a Jews-only enterprise. The principals were Hammer, Saul Eisenberg, Albert Reichmann (Canadian billionaire), Robert Maxwell (British billionaire, 'taken out' by the Mossad) and, strangely enough, Sen. Al Gore Jr., who is officially described by the establishment media as a gentile. Why would a supposed gentile be included in the 'Elders of Zion' operation which was intended to be directed only by Jews?[52]

The Elders of Zion operation had a two-fold purpose. It was another three-way secret split between and among Russia, the United States, and Israel, which promised to make that tiny Mideast country a major international aircraft manufacturer.

The second purpose was a campaign to cover up Jewish involvement in the Bolshevik Revolution and subsequent Soviet Communism; i.e., to transform the pivotal role-played by the Ashkenazi descendants of the Khazarian tribe as the major leaders of the Bolshevik Revolution, of the Soviet Cheka secret police under Iron Felix Dzurzinsky and of the Red army under Trotsky. The new image would depict the Jews as victims of Bolshevism and martyrs under the reign of Stalin.

Thus, the establishment in Moscow of the Solomon Mikhoels Jewish Cultural Center (1989). Hoffman describes this center as the hub of Jewish disinformation now being promulgated about Soviet Bolshevism (Communism).

> A major player in the promulgation of this disinformation is *Jerusalem Post* news editor Louis Rapaport, who acknowledges the central role of the Mikhoels Center in his book exonerating the Jews of responsibility for the crimes of the Soviet regime.[53]

We can now begin to understand why Al Gore, Jr., as vice president, was so chummy with Russian Prime Minister Viktor Chernomyrdin (dismissed by Yeltsin in 1998), whom Bob Zelnick describes in his book, *Gore*, as a crook and an inept, corrupt troglodyte.

It is no secret that many of the billions of dollars funneled to Russia through him by the United States and other members of the International Monetary Fund wound up in Swiss bank accounts. In November 1998, the *New York Times* reported that by 1995 the CIA had accumulated what they considered to be 'conclusive evidence of the personal corruption' of Chernomyrdin and had sent it to the White House, expecting the administration to take appropriate steps to protect American interests. 'Instead, when the secret CIA report on Mr. Chernomyrdin arrived in the office of Vice President Al Gore, it was rejected and sent back to the CIA with a barnyard epithet scrawled across its cover.[54]

Zelnick concludes that "the kindest interpretation is that Gore, a diplomatic neophyte, had become so infused with a sense of self-importance regarding the 'Chernomyrdin channel', that he was simply unable to process bad news about his Russian chum, however well-documented it might have been."[55]

There seems to be a trend here, although Zelnick certainly doesn't flag it as such; that is, of Jewish personnel in high US government positions seeking out, and dealing on a friendly personal basis, with known Jewish personnel in high Soviet or Russian government positions. We saw that with Madeleine Albright and her dealings, both official and social, with the then replacement of Chernomyrdin, one Yevegeny Primakov, as prime minister. Both of these PMs had come up the KGB ladder, both had undergone early name changes.

Indicative of that trend to please and appease the Zionists was the hiring by Gore of a Tennessee farm boy and former Christian minister, Richard Marius, who had become a writer and teacher. Gore needed a speech to be delivered at Madison Square Garden on 18 Apr 1993 to commemorate the 50th anniversary of the uprising against the Nazis by the Jews of the Warsaw ghetto.

Zelnick writes that Marius, en route to Washington, "dwelled on an unforgettable image of the event, a photograph of a young boy with hands raised over his head, walking at the head of a long, doomed line of Jews marching out of the smoke and ruin of the Ghetto when the Nazis had finally reduced it in May 1943. On the side of the street a leering Nazi trooper held a rifle."[56]

Marius played with this image to produce a memorable oration. As Gore later recited:

> I am always arrested by the image of one frightened little boy. He wears a coat that reaches to his bare knees over his short pants. On his head is a wool cap, as if some mother had dressed him to ward off the morning chill on his walk to school. Yet, here he is, trudging at the head of a weary column of doomed humanity, his hands lifted in the air in a gesture of harmlessness under the scornful laugh of a German soldier who holds an automatic rifle in his hand.

This child is not on his way to school. He is going to his death....

Before that image, words fail. We are reduced to silence – silence filled with the infinite pool of feeling that has created all the words of humility, heartbreak, helplessness, and hope in the language of the world.

How could the human race have allowed such a calamity as the Holocaust to fall upon us? What terrible darkness lies coiled in the human soul that might account for this venomous onslaught in the middle of a century that was hailed at its birth as a 'century of progress?'

The story of the Warsaw ghetto is sacred text for our time. It warns us of the unfathomable power of evil, the pestilence of the human soul for a time can dissolve nations and devastate civilization....

But the uprising in the ghetto also warns tyrants wherever they rule for a season that a fierce, bright light blazes eternal in the human breast, and that the darkness can never put it out....[57]

Well... doesn't that kind of grab you? Of course, it was meant to, just as the *Diary of Anne Frank* was meant to do when it was concocted by her father and a Dutch writer some six years after her untimely death.

As Paul Harvey says, "Now, for the rest of the story!"

The rest of the story has to do with that heart-rending photo of a little seven-year-old boy, hands raised aloft, along with other children; and behind them, a German soldier with a rifle... little

Jewish children on their way to the gas chambers of Auschwitz and "extinction" or "extermination." Anyone over 50 must recall that photo and the accompanying story.

Using that poignant picture, the compliant media told over and over again how this little boy's fate was sealed. He became one of six million Jews exterminated by the evil Germans during the "Holocaust."

An article on the subject (28 June 1982), "Jewish Physician Accidentally Explodes a 'Holocaust' Myth," explains that "The historic picture was one of several dozen taken by official German photographers during the military operation against the Jewish Warsaw uprising of 1943. Now, almost 40 years later, Dr. Tsvi C. Nussbaum, a physician in Rockland County, New York, says that he is the famous boy in the photo."[58]

The *New York Times* broke the startling story (28 May 1982), reporting that Dr. Nussbaum's statement has upset Jewish "Holocaust" publicists who are "convinced that the symbolic power of the picture would be diminished were the boy shown to have survived."

The *Times* wrote, "Holocaust historians have long considered the photograph a sort of sacred document."[59]

They quote Dr. Lucjan Dobroszycki of the Yivo Institute of European Jewish History in New York: "This great photograph of the most dramatic event of the holocaust requires a greater level of responsibility from historians than almost any other. It is too holy to let people do with it what they want."[60]

And what of poor Dr. Nussbaum after all this?

"I never realized that everyone puts the entire weight of six million Jews on this photograph," he said. "To me it looked like an incident in which I was involved and that was it."[61]

Thus are legends made...and hoaxes too.

Nussbaum recalls the incident: "In response to rumors that Germans planned to exchange Jews for German citizens abroad, many of the Warsaw Jews emerged from hiding and gave themselves up in 1943. Their names were entered on a "Palestine list" and the group was sent to Bergen-Belsen detention camp in Germany."[62]

The young Nussbaum, then 9, was liberated from Bergen-Belsen by American soldiers in 1945. He spent the next eight years in Israel and moved to New York in 1953 where he became a doctor and "holocaust survivor."

SECOND LADY'S "FAMILY VALUES"

We read a moment ago of Richard Marius and the speech he composed for Vice President Gore to deliver. According to Bob Zelnick, this led Gore to offer Marius a permanent position on his staff at $70,000 a year. Marius duly gave notice at Harvard and headed for Washington.

Some months later, Tipper Gore's chief-of-staff asked Marius to write a speech for Mrs. Gore, who would be addressing a family values conference in Nashville. Zelnick relates that the evening before her speech, Tipper told the press it would be very special. 'I've worked very hard on it,' she said."[63]

A few days later, the Second Lady's chief-of-staff called Marius to inform him that she had some very bad news for him. "As you know," she said, "we have very close relations with the Jewish community...." Zelnick writes that she told him, "during the past week, several in that community had complained bitterly about his appointment. She said the vice president had now read Marius's 1992 book review of *Season of Stones* and had decided not to hire him after all."

It seems that Marius had indeed written a review of the book by Helen Winternitz in which she described the excesses of Shin Bet – Israel's secret police – during the sustained period of Palestinian civil unrest in the late 1980s known as the Intifada. Marius wrote:

> Many Israelis, the Holocaust fresh in their memory, believe that the horror gives them the right to inflict horror on others. Winternitz's account of the brutality of the Shin Bet, the Israeli secret police, is eerily similar to the stories of the Gestapo, the *Geheimstaatspolitzei* in Nazi-

occupied territories in World War II – arbitrary arrests in the middle of
the night, imprisonment without trial, beatings, refined tortures, murder,
punishment of the families of suspects.[64]

"I have never had an anti-Semitic thought in my life,"
Marius protested.

The chief-of-staff then asked Marius to provide a cover for
the vice president, that it was his own decision not to accept the
political appointment.

In the end, Marius wouldn't lie, even for the vice president.
He told Zelnick in a letter that he had no regrets. "I consider
myself lucky not be a part of the trashy behavior that's part of this
administration's life – though I voted for that sleezebag Bill
Clinton in both his presidential elections."[65]

Enough of this sleezebag! And, what about Hillary, the
consumate politician and opportunist?

HILLARY AS "GRIEVING WIDOW"

No kidding, friends, it's in the cards. The gal we know as
the First Lady, a devout Methodist, could become the "grieving
widow." A recent cartoon by Kevin Siers of the *Charlotte
Observer* depicts St. Hillary tied to a stake, emblazoned by the face
and protruding proboscis of "her man." St. Hillary, with those
devout Methodist hands clasped, says, "I stay tied because of my
deep insight into the nature of sin.... Is it my fault people love a
martyr?"

Cal Thomas, in a related column (5 Aug 99), boldly states
that Hillary Clinton puts the spin on religion. "Only a couple that
has been emboldened by their escape from impeachable offenses
would try to spin God." Thomas quotes the indomitable Hillary:
"Peter betrayed (Jesus) three times, and Jesus knew it but loved
him anyway." According to Thomas, "Bill Clinton is no Peter, and
she is certainly no Jesus." He concludes that we have moved to
another level. "The Clintons are beyond all accountability
because, like the Blues Brothers, they are on a 'mission from God'.
God help the rest of us sinners."[66]

We have indeed moved to another level. Will it become "Level 5," which portends a "grieving widow"? Consider what has happened elsewhere in our time. Recall Representative Hale Boggs "disappearing" in a flight over Alaskan waters (Oct 1972). His wife, Lindy, was quickly appointed to take his seat in Congress. Sonny Bono, Representative from California, being killed in a skiing "accident"; his grieving widow took over as the Bono rep to Congress.

Mireya Moscoso took over as president in Panama on 1 Sep 99. Gen Omar Torrijos took out her husband, President Arnulfo Arias, in a coup (1968). Torrijos also signed the Panama Canal Treaty with Jimmy Carter (1977). This "grieving widow" of Arnulfo Arias could be of immense help to us if we dispatch the 82d Airborne to make that treaty null and void.

A quick look back at recent history: Gen Juan Peron was elected president of Argentina in 1946. He and his former girlfriend-turned-wife, Eva Durate, ran Argentina as a team. This author's cousin, Leonard Greenup, was on the scene as a reporter for the *Buenos Aires Herald* (1941-45): he and his lovely wife, Ruth, wrote a best seller in 1947, *Revolution Before Breakfast*, in which they describe Evita, who was 30 at the time. They could well have been describing Hillary:

> Evita is also notable for her ability to flaunt the conventions. In the first place, she had virtual public recognition as Peron's lady love long before they were married and the conventional folk of Argentina were scandalized at the prospect of Peron's becoming president without legalizing their relationship. The political convenience of a wedding played into Evita's hands, and a few months before the election they took their vows in a church ceremony. Evita also received the Pope's blessing for the marriage, which was an enviable achievement considering she had been the most gossiped about woman in many a year.
>
> When Evita first came out of obscurity in the early days of the revolution, she had dark hair worn in a rather long bob. She was good-looking even then, but not in the smoothly dazzling way she is as the President's wife. Evita has become a blonde, her hair done in an elaborate up-sweep style. Her clothes are designed by some of the most exclusive French houses in Buenos Aires, and she is said to own at least a dozen fur coats....

Her presence on the campaign train marked a beginning of a new political way of life for the Argentines, who are accustomed to their first ladies being gracious and entertaining, but completely removed from political activities. Evita blithely kicked over the traces of such tradition and became one of her husband's closest political advisers, sitting in at conferences and helping the new president divide the spoils of office among his henchmen. She began going out on her own to the working districts and inspected factories, housing projects, and made speeches in behalf of the new government of Argentina. She was installed in an office of her own and did not hesitate to call cabinet members into her headquarters to administer tongue-lashings or to distribute largesse. And while Peron was known as a 'strong man' abroad, some Argentines suspected that at home he was a hen-pecked husband.

Evita's own ideas on politics are a great influence on the new president. This may be a handicap. Evita can't tolerate opposition and is satisfied to have 'yes' men in the highest government posts. She is also known for her spiteful nature. Evita has compiled a 'black list' of persons who have gotten into her bad graces and she awaits her opportunity to get even with them, to engineer their fall from power or influence. When she accomplishes this, she scratches off the name, and is ready to eliminate the next one on the list.[67]

THE KING IS DEAD... LONG LIVE THE QUEEN

Evita died in 1952, Peron was exiled in 1955 after a coup, but returned triumphant in 1973, and with a new wife, Maria Estela Martinez, better known as Isabel. He was re-elected as president and appointed Isabel as his vice president. Ten months later he died; the "grieving widow" took over the reins of government, but was ousted by a coup in 1976.

In the Philippines, it was opposition leader Benigno Aquino who was assassinated in 1983. His "grieving widow," Corazon Aquino, ran against Marcos in 1986, becoming president. Marcos fled the country. It was a different spin in Nicaragua, with Violeta Barrios de Chammoro defeating Daniel Ortega in 1990 (don't know if she was a "grieving widow").

Still a different spin in India; Indira Gandhi, daughter of India's first prime minister, Pandit Nehru (1949-64), was declared prime minister in 1966. She ruled "democratically" until 1975 when she declared a "national emergency." Forced out in 1977, she was re-elected in 1980, only to be assassinated by two of her Sikh bodyguards, hired by her son, Rajiv, who replaced her, but he was swept from office in 1989 and assassinated in 1991. Several years later, Indira's assassins were freed from their country club prisons undoubtedly with a Swiss numbered account full of money. Indira Gandhi's Marxist handlers had her blown away for falling behind the timetable to take over Pakistan, which was then developing A-bomb capabilities.

And, of course, in neighboring Pakistan, Army Chief, Gen Pervais Musharraf, pulled a *coup d'etat* on 12 Oct 1999, placing Prime Minister Nawaz Sharif under house arrest.[68] Waiting in the wings is the former prime minister, Benazir Bhutto, the "grieving daughter" of another former prime minister, Zulfikar Ali Bhutto, who had been judicially executed in the 1970s following another coup.

Benazir Bhutto, speaking with BBC World TV in London on 13 Oct 1999, said she doesn't support coups, "but ultimately I blame Sharif for ruthlessly trampling on the rule of law and attempting to divide the army politically." She said the army should set a firm date for elections and "go back to the barracks."[69]

POWER OF ILLUMINISM

Through the eyes of Mrs. Nesta Webster, we can get an early portrait of Bill Clinton and his Oxford-trained cabinet members, as painted by a special commissioner of police in Mayence, France when it was part of the Napoleonic Empire. Francois Charles de Berckheim reported in 1810 that the *Illuminati* had initiates all over Europe and were working hard to introduce their principles into the lodges of Freemasonry.

Berckheim was a Freemason. He said,

> Illuminism is becoming a great and formidable power... kings and peoples will have much to suffer from it unless foresight and prudence break its frightful mechanism.[70]

Berckheim also painted a picture of the organization and methods of the *Illuminati* which ties back to the Weishaupt papers of 1786. The commissioner stated in 1813:

> It is above all in the universities that Illuminism has always found and always will find numerous recruits. Those professors who belong to the Association set out from the first to study the character of their pupils. If a student gives evidence of a vigorous mind, an ardent imagination, the sectaries at once get hold of him, they sound in his ears the words Despotism, Tyranny, Rights of the People.... Before he can even attach any meaning to these words, as he advances in age, reading works chosen for him, conversation skilfully arranged, develop the germ deposited in his youthful brain....
>
> At last when he has been completely captivated, when several years of testing guarantee to the society inviolable secrecy and absolute devotion, it is made known to him that millions of individuals distributed in all the States of Europe share his sentiments and hopes, that a secret link binds firmly all the scattered members of this immense family, and that the reforms he desires so ardently must sooner or later come about. The propaganda is rendered the easier by the existing association of students who meet together for the study of literature, for fencing, gaming, or even mere debauchery.
>
> The illumines insinuate themselves into all these circles and turn them into hotbeds for the propagation of their principles... it is by convening from childhood the germ of poison into the highest classes of society, in feeding the minds of students on ideas diametrically opposed to that order of things under which they have to live, in breaking the ties that bind them to sovereigns, that Illuminism has recruited the largest number of adepts....[71]

As we saw so clearly in the meeting in the ammunition bunker, it matters not whether the "adepts" are "Republican" or "Democrat." Professor Carroll Quigley explained in *Tragedy and Hope* that the Money Power "intended to contribute to both and allow an alternation of the two parties in public office in order to conceal their own influence, inhibit any independence by politicians, and allow the electorate to believe that they were exercising their own free choice."[72]

We are indeed living in the Kingdom of Darkness.

CHAPTER XIII

WILL BOLSHEVISM TRIUMPH?
(Where do we go? What shall we do?)

Universal peace can be founded only on the unity of man under one law and one government.... All states, deflated and disciplined, must align themselves under the law of the world-state... the new order....

William Yandell Elliott, The *City of Man,* 1941

PART ONE
BOLSHEVIZING *LOS DIABLOS*

I T is entirely appropriate, as we wind down the *Black Book of Bolshevism,* to retrieve gingerly a slide labeled *Los Angeles – breeding ground for the Bolshevik bacillus*, and slip it under our microscope.

To bring this modern-day Sodom and Gomorrah into sharper focus, we must consider a most startling article published in the Hollywood Issue of *Los Angeles* magazine for March 1999. Under the strange title, "MOSCOW 90210," Thomas Carney leads us into the sordid world of high crimes and misdemeanors carried out on a daily basis in what has become our most populous city, inappropriately named Los Angeles, which could easily pass as Los Diablos.

The lead-in tells us much:

> More than 600,000 émigrés from the former Soviet Union now live in Los Angeles. They've brought with them vodka and ravishing cheekbones. They've also brought shadowy former KGB with a taste for cash transactions and high security mansions, and criminals so ruthless that even the FBI is in awe. The Russians are here. And they are changing the face of LA forever.[1]

Carney's exceptionally revealing article stresses that this influx of Russian émigrés has introduced a heightened degree of both violence and criminality into LA.

> From Russian Hill in Hollywood [Mount Olympus] to the mansionized yurts of Beverly Hills, from the steppes of Glendale to the North Hollywood tundra, card-carrying capitalists – some carrying into the country, literally, suitcases full of cash – have transformed Los Angeles into Moscow on the Pacific.

According to Carney, they are smarter than we are, better educated and more ambitious, tougher and slyer, "but their crooks, according to our cops, are the smoothest thing since iced vodka."[2]

Although hard figures are scarce, about 600,000 Russian-speaking émigrés from the 15 republics that once made up the Soviet Union now live in Los Angeles. It all began, according to Carney, in the mid-1970s when Soviet Jews emancipated by the Jackson-Vanik Amendment began landing in LA... "waves of Russian-speaking émigrés have hit these shores like surfing sets."

He elucidates about the suitcases full of cash. These are the "new Russians":

> ...former Communist party *apparatchiks* who in 1989 saw the handwriting on the Berlin Wall before it fell and began spiriting an estimated $66 billion out of party and state coffers into Swiss bank accounts and American real estate, according to US officials. Many are reputed to have connections with organized crime. And it is these Russian nouveau riche who have gravitated not to New York or Miami but to America's leader in unbridled capitalism and unapologetic behavior: Los Angeles, California.[3]

SEN. JACKSON "SCOOPED" BY BOLSHEVIKS

The principal individual in Washington responsible for opening the floodgates to unbridled Jewish emigration from Eastern Europe into the US was Sen. Henry "Scoop" Jackson (D-WA). He was always *dans le poche* of the Israel-first crowd of influential Bolsheviks here in the United States.

One of the Representatives of that time who knew "Scoop" Jackson very well indeed was Paul Findley (D-Oh) who wrote extensively about him in his book, *They Dare to Speak Out* (1985).

All too typical of the Israel-first political action committees financing Sen. Jackson (and other Congress members) was the National Bipartisan Political Action Committee headed by Mark Siegel. This group was formed originally to help in the late Senator Jackson's 1978 presidential bid.

Findley explains how a top Defense expert outlined to him an event involving President Carter's Secretary of Defense, Harold Brown (whose father was a Russian Jew):

> I remember once Israel requested an item on the prohibited list. Before I answered, I checked with Secretary Brown and he said, 'No, absolutely no. We're not going to give in to the bastards on this one.' So I said no.
>
> Lo and behold, a few days later I got a call from Brown. He said, 'The Israelis are raising hell. I got a call from (Sen. Henry) Scoop Jackson, asking why we aren't cooperating with Israel. It isn't worth it. Let it go.'[4]

Findley stresses that Israeli penetration of State and Defense reached an all-time high during the Reagan administration:

> In 1984 people known to have intimate links with Israel were employed in offices throughout the bureaucracy and particularly in the Defense Department... headed by Fred Ickle, undersecretary for international security. The three personalities of greatest importance in his area are Richard Perle, Ikle's assistant for international security policy; Stephen Bryen, Perle's principal deputy, whose assigned specialty was technology transfer; and Noel Koch, principal deputy to Richard Armitage, assistant secretary for international security affairs. Koch was formerly employed by the Zionist Organization of America. Perle previously served on the staff of Democratic Senator Henry Jackson of Washington, one of Israel's most ardent boosters, and had the reputation of being a conduit of information to the Israeli government. Stephen Bryen came to the administration under the darkest cloud of all.[5]

Bryen was on the staff of the Senate Foreign Relations Committee in 1978, at which time he offered a top-secret document on Saudi air bases to a group of visiting Israeli officials. He later left the committee and became executive director of the Jewish Institute for National Security Affairs (JINSA), an organization founded – according to the *Jewish Week* – to "convince people that the security of Israel and the United States is interlinked." When Bryen moved to the Defense Department, his wife, Shoshona, replaced him at JINSA.

Later, a Justice Department memo (26 Jan 1979) revealed that "Bryen is (a) gathering classified information for the Israelis, (b) acting as their unregistered agent and (c) lying about it...." The file was closed in late 1979 without action.[6]

Early in 1981 Bryen was hired as Richard Perle's chief deputy in the Pentagon. Perle himself was picked up in an FBI wiretap discussing classified information with someone at the Israeli embassy. In 1983 Perle received substantial payment for representing the interests of an Israeli weapons company. He would claim that he was between government jobs when he worked for the Israeli firm. In 1999 Perle was a principal adviser to Governor George W. Bush in his campaign for the presidency.

Another glimpse of "Scoop" Jackson and his Zionist/ Bolshevik handlers is found in Walter Isaacson's voluminous work *Kissinger* (1992), wherein the Jackson-Vanik Amendment became an all-consuming part of the then Secretary of State, Henry Kissinger's, efforts to ram through Congress a bill to grant most-favored-nation (MFN) status to the Soviets.

According to Isaacson, "Jackson was not the type of leader who needed an impassioned aide to tell him what to think, but he had one anyway: Richard Perle, an intense, razor-sharp scourge of the Soviets who, despite his cherubic smile, earned the sobriquet Prince of Darkness from the legions he had engaged in bureaucratic battle. Among the kinder things Kissinger called him at the time were 'ruthless', 'a little bastard', and 'a son of Mensheviks who thinks all Bolsheviks are evil.'"[7]

Isaacson includes such other Israel-firsters then riding high in Washington as Morris Amitay, then of Sen. Abraham Ribicoff's staff and later head of the American Israel Public Affairs Committee (AIPAC). Jackson's main supporters in his efforts to get the Jews out of Soviet Russia also included Senators Ribicoff and Jacob Javits, both of whom were pushing for annual quotas of around 100,000 Jews.

In January 1975, following passage of the trade bill, the Soviet Union repudiated it and informed the US that it would not seek most-favored-nation status or comply with provisions of the bill. The Jackson-Vanik amendment, however, was now part of American law. For the next 15 years, the numbers of Jews emigrating fluctuated based on the warmth of Soviet-American relations. In 1979, after a new wheat deal and the negotiation of a SALT II treaty by President Carter, it jumped to 51,000. It was only during the Gorbachev revolution of 1989 that emigration restrictions were suddenly lifted. In 1990, the number of Jews leaving the country exploded to 150,000.[8]

Richard Perle, along with a strange mix of neo-cons and Israel-firsters, urged President Clinton (by letter dated 29 Jan 1999) to use "strong action and sustained US leadership to address the largest security crisis in Europe today. Serbian forces under the command of President Slobodan Milosevic are again slaughtering civilians and threatening the stability of the region, as many of the same forces did in Croatia and Bosnia."[9]

Perle and his fellow "patriots," such as Morton Abramovitz, Richard Burt, Zbigniew Brzezinski, Bob Dole, William Kristol, Mel Levine, Helmut Sonnenfeldt and Jeane Kirkpatrick, want NATO to use air power as necessary to compel the removal of Serbian forces and prepare the way for the introduction of NATO ground troops. The next logical step would be to agitate for NATO troop involvement in a contrived crisis anywhere outside of Europe – say, in the Middle East, or even on East Timor island, one of 13,000 islands making up Indonesia, situated on or near the equator to the north of Australia. To the global government advocates, no country, however remote, is safe from the Talmudic tactics designed to destroy utterly any nation or peoples standing in the way of total subjugation by the chosen few.

It would seem a far cry from the build-up of Eastern European émigrés (say criminals) in Los Angeles to their fellow Bolsheviks wanting once more to bomb a country (any country but

Israel) back into the stone age, but, oddly enough, there is a relationship.   And perhaps even stranger, a relationship to the planting of a young, innocent "intern" into the White House in 1993.   Remember that sweet Monica was also a product of the influx of aliens into Hollywood.

THE COMING OF TINSELTOWN

In mid-century, the noted British journalist and author, Douglas Reed, came to America and toured about the country, generally liking what he saw. In his work *Far and Wide*, published in 1951, Reed takes us on his travels, which began on the rockbound coast of Maine, took him into the deep South and eventually Westward until, mid-1950, he reached Los Angeles.

> Los Angeles stands on the opposite coast from the first settlement and is the opposite of all the earlier American Republic meant. Thirty-five years ago it was but a name on a map, and now it is of the world's biggest cities. What it yet may become, the mid-century traveler might ask in borrowed word:
>
> Be thou a spirit of health or goblin damn'd;
>
> Bring with thee airs from heaven or blasts from hell.
>
> Be thy intents wicked or charitable?
>
> Thou com'st in such a questionable shape.[10]

Reed's reaction was "a tinselled impermanence in this city, built on the irrigated sands.   It has the all-denying spiritual desolation of New York."

The recent immigration to California, and especially to Los Angeles, Reed saw as politically instigated. "Growing population means growing political power, in the capital at Washington, in the United Nations building at New York, and thus in the world."

Reed reveals that a careful study of the American electoral system shows the points where power may be obtained:

> Of the 150 million American in 49 states, about 60 millions live in seven states, the thickly-populated industrial ones of New York, Pennsylvania, Illinois, Michigan, Ohio, Massachusetts and California. Each state, large or small, sends two senators to Congress, but the numbers of Representatives rise or fall according to states-population.

The concentration of population in these seven states gives them the balance of power in presidential elections. The political control of these states, therefore, is a major prize in the contest for power....

Into these states the new immigration from Eastern and Southern Europe, after the Civil War, mainly flowed. It is fairly clear today that this movement was largely directed, in the case of the Jewish immigration, by the Political Zionists. In 1940, according to Jewish reference books, more than half of all Jewish immigrants went to California.

Simultaneously an increasing number of Negroes is being drawn from the South into these seven states by Communist-dominated unions. The powerful waterside union in California chiefly instigates this movement. These unions are under the control of leaders of Eastern European origins.... By these means the vote of the seven key states has been mobilized for Democratic or Communist candidates.... Los Angeles is growing into a political stronghold of the new immigration on the Pacific, as New York is already its chief one on the Atlantic and in the world.[11]

NEW YORK-MOSCOW-TEL AVIV TRIANGLE

A man who saw first-hand the fatal workings of what he called Bolshevik/Zionism was Jack Bernstein, an American Jew who moved to Israel shortly after its founding in 1948. He returned in abject disgust to the United States after witnessing the machinations of a political triad of countries during the so-called Yom Kippur War in 1973. He would later publish a book, *The Life of an American Jew in Racist Marxist Israel.*

Perhaps the key to understanding what is currently transpiring in the Middle East, especially in Israel, is what Bernstein calls the "Golda Meir/Stalin/Kaganovich Pact."

Bernstein denies that because Soviet Russia sold military equipment to Egypt and the Arab countries, the Soviets supported the Arabs in the 1973 War. "This is a false impression," Bernstein emphasizes, and in order to comprehend the blatant deceit behind it, one must understand the Golda Meir/Stalin/Kaganovich Pact.[12]

Golda Meir (Meyersohn), born in Russia in 1898, grew up in Milwaukee, Wisconsin, and in 1921 moved to Palestine. In 1949, she became Israel's first ambassador to the Soviet Union. It was here that she met with Josef Stalin and his brother-in-law, Lazar Kaganovich. From this fortuitous gathering emerged a top-secret pact, in which Israel (1) would not allow the US or any Western country to build military bases on Israeli territory; (2) would allow an official Communist party to function in Israel; (3) would never make any agreement to solve the Palestinian problem; (4) would work with world Jewry to adopt a policy of Western powers favoring Israel over the Arabs; and (5) would continue its Marxist economic policies.[13]

In return, the Soviet Union was to (1) institute a pro-Arab policy solely as a camouflage for its true intention, which was to furnish military aid to the Arabs (and Egypt), but never enough to enable them to destroy Israel; (2) encourage Jewish immigration to Israel from the Soviet satellite countries, and, if insufficient, then allow Jewish emigration from Soviet Russia; and (3) absolutely guarantee the security of Israel and, in that connection, authorize the free exchange of intelligence reports between Israel and the Soviet Union.[14]

The third leg of the tripod (the United States) would come into play during the 1973 Yom Kippur War, when the Egyptian armies penetrated deeply into Israeli defenses in the Sinai. Bernstein stresses, "as pre-planned, the US airlifted massive amounts of military equipment and supplies to Israel..." and placed the US 82d Airborne Division at Ft. Bragg, as well as US troops stationed in Germany, on alert, fully prepared to be airlifted into Israel to assist the Israeli forces against the combined Arab/Egyptian armies, if necessary.[15]

Bernstein also explains how the New York-Moscow-Tel Aviv triad functioned during the 1982 invasion of Lebanon, stressing that the real reasons for Israel's attack on Lebanon were (1) to carry on a perpetual war in the Middle East, with the attack on Lebanon merely another phase of its Zionist/Marxist "wars of aggression"; (2) to capture the waters of the Litani River for use in water-scarce Israel.[16]

Bernstein states that the terrorist attack on the Marine base in Lebanon, causing the death of 250 US Marines, "was planned by

Israeli military personnel... the Mossad, Israel's secret service....
By instigating the attack on the Marine base, the Israeli 'war
hawks' had hoped the attack would turn the American people
against the Arabs, and that the US could be drawn into the war and
further help Israel in its aggression."[17]

PART TWO
A "FIFTH COLUMN" WITHIN THE GATES

YOU may not recall a play staged in 1938 called *The Fifth Column*. It was based on the phrase, which originated in a radio address by one of Franco's generals, Emilio Mola, during the Spanish Civil War (1936-1939). Mola was leading four columns of troops against Madrid, and boasted that he had a "fifth column" of sympathizers within Madrid who would support him.

Spain in the 1920s was controlled by the Socialist party (PSOE) under Francino Largo Caballero, who served the new Spanish Republic until a failed military coup by the Falangistas (Aug 1932) brought disaster. The following year, the Socialists lost the election. Spurred on by alien Bolshevists, they resorted to terror.

Gen Francisco Franco, a highly capable career officer, a nationalist and devout Catholic of Jewish heritage, was reluctant to use military force; however, seeing his country threatened by a deadly foreign bacillus and sensing the alien effort to divide the army, he was prepared to act "if worse came to worse." By February 1936, he knew that a take-over by the Bolshevist left was imminent and that it would lead to forced collectivization, destruction of the Church and brutal repression by the agents of Soviet Russia.

"Their fronts are Socialism, Communism and Bolshevism which attack civilization to replace it with barbarism," he told his army commanders after the Socialists regained control in the elections of 1936, only to be overwhelmed by their brother Bolshevists who had penetrated the PSOE.[18]

Just as in Russia in 1917 and onwards, the Zionist Bolshevists zeroed in on two principal targets: the military and the Church. By March, the first burnings of churches and convents took place, as the militant Communists formed a revolutionary Marxist party, *Partido Obrero de Unificaion Marxista* (POUM) which began in May to take over the factories. By June, the POUM had burned 160 churches, committed 269 political murders, called 113 strikes and sacked ten newspaper offices. The government failed to act. In fact, the new republican riot-police, the Assault Guards (similar to BATF and FBI) actually joined in the violence.[19]

Sensing imminent disaster, the civilian authorities pleaded for Franco to act. Recognizing that he now had "respectable civil backing," the General struck with military force, triggering the Civil War, which pitted the Republicans (controlled by the Comintern, i.e., Bolshevists) against the Nationalists (Franco and his regular and colonial forces).

Franco was appointed chief of state in October 1937, when the siege of Madrid began. By mid-1938, he launched an offensive which carried him to victory over the Bolshevists in 1939. He continued as chief of state until his death in 1975. In 1957, he announced that the Spanish monarchy would be restored at his death. King Juan Carlos I assumed the throne in 1975, the first king of Spain in 44 years; Generalissimo Franco had reigned as chief of state for 36 of those years.

Paul Johnson points out in his masterful work *Modern Times:* "For the Republicans (Bolshevists), the Catholic Church was the chief object of hatred." He states that Arthur Koestler, in *The Invisible Writing,* described how Fascist atrocities were fabricated in the lie-factory run by Otto Katz from the Comintern office in Paris.

It wasn't only the lie factory that aided and abetted the subversive Communists/Bolshevists; they were glorified by such writers as Ernest Hemingway (*A Farewell to Arms*), and by the Abraham Lincoln Brigade made up of American volunteers fighting for the Marxist Republicans. Johnson reports:

> No episode in the 1930s has been more lied about than this one, and only in recent years have historians begun to dig it out from the mountains of mendacity beneath which it was buried for a generation. What emerges is not a struggle between good and evil but a general tragedy.[20]

Upon this Millennium, we are faced with a general tragedy far worse than the events of the Spanish Civil War. Identical forces are at play, but with far more concentrated power at their disposal, including such weaponry as nuclear, chemical, biological agents, as well as weather manipulation. With the seven levers of power now virtually totally in the hands of the Barbarians within our gates, we seem to be headed down the slippery slope to unprecedented destruction, depression and decay. Even our once proud and loyal military – the Muscle, if you will – has apparently been co-opted to subvert the Constitution and support the global oligarchs.

US PUSHES MALAYSIAN COUP

We have seen in this work how two other countries separated by distance and time resorted to the technique of violence to save their countries and culture from the great menace of this century – atheistic Bolshevism. General Francisco Franco saved Spain in the 1930s from this deadly bacillus. General Augusto Pinochet saved Chile from the identical deadly disease in the 1970s.

Today, at least two leaders of other countries also separated by a vast distance are fighting to stave off the global gangsters and their financial manipulations – Malaysia and Venezuela.

"The prime minister of a friendly nation has been targeted for elimination. His crime is that in a world order built on lies, this man tells the truth." This was the kicker for a factual reportage by Warren Hough in the *Spotlight* weekly (7 Dec 1998). President Clinton was pushed by his handlers to sign on to a series of covert actions designed to overthrow Malaysian Prime Minister Mahathir Mohamad, "an elected, democratic and long-established Asian leader."[21]

Hough cites a report by Russell E. F. Faulkner, a British broadcast correspondent stationed in Hong Kong. The campaign to destabilize the Malaysian government was driven by Israel's aggressive Washington lobby, its secret service, the Mossad, and its powerful allies on Wall Street, George Soros and the Establishment media. Faulkner related:

> They have never forgiven Mahathir for publicly denouncing the international financiers [whose currency raids ruined Southeast Asia's hard-working economies last year] as 'Jewish speculators' and criminal Zionist money manipulators.[22]

In addition, Mahathir "has established himself as a leader among critics of the unfettered global markets and the IMF's economic prescriptions," reported *Washington Post* staff writer Paul Blustein from Kuala Lumpur, Malaysia's capital, on 21 Nov 98.[23]

Blustein also related that the IMF and the Clinton administration are more eager than ever "to discourage other countries from following Malaysia's lead in imposing financial controls on speculative 'hot money' maneuvers."

Hough states, "Zionism's worldwide agent network and the web of dual-loyalist policy makers in Washington, led by Vice President Al Gore, are doing more than just discouraging neighboring governments from emulating the Malaysian leader's patriotic reforms. They are encouraging a *coup d'état* against him, diplomatic sources say."

FROM FAILED COUP TO JAIL TO PRESIDENT

In our own Western Hemisphere, we witnessed an aftermath of an attempted *coup d'état* in Venezuela in 1992. The leader of that failed coup attempt, then Lt Col Hugo Chavez, marched out of the darkness on the night of 4 Feb 1992, with 10,000 troops behind him, to try and overthrow the corrupt government of Carlos Andres Perez (CAP) who, along with his thuggish underlings, had bled off over $250 billion of oil wealth, and, in the words of columnist Georgie Anne Geyer (*Washington Times,* 1 Dec 1998), "built up huge voracious bureaucracies (33% of the country works for the government) and left Venezuela today with 80% of the population of potentially the richest country in Latin America living in miserable poverty."[24]

Geyer informed us that the coup attempt "didn't work, some dozens were killed, and [Chavez] went briefly to prison, only amazingly to emerge where he is today."

So, where is this failed coup leader today? As the *Agence France-Presse* reported from Caracas, Venezuela (1 Dec 1998), "Former coup leader Hugo Chavez will win Sunday's presidential election by a landslide, according to a poll released two days ago, a week ahead of the vote."[25]

And win he did! The young, charismatic nationalist and former soldier easily defeated the runner-up Henrique Salas Romer by 59% to 36%. He appears to be cut from the same cloth as General Aleksandr Lebed of Russia, who is also a former patriotic soldier, and poised to take over as the Russian president by "ballots or bullets."

WHICH WILL IT BE IN THE NEW MILLENNIUM?

As we put behind the totally decadent 20th century, we are bound to see more patriots and soldiers rise up to follow in the footsteps of such as Gen Simon Bolivar, the Latin American leader whom President Chavez admires above all others:

> Today, we continue with the same dream, with the core idea being Bolivarian, because he was the author not only of a physical, but of a moral ideal – for all of Latin America and for all of the world.[26]

Bolivar had become dictator of Venezuela in 1813 and, in 1817, established the independent government of Venezuela. In 1821, by defeating the Spanish army at Carabobo, he ensured the independence of his country. In 1824 he was proclaimed emperor of Peru. Revered as Latin America's "soldier-statesman," he died in 1830 at the age of 47.[27]

President Hugo Chavez, 44, also has great plans for his country; but, so did Prime Minister Mahathir Mohamad before the international bankers and the speculators, as well as the IMF, got hold of it. Horrendous debt and devaluation of their currency has virtually destroyed the Malaysian economy. Horrendous debt and grand internal theft by CAP and company virtually destroyed Venezuela.

THE COMING "SIEGE"

Hollywood has produced a so-called blockbuster movie entitled *The Siege* (1998) which depicts in living color the imposition of martial law in New York City following a series of terrorist acts there. William Norman Grigg, one of the editor/writers of the *New American* magazine, reviewed the film in the 7 Dec 1998 issue under the banner, "Could it Happen in America?"[28]

Of course it could. Grigg asks an all-important question: Should this film be regarded as a cautionary tale or a trial balloon? Recall the political satire *Wag the Dog* which eerily depicted, incisively and accurately, an event that was to take place months later (Aug 98) when President Clinton, caught in his peccadilloes with a purposely-planted intern, decided to bomb two sovereign nations as a technique of fighting terror.

Is *The Siege* similarly a sign of things to come? Grigg states that the intended purpose was to gauge the public's response to a specific scenario.[29]

One should compare it to *Seven Days in May*, which, rather than imposition of martial law, showed a planned *coup d'état*. There is a difference. The new film depicts the hero/villain as a two-star commander, Gen Devereaux, of an elite force of paratroopers who, rather than attempting to overthrow a corrupt government, is simply following the orders of his commander-in-chief, Bill Clinton.

There is another villain, of course, namely the Muslims. As the *New York Times* observed (1 Nov 1998), referring to the Muslims and Arabs undertaking a leaflet-distribution campaign outside the theaters showing *The Siege*:

> They point out that there is no avoiding the fact that its villains are Arabs who quote the Koran and perform ablutions before heading off to blow up innocent civilians.[30]

Dare we ask, just who benefits when Christian America is pitted against the Muslim world, or, for that matter, against the "Yellow Peril"? Just who is it that orchestrates these scenarios, defines these enemies and cunningly sets us up for further police-state repression?

Grigg asks another pertinent question: "Why is America so vulnerable?"[31]

UNRESOLVED QUESTIONS REMAIN

We were close to a coup here in the United States at the time of the Kennedy assassination in November 1963. Tapes recently released indicate that what transpired at that time was in fact a double coup – one in South Vietnam, the other, just a few days later, when the author of the Vietnamese coup was himself taken out.

Two unresolved questions remain: who specifically was behind both events; and, most important, what was the *raison d'être*?

We get a partial answer from Christopher Mathews, a nationally syndicated columnist writing in the *Washington Times* (29 Nov 1998). His column, "Echoes of Vietnam," is based on the release of tapes in late November 1998 which reflect "the most fateful American action of the Vietnamese War: the August 1963 decision to dump the existing government in Saigon led by President Ngo Dinh Diem and replace it with a military junta more responsive to US war aims."[32]

From the tapes made by JFK himself (4 Nov 1963) immediately following the bloody butchery of President Diem and his brother Nhu in an armored personnel carrier in the early morning hours of 2 November, Mathews lays out the Machiavellian sequence which ultimately led to the butchery of over 55,000 American boys in a jungle war half-way round the world which was unwinnable from the start. Mathews stresses:

By eliminating the last Vietnamese leader with the legitimacy to tell us to leave that country, we lost the last leader with the legitimacy to ask us to stay.

Here are those events, along with the perpetrators:

Kennedy's fateful command was delivered in a 24 Aug 63 cable to his hand-picked ambassador in Saigon, Henry Cabot Lodge, approving a military coup against Diem....

'We are launched on a course from which there is no respectable turning back,' Lodge responded; 'the overthrow of the Diem government.' On 1 Nov... the coldblooded Lodge had breakfast with Diem, assuring him he had nothing to fear. Later, when an anguished Diem called for help, Lodge waffled, saying people were asleep back in Washington and he couldn't get a decision on what to do....[33]

Kennedy places the blame on the divided counsel he was getting from his experts. On the 4 Nov tape, he lists those backing the coup, Averill Harriman, Roger Hilsman and George Ball of the State Department, and National Security aide, Michael Forrestal – and those opposed: military aide Maxwell Taylor, Attorney General Robert Kennedy, Defense Secretary Robert McNamara and CIA chief John McCone.[34]

So, the questions remain: What will happen? Will it be war rather than reconciliation in the Middle East? Will it trigger World War III?

In fact, unpayable debt, financial currency speculation and devaluation, ever-increasing unemployment and wild fluctuations in the world stock markets all point toward a gigantic global financial collapse. Will it collapse the US economy? Will the President, whomever he (or she) may be, declare martial law? Could a civil war not unlike that of Spain break out in the United States?

As one disgruntled general officer remarked in June 1999, "it may be time for Hugh [chairman of the Joint Chiefs, Gen Henry Shelton] to say what Franco said in 1936 – 'enough is enough.'"

It may already be too late. Maybe we too, not unlike the Russians of 1917, were conquered by a *coup d'état* carried out by a relatively small group of determined and deadly Bolshevists. They now appear to have absolute control over six of the seven levers of power. Could that seventh lever – the military – launch a counter-coup?

Or has it come to pass – as many believe – that the sacred tenets of Duty – Honor – Country have been bred out of them, and that they are now the fawning, boot-licking puppies of our fearful masters?

Patrick J. Buchanan perhaps said it best in a bold commentary published in the *Washington Times* (22 Feb 1999). He states that: "[W]ith the Senate's failure to muster even a bare majority for the conviction of Bill Clinton, some conservatives are near despair."[35]

"Is the culture war over?" Buchanan asks. He stresses that "looking back over recent decades, it is impossible to deny that an anti-Western culture has completed its long march through America's institutions, capturing the arts, entertainment, the public schools and colleges, the media, and even many churches."

"Politics is the last contested battlefield of our culture war, for only through politics can the new cult, a militant and intolerant secularist faith that will abide no other, impose its values on us."[36]

Buchanan, in his own inimitable style, asks the gut-wrenching question… Where do we go? What shall we do? Is the battle truly lost?

We find the clincher – and perhaps the courage to withstand the onslaught and even to mount a last desperate counterattack – in his final paragraph, for this country has been there before. Leaders did emerge, sword in hand, to take a stand against fearful odds and go toe to toe against the alien forces within the gates. Here is Buchanan:

> What is needed today is the same awareness that finally hit the conservative men of America in the early 1770s. Loyal to their king, they had rejected the counsel of Sam Adams to rebel against him and fight.
>
> Finally, it dawned on these conservatives that they had to become radicals; they had to overthrow the king's rule to keep what they

had. And they found in George Washington a conservative leader with the perseverance to take us to victory over an enemy superior in every way but courage and character.[37]

Is there not today, among that vast array of sheer military force, just one leader who will sound the trumpet and mount the charge against a totally tyrannical despot and his imperial court lackeys, and bring them to a court of military justice and/or the gallows?

A lesson can be learned from the *Book of Judges,* which outlines how Gideon saved Israel from the fearsome Midianites. From a force of 32,000, Gideon, guided by the Lord, chose only 300, and with that comparatively small number, which he split into three forces of 100 each, he attacked the Midianite hordes at night. Each man carried a lamp and a trumpet, and, with the flickering lamps and the blowing of trumpets, Gideon surrounded the enemy, who fled in panic. Gideon's forces pursued them, captured their princes and slew them, "and brought the heads of Oreb and Zeeb to Gideon on the other side of the Jordan."

There is a lesson here for the more astute, perhaps best epitomized by America's national motto: "In God we trust," as well as in our military oath, which ends: "So help me God." We can add to those as a natural continuum: "God plus One is always a majority."

And perhaps finally, "If God be for us, who can be against us? (Romans 8:31)

We have a much bigger objective. We've got to look at the long run here. This is an example – the situation between the United Nations and Iraq – where the United Nations is deliberately intruding into the sovereignty of a sovereign nation.... Now this is a marvelous precedent [to be used] in all countries of the world...

Former CIA Director, Stansfield Turner, July, 1991

CHAPTER XIV

THE COMING COUP
(Destabilize from Within)

I came in on a tank, and only a tank will evict me.
Abu Zuhair Yahya, Iraqi prime minister, 1968

PART ONE
WHEN YOU STRIKE AT A KING...

HAVING stood in the shadows of four *coups d'état* since 1967, this author has more than a passing interest in why and how they come about.

A *coup d'état* (stroke of state), Webster tells us, is the sudden, forcible overthrow of a government. Generally, over the 50 years since the end of WW II, it has been used by disgruntled military factions in the so-called developing or emerging nations, particularly in the Mideast, Africa and Latin America.

And conversely, seldom used in developed countries.

However rare, coups have indeed been successfully staged in certain advanced societies during those same 50 years. Probably most important, a coup could be attempted over the next few months in such states as Russia, Italy, France, Britain or even the United States.

What conditions would make an advanced country ripe for a coup?

There are certain factors we can watch for, the most important flags of danger being four in number, and a combination of the four indicating that traditional strengths and resilience of a developed country have been dangerously weakened:

1) Rising instability within the major parties making up the political system, leading to gross disaffection on the part of the electorate;

2) Rising financial/economic instability, characterized by rapidly escalating interest rates and hyperinflation, coupled with astronomical debt, both public and private, business bankruptcies, spiraling unemployment and a markedly decreased standard of living of the people;

3) A major military/ political defeat, following a long-drawn-out conflict, with no apparent benefits accruing either to the military or to the populace at large, but rather leaving both segments with a loss of integrity and sense of personal worth.

4) .Political and socio-economic power increasingly centralized, characterized by a plethora of statutes and regulations, a bloated bureaucracy, confiscatory taxes and the building up of a national secret police force.

Perhaps the greatest danger as regards the possibility of a coup is the utter humiliation in defeat suffered by the military leaders. We see this most starkly in Russia.

'WAITING FOR THE RUSSIAN STRONGMAN'

This was the intriguing title of an op-ed by Neil H. G. Glick (*Washington Times*, 21 Sep 1998). He was formerly program director of the American Chamber of Commerce in Russia from 1993-1997.

Glick considers that the Russian people are at the end of their rope. "The people are angry, and there is fear of a new revolution," Glick wrote. "The Russian people long for a strong, unifying leader to pull them out of this economic and social turmoil.... A future leader could be found in the Russian military – a historically respected part of society," Glick said, pointing out that the government was taking the threat of a military strongman seriously. "All major military figures of the past five years were pushed out of the Kremlin. One example is Gen. Alexander Lebed who was thrown out of his government position a few weeks after

he effectively negotiated an end to the Russian war in Chechnya –
a war extremely unpopular with the people, yet strongly supported
by the government."[1]

Glick outlined a scenario for another Russian revolution:

- Small protests spread to national level;

- Discontented masses hit the streets of Moscow and St. Petersburg;

- A new leader would emerge, who could blame "minorities and the
  West." He would showcase how the once- powerful military has lost
  its glory. By simple promises, a leader could have support of the
  military, which creates a short path to the Kremlin.[2]

Glick stated that the scenario of an "unknown force taking
power is frighteningly close to what happened to Russia in 1917,
ushering in Lenin and the Communist Party."

In his final analysis, Glick stressed that we should push
President Yeltsin and Prime Minister Primakov to make the major
reforms that had never occurred, "otherwise a people's revolution
and a frightening New Russian Order would emerge."[3]

STRIKE TO KILL

Those four conditions making a country ripe for a coup are
also present in the United States to a greater degree than they have
been in the past 50 years. The Korean police action of the 1950s,
followed by the protracted Vietnamese fiasco of the 1960-70s,
created a long-festering wound in the military body – a stab in the
back, if you will – as well as a suppurating sore in the body politic.

Neither was assuaged by the massive effort on the part of
the Bush administration in 1991 to defeat a contrived enemy in
what we call Desert Storm. Many of the leaders who took part in
that engagement feel no sense of pride and accomplishment in the
results. "It was a bloody massacre," one general grimly recounted,
"and we handed out like crackerjack prizes over 40,000 medals for
heroism."[4]

We were close to a coup in the early 1970s as President
Nixon was dragged through the contrived Watergate affair, and
again when President Ford was shot at twice in 1975. Later, in

1981, following the shooting of President Reagan, the situation was ripe for a possible coup, but the four elements listed were not present in sufficient detail. The same can be said for the assassination of President Kennedy in November 1963. Remember too that in each of these instances, elements of the federal government were directly involved... complicit would perhaps be a better word. Several high-level military officers believed that the killing of JFK was in fact a *coup d'état* carried out by elements of the CIA working with the Israeli Mossad. Kennedy was attempting to halt the development of nuclear weapons by the Israelis, while simultaneously planning to disband the CIA and disengage our military troops from the Indo-China area. (Read *Final Judgment* by Michael Collins Piper for more details.)[5]

Consider that since the end of WW II, there have been 140 coup attempts about the world and that over 100 of them were successful. Bear in mind that we are only addressing coups and disregarding other types of conflicts, such as revolts, guerrilla wars, insurrections, civil wars, border conflicts, limited war, or covert invasions.

There is a pattern in coups, in that the successful ones involved elements of at least two of the traditional three military services; where one faction attempted to go it alone, or when a political faction attempted a coup, it generally failed. Syria is perhaps the only exception. Since 1949, army factions have staged 12 successful coups and failed but twice.[6]

LIKELIHOOD OF A BLOODY REVOLUTION

Before we look more closely at the distinct possibility of a coup in one of the developed countries, let's look briefly at the likelihood of a more bloody revolution. In fact, the coterie of Marxists-Leninists, modern-day Socialists, and their fellow travelers have been cunningly manipulating various factions and events, not only in the European countries, but throughout the Americas, hoping – and perhaps praying – for a "proletarian" revolution. Their strategy is the age-old *divide et impera*. We saw it in spades during the Rodney King riots in Los Angeles and witnessed it *ad nauseam* in the never-ending OJ Simpson murder trial. Had Ron Goldman been a gentile, O. J. would have been back in the good graces of Hollywood instead of a pariah. Who was really in charge? Take a look back at the entourage of pricey defense lawyers, cunningly working the system to strip their client of all of his assets and then get him acquitted. His guilt or innocence was not even secondary; of exclusive import is the matter of race, which could be the trigger for our own bloody revolt of the masses.

Wilmot Robertson stressed the factor of race in his international best seller *The Dispossessed Majority* (1981). He states that if a revolution ever breaks out in the United States, it will not be because of the hardening of class divisions or capitalist exploitation, but because of the heterogeneity of the American population, the racial dynamism of minority elements within this population, and the deracination (uprooting) of the American Majority.

> The order of battle is already drawn up. On the revolutionary side of the barricades will be the fire-breathing militants of the unassimilable minorities... and the more desperate and more compromised Majority liberals. On the counterrevolutionary side will be the Majority core and the assimilated members of the Assimilable Minorities. As in all revolutions most of the population will assume, or try to assume, a very low and very neutral profile.[7]

A so-called proletarian revolution would obviously put the finishing touches on the dispossession of the Majority. Robertson warns that to speed the day, the inflammatory rhetoric, the urban insurrections, and the guerrilla war which the media still prefer to call a crime wave are putting so many Americans in such a revolutionary mood that a further escalation of violence will hardly be necessary. He further states:

> A few more decades of this softening up, this preparation for the kill, could be as damaging to the Majority as an all-out Marxist putsch.[8]

Herewith, a timely word of warning as regards the possibility of a coup in the United States. Most of us will probably agree with Gen Barney Rutkowski's statement in *Seven Days in*

May: "People always say it couldn't happen here, and I am one of those people... but...."[9]

The federal administration, ostensibly run by the President, but actually under the total control of his handlers (made up of unassimilable minorities and liberal intelligentia), could accomplish a *de facto* coup by declaring a national emergency, suspending the Constitution, and turning the nation over to its Federal Emergency Management Agency (FEMA). We can look back to that time in the 1930s, prior to World War II, when we were in fact living under a national emergency enforced by a virtual dictator – FDR – and his alien handlers. We can look forward to more of the same.

On 21 January 1999, Bill Clinton announced that he is thinking about setting up a "Domestic Terrorism Team headed by a military "commander in chief" with a $2.8 billion budget to combat alleged terrorism on US soil. (*New York Times*, 22 Jan 1999). But the danger from terrorism on US soil was the direct result of President Bush and Clinton's reckless bombing of six countries: Yugoslavia, Sudan, Afghanistan, Bulgaria, Albania, and Iraq. That's what motivated the world's number one terrorist Osama bin Laden, to state that all Americans, including "those who pay taxes," are now his targets.

Using terrorism as an excuse, the Clinton Administration made extraordinary plans to use military force against American citizens.

Secretary of Defense Wiliam Cohen said in an *Army Times* interview that "Americans soon may have to choose between civil liberties and more intrusive means of protection."

Deputy Secretary of Defense John Hamre has been floating the idea of designating some US troops as a "Homelands Defense Command" to impose military rule within the United States.

The Army War College journal *Parameters* (Autumn 1997) predicted that "terrorism" will "almost inevitably trigger an intervention by the military" and "legal niceties...will be a minor concern."

Clinton's Executive Order 12919, entitled National Defense Industrial Resources Preparedness, gives FEMA dictatorial authority over communications, energy, food, transportation, health, housing, and other resources. The president can invoke "emergency" powers to deal with a perceived emergency.

There are two elements within our current structure which give them pause: one is the fact that the hard core units of our military force structure are still under the direct command of Majority officers and noncoms; the second is that we have within the heartland a heavily-armed and patriotic citizenry, many of them now formed into what can best be called an unorganized militia.

These two can be broken in two ways. Recognizing the psychological import of the territorial imperative – men and women fighting to the death for their piece of real estate – the Federal juggernaut has the power and coercive force to disarm the citizens completely by the use of mercenary UN forces already located about the US, and then destroy their economic base by a calculated financial collapse. It just might take such an awakening call to cause a normally docile and peace-loving citizenry to rise up in righteous wrath and slay the Midianites, delivering the heads of their "princes" and other assorted "royalty" to our own Gideon.

Does anybody out there hear the sound of the trumpet?

"FEAR OF THE FEDS" ENDEMIC

We are now at the stage where there seems to be a general breakdown in the dialogue between the citizenry and their duly constituted government in Washington DC.

Nowhere is this more evident than in the best seller *The Secret Life of Bill Clinton* written by Ambrose Evans-Pritchard (1997). He was Washington correspondent for the London *Daily Telegraph* for four years, prior to his sudden recall to London by the paper in late 1997. Because of the nature of his subject – the wrongdoings of a sitting president of the United States – and his impeccable and thorough research, we should consider his statements in the same light as we look upon the revelations of

Alexis de Tocqueville about the US, which he made during a visit to this country in 1831. Usually the most accurate portrayal of a country comes from the pens of foreign historians, rather than a native of the country.

Evans-Pritchard reveals key features of what he sees as the disintegration of a once-great nation, the United States of America, in his parting shot at the Clinton administration. Carried as an editorial under the banner "Good-bye, good riddance" and featured in the *Daily Telegraph* in 1997, it included *inter alia*:

> The Clintons wasted little time taking charge of the US Justice Department. All US attorneys were asked to turn in their resignations (1993). It was a move of breath-taking audacity, one that gave the Clintons control over the prosecutorial machinery of the federal government in every judicial district in the country.
>
> They then set about eliminating the Director of the FBI, William Sessions, who was known for his refusal to countenance White House interference in the affairs of the Bureau. The post of FBI director is supposed to be a 10-year appointment that puts it above politics... Sessions was toppled in a Washington putsch... and replaced by the hapless errand boy Louis Freeh.[10]

Upon the firing of Sessions by his boss, Janet Reno, he emerged from her offices visibly shaken; so much so that, while stepping off the curb to enter his car, he tripped, fell, and broke his arm. We will shortly discover that this was not the first time a director of the FBI was removed. First, let's look more closely at Evans-Pritchard's revelations:

> When you are living through events day by day, it is hard to know whether you are witnessing a historic turning point, or just mistaking the usual noise of politics for something meaningful.... There is no doubt that strange things have been going on in America.
>
> The Clinton era has spawned an armed militia movement involving tens of thousand of people. The last time anything like this occurred was in the 1850s with the emergence of the southern gun clubs. It is easy to dismiss the militia as 'right-wing nuts'; it is much harder to read the complex sociology of civic revolt. At the very least the militias reveal the hatred building up against the irksome yuppies who run the country.... It is under the president that domestic terrorism has become a feature of life in America, culminating in the destruction of the Oklahoma federal building on April 19, 1995. What set the deadly spiral

in motion was the Waco assault two years before, and the cover-up that followed.

No official has ever lost a day's pay for precipitating the incineration of 80 people, most of them women and children, in the worst abuse of power since Wounded Knee a century ago. Instead of shame and accountability, the Clinton administration accused the victims of setting fire to themselves and their children, a posthumous smear that does not bear serious scrutiny. It then compounded the injustice by pushing for a malicious prosecution of the survivors.

Nothing does more to sap the life of a democracy than the abuse of power. Public trust is dangerously low. According to polls, barely a quarter of the American people now feel that they can count on the federal government to do the right things.

A majority refuses to accept that Vincent Foster committed suicide, and they have good reason for their doubts. The paramedics and crime scene witnesses in Fort Marcy Park on July 20, 1993, tell a story that flatly contradicts the official findings. A police Polaroid shows a .22 caliber bullet wound in Foster's neck that the autopsy somehow failed to show. Are Americans to believe that Hillary Clinton's closest friend shot himself twice, with two different guns?

The worst thing Clinton has done to America was to make the FBI the mutated clone of the Arkansas State Police resulting in their becoming a mere rubber stamp for whatever the Clinton administration declares as truth.... Whether it is the persecution of dissident investigators in the air disasters of Pan Am 103 and TWA 800, or allowing the White House to peruse the secret files of political opponents, or the alleged intimidation of key witnesses in the Foster case, the FBI is starting to look like the enforcement arm of a police state....

The FBI has now been politicized to the point where it cannot be trusted.[11]

BACKGROUND TO BETRAYAL

Let's consider two alphabet-soup organizations we know best by initials: the CFR which we discussed earlier; and the FBI which has had from its date of inception the mission of protecting the country from subversion and espionage. During the 1930s and through the war years of the 1940s, the FBI was especially active in the area of monitoring organizations with possible links to both Communism and National Socialism.

The actual FBI investigation of the CFR began about the time of the outbreak of war in Europe and continued throughout the US involvement in that war. The FBI, under the able leadership of J. Edgar Hoover, continued to monitor the CFR through the Eisenhower, Kennedy and Johnson administrations. An examination of their cabinets and close advisers will reveal that the vast majority were CFR members.

In 1972 J. Edgar Hoover launched a major investigation of the CFR. A few weeks later, he was discovered dead at his home. L. Patrick Gray III, a retired Navy captain, was appointed as director; however, in less than a year, following an exchange of data stamped SECRET between Gray and his top agent in charge of the Oklahoma City office concerning Gary Allen's book, *None Dare Call It Conspiracy*, Gray was fired by President Nixon and replaced by Clarence Kelley. He scrubbed the ongoing investigation of the CFR and lasted as head of the FBI for five years.

The thrust of the book, *None Dare Call It Conspiracy*, is that the CFR holds absolute sway over the United States Government, with the objective of destroying the Constitution and forming a socialistic one-world government under the United Nations.[12]

To refresh your memory on just what the CFR does, we can look to a book by Senator Barry M Goldwater, *With No Apologies*, in which he defined the CFR members as being "the most elite names in the world of government, labor, finance, business, communications, the foundations and the academies."[13]

While, according to Goldwater, many of the CFR policies were damaging to the cause of freedom and particularly to the United States, this is not because the members are Communists or Communist sympathizers. He further stated:

> I believe the Council on Foreign Relations and its ancillary elitist groups are indifferent to communism. They have no ideological anchors. In their pursuit of a new world order they are prepared to deal without prejudice with a communist state, a socialist state, a democratic state, monarchy, oligarchy... it's all the same to them....[14]

One CFR member (for 16 years), Admiral Chester Ward, authored a book with Phyllis Schlafly, *Kissinger on a Couch*, after he broke away from the organization. The Admiral warned:

> The most powerful clique in these elitist groups have one objective in mind... they want to bring about the surrender of the sovereignty and the national independence of the United States.[15]

Since William Webster, an active member of the CFR, took over the FBI in 1978, that organization has provided the heads of all the major intelligence and security agencies – not only the FBI, but the CIA and the NSA. It has also made deep penetrations into the higher echelons of the military.

This would seem to indicate little chance of a coup d'état taking place in the United States... unless one is deliberately staged, as was the case in the Soviet Union in 1991.

Let's look at further aspects of the typical *coup d'état* in order to determine whether here in the United States, or in other advanced nations, such a usurpation of the existing government is possible or even feasible.

SETTING THE STAGE FOR A COUP

When we examine the situations existing in other countries prior to a coup being attempted, we will see that there is generally a breakdown in communication between the government and the governed. The dialogue is either nil or meaningless.

Let's look briefly at what happened to Chile in the 1970s. William Norman Grigg, senior editor with the *New American* magazine, wrote an outstanding piece, *"Justice" for Pinochet,* in the 23 Nov 1998 issue. The thrust of this fine article was that Augusto Pinochet, former Chilean leader, was "arrested" in London (16 Oct 1998) while seeking treatment for a heart problem and diabetes. Pinochet was 82 at the time.

> Salvador Allende, who was elected president in 1970 with a 37 percent plurality, was an unabashed Marxist who was eagerly imposing Cuban-style socialism on what had been a prosperous and stable country.[16]

By 1972, former President Eduardo Frei said:

> Chile is in the throes of an economic disaster. Not a crisis, but a veritable catastrophe no one could foresee would happen so swiftly nor so totally…. The hatred is worse than the inflation, the shortages, the economic disaster.[17]

Grigg writes:

> Less than a month before the coup, Allende told his cabinet that 'the armed forces and the popular parties (that is, the various Communist-controlled groups) would move against those representing the 'fascist sectors' in Chile – which included anyone who opposed the conversion of the country into a Marxist 'utopia'.[18]

Allende created a praetorian guard and drew up lists of enemies to be purged or liquidated, including the top military leadership. Pinochet's lightning coup of 11 Sep 1973 resulted in the death of Allende and the removal of his Communist co-conspirators.

Frei declared after the coup, "The military has saved Chile and all of us. A civil war was being well-prepared by the Marxists."

Grigg reports that in the preemptive action undertaken by the military junta, about 600 Communists either died or disappeared, and another 4,800 were either imprisoned or exiled (most of those incarcerated were released within five years).

> Pinochet was indeed a dictator, but in the old Roman sense of the expression: he took power in a moment of crisis, restored lawful order, renounced his extraordinary powers and relaxed temporary restrictions as soon as events permitted, and surrendered power altogether once he was no longer needed.

> Under Pinochet's stewardship, state-run businesses were privatized, interventionist measures were abolished, the standard of living for all Chileans – including the poor – improved dramatically, a private system of retirement insurance was created, and the Chilean economy enjoyed unprecedented growth.

As Grigg states:

> Under Pinochet, Chile enjoyed the prosperity and ordered liberty which was anathema to Allende's Marxist regime. Predictably enough, Pinochet became the international focus of Communist-inspired

enmity. The Marxist Left never forgets and cannot forgive, and with the aging Pinochet – who suffered from a heart condition, a urinary tract infection, and diabetes – recuperating from surgery, the opportunity for revenge presented itself.[19]

COULD IT HAPPEN IN THE UNITED STATES?

When we look at the situation in our own country, we see a pattern, ever-intensifying since 1964, where the three branches of government not only neglect but deliberately alienate the majority. Using the psychological tactic of *divide et impera*, successive governments, whether under a Democratic or Republican president, have showered blessings on the "minorities," to the financial, social and ethnic degradation of the majority.

Governmental edicts, coupled to a controlled and complicit media deliberately divorced from the majority, are designed specifically to create further divisiveness between various groups, such as black against white, Christian against Muslim, child against parent, man against woman, and especially homosexual against heterosexual.

We witnessed this in spades in the 1990s where, in the interest of diversity, Clinton chose what he (and Hillary) considered to be equal representation of society in general in his cabinet and other appointments. Far from being representative, we saw a heavy concentration of minorities such as militant women and homosexuals. In fact, in the cabinet, in the Supreme Court selections, in Justice, in the FBI and CIA and in key advisory positions, Jews predominate.

This, of course, is not a new revelation. The majority of Woodrow Wilson's key advisors were also Jewish, as were those of FDR during his 12-year reign. (52 of his top cabinet officers and close advisors, out of a total of 75, were Jewish.)

Throughout the Clinton administration, Jews occupy at least 65% of the key slots of federal government. Many of them were selected from the CFR, whose total membership of over 3,100 is roughly 50% Jewish.

This is a fact and must be considered. The trigger to past coups and other forms of conflict has often been ethnic, moral, cultural, or religious difference, where one group strives to dominate another within a nation. Rather than coups, they develop into what we call indigenous upsurges, similar to what is happening today in the former USSR and Yugoslavia. The result is gross instability.

Such British "royalty" as Lord Rees-Mogg, Peter Carrington and Lord Owen, coupled with members of our own "royalty" here in the US, e.g., Henry Kissinger, Brent Scowcroft and Lawrence Sidney Eagleburger, operating under the banner of Kissinger Associates, have created these upsurges, using the manipulative techniques developed by the London Tavistock Institute and practiced as well by such anti-nativist organizations as the Stanford Research Institute (SRI), the Hudson Institute and the Institute for Policy Studies (IPS).

Most ruling cliques hope for stability; however, faced with a threat to their power base, they can generally create instability at will, usually to the detriment of the ruled. Any government, whether of a developed or developing nation, makes use of certain tried and true techniques of physical and psychological control and coercion of its populace, among them mass manipulation.

THE MONOPOLY OF MASS MANIPULATION

Mass manipulation by government is accomplished by controlling – either directly or indirectly – the '7 Ms': Money, Media, Markets, Medical, Mind, Morals, and Muscle, the last of which is embodied in the Military. The primary function of our armed forces is to defend the Constitution of the United States of America. That primary function, however, has slowly been subverted by an enemy within.

The Muscle has been slowly and systematically exhausted by thrusting that military into wars of attrition – no-win wars of both psychological and physical defeat, as planned by that amorphous group of self-aggrandizing and self-promoting one-worlders who are slowly, slowly strangling us and our freedom with the binding chains of despotic World Government.

That same group has now created a Monopoly over five of the seven Ms and is currently engaged in a two-fold task to subvert the military's role of defending the Constitution from all enemies, both foreign and domestic, by such missions as peacekeeping, humanitarianism, nationbuilding. At the same time, this amorphous group seeks to forge elements of our military – including National Guard units – into a global military force under the United Nations and/or NATO, which is nothing but a subgroup of the UN.

Coupled with suborning the roles and missions of the military is the progressive and systematic weakening of that force by a process of downsizing, feminizing and sodomizing. Such menacing malevolence was hatched in various Talmudic think tanks, e.g., the Institute for Policy Studies, the Hudson Institute, the Tavistock Institute for Political/Psychological Warfare, and an offshoot of the Frankfurt School, the Institute for Social Research.

Simultaneous maneuvering is still being waged to bring the entire medical industry (which constitutes 14% of the GDP) under "managed health care." The overall supervisor of this sinister plot was that Talmudic scholar and Oxonian, Ira Magaziner, while his colleagues of those very same schools – Mickey Kantor and Robert Reich – dominated the NAFTA-GATT free trade scam. Much of their control was assumed by Charlene Barshefsky, trade representative, who in 1998 was actively pushing for legislation to give Clinton fast-track negotiating authority.

These situations continue to develop because of the general passivity of the electorate. A large part of any population is generally indifferent to its government, seeking a combination of bread and circuses. Media moguls and politicos have appeased them with never-ending sex, soaps, sports, sweepstakes and subsidies, as well as a steady diet of sensationalism and propaganda passing as news on the idiot box.

Although this process of converting our Republic to a 'social democracy' and eventually to a segment of a one-world despotic government has been ongoing for the entire century, the four factors leading to a coup have never been present to a degree sufficient to trigger a coup.

Until now.

PART TWO
GRAND STRATEGY OF A COUP

UNLIKE other forms of conflict, a coup is of short duration and relatively bloodless. To be successful, however, strategy and planning must be detailed, precise and complete. 'C-cubed' must be uppermost: Command, Control, Communication.

A coup, to be successful, must be executed with maximum speed, and all units capable of supporting or interfering, whether police, security, intelligence or military, must be considered and identified. All of these units must either be active participants or effectively neutralized during that critical time of execution and shortly thereafter.

Initially, units should be divided into potential allies and neutrals; only the allies will be infiltrated in depth.

There is a third group, much larger in size, consisting of those units in isolation, either by geographic location remote from the coup site, or incapable of intervening because of their peculiar roles and missions or lack of weapons and transportation. They can be disregarded.

Although the core of the coup planners must be kept relatively small, the multi-faceted operation demands support from key individuals within those elements that will participate or that could rise up against it. This requires infiltration and cooperation – or subversion from within the force structure – of two types of individuals… leaders and technicians.[20]

Before selecting key personnel, the location, physical makeup, force structure and function of all units capable of intervening must be known. The selection of individuals then becomes the critical factor which requires a fundamental understanding of human nature. Every man approached is a potential informer. A thorough screening of all potential key personnel must be made, followed by verbal contact only: there will always be the danger of a tattler.

Technicians become invaluable for neutralizing those units capable of intervening by sabotaging or neutralizing communications, transportation, and internal lines of command and control. Technicians will also be needed on the teams given the task of neutralizing civil communications, including TV and radio stations, telephone and telex, as well as the major newspapers within the target area, usually a nation's capital. The technical interruptions of these media forms must be of a temporary nature, as they will become most important in the post-coup phase.

Choosing leaders is perhaps the most critical aspect of coup planning. Look for tried and true leadership characteristics, coupled with good relations with subordinate officers and men. Big question: Will their troops follow them?

NEUTRALIZING POLICE AND SECURITY FORCES

Police units at state and local level have a limited degree of capability to assist in the coup, but become a valuable source following the coup for maintenance of law and order, crowd control and curfew enforcement.

Federal security forces – all of the alphabet-soup groups – must be identified precisely, and determinations made as to their location, strength, armaments, transport, communications and physical ability to intervene. One must also consider the various foreign elements now scattered throughout the country, both military and police. These elements, flying the blue-and-white banner of the United Nations, both integral units and individuals infiltrated into the ranks of our fighting forces and police, must be identified and neutralized.

Counter-intelligence agencies, such as Division 5 of the FBI and Internal Security of the CIA, become critical during the planning phase of a coup, which adds emphasis to the continuing need for preservation of internal security. Beware the *agent-provocateur*!

POLITICAL FORCE – THE WILD CARD

There is a continuing danger in the post-coup phase from various political forces which possess real political power, whether inside or outside the government. These are the elements making up the major political parties, pressure groups, trade unions, civil service, academics, religious, business, and the media, or any other group having the capability to influence major segments of the populace. Here, we must reemphasize the interlocking directorate that presently has absolute control over most of the 7 Ms: Money, Media, Markets, Medical, Morals, Mind, Muscle.

The term "interlocking directorate" is most appropriate, for the nature of the Monopoly of Mass Manipulation is such that the control of one factor often leads to control of the others. Suffice it to say that provisions for the neutralization or breaking up of such control must be considered in great detail during the strategy and planning phase, and definite actions must be taken by special teams during the actual coup, as well as by political specialists during that critical phase immediately after the coup.

We must bring up once more the cardinal reason for a coup, and that is to replace an existing government. Here again is a shorthand version of the four necessary conditions that must be present in a society in order for a coup to be successful and to emerge as a legitimate government in its own right, i.e., one that will receive the support of the electorate:

1) Severe and prolonged economic crisis;

2) Unsuccessful war leading to defeat and occupation;

3) Chronic political instability;

4) Concentration of police-state power at the national level.

During the planning phase, a long, hard look must be taken at personalities inside and outside the government, and a determination made as to which ones constitute a major threat to the ultimate success of the coup. We should include in this category cabinet heads, members of Congress, advisors and all others making up the *sanctum sanctoris* or inner circle, i.e., the oligarchy. Additionally, and occasionally overlapping, we have a few powerful individuals controlling organizations with a large-scale impact on the political process, particularly in finance, the media and the market place. This is a fact, whether we are speaking historically of such coups as Greece in 1967 or Chile in 1973, or considering the likelihood of a coup in Russia, particularly, and, to a lesser degree, to such southern neighbors as Brazil, Argentina or Mexico.

And, while it may be highly unlikely that a coup would be precipitated here in the United States, the identical factors would apply. Special teams must be dispatched during the execution phase to pick up and detain all of these individuals in secure and secret conclaves until such time as the most critical transition phase has passed. Other special teams will simultaneously be dispatched to take over certain physical facilities, among them: TV and radio stations, and other fixed communication systems, such as telephone, telex links, and the internet.

Still other teams will cut off ingress/egress to the capital city by a series of roadblocks at key highway junctures, and by preventing landing and takeoff from area airports, both civil and military. One of the most effective means of neutralizing an airport is to block runways with trucks or autos, and cover them with concealed fields of fire to prevent their being removed.

Strategic buildings must be seized by team deployment within the capital. These are identified as edifices whose possession connotes political power.

Most of the factors of a military operation in combat enter into the conduct of a coup, except that no "reserve forces" are held back, nor is there any need to plan for replacements of key individuals or teams. It is a one-shot deal where every resource is fully committed and the actual event lasts only a few hours. Hence, the absolute need for extensive preparation, detailed planning, flexible timing, controlled sequence, internal security, skills in diplomacy, personnel management, and *cojones,* participation in a coup is not for the faint of heart.

The immediate objective of a coup is to destabilize the seat of government so that it can be overthrown. During the post-coup phase, all effort is geared toward restabilization. By constantly emphasizing C-Cubed – Command, Communication, Control – we retain stability within the coup forces and eventually expand them to include all elements of the military.

By control over such infrastructure as communications and transport the various bureaucratic elements, such as the police and security forces, as well as the civil service, can be stabilized. Regarding the civil populace, the immediate aim is to enforce public order. This is a two-stage process of physical coercion, followed by political steps to gain acceptance.

The immediate post-coup goal is total immobility. This can be accomplished by a no-exceptions curfew for a defined period of time. The rule is "nobody moves." Coupled with a rigid curfew is a stoppage of all forms of public transport, including aircraft, trains, buses and metro-lines. The rule is "nobody leaves."

All public buildings and government offices will remain closed for a specific time. All telecommunications will be disrupted for a like period of time. The rule is "nobody talks." In effect, the plotters now have a captive audience who will listen attentively to their broadcast monopoly via radio and TV. The purpose is not to explain or entertain, but to discourage resistance and relieve fear of personal safety. The technique will be to emphasize that the plotters are in charge and have restored law and order.

And a degree of sanity to a society gone insane.

PART THREE
COUPS D'ÉTATS IN RUSSIA AND US

LET'S have another look at the 1948 interrogations of the Gestapo Chief, Heinrich Muller, which author Gregory Douglas headlines as *The Coup d'État in Russia and the United States.*[21]

Muller was considered to be one of the foremost experts on the political and intelligence structures of the Soviet Union. Douglas states that his views on Lenin's seizure of power in 1917 by a brilliant *coup d'état* are coupled with his suggestions about how such a coup might be conducted in the United States or another democratic society.

Muller states that the actual coup in 1917 was not carried out by Lenin, the man of words, but by Trotsky, the man of action. It was Leon Trotsky who planned to seize power by a coup using no more than a thousand men – to be used against over 20,000 loyal armed troops and police, all in physical possession of the city:

> What Trotsky did was to select the key targets for control, send his men out in small groups into a city filled with deserters, frightened workers and so on, and in the confusion, get them to infiltrate into those key points. They made no attempt to seize them but merely to do a military style reconnaissance.

> While Lenin was eagerly planning his mass rising, one day and without telling anyone, Trotsky and his men struck the establishment, seized the key points, and let in Lenin and his ponderous units – something they could not have done themselves against a well-organized defense.

> This done, Trotsky then presented Lenin with the city and eventually, the whole of Russia. I stress that Trotsky was a very dangerous man and his idea is of the greatest importance in the study of how to either perform or defend against the only form of the coup that can work quickly.[22]

Upon the urging of his interrogator, Muller shed added light on the question of whether such coups were possible anywhere, "even in your peaceful country" (meaning the US in 1948).

Muller outlined the conditions that must exist before a really successful coup could be launched. Here are his key points, including the key points made by Gregory Douglas in his analysis of that segment of the secret Intelligence Report:

> Decline in the standard of living; leads to distrust of the bureaucracy which leads to the bureaucracy launching repressive actions against the unhappy citizens.

> If this repression is coupled to weak leadership at the highest levels, the public becomes frightened, unhappy, and demanding of change.

> The leadership in turn becomes frightened and demands more and more police who antagonize the people even further.

> There will be outbreaks of civil disobedience...religious agencies will become involved against the government, which will make a cardinal error and try to repress them as well. This will anger the neutralists who will side with the churches and, at some point, some group will seize power by a coup.

> A right-wing coup is the best assumption. The public wants a return to stability and only a dictator can supply this. They will willingly surrender the authority to him if he will assume all responsibility.

> The fewer number of actual coup plotters the better... a few key military units, preferably elite ones, in proximity to the capital, a few key units specializing in communications and you have a successful coup.

> Control of the news is of utmost import... send armed technicians into the main sending stations and put out just the right kind of news at the critical moment. You don't need to subvert newspapers and radio stations if you control their news....

> There must be a common enemy against whom the new government will ruthlessly proceed to bring law and order back to the people whom they serve.

> In developing a secret police to combat these menaces (of staging a coup), one can place too much power in their hands and place too much reliance on their honesty... the Russian secret police became a state within a state... you will have the same problems in your country (the US) if you give too much power to an agency designed to protect you (the FBI).

I think (the danger of armed militias) lay more in their lack of proper training rather than any menace to the government. Most of these small farmers and businessmen would support the government and essentially be of a conservative nature.... You would want to disarm them? That probably wouldn't be very wise. With your natural inclination to rebel, the farmers would shoot back....

A stable society does not need such groups (militias), but in an unstable one, many citizens would feel threatened by their government's lack of protection, and no doubt, form such groups. And, if the governments were left-wing, they would fear such private armies very much because of their inherent threat.[23]

Here, Gregory makes certain reflections on the historical significance of Muller's comments:

The continued discussion about the bearing of arms by non-military citizens is much more interesting... the first government of the United States viewed the citizen-soldier as an important element of defense [as] is reflected in the Constitution where the subject is specifically addressed.

A conservative government might be dull but it does not, in general, attempt to exert control over its citizens, other than to maintain law and order. A radical government, on the other hand, cannot feel safe in its power until it has established an ever-intrusive control over its people.

Control of weapons is certainly a prime goal for such an entity and this would work in tandem with discrediting and eventually destroying, any institution that might be able to mount an attack on it.

The first target (of a radical administration) would be any religious group who might find a moral, and hence religious, fault with its goals or techniques. The second target would be any other organization that could conceivably organize against it.

By a *de facto* control over the reporting of news, an administration bent on complete domination can accomplish the implementation of their goals with relative ease, given a receptive and passive audience.

Faked opinion polls and heavily slanted pro-administration reportage might have had a strong effect on this audience when there were no other sources of information. But, with the advent of alternative information sources... propaganda is far less able to influence, dominate, and control public perceptions.[24]

One should obtain the four-volume set of *Gestapo Chief* and study it in its entirety. The similarities between what is currently happening to citizens in the United States and what happened to citizens of Russia from 1917 on – until they were either completely destroyed, cast into Gulags, or became slave laborers in the grain factories (collective farms), the mines and the arms plants – will mesmerize you, may even enrage you, but the question remains: what can we do about it; i.e., becoming slaves to the Bolsheviks?

Prof. Carroll Quigley, in his monumental work, *Tragedy and Hope: A History of the World in our Time*, points out that when the Bolsheviks seized the centers of government in St. Petersburg (7 Nov 1917), they were able to hold them because of the refusal of the local military contingents to support the Provisional Government.[25]

PART FOUR
SEVEN DAYS IN MAY

FOR a better grasp of the how and why of a coup, let's turn to *Seven Days in May,* a fictional account of a coup to take place in May 1973 by a group of high-ranking US military, led by the Chairman of the Joint Chiefs. The book came out exactly 12 months before the assassination of JFK and just prior to the beginnings of what came to be known as the Vietnam War. It appears that *Seven Days in May* was a psychological precursor to both events, designed to place the US military in a defensive position politically, which would ultimately lead to degradation and defeat of that same military force.[26]

Seven Days in May was written by Fletcher Knebel and Charles W. Bailey II and published in November 1962. (Originally the story was written by Charles Bailey, but it didn't sell, so he joined forces with a better-known writer, Fletcher Knebel, his colleague at the Washington Bureau of Cowles Publications. Bailey had been a reporter with the Minneapolis Star and Tribune; Knebel had been a reporter in Ohio and wrote a column from Washington, *Political Fever.*) A significant factor about the book: nowhere within its covers is there a name of a publisher, only the date 1962. Neither is there any other customary copyright data nor any Library of Congress catalog card number.

This author was given a copy by his then Pentagon boss, Gen Robert H York, who would go on to command the 82d Airborne in the invasion of the Dominican Republic (1965) and later take over the three-star slot as commander of the XVIII Airborne Corps at Fort Bragg.

That slot in the fictional book was held by Lt Gen Thomas R. Hastings, commander of the First Airborne Corps, US Army, Fort Bragg, NC. His command was a very important element of the coup plot. It provided 3,500 special forces soldiers being trained at a secret base in New Mexico and would provide the aircraft out of Pope Air Force Base for the troop lift to key cities and installations about the US during the coup.

It is fairly easy to categorize the mind-set of the authors as "liberal" or "left-liberal." There is a definite anti-military tone throughout the book, epitomized at the frontispiece by the quotation of President Eisenhower's valedictory address at the end of his second term, 17 January 1961:

> ...In the councils of government, we must guard against the acquisition of unwarranted influence, whether sought or unsought, by the military-industrial complex. The potential for the disastrous rise of misplaced power exists and will persist. We must never let the weight of this combination endanger our liberties or democratic processes.[27]

Of course, if we really want to look at a military-industrial complex, we can look back to WW I when Bernard Baruch regimented American industry to meet the requirements of total warfare. (As part of the Industrial Mobilization Plan, it was revised during WW II, developed under Louis Johnson, assistant secretary of war, and approved by President Roosevelt.)

To put the book in its proper context, one must also understand that in the overall strategy on the part of this same liberal-minority intelligencia, the specter of a military-industrial complex is constantly depicted as a sort of wholesale conspiracy against the American people by WASP military brass and WASP industrial leaders.

Analyzing the book from a psychological standpoint. First, it is a real page-turner, well worth the read, particularly at this time, as there are remarkable similarities between the politico/economic situations in the US at the fictional time of the story (1973) and today.

The President, Jordon Lyman, is called "Governor" by many of his court followers – he had served two terms as Democratic governor of Ohio – and his current poll rating at mid-term is 29%, "lowest in the history of such poll taking." The Presidency was previously held by a Republican. Senator Prentice of California (in on the coup) explains the rating: "It's very simple, the President trusts Russia, the American people don't."[28]

The President has just signed a nuclear disarmament treaty with the head of the USSR (Premier Georgi Feemorov) and forced it through the Senate with only two votes to spare for the required two-thirds majority. Under the agreement, each country (under the eyes of Indian and Finnish inspectors) on 1 July would disarm ten neutron bombs. Each month thereafter more bombs would be dismantled, not only by the US and USSR, but by all nuclear powers, including Red China which had ratified the treaty. Two years hence, all nuclear lockers would be bare.

Let's set the scene; it is May and on the weekend the military is to run another test against a simulated nuclear attack, called Red Alert. The President would go to his weekend retreat at Camp David in the Maryland hills and then fly south by chopper to the underground command post at Mount Thunder in the Blue Ridge Mountains of Virginia, where the five members of the Joint Chiefs would have already assembled.

At the President's command, "All Red," the emergency communications lines would be opened, all missile bases would be armed within five minutes, all SAC bombers would be airborne in ten minutes, all Nike Zeus anti-missile missiles would be armed and tracking, and every warship of the fleet would be on the way to sea.

The Army airborne divisions at Bragg and Campbell would each have a regiment combat-loaded and ready for takeoff within a half-hour. The Air Defense Command interceptors, armed with air-to-air missiles, would be allowed ten minutes to get their flights to 50,000 feet.

Also to be tested Saturday is the master communications control system. "A flick of a switch at Mount Thunder would cut into every radio and television network in the US, placing control over broadcasting in the hands of the command post." Such a switch (if one exists, and it probably does) would become perhaps the most important lever to be controlled by the coup plotters.[29]

So much for the general layout; let's look at some of the actors.

Senator Clark of Georgia is talking with Gen Barney Rutkowski, head of SAC about the possibility of a coup: "You don't seem surprised, General. Aren't you a little thrown by this thing?"

"I did a lot of putting two and two together on the way over here, Senator. People always say it can't happen here, and I'm one of those people. But all of a sudden I figured out I was wrong. Given the right circumstances, it can happen anywhere. And don't quote me in the Senate, but the military has been riding awful high-wide-and-handsome in this country ever since World War II...."[30]

Todd, Secretary of the Treasury, without telling the President or others, had assembled 30 agents of the Narcotics Bureau and the Alcohol Tax unit – both under the jurisdiction of the Treasury – in his office across the street from the White House.

Perhaps the most revealing passage is toward the end when the President calls in the Joint Chiefs' Chairman, Gen Scott, with the intent of forcing him to resign. (We learned early on through a Marine Colonel Casey that Gen Scott is head of the coup and will become President in order to legitimatize the coup.) "The President felt inadequate and puny sitting under this tall and imposing officer who held a cigar pointed at him like a weapon. The President stood up and took a step forward, putting the two men on more equal physical terms as they stood facing each other. Scott kept on talking."[31]

> The information put together yesterday by the NIC and reported to both of us by Lieberman substantiates all the misgivings of the Joint Chiefs. We told you time and again that the Russians will never adhere to the spirit of the treaty. And we emphasized until we were blue in the face that it was folly to sign a document which left a clear loophole – namely that one country or another could assemble warheads in one place as fast as it took them apart in another under the eyes of the neutral inspectors.
>
> The US of course would never do that, but the Russians would – and are doing precisely that.... I must say further, Mr President, that it borders on criminal negligence not to take some immediate action. If you persist in that path, I'll have no recourse as a patriotic American but to go to the country with these facts.

'Listen, Mr President,' Scott spoke softly, but his voice seemed like a hammer at Lyman. 'You have lost the respect of the country. Your policies have brought us to the edge of disaster. Business doesn't trust you. Labor flaunts its disdain for you with strikes. Military morale has sunk to the lowest point in 30 years, thanks to your stubborn refusal to provide even decent minimum compensation for service to the nation.

Your treaty was the act of a naive boy.[32]

Art Corwin (head of the Secret Service) had 24 Secret Service agents scattered through the White House and around the grounds. We are led to believe that Art is tough, but not very bright, as compared to, say, Lieberman.

Saul Lieberman was Director of Central Intelligence. If Lyman had required IQ tests for his appointees, Lieberman would have led the field with 20 points [see the book *The Bell Curve* for import] to spare. He had been an enlisted man in the Army Counterintelligence Corps during WWII, then went home to Detroit to found a retail credit agency that spread into half the states and made him rich. Two private missions behind the Iron Curtain and service on several presidential committees which weighed the shortcomings of the CIA gained him a small reputation in the elite world of espionage... Lieberman was almost aggressively uncouth....

Morty Freeman [a TV script writer in NY] promptly plunged into a passionate denunciation of nuclear weapons and previous US policies, praising Lyman for 'having the courage' to understand that 'the Communists want to live too.' When he went on to declare that Eisenhower-Kennedy distrust of the Russians had set civilization back two decades, Casey [the Marine colonel] offered mild dissent. Freeman blasted military officers as 'latter-day Francos', damned the Republican Party, the Chamber of Commerce and the American Medical Association, and called Lyman 'the only world statesman since Nehru'.[33]

Finally, after forcing the resignation of the top military officers, President Lyman goes on national TV to address the nation. Among his cogent comments:

No matter what convictions and deeply felt motives moved General Scott and his colleagues to act as they did, I had no choice as President and commander in chief of the armed forces, but to act as I did. To have done otherwise would have been to betray the great trust handed down to us across two centuries by the men who wrote the Constitution. This is a republic, managed by a President freely elected by all the people... he must assume full responsibility, under the Constitution, for the foreign relations and defense of the United States....[34]

The takeaway for all this blather – I assume intentionally by the authors – is that the military is a bunch of damned Fascists, intent on subjugating the American people and destroying the Constitution, replacing it with a dictatorship of "far right Birchers" (the authors use this expression, perhaps already fearful of the John Birch Society, which was founded in 1958). The fact is that by 1962, when the book was published, we had long since ceased to be a Republic and were well on the road to becoming a true social democracy, patterned after that other social democracy in the USSR. In order to bring these two world powers into alignment, the powers that be (such as the CFR, the ADL and the Trilateralists) totally disregard the principles of the Constitution.

We have nurtured that social democracy in the USSR right along and without fail from day one up through today. Whether we now choose to call it social democracy or by some other name matters little, for the ultimate goal of our fearful masters is to align the two powers – United States and Russia – as the absolute rulers of the world.

And now, what goes around, comes around, for the last of the Soviet dictators under the Soviet Union, Mikhail Gorbachev by name, is ensconced in the commandant's residence of the Presidio in San Francisco. He lives there, friends, and operates his Gorbachev Foundation USA from those beautiful grounds.

And from its confines issues pronouncements about the coming global despotism envisioned by his Soviet predecessors, such as Lenin, Stalin, Brezhnev and Andropov.

His world forum concentrated on "fundamental challenges and opportunities confronting humanity as we enter the next century... we are giving birth to the first global civilization.... Inherent within the forum is the potential for establishing a global brain trust to continue into the next century... and to provide the framework for stability and regulated human interactions...."[35]

Truly, we have not only helped wheel this latest Trojan Horse inside the gates, we are stabling it in the finest of sumptuous quarters and feeding it the most delectable of our abundant produce – the fertile, febrile brains of our highly impressionable youth.

Remember that Gorbachev has never renounced his love, admiration and respect for Marxist/Leninist ideology. He in fact is ushering in – with an able assist from his colleagues in the CFR – the brave new world of Socialism, which Dr. John Coleman defines as *The Road to Slavery* in his 1994 book of that title.[36]

Dr. Coleman, in his epic work, not only gives us the history of Fabian Socialism, but explains why it leads to slavery by making use of the following techniques: - Socialist-Controlled Education - Subverting the Constitution - Socialist Penetration and Permeation of Religion - Destruction of the US through Free Trade. In his Introduction, the good doctor calls Socialism "the principal, fatal political disease of modern nations," and quotes Lenin, "Communism is Socialism in a hurry." He explains that Socialism is the liquidation of the free enterprise system and is "revolution without openly violent methods but nevertheless does the utmost violence to the psyche of the nation."[37]

Dr. Coleman points to such of our presidents as Wilson, Roosevelt, Eisenhower, Carter, Kennedy, Johnson and Clinton, who were eager, willing servants of Fabian Socialism. Dr Coleman boldly states:

> All United States presidents since Wilson have repeatedly stated that the United States is a Democracy, when in fact, it is a Confederated Republic.... The bland smooth surface of Socialism hides its true intent: A Federal World Government under Socialist control, in which We, the People, will be their slaves in a New World Order of the New Dark Age.[38]

WHERE IS THE AMERICAN LEGION?

That once-great organization was founded by a group of patriots after the needless involvement of the United States in WW I. Charter members included this author's father and two uncles, one, Donn Stowell, an American flying ace of the famous Hat in the Ring Squadron, whose best friend, Eddie Rickenbacker, was the leading ace with 26 kills. Eddie also was a charter member of the American Legion.

The Legion was originally set up to combat Communist infiltration. A group of concerned former officers, who had served with the American Expeditionary Force in France, bankrolled it, including Grayson Murphy, William Doyle and Gerald MacGuire of a New York brokerage house. Others were businessmen, such as Robert Sterling Clark, a Wall Street banker, John W. Davis, a one-time candidate for the presidency of the United States, Alfred E. Smith, former governor of New York and another presidential contender, as well as a leading industrialist, Iréné du Pont, founder of the American Liberty League.

This was the group behind the genuine attempt to pull a *coup d'état* in 1933. Their representative approached a famous American hero, known as "the fighting Quaker," Maj Gen Smedley Darlington Butler, the retired commandant of the US Marines.

Butler would later appear before the McCormack-Dickstein Committee of the House of Representatives, which was set up to investigate Bolshevik activity in the United States. According to his testimony, he was offered the job of leading a 500,000-man army comprised of veterans, which would spearhead the coup.

Corroborating testimony was provided by Paul Comly French, a reporter for the *Philadelphia Record*. French testified that the contact man for the group plotting the coup, Gerald MacGuire, told French of the need for a "government in this country to save the nation from the communists who want to tear it down and wreck all that we have built in America. The only men who have the patriotism to do it are the soldiers, and Smedley Butler is the ideal leader. He would organize a million men overnight." [39]

The McCormack-Dickstein Committee released a watered-down report of the Butler testimony, but claimed there was no evidence of a plot led by prominent Americans.

In the new States not only a man's property and his work, but his family, his leisure and his thought are controlled by the immense and complex machinery of party and police and propaganda which are gradually transforming society from a commonwealth of free citizens into a hive or an ant-heap. For the new tyranny is not merely a matter of subjugating the people by force to the rule of a master, like the tyrannies of the past; it uses the new techniques of psychology and behaviorism to condition the personality and to control the mind, as it were, from within. By continued repression and stimulation, by suggestion and terrorization, the personality is subjected to a methodical psychological assault until it surrenders its freedom and becomes a puppet which shouts and marches and hates and dies at its masters' voice, or in response to their unseen and unrecognized stimulation. In such an order...the new power [becomes] means for conditioning and controlling the psychic life of the masses.

Christopher Dawson, *The Judgment of the Nations*

EPILOGUE
THE INSANITY OF EMPIRE

What's the point of having this superb military that you're
always talking about if we can't use it?
Secretary of State Madeleine Albright to Gen Colin Powell, 1994

REIGN OF MASS MURDERERS

"IT is natural to man to indulge in the illusions of hope," led off
Patrick Henry at the Second Virginia Convention (23 Mar
1775) at St. John's Church in Richmond. "We are apt to shut our
eyes against the painful truth – and listen to the song of that siren,
till she transforms us into beasts...."[1]

Today, we of the military – whether active or retired – are
being fatally neutralized by the songs of other sirens. Yes,
collectively, we have become beasts, and our crimes are legendary,
whether under such leaders and traitors as George Catlett Marshall
or Dwight David Eisenhower. We soldiers have marched to the
drum beats of such traitors of today as George Herbert Walker
Bush and his fellow drug-runner of the 1980s, that psalm-singing,
Bible-toting non-soldier and war-monger, William Jefferson
Clinton.

Just what in God's name are they after – these traitors to
our country and Constitution? What is that they crave beyond all
else? What do they mean when they grandiloquently speak of the
New World Order? Above all, just who are their masters, clever
ventriloquists whose words they mouth?

We saw that it was FDR who used his imperial powers to
promote the basic principles of a mysterious clique whose
diabolical plans for redistribution of the earth and its resources
were first published in 1942, but clearly prepared much earlier.

The Group for a New World Order, headed by Moritz Gomberg, proposed:

- that the Bolshevist/Communist Empire should be extended from the Pacific to the Rhine, with China, Korea, Indo-China, Siam and Malaya in its orbit;

- that a Hebrew State should be set up on the soil of 'Palestine, Transjordan and the adjoining territories';

- that Canada and numerous 'strategic islands' were to pass to the United States;

- that the remaining countries of Western Europe were to disappear in a 'United States of Europe';

- that the African continent was to become a 'Union of Republics';

- that the British Commonwealth was to be left much reduced, the Dutch East Indies joining Australia and New Zealand in it.[2]

Much of this "Gomberg Plan" (as it was termed by FDR and others) came to pass; much of it is still being implemented by a brotherhood made up of a curious mix of "JEWS WHO ARE NOT JEWS" and "CHRISTIANS WHO ARE NOT CHRISTIAN" – in fact, the BICEPHALOUS MONSTER, BARBARIANS WITHIN THE GATES.

If we are to save the once-sovereign nation known as the United States of America, we had better heed that patriotic address made in Richmond, Virginia some 225 years ago by Patrick Henry:

> Sir, we have done everything that could be done to avert the storm which is now coming on. We have petitioned – we have remonstrated – we have supplicated – we have prostrated ourselves before the throne, and have implored its interposition to arrest the tyrannical hands of the ministry and parliament. Our petitions have been slighted; our remonstrances have produced additional violence and insult; our supplications have been disregarded; and we have been spurned with contempt from the foot of the throne....

> There is no longer any room for hope. If we wish to be free – if we mean to preserve inviolate those inestimable privileges for which we have been so long contending... we must fight! I repeat it, sir, we must fight!

> An appeal to arms and to the God of hosts is all that is left us![3]

Certainly those stirring words could be repeated in truth today; only the "throne" has changed, along with substituting the "administration and Congress" for the ministry and parliament. Today, however, we are no longer separated from the oppressor by a large body of water. Our oppressor is here... inside the gates.

We ignore at our peril the explicit words in Chapter 14, "The Coming Coup":

When you strike at a king, strike to kill.

John Atkinson Hobson, in his epic work, *Imperialism: A Study* (1902), stated:

> The direct influence exercised by great financial houses in 'high politics' is supported by the control which they exercise over the body of public opinion through the Press, which, in every 'civilised' country, is becoming more and more their obedient instrument... the City has notoriously exercised a subtle and abiding influence upon leading London newspapers, and through them upon the body of provincial Press, while the entire dependence of the Press for its business profits upon its advertising columns has involved a peculiar reluctance to oppose the organised financial classes with whom rests the control of so much advertising business.[4]

John Swinton, a leading editor of note prior to WW I, also passed judgment on the Press at an annual dinner of the American Press Association:

> There is no such thing as an independent Press in America, if we except that of little country towns. You know this and I know it. Not a man among you dares to utter his honest opinion. Were you to utter it, you know beforehand that it would never appear in print. I am paid one hundred and fifty dollars a week so that I may keep my honest opinion out of the newspaper for which I write. You too are paid similar salaries for similar services. Were I to permit that a single edition of my newspaper contained an honest opinion, my occupation – like Othello's – would be gone in less than 24 hours. The man who would be so foolish as to write his honest opinion would soon be on the streets in search of another job. It is the duty of a New York journalist to lie, to distort, to revile, to toady at the feet of Mammon, and to sell his country and his race for his daily bread, or what amounts to the same thing, his salary. We are the tools and the vassals of the rich behind the scenes. We are marionettes. These men pull the strings and we dance. Our time, our

talents, our lives, our capacities are all the property of these men – we are intellectual prostitutes.[5]

Advancing up the slippery slope of time, as trod by both men of wealth and their wordsmith lackeys, we come to June of 1991 and a Bilderberger gathering in Baden Baden, Germany (attended by Gov Bill Clinton of Arkansas), wherein David Rockefeller spoke thusly:

> We are grateful to the *Washington Post*, the *New York Times*, *Time Magazine* and other great publications whose directors have attended our meetings and respected their promises of discretion for almost 40 years.... It would have been impossible for us to develop our plan for the world if we had been subjected to the lights of publicity during those years. But, the world is more sophisticated and prepared to march towards a world government. The supranational sovereignty of an intellectual elite and world bankers is surely preferable to the national auto-determination practiced in past centuries.[6]

Americans view the passing scene through the beady eyes of the global Bolsheviks shaping the world. Wearied by the intense struggle to make a living, they are soothed into comfortable mental lethargy by a quadripartite of pain-relievers – the radio, the television, the newspapers and the movies. With unbounded tolerance for those who entertain them with the spoken and written word emanating from those four anodynes, they willingly embrace as truth the various untruths and outright lies being regurgitated regarding the state of their country and of the world. Having been deliberately dumbed down in the public schools since their kindergarten days, they enter adulthood with sensibilities so dulled that they are oblivious to the fact they have become but discardable pawns on the gigantic chessboard of the New World Order.

This, my friends, is the fatal flaw brought about by media manipulation. It makes the subversion of our democracy, as limited by the Constitution, an accepted fact to the unthinking masses who cheer our departing brave boys (and girls) of the military as they sally forth into the latest foreign adventure, inexorably leading to a New World Order under the control of the United Nations Command, while destroying the sovereignty of the United States.

Sure, this is totalitarianism... but... with a kinder, gentler face. The techniques are the same, whether in a free society or a slave state, namely, the use of disinformation, dissimulation, propaganda and the spiking or killing of stories or events or manuscripts, no matter how promising, that do not hew the party line; i.e., the New World Order.

Such has been the case in Soviet Russia since the Bolshevist invasion, or bloody revolution, of 1917; and in this country, since the Fabian Socialists locked step with International Zionism to take back the Colonies in a quiet and peaceful revolution, beginning under Woodrow Wilson in 1912, and reaching fruition in 1933 with the advent of FDR and his New Deal.

We saw in Chapter 4 how FDR and his fellow Bolshevik New Dealers set out to socialize America and set it up for a one-world globalist government. They desperately needed a war, in order to destroy Germany, to save Uncle Joe's Russia and to spread Soviet bolshevism throughout Western Europe. FDR began a search for a military man who could lead the US forces into combat in Europe, with the goal of bringing this seemingly impossible task to fruition. With a little help from his daughter, Anna, he found Dwight David Eisenhower.

The beleagured Bill Clinton, in March of 1999, was also looking for a war – any war – to bemuse the fickle public; perhaps Kosovo, or once more into Iraq... or maybe both! Let's take a look at what he tried with a clumsy attempt in December 1998 to arrange a coup, a la JFK in 1963.

OPERATION DESERT FOX

As the showdown at High Noon approaches, we must consider the operation designed by Clinton's handlers to divert attention away from his impeachment and trial. Perhaps the best intelligence report on that fiasco is one issued by Donald S. McAlvany, editor of the *McAlvany Intelligence Advisor* (Feb 1999 issue). Following are key excerpts:

Several months before the launch of Desert Fox in December (1998), Clinton commissioned the CIA and British Intelligence to recruit Sunni Muslims to overthrow Saddam. The US was to provoke Saddam by pushing a confrontation over weapons inspections and then launch a four-day air attack against Iraq.

On the fifth day, 5,000 US troops in Kuwait were to join up with 3,000 SCRI Iraqi soldiers (i.e., Iraqis opposed to Hussein) and 15,000 Saudi, United Arab Emirates, and other Gulf State troops. Kurdish troops were to move south. Iraq's Third Corps (whose commanders were anti-Saddam) was to move in conjunction with the coalition forces and on Day Five launch a coup against Saddam. The US was to provide the air cover and destroy Republican Guard units. Anti-Saddam Shi-ite units in the South were to attack Republican Guards and pin them down, and also take over key television stations. Saddam would be overthrown. Clinton would be a hero at home, and the Republican drive for impeachment would be derailed.

In early December the green light was given for US and British special ops to infiltrate Iraq. On 10 December Iraq would not let UN inspectors in. On 14 December a Saudi special ops soldier was shot crossing the Saudi border and the US forces went on Defcon Charlie (the highest state of alert short of war). It is believed the Saudi carried maps and other documents that tipped off Saddam regarding the coming attack.

The tipoff could also have come through leaks from the US, British, or French governments. Clinton told French President Chirac of the coming attack, but gave him the wrong date, and Chirac leaked word to Russia – but with the wrong date. Also, undoubtedly, Russia put Iraq (which is a client state of Russia's) on alert that an attack was coming.

Early on the morning of 16 December, a countercoup took place. Saddam issued Presidential Decree 98 which called for a dramatic restructuring and redeployment of commanders and subcommanders in the Iraqi Third Corps (which was to lead the revolt against him). The two top officers in the Third Corps and five top officers in Camp Rashid (a training camp attached to the Third Corps) were arrested and summarily executed. Later that day, the US government learned of the executions and, hence, the total exposure of the coup plot. At that point, Desert Fox had a greatly reduced chance of succeeding in overthrowing Saddam.

Nevertheless, President Clinton, desperate for a distraction from the impeachment juggernaut… gave the order to commence the air strikes on 16 December…. Then on 18 December, confirmation came that all the primary coup participants were dead. The air strikes were halted and Desert Fox was aborted.[7]

SHOOTOUT AT HIGH NOON

The glaring headlines of the *Culpeper Star Exponent* (12 Feb 1999) announced "Decision at High Noon":

WASHINGTON - The Senate is poised to acquit President Clinton at high noon, putting an end to the rancorous impeachment trial but not, perhaps, to the rancor on Capitol Hill.[8]

Some savvy journalist will shortly pen an entire book dedicated to the proposition that the impeachment hearings, the trial and indeed the entire sexcapade with the young "princess" intern, Monica Lewinsky, were part of a script written as early as 1992 when a very wealthy entrepreneur paid a million bucks into the coffers of the Democratic National Committee and the Clinton election campaign, with the only caveat being that the former Hollywood high school student be given a top security clearance as a White House intern.

This was but one of the second mortgages taken out on William Jefferson Clinton – call it blackmail – to ensure that he carried out the will of his fearful masters. As the holders of second mortgages are wont to do, these obligations were to be called in at critical junctures in the political/financial world of high crimes and misdemeanors.

The sexual peccadilloes were both lascivious and titillating to the generally unthinking public – great entertainment! They masked the really high crimes and related misdemeanors. Many members of the Senate and House on both sides of the aisle belong to the same secret societies whose codes of honor demand protection of their own, even when the highest crime of treason is known and recognized. Such was the case with William Jefferson Clinton.

Following the Revolutionary War in 1787, Benjamin Franklin recognized the inherent danger of choosing a country's leader who could for whatever reason resort to tyranny and treason. Franklin said, "Impeachment is the alternative to assassination."[9]

To put this in its proper context, recognize that Kenneth Starr was severely restricted as to the charges he could send to the

Congress for consideration of impeachment. The really criminal activities of this sitting president – up to an including treason – were set aside and only *l'affair Monique* was allowed to be considered. Thus our sitting president was more than satisfied with the charges. He had read the script (as had Hillary). He knew, as did most of the Representatives, and perhaps all of the Senators, that the outcome announced on 12 February was foreordained.

So, now it's back to business as usual, right?

Not quite. Recall that in Chapter 2 we discussed the money and media monopoly which led to the destruction of France and what Prof. Quigley calls "the excesses of frenzy and fraud displayed in the United States."

WHERE IS OUR MILITARY LEADERSHIP?

We witnessed the media, the money power and the administration back the bombing of Serbia – albeit under NATO auspices – for 78 murderous days and nights, then support the dispatch of thousands of American soldiers – under UN control – into Kosovo as peacekeepers.

For those of us who keep track of such ventures, it is *deja vu* all over again. When George Bush was vacating the White House for Bill Clinton in 1993, the endangered country was Somalia. Reporter Gil Klein explained that military adventure in the *Richmond Times-Dispatch* (17 Jan 1993), under the header, "Crises Pushing Packing Into Background." In that prescient article, reporter Klein outlined the last major address by the outgoing president (Bush) to the US Military Academy cadets where he warned them:

> We would risk the emergence of a world characterized by violence, characterized by chaos, one in which dictators and tyrants threaten their neighbors, build arsenals brimming with weapons of mass destruction and ignore the welfare of their own men, women and children.[10]

While he cautioned that we should not become the world's policeman, he said that: "Once we are satisfied that force makes sense, we must act with the maximum possible support."[11]

Klein also quotes defense analyst Lawrence Korb of the Brookings Institute who explained our sending troops into Somalia thusly: "Somalia is an experiment to show we can do something in concert with the United Nations in an area where we have no vital interests."[12]

Robert Hunter, with the Center for Strategic and International Studies, was also quoted: "It is important that it goes right because it is getting the American people used to this kind of operation... *it is creeping the American people up on the idea of accepting the use of American forces under United Nations command.*" (Emphasis added.)[13]

Here we are, still busily creeping the American people (and Congress) up on the idea of accepting the use of American forces under UN command.

The Undersecretary of State, Thomas Pickering, appeared before the House International Affairs Committee on 10 Feb 1999 and defended Bill Clinton's unilateral decision to commit troops to Kosovo, claiming that "there is ample constitutional precedent for this type of action."

Representative Tom Campbell (R-Ca) quickly informed Pickering that "previous constitutional violations do not justify subsequent ones."

Representative Pat Danner (D-Mo) added: "We are indeed going into a second Bosnia."

Representative Ron Paul (R-Tx) referred to Clinton's promise that the troops he deployed to Bosnia would be home in six months. "The years have passed," Paul states, "more than $20 billion has been spent, and our soldiers are still there. Very few seriously ask anymore when these troops are coming home – or even what it is they are supposed to be accomplishing."

In November 1995, as a means of compelling Congressional acquiescence in his Bosnia deployment, Clinton inserted a small advance contingent, before unilaterally dispatching a force of 20,000 peacekeepers. By this tactic, Clinton used our

GIs as hostages. Congress was unwilling to defund the Administration's unconstitutional venture lest it be accused of abandoning our soldiers in the field.

The *Washington Post* (12 Feb 1999) indicated that Clinton is prepared to pursue the strategy once more by kidnapping a 2,200-man Marine expeditionary force deployed in the Adriatic and relocating them in Kosovo in advance of the main body of NATO peacekeepers.[14]

Using such time-honored tactics, Clinton was re-creating the Somalia debacle of 1993; US troops assigned to a UN-supervised peacekeeping mission, under foreign command, deployed to a region in which no peace nor US vital interest exists, while "battlin' Madeleine, the mad bomber," along with her willing handmaidens – the US military – used the aging 8-engine B-52 bombers to rain death and destruction on both friend and foe by precision bombing Kosovo – and the rest of Serbia – from 15,000 feet for 78 unending days and nights of Talmudic-instigated terror.

We saw in an early chapter where the widespread terror-bombing of German civilians was first instigated by the British in 1942 under the dictates of the Lindemann Plan. Shortly thereafter, this drumbeat of merciless destruction was picked up by the former vice president, Henry A. Wallace (Walinsky) in his work, *The Century of the Common Man*. Wallace declared, in Chapter 11, "Business Measures":

> No businessman can plan for the future with any certainty so long as there is fear of war on the horizon. It is vital, therefore, that the United Nations' covenant must provide the machinery to assure 'freedom from fear' – an international peace law, an international peace court, and an international peace force. If any aggressor nations take the first step toward rearmament, they must be served at once with a 'cease and desist' order and be warned of the consequences.
>
> If economic quarantine does not suffice, the United Nations' peace force must at once bomb the aggressor nation mercilessly.[15]

IS THE MILITARY READY TO MUTINY?

Until our successful slaughter of Serbs – and others – by interdicting them with a thousand cruise missiles and 40,000 tons of aerial high explosives, the use of air power to compel subjugation of an enemy had a sordid history of miserable failure. One only has to look back to our aerial assault of North Vietnam during the Johnson and Nixon administrations, where we dropped more military ordnance than previously used in the history of aerial warfare. The results are well known: ignominious and utter defeat of the world's greatest power, the United States of America.

What the military learned was that air strikes, uncoupled from a general war-making strategy, do not convince an adversary of our firm resolve, but reflect a fatal weakness of our overall policy. In fact, military leaders warned President Clinton prior to the Kosovo campaign that such action would create more problems than it solved. They urged the president to use continued diplomacy; however, with such foreign policy lightweights as Madeleine Albright and Richard Holbrooke leading the diplomatic effort, such a course was doomed from the start.

One high-level Pentagon source said, "This campaign is a White House operation, not a military action. We are following the orders of our commander-in-chief; that doesn't mean we agree with him."

The disagreement between the military and the White House grew so heated just prior to the beginning of the air strikes in late March 1999 that Secretary of Defense William Cohen warned the Joint Chiefs to "keep your troops in line on this one."

So, we were caught in another effort to bomb a sovereign nation back to the stone age through the use of air power alone, this one covered by the transparent fig leaf of a combined NATO effort – with no overall plan or strategy, except to convince the American people that our valiant efforts at peacekeeping were noble and moral, to quote our draft-dodging commander in chief, Bill Clinton.

"The tension here is incredible," one military source told reporter Doug Thompson of the Capitol Hill Blue web site. "We have high-level officers talking privately of defying orders, but no one is willing to risk their career to stand up to the president of the United States."[16]

In a revealing article carried in *Chronicles* magazine (July 1998), William J. Corliss, an associate of Boston University Center for Defense Journalism, stressed that the onslaught of political correctness has resulted in the lowest military morale in history.[17]

"Outside of religious orders, there is no institution that demands so much in the way of obedience and conformity as the military. Precisely because the imperatives of political correctness are so frequently contrary to human nature, the effects on a comparatively closed society like the military are devastating."

Corliss fingers the major problem within the rank and file of our fighting forces – that is, the feminization of our fighting forces and the social experimentation which flies in the face of good order, morale and discipline. It has "finally matured into a criminal neglect of the concrete exigencies of war-fighting."

Who is to blame? Corliss points out that:

> ... there exists a thin crust of officers at the very top who are there because they have shown themselves willing to carry out the directives of the civilian culture warriors. Serving below them is a vast sea of disgust, complemented by highly trained professionals who have retired in droves citing morale, a changed culture, and lowered standards of every sort."[18]

In an interview with former Chairman of the Joint Chiefs of Staff, Admiral Thomas H. Moorer, that "thin crust" is revealed by name; regrettably, they have gone over to the enemy. In the *New American* magazine (2 Aug 1999), Publisher John F. McManus points out that:

> The CFR Annual Report lists the organization's members. Currently appearing on the list are the names of the chairman of the Joint Chiefs of Staff, Gen Henry Hugh Shelton; the chief of Naval Operations, Adm Jay Johnson; the commandant of the Marine Corps, Gen Charles Krulak; the chief of staff of the Air Force, Gen Michael Ryan; the NATO

commander, Gen Wesley Clark, and other high-ranking military officers.[19]

Forget the hype and rhetoric of ethnic cleansing and atrocities being peddled by a besieged White House. The fact is that both sides of this latest Balkan set-to have been doing this to each other for at least 500 years. If the think-tank strategists and academic gurus, whose flawed reasoning has sucked us once more into a bottomless quagmire, believe that we can stop those ethnic upsurges in Yugoslavia – or anywhere else in the troubled world – by bombing alone, they are badly and criminally mistaken. The only way we can win – if indeed that is our intent – is to send in a massive force of ground troops with fixed bayonets to take and hold the high ground of the rugged terrain of Yugoslavia in its entirety.

As Clauswitz saw clearly, the only purpose of invading an enemy's territory is to destroy his ability to wage war primarily by rendering its armed forces inoperable. This noble endeavor would pit our young men (and women) – untried, unseasoned – against combat veterans who would be defending their homeland. This is the territorial imperative; its end result is the slaughter *en masse* of the invading force, who may or may not emerge victorious. Recall the sieges of Leningrad and Stalingrad during World War II.

Now, our esteemed president and commander-in-chief wants the warm and tender bodies of our kids to feed the insatiable appetite of the god of war. He is insanely creeping us up on the idea of accepting the use of American forces under United Nations command so we can enter the new millennium under a despotic global government.

Weep, mothers.

Charley Reese, who writes incisively, stressed (20 Apr 1999) that:

> In the fog of war propaganda, let us remember the facts. The North Atlantic Treaty Organization is in the wrong. NATO is in violation of the United Nations charter, which forbids military aggression against a sovereign state at peace with its neighbors. Yugoslavia was at peace with its neighbors. NATO is in violation of its own charter

because it was supposed to be a defensive alliance only. No attack was launched against any NATO country. The United States, which has orchestrated this war against Yugoslavia, has no legitimate, vital, strategic or even marginal interests in the Balkans.[20]

Reese pointedly indicates that in an age of lies, it is always better to look at actions rather than words:

By expanding the alliance and immediately launching an offensive war against a sovereign nation, NATO has shown that its purpose is to be a weapon to enforce US domination of Eastern Europe.[21]

It is close to high noon. The real enemy is not only inside the gates, but has taken over the presidency and its subservient minions on Capitol Hill.

ARE CLINTON'S HANDLERS PLOTTING WW III?

The illegal, unconstitutional and murderous aerial warfare waged against Serbia on the part of NATO came to a halt, and a peace of sorts was brokered, which allowed NATO ground forces access to the Serbian province of Kosovo. Of course, as was planned all along, Russia now entered the fray: some called it the Russian surprise. Samuel L. Blumenfeld wrote knowledgeably about this aspect on the *WorldNet Daily Communications* (16 Jun 1999). Here are key points of the Blumenfeld analysis:

As is well known, the Russians are superb chess players. They are well aware of NATO's geopolitical agenda and are not about to be told by NATO what they can and cannot do in Kosovo.... A Russian unit of 200 paratroopers entered Kosovo and reached Pristina, the capital, before a single NATO soldier had crossed the border into Kosovo. The move not only took NATO by surprise, but undercut what was to be a total and exuberant NATO victory....

In a sense, the Russians have us where they want us. We can't deny them the economic aid they need, because then it would be like blackmail by NATO and simply confirm their fears that the West wants hegemony over them....

It is clear that the US and NATO acted in violation of the United Nations charter in bombing Yugoslavia, which had attacked no one. Kosovo is a province of Yugoslavia. The latter had a perfect right to quell an insurrection by ethnic Albanians in its territory... apparently, the NATO allies want the freedom to set up their own New World Order –

their own kind of hegemony – without having to consult all of those other nations at the UN.

Why? Perhaps it has a lot to do with the ideology of Cecil Rhodes, the prime mover of a plan for world government to be dominated by the Anglo-Saxons....

One of the important components of Rhodes' plan was the creation of Rhodes Scholarships at Oxford whereby the 'best souls' could be recruited to further the progress of the Order and its plan. Strobe Talbott, as well as Bill Clinton, are Rhodes Scholars. In an article entitled 'The Birth of the Global Nation' published in *Time* (20 Jul 1992), Talbott wrote: 'The big question these days is, which political forces will prevail, those stitching nations together or those tearing them apart? Here is one optimist's reason for believing unity will prevail over disunity, integration over disintegration. In fact, I'll bet that within the next hundred years (I'm giving the world time for setbacks and myself time to be out of the betting game, just in case I lose this one), *nationhood as we know it will be obsolete, all states will recognize a single, global authority.'* (Emphasis added.)

Strobe is on the mark according to Rhodes' timetable. The plan has been in effect for about 100 years, with a 100 more to go. The Order already controls the wealth of the world. Now, if we can keep recruiting the 'best souls' (like Bill and Strobe) to complete the job, Rhodes' dream of world government may indeed be realized. The only problem is that human nature won't let it happen.[22]

Here is another view regarding "NATO's Victory," taken from the highly informative *Weekly Analysis* (21 Jun 1999) by STRATFOR's Global Intelligence Update:

NATO has won the 1999 Serbia War. Of that there can be no doubt. There are two questions to be asked. First, how did it manage to win the War? Second, what are the ramifications of this victory? NATO did not win the war militarily. It won the war with a breathtaking diplomatic performance in the last week that was duplicitous, disingenuous, and devious – precisely what brilliant diplomacy is supposed to be. Yet, at the same moment that NATO's diplomacy snatched victory from the jaws of stalemate, its very characteristics have set the stage for an ongoing and perhaps insoluble problem not only in the Balkans, but within the councils of NATO and ultimately, in the global geopolitical reality.

The issue of whether NATO won the war militarily will be debated for many years. The question of air power's efficacy is always debated with religious zeal. In this case, the question comes down to this: why did Slobodan Milosevic agree to the G-8 accords during his meeting with Chernomyrdin and Ahtisaari?

...Implicitly, the very question means that Milosevic had a choice. If he had a choice that means that the weight of the air war was not so unbearable that he could not endure it. At the same time, Milosevic chose not to endure it..

NATO came out of the war internally weaker than it went in. Russia and China came out of the war more, rather than less, hostile. The stability of the Balkans is now a permanent and impossible responsibility for the West. It was a victory. A few more victories like this and....[23]

That unfinished sentence in the global intelligence report tells us much – perhaps more than we care to think – about where we are heading. More and more, it appears that the group to which Blumenfeld alluded is in fact the Bicephalous Monster, that two-headed Leviathan about which we have been reading throughout this work, one head comprised of "JEWS WHO ARE NOT JEWS," and the other, "CHRISTIANS WHO ARE NOT CHRISTIAN."

For further elucidation of this critical point, we must turn to an expert on the geopolitical scene, who has proven time and again to be uncannily correct in his surmises, and way out front of the mainline media's mavens. Warren Hough, writing under the banner, "Mysterious Financier Brokered Kosovo Deal," says in part:

The real back-room negotiator who brought the air war over Yugoslavia to a halt this month is a shadowy international financier identified as Peter Castenfelt.

Castenfelt has served as an agent for Israel, Russia, the World Jewish Congress and the International Monetary Fund (IMF), according to Wall Street insiders and seasoned UN diplomats.

These sources agree that none of the headline figures hailed as the 'peacemakers' of Kosovo – Finnish President Marti Ahtisaari, former Russian premier Victor Chernomyrdin or US Deputy Secretary of State Strobe Talbott – deserve the credit for settling this conflict.

'Castenfelt is the interlocutor who brokered the cease-fire deal between Clinton and Milosevic,' says Dr. Emile Roque, a legal adviser to the Balkans Task Force of the UN High Commission on Refugees....

Castenfelt apparently emerged as the key behind-the-scenes fixer of the Balkans upheaval after four Moscow 'oligarchs' – a group of Zionist billionaires headed by Boris Berezovsky and Roman Abramovich – flew to Washington in mid-May for a secret crisis meeting with senior White House officials, the *Spotlight* has learned.

The terms of the Balkans settlement laid out at this conclave and subsequently negotiated by Castenfelt... include the following agreements:

- Russia will receive a total of some $8.7 billion from the IMF and the World Bank in stabilization and development funds before the end of the year. Half of the this amount will stay in Washington to clear past IMF credits, but the Zionist financiers and sticky-fingered Moscow bureaucrats who control the Russian economy will be allowed to keep – and divide – the other half.

- In the eventuality that the position of Milosevic, now an indicted war criminal, becomes untenable in Yugoslavia at some future date, he will be allowed to move to Russia. Neither he nor the substantial funds the Serbia strongman has accumulated and stashed in Greece will be 'pursued or seized' by NATO.

- As Yugoslavia's former energy czar, Milosevic will be allowed to join the merger between Yukos and Sibneft, Russia's two leading oil companies, as an executive.

- Sergei Stephashin, Russia's new prime minister, will work closely with Russian billionaire Vladimir Gushinsky, head of the Russian Jewish Congress. They are expected to work in close cooperation with US liquor baron Edgar Bronfman and his World Jewish Congress to curb Russian anti-semitism by whatever means necessary. [24]

In a special broadcast on "Our Revolutionary Right," carried nationwide on the *American Dissident Voices* of 12 Jun 1999, Dr. William Pierce of the National Alliance group stressed that it was the adult citizens of the United States and Britain who were responsible for the wanton carnage committed by Bill Clinton and Tony Blair against the Serb population in Yugoslavia. He quotes Abraham Lincoln in his first inaugural address (4 Mar 1861); "Whenever our people shall grow weary of the existing government, they can exercise their constitutional right of amending it, or their revolutionary right to dismember or overthrow it."

Dr. Pierce stated that rights never stand alone; they always entail responsibilities; in particular that revolutionary right mentioned by Lincoln. It is accompanied by the inescapable responsibility to exercise it when it becomes appropriate to do so.

When our constitutional right of amending the government has been taken away from us by the subversion of the democratic process in the Clinton era, the appropriate time has arrived.

Dr. Pierce points out that it was not just an attack on Serbia, it was an attack on America as well.

This was the case of the common enemies of Serbia and America using American military and economic resources against Serbia now, with the plan to use them against America in the future. If the New World Order gang successfully compels everyone to toe the line, it will be American freedom which will be sacrificed as well as Serb freedom.[25]

In an explosive article (5 Aug 1999), "The Kosovo End Game: Open Season on Serbs," Bob Djurdjevic of *Truth in Media* states that every week since NATO's 'peace' commenced on 10 June, 30 or so Serbs have been killed – which adds up to over 200 dead Kosovo Serbs, according to the *Washington Post* front page story (4 Aug 1999). "In other words," Bob writes, "there are more Serbs being killed now than there had been casualties on both sides of the 'civil war' prior to the start of NATO's bombing on 24 Mar, ostensibly launched so as to prevent such violence in Kosovo."

The West (meaning the closet-Bolsheviks now occupying the western government offices in Washington, London or Bonn), planned executed and delivered their Balkans Grab of the 1990s to the Wall Street and the City Banksters, and to other multinationals now setting up shop there. The West snatched the centuries-old Serb lands and cities, turned them over to the local Croat or Muslim western vassals, and then sent tens of thousands of NATO troops to protect the stolen property and keep the dispossessed owners out.

Which is exactly the kind of end game now taking place in Kosovo. And it has all been planned in Washington, London, Bonn… years ago.… It's just that so many people, especially the Serbs, refused to believe that their beloved West, with which they had been allied in two world wars, is capable of such evil deeds.

Which is why the *Post*'s effort to deflect the western culpability for the slaughter of the Christian Serbs, now being carried out by the

Albanian M&Ms – the western Muslim-Marxist proxies (KLA) – is the most pathetic part of its tragic 4 August Kosovo story. The goal of the West has been all along an ethnically pure Kosovo, with subservient Albanians licking the boots of the foreign occupiers, just as the Slovenians, Croats and Bosnian Muslims are doing. That's something the western neo-Bolsheviks knew the fiercely independent Serbs would never have done. Which is why they first bombed the Serbs into the stone age, and then stood guard as the KLA ran them out of Kosovo.[26]

Although Djurdjevic doesn't say it, this is exactly what the Ashkenazi Bolsheviks have been doing to the Palestinians for over 50 years, and with the willing complicity of those now culpable countries, namely the United States, Britain and Germany.

THE NIGHT OF THE LONG KNIVES

We are on the eve of entering the nuclear phase of World War III.

Actually WW III began during the Korean police action, which we were foreordained to lose. The 12 unending years of the Vietnam fiasco, which we were also slated to lose, was a diversion. Its principal *raison d'être* was to humiliate the US Armed Forces and set them up for further weakening by downsizing, sodomizing and feminizing.

All of these diversionary tactics dovetail nicely into a program of economic destabilization and deindustrialization, now coming to a head, and cunningly planned by the Barbarian within to coincide with a gigantic media blitz of deception, disinformation and blatant propaganda, coupled with outright lies.

The target continues to be the American public, which seems to be coming awake after a long, long sleep. The technique has been and continues to be *divide et impera*.

By other techniques, the Enemy within has revealed to us that most aspects of our government are unreliable and unworkable. The peoples' faith in their government and in the Constitution has been slowly and maliciously destroyed. The immediate objective of the Barbarian within is fourfold:

1) Destroy the Constitution

2) Disarm the citizens

3) Collapse the economy

4) Introduce "the terror"

By the use of psychological techniques discussed in Chapter 11, especially those involving psychopolitics and related skills of terror, force and coercive obedience developed by the Soviet Bolsheviks, the Barbarian within the gates has virtually taken over our government, our culture and our very way of life. They continue to use these techniques in order to destroy the executive office of the president. In that regard, we are essentially in the same boat as another once-powerful country, Russia, which is also both bankrupt and leaderless.

DISPOSSESSING THE MAJORITY

Like Prometheus, we are bound and chained against a mountain and are slowly being tortured by these collective lords of the world; our crime is stealing fire (technology) from heaven and giving it to man. By a systematic looting of our lands and wealth and culture and morals, we are being emasculated and taken over. By excessive regulation and taxation and litigation (statutes and judgments), our businesses are failing at a record rate – and the end is not yet.

We had at one time two solid underpinnings to our society – Christianity and the military. Both were targeted early on. We have, for any number of reasons, stood helplessly by as our moral/cultural pillars have been pulled down. The collectivist media have trivialized our faith and feminized our fighting forces.

The Collectivists have simultaneously torn down the pillars of our ivory towers, the institutions of higher learning, and looted our land by driving off countless farmers and ranchers on the pretext of environmentalism.

IVORY TOWER OFF LIMITS TO CHRISTIANS

Even the mainline media are now admitting that, yes, these things are happening. Patrick J. Buchanan, perhaps the premier nationally syndicated columnist, slams the obvious unfairness of underrepresentation of white Christians in our elite schools of higher learning. In his column, "In Quest of Fairness by Numbers" (*Washington Times* 30 Nov 1998), Buchanan cites a 16 Nov 1998 *Wall Street Journal* story by Ron Unz, a Harvardian of 20 years ago, now a California political activist and entrepreneur. Here are the most revealing statistics:

> According to Mr. Unz, today at Harvard College, Hispanic and black enrollment has reached 7% and 8%, respectively.... He [Unz] goes on to report that nearly 20% of the Harvard College student body is Asian-American, and 25 to 33% is Jewish, although Asian-Americans make up only 3% of the US population and Jewish-Americans even less than 3%. Thus, 50% of Harvard's student body is drawn from about 5% of the US population.

> When one adds foreign students, students from our tiny WASP elite, and children of graduates, what emerges is a Harvard student body where non-Jewish whites – 75% of the US population – get just 25% of the slots. Talk about underrepresentation! Now we know who really gets the shaft at Harvard – white Christians. Mr. Unz, in his *Wall Street* article, says that the same situation exists at other elite schools like Yale, Princeton, Columbia, Berkeley and Stanford, where Chelsea Clinton goes.

> As Hispanics, Asians, African-American and Jewish-Americans also vote overwhelmingly Democratic, the picture that emerges is not a pretty one. A liberal elite is salving its social conscience by robbing America's white middle class of its birthright, and handing it over to minorities, who just happen to vote Democratic.

> Not to put to fine a point on it, the white Christian middle class is being dispossessed.

> If elite colleges and grad schools enroll 75% of their students from the small Democratic minorities while white Christians and Catholics, who make up 75% of the population,. are relegated to 25% of the seats, there is no doubt who is going to run America in the 21st century.[27]

Three highly important books support this contention: one by James Yaffe, *The American Jews* (Random House: 1968); another by Martin Mayer, *The Lawyers* (Harper & Row: 1967); and the third, *The Dispossessed Majority* (Howard Allen: 1981) by Wilmot Robertson, who anticipated Untz' thesis.

Yaffe stressed that in the 1960s the faculty at Harvard was "dominated by Jews," and 15 to 25% of the faculty at other leading universities were Jewish.   Jews comprised 25% of the undergraduates at Harvard, 18% at Yale, 15% at Princeton, and 40% at Columbia.[28]

Martin Mayer, in his work, *The Lawyers*, gave us these statisticss: nationwide, 20% of all lawyers were Jewish – in New York City, 60%. In the top law schools, Jews accounted for almost a third of the entering class. At Harvard, the most influential law school of all – 25% of the nation's law professors were Harvard alumni – almost half the faculty was Jewish.[29]

As we read in Chapter 7, the liberal dilution of the bloodlines of Anglo-Saxon law was demonstrated in the fraudulent Nuremberg Trials. The late Senator Robert Taft looked on those farcical trials as "a blot on the American record that we shall long regret." As he pointed out, "the verdicts violate that fundamental principle of American law that a man cannot be tried under an *ex post facto* statute." Sen. Taft stressed that the purpose of the trials was to "clothe vengeance in the form of legal procedure." Surprisingly, his views made the front page of the *New York Times* (6 Oct 1946).[30]

WILL BOLSHEVISM TRIUMPH?

Let's turn back the clock just a few short years and move the setting from Washington, DC to London, England. A Jew of immense standing and respect, both in England and in America, was Dr. Oscar Levy. In July 1920, in response to a request from his dear friend, Prof. George Pitt-Rivers of Worcester College, Oxford, for a review of his manuscript entitled *The World Significance of the Russian Revolution,* Dr. Levy wrote the following letter – one well worth reading:

> When you first handed me your MS on *The World Significance of the Russian Revolution*, you expressed a doubt about the propriety of the title. After a perusal of your work, I can assure you, with the best of consciences, that your misgivings were entirely without foundation.

No better title than *The World Significance of the Russian Revolution* could have been chosen, for no event in any age will finally have more significance for our world than this one....

What I appreciate more than this new light thrown on a dark subject, more than the conclusion drawn by you from this wealth of facts, is the psychological insight which you display in detecting the reasons why a movement so extraordinarily bestial and so violently crazy as the revolution was able to succeed and finally to overcome its adversaries. For we are confronted with two questions which need answering and which, in my opinion, you have answered in your work. These questions are: (1) How has the Soviet government, admittedly the government of an insignificant minority, succeeded not only in maintaining but in strengthening its position in Russia after two and a half years of power? and (2) Why has the Soviet government, in spite of its outward bestiality and brutal tyranny, succeeded in gaining the sympathies of an increasing number of people in this country [Britain]?....

You rightly recognize that there is an ideology behind it and you clearly diagnose it as an ancient ideology. There is nothing new under the Sun, it is even nothing new that this Sun rises in the East....

For Bolshevism is a religion and a faith. How could these half-converted believers ever dream to vanquish the 'Truthful' and the 'Faithful' of their own creed, these holy crusaders, who had gathered round the Red Standard of the Prophet Karl Marx, and who fought under the daring guidance of these experienced officers of all latter-day revolutions – the Jews?

I am touching here on a subject which, to judge from your own work, is perhaps more interesting to you than any other. In this you are right. There is no race in the world more enigmatic, more fatal, and therefore more interesting than the Jews.

Every writer, who, like yourself, is oppressed by the aspect of the present and embarrassed by his anxiety for the future, must try to elucidate the Jewish Question and its bearing upon our Age.

For the question of the Jews and their influence on the world, past and present, cuts to the root of all things, and should be discussed by every honest thinker, however bristling with difficulties it is, however complex the subject as well as the individuals of this race may be....

You point out, and with fine indignation, the great danger that springs from the prevalence of Jews in finance and industry, and from the preponderance of Jews in rebellion and revolution. You reveal, and with great fervor, the connection between the Collectivism of the immensely-rich international Finance – the Democracy of cash values, as you call it – and the international Collectivism of Karl Marx and Trotsky – the

Democracy of and by decoy-cries.... And all this evil and misery, the economics as well as the political, you trace back to one source, to one *'fons et origo malorum'* – the Jews....

There is scarcely an event of modern Europe that cannot be traced back to the Jews. Take the Great War that appears to have come to an end, ask yourself what were its cause and its reasons: you will find them in nationalism. You will at once answer that nationalism has nothing to do with the Jews, who, as you have just proved to us, are the inventors of the international idea.

But no less than Bolshevist Ecstasy and Financial Tyranny can National Bigotry (if I may call it so) be finally followed back to a Jewish source – are not they the inventors of the Chosen People Myth, and is not this obsession part and parcel of the political credo of every modern nation, however small and insignificant it may be?

There is no doubt that the Jews regularly go one better or worse than the Gentile in whatever they do, there is no further doubt that their influence today justifies a very careful scrutiny, and cannot possibly be viewed without serious alarm. The great question, however, is whether the Jews are conscious or unconscious malefactors. I myself am firmly convinced that they are unconscious ones, but please do not think that I wish to exonerate them on that account.... A conscious evildoer has my respect, for he knows at least what is good; an unconscious one – well, he needs the charity of Christ – a charity which is not mine – to be forgiven for not knowing what he is doing. But there is in my firm conviction not the slightest doubt that these revolutionary Jews do not know what they are doing; that they are more unconscious sinners than voluntary evildoers.... You have noticed with alarm that the Jewish elements provide the driving forces for both Communism and Capitalism, for the material as well as the spiritual ruin of this world....

It is from this quality, no doubt, that springs his mysterious force – that force which you no doubt condemn, but which you had to admire even in the Bolshevists. And we must admire it whether we are Jews or whether we are Christians, for have not these modern Jews remained true to type, is there no parallel for them in history, do they not go to the bitter end even in our day?

Who stirred up the people during the late war in Germany? Who pretended to have again the truth, that truth about which Pontius Pilate once shrugged his shoulders? 'But these visions are all wrong,' you will reply. 'Look where they have led the world to. Think, that they have had a fair trial of 3,000 years' standing. How much longer are you going to recommend them to us and to inflict them upon us? And how do you propose to get us out of the morass into which you have launched us, if you do not change the path upon which you have led the world so disastrously astray?'

To this question I have only one answer to give, and it is this: 'You are right'. If you are antisemite, I, the Semite, am an antisemite too, and a much more fervent one than you are.... We Jews have erred, my friend, we have most grievously erred. And if there was truth in our error 3,000, 2,000, nay, 100 years ago, there is now nothing but falseness and madness, a madness that will produce an even greater misery and an even wider anarchy.

I confess it you, openly and sincerely, and with a sorrow, whose depth and pain an ancient Psalmist, and only he, could moan into this burning universe of ours.... We who have posed as the saviors of the world, we have even boasted of having given it 'the' Savior, we are today nothing else but the world's seducers, its destroyers, its incendiaries, its executioners.... We have promised to lead you to a new Heaven, we have finally succeeded in landing you into a new Hell.... There has been no progress, least of all moral progress.... And it is just our Morality, which has prohibited all real progress, and – what is worse – which even stands in the way of every future and natural reconstruction in this ruined world of ours.... I look at this world, and I shudder at its ghastliness; I shudder all the more as I know the spiritual authors of all this ghastliness....

Yes, there is hope, my friend, for we are still here, our last word is not yet spoken, our last deed is not yet done, our last revolution is not yet made. This last Revolution, the Revolution that will crown our revolutionaries, will be the revolution against the revolutionaries. It is bound to come, and it is perhaps upon us now. The great day of reckoning is near.... Then you, my dear Pitt-Rivers, the descendant of an old and distinguished Gentile family, may be assured to find by your side, and as your faithful ally, at least one member of that Jewish Race, which has fought with such fatal success upon all the spiritual battlefields of Europe.

Yours against the Revolution and for Life ever flourishing,

– OSCAR LEVY [31]

More recently, Ben Stein, a TV personality and most principled man of letters, spoke to a Jewish pro-life group gathered at Catholic University on Thursday 12 Nov 1998. A portion of his stirring talk was printed in *The Washington Times* (17 Nov 1998), under the heading, "Jewish Influence?"

Not so long ago, it was unheard of for Jews to be in the major law firms in Washington DC.... Jews were not allowed to live in huge swaths of Bethesda and Chevy Chase, not allowed in any of the major country clubs.... I think about what the Jewish position is [now] in America. The secretary of state is Jewish...the secretary of defense is half-Jewish.... The secretary of the treasury is the only one who is Jewish and admits he's Jewish. We have many Jewish senators and congressmen.

The head of every major Hollywood studio is Jewish. The heads of all the networks are Jewish. The heads of two out of the four national newspapers are Jewish. The heads of every Ivy League university are Jewish. So the idea that Jews are in a position of particular vulnerability – I think perceived vulnerability for sure – but real vulnerability? I'm not sure any more in America. It seems that this country is so generous, so openhearted and so kind and good that I cannot foresee [anything]....

I'll tell you how I knew beyond a shadow of a doubt that the Jewish position in America had changed dramatically.... The wife of a very close friend of my father died a few weeks ago and they had the memorial service at the Chevy Chase Club. And there was a cantor with a yarmulke giving the service at the Chevy Chase Club. And I cannot describe to you how astonishing a turn of events this was.[32]

KNOW THE ENEMY

In *Fabian Freeway*, Rose Martin cites the incident where General Andrew Jackson, just before the Battle of New Orleans, is confronted by an unusually dense fog on the fields just outside the city. He is asked by a young soldier: "But General, sir, how can I fight and defend myself against an enemy I can't see?"

"Sooner or later, your enemy will show himself," replied the General. "And you will know what to do.... In your future life, if you survive this – and by God, you will – you will be confronted by many unseen enemies of your hard-fought liberty. But they will show themselves in time – time enough to destroy them."[33]

In her epilogue, Martin emphasizes that: "While peace is undoubtedly wonderful, the motives of those who organize so-called peace movements and peace demonstrations of varied degrees of violence, are often suspect.... In the final analysis, World Government under Socialist rulers becomes the pacific sea toward which all tributary movements flow. With the end so nearly achieved, it seems more than ever unfair that the American people should not be permitted to know the identity of their betrayers...."[34]

CONSIDER THE OPTIONS

We should consider our options and consider them very carefully:

(1) Either a unified Rising against the New World Order of economic and political slavery; and for restoration of our Constitution and the Republic for which it stands;

(2) Or a submissive surrender to the global oligarchy and preparation for a journey into the long dark night of no return.

Saying all that, let's consider that great playwright, Robert Ardrey's, guidance that there is a wisdom of confronting today's problems today – so long as we confront them – and leaving tomorrow's until we have all had a good night's sleep.

> Otherwise we run that risk of sinking back into inertia's pool from which nothing can emerge but low whimpers, sad whines, and finally from somewhere in its dankest depths a few last unremarkable bubbles....[35]

Some of the biggest men in the United States, in the field of commerce and manufacturing, are afraid of somebody, are afraid of something. They know that there is a power somewhere so organized, so subtle, so watchful, so interlocked, so complete, so pervasive, that they had better not speak above their breath when they speak in condemnation of it.

President Woodrow Wilson, 1913

AFTERWORD

Open Letter to Our Military

(Time to Define the True Enemy)

If the trumpet give an uncertain sound, who shall prepare himself for battle?

I Corinthians XIV: 8

S IRS, you are doing none of the things that should be done to avert the storm which is impending.

We have petitioned – we have remonstrated – we have supplicated – we have prostrated ourselves before that great citadel on the Potomac known worldwide as the Pentagon and have implored your interposition to arrest the tyrannical hands of the totally corrupt Clinton administration and his minions on the Hill who have jointly and severally sold out our people and their Constitution. Collectively, they have abdicated governance under a Constitution by declaring us out of their protection and waging war against us.

Our petitions you have slighted; our remonstrances have only produced additional violence and insult as you have steadily and unceasingly waged war against innocent peoples and their once-sovereign nations about the world, wantonly murdering not only their soldiers by ignominious and inglorious use of high technology weaponry, but their women and children by the same weaponry, and enforcement of criminal embargoes of foodstuffs and medicine.

Our supplications you have disregarded; and you – our supposed military leaders – all of whom took a solemn oath to defend our Constitution against all enemies foreign and domestic, have spurned us with contempt as you grovel at the foot of the throne of His Mightiness, William Jefferson Clinton.

Sirs, while you have not only tolerated but have actually authorized and ordered our soldiers, sailors and airmen to take up positions in some 140 countries about the world – to become *de facto* the world's cops and oppressors in the name of peacekeeping, humanitarianism and nationbuilding – you have acquiesced to and often directly assisted the enemy within – the Barbarians – to seize the seven critical levers of power and to further oppress and enslave our people.   You have performed these criminal and malicious acts in the name of national security and vital interests.

Sirs, while you have curried favor of your fearful masters, eagerly sought membership in their secret societies, fawned over their weird and diverse proclivities, you have not only allowed but have aided and abetted their alien scientists in their continuous search for the absolute weapon and the ultimate destruction of all Christians and the rule of law.   From development of atomic, hydrogen and neutron bombs, these evil genii have advanced to the ultimate crimes against a nation and a people – weather manipulation and the insidious spread of biological agents.

All experience has shown that people are more disposed to suffer, while evils are sufferable, than to right themselves by abolishing the forms to which they are accustomed.   But when a long train of abuses and usurpations pursuing invariably the same object, evinces a design to reduce them under absolute despotism, it is their right, it is their duty, to throw off such government, and to provide new guards for their future security.

Sirs, while you have sought personal glory and promotion in fraudulent combat, in vainglorious command of such one-world imperial armies as NATO, and in obtaining knighthood from the pathetic figurehead of a tiny island off the coast of Europe, our citizenry – your friends, relatives, neighbors and countrymen – have been raped and pillaged by the Barbarians within the gates.

In vain, after these most evil of deeds against us, may we now indulge the fond hope of peace and reconciliation?

There is no longer any room for hope.   If we wish to be free – if we mean to preserve inviolate those inestimable privileges for which we have been so long contending – if we mean not basely to abandon the noble struggle in which we have been so long engaged, and which we have pledged ourselves never to abandon until the glorious object of our contest shall be obtained – we must fight! Sirs, I repeat, WE MUST FIGHT!

They tell us, sirs, that we are weak – unable to cope with so formidable an adversary. But when shall we be stronger? Will it be next week or the next year? Will it be when we are totally disarmed, and when a federal agent shall be stationed in every house? Shall we gather strength by irresolution and inaction? Shall we acquire the means of effectual resistance by lying supine, and hugging the delusive phantom of hope, until our Barbarians within the gates have bound us hand and foot?

Sirs, we are not weak, if we make a proper use of those means which the God of nature has placed in our power. Thirty millions of people, armed in the holy cause of liberty, and in such a country as that which we once possessed, are invincible by any force which our enemy can send against us. Besides, sirs, we shall not fight our battles alone. There is a just God who presides over the destinies of nations; and who will raise up friends about the world to help fight the battle with us.

The battle, sirs, is not to the strong alone; it is to the vigilant, the active, the brave. Besides, sirs, we have no choice in this matter. If we were base enough to desire it, it is now too late to retire from the contest. There is no retreat but in submission and slavery!

Our chains are forged. Their clanking may be heard on the plains and in the valleys and on the very top of the mountains. Let their clanking be as the resounding notes of the trumpet, calling the courageous, the loyal and the stalwart to our just cause.

Sirs, this war is inevitable, then let it come! I repeat, sirs, let it come! Will you lead us? Or will you continue on your present course to sell out the country and its constitution and its peoples? And, to what end? The next pretty bauble? The next promotion? The next adulation by the mainline media? The next title of nobility?

In every stage of these oppressions we have petitioned for redress in the most humble terms. Our repeated petitions have been answered only by repeated injury. A prince, whose character is thus marked by every act which may define a tyrant, is totally unfit to be a ruler of a free people.

Consider carefully your ultimate decision, for the choice is yours; you alone have the power to absolve us from all allegiance to the present government and its coterie of arch-criminals and opportunists. You alone – the military – have that power to release us totally from this absolute tyranny and restore our beloved country to the Constitution which authorizes our 50 free and independent states to levy war, conclude peace, contract alliances, establish commerce, and to do all other acts which independent states may of right do.

A last supplication, a last entreaty...hesitate no longer...vacillate no longer, for *THE BARBARIANS ARE INSIDE THE GATES!*

With apologies to Thomas Jefferson and Patrick Henry,

Donn de Grand Pré

a soldier... once young....

REFERENCES

PROLOGUE

1. Tom Bethell, *American Spectator,* Jan 98
2. Ibid.
3. J. Lawton Collins, *War in Peacetime* (1969)
4. Theodor Herzl, "father of International Zionism" 1902
5. Representative (ND) Usher Burdick, speech 17 Jan 57
6. Trygve Lie, *Cause for Peace* (1949)
7. George Knupffer, T*he Struggle for World Power* (1958)
8. *The Barnes Review,* Mar-Apr 98
9. Alfred M. Lilienthal, *The Other Side of the Coin* (Devin-Adair: 1965) 16
10. Ivor Benson, *The Zionist Factor* (Noontide Press 1986) 116
11. Israel Shahak, J*ewish History, Jewish Religion: The Weight of Three Thousand Years* (Pluto Press: 1994) 35
12. Dr. Theodor Herzl, in a proposal to the Rothschild Family Council in 1881
13. Bruce Nelan, *Time,* 9 Feb 98
14. Senator John McCain, *Washington Times,* 4 Feb 98
15. Israel Shahak, 37
16. Ibid., 39
17. Lisa Beyer, *Time,* 9 Feb 98
18. Robert Kaplan, *The Ends of the Earth* (1996)
19. Walter Laqueur in the foreword to Edward Luttwak's *Coup d'état: A Practical Handbook* (1968)
20. Edward Luttwak, 67

CHAPTER I
We Are at War

1. Dr. Alfred Lilienthal, "What Price Holocaustomania?" in *The Washington Report on Middle East Affairs,* Apr 98
2. Ibid.
3. Ibid.
4. Paul Hendrikson, *The Living and the Dead: Robert McNamara and Five Lives of a Lost War* (Knopf: 1997) 47
5. Christopher Hitchens in "Young Men and War" *Vanity Fair,* Feb 97
6. Ibid.
7. Adolph Hitler, *Mein Kampf* (1925), English translation 1939
8. I served as Deputy Chief of the International Division on the Army staff until 1966 when, following a successful negotiation in London which I chaired, I was requested by Secretary of Defense McNamara to join his office of International Security Affairs (ISA), then under Assistant Secretary of Defense, John McNaughton. I served as Director, Ground Weapons

Systems and as an international negotiator.

9. ISA Memo "Future Actions in Vietnam" 19 May 67

10. Hendrikson, 62

11. ISA Memo of 19 May 67. The memo was actually drafted in our office in ISA, then headed by John McNaughton. Later, the reporter Neil Sheehan called it an act of abundant moral courage. The paper wasn't declassified until 1984, during the Westmoreland/CBS trial.

12. Internal Defense Memo, 14 May 67

13. See *Final Judgment*, by Michael Collins Piper, which points out that JFK was planning to pull our relatively small commitment of troops and CIA operatives out of Vietnam.

14. Listed names taken from news stories in *Washington Post, Washington Times* and *USA Today,* Mar 98

15. Col David Hackworth, quoted in an interview by Bob Drury, *Men's Journal,* Feb 94

16. Ward Just, *Washington Post,* 12 Sep 68

17. David Halberstam, *New York Times,* 1979

18. Hendrikson, 67

19. Elizabeth Bentley, special subcommittee on internal security of the US Senate, in 1953

20. Subcommittee report to the Senate Judiciary Committee, "Interlocking Subversion in Government Departments," 30 Jul 53

21. Ibid.

22. McNamara, *In Retrospect: The Tragedy and Lessons of Vietnam,* reviewed in the *Washington Post,* 9 Apr 95

23. Hendrikson, 123

24. Ibid., quoting McNamara 124

25. Ibid., 125

26. G. Edward Griffin, *The Creature from Jekyll Island* (American Opinion: 1994) 527

27. Ibid., 528

28. Leonard Lewin, ed., *Report from Iron Mountain on the Possibility and Desirability of Peace* (1967), as reported by Griffin 523

29. Ibid., 524

30. Ibid., 524

31. Griffin, 532

32. David Rockefeller, as quoted by Prof. Roger Rusk in *The Other End of the World* (1988) 24

33. Col L. Fletcher Prouty, *The Barnes Review,* Dec 95

34. Col Harry Summers, *Washington Times,* 28 Apr 99

35. Sec Def Clark Clifford, 21 May 68

36. Prouty

37. Extract from NSAM #263, 11 Oct 63

38. Alexis de Tocqueville, *Democracy in America* (1835)

39. Ibid.

40. Prouty

41. Ibid.

42. NSAM # 263

43. Prouty quoting *Atlantic Monthly,* 19 Jul 73
44. President L. B. Johnson's NSAM # 288, 16 Mar 64
45. Prouty
46. Senate Internal Security Report, 1953
47. Tom Bethell, "Losing the War" in *American Spectator,* Feb 97
48. Ibid.
49. Ibid.
50. Ibid.
51. B. K. Eakman, *Cloning of the American Mind* (Huntington House: 1999)
52. Ibid.

CHAPTER II
High Noon

1. Carroll Quigley, *Tragedy and Hope* (Macmillan: 1966) 519
2. Ibid., 522
3. Ibid., 523
4. Ibid., 525
5. Ibid., 525
6. William L. Shirer, *The Collapse of the Third Republic* (1971)
7. Quigley, 528
8. Shirer, 50
9. Ibid., 51
10. Ibid., 52
11. Ibid., 53
12. Quigley, 244-45
13. Robert Welch, *The Politician* (1963) 8
14. John Gunther, *Eisenhower: The Man & the Symbol* (1951)

15. Dwight Eisenhower, *Crusade in Europe* (1948) 10
16. Ibid., 11
17. Welch, 9
18. Ibid., 9
19. *Boston Herald,* 17 Jul 70
20. Douglas Reed, *Far & Wide* (Dolphin Press: 1951)
21. James Bacque, *Other Losses* (Canadian Intelligence Service, Alberta, Canada: 1989)
22. Ibid., 32
23. Ibid., 34
24. Eisenhower, *Crusade in Europe*
25. Welch, 108
26. Ibid., 76
27. Ibid., 77
28. Rabbi Stephen Wise, quoted by Douglas Reed in *Controversy of Zion* (1956) 215
29. Ibid., quoting Edward Mandell House, 231
30. Ibid., 233
31. J. Edgar Hoover, *Elks Magazine,* Aug 56
32. D. D. Eisenhower
33. Reed, quoting Ben Hecht, 472
34. Ibid., re Bernard Baruch 473
35. Ibid., 474
36. Robert A. Taft, *A Foreign Policy for Americans* (1952)
37. Reed, quoting Eisenhower, September 1952
38. Ibid., 535
39. Reed on the Chazar tribe
40. Eisenhower's request to Congress, 5 Jan 57
41. Welch, *The Politician* 216

42. *New York Times,* 12 Dec 56

43. Livia Rokach, *Isarel's Sacred Terrorism* (1980) 47

44. Ibid., 45

45. Moshe Sharett's Personal Diary (Mar 55) 39

46. Ibid., (14 Apr 55) 46

47. Rokach quoting Ben-Gurion (8 Aug 55) 46

48. Sharett's entry (1 Oct 55) 47

49. Ibid., (3 Oct 55) 47

50. Rokach 48

51. Welch quoting Webster

52. Welch quoting Madame Roland 251

53. Welch on Eisenhower 264

54. *New York Times* article on Gen Wesley Clark, 3 May 99

55. Ibid.

56. *Counterpunch,* a Washington DC newsletter, 5 May 99

57. Robert Novak, syndicated column, 5 May 99

58. Ibid.

CHAPTER III
Bolsheviks Rule Russia

1. Albert Einstein, *The Atlantic Monthly,* Nov 1945

2. Richard Pipes, *Russia Under the Bolshevik Regime* (1991)

3. Robert Wilton, *The Last Days of the Romanovs* (1920) 25-29

4. Winston Churchill, "Zionism versus Bolshevism" *London Sunday Herald,* 8 Feb 1920

5. Sir Eyre Crowe, British Foreign Office, 1920

6. Churchill, 15 Sep 1919

7. Churchill, 1920

8. British White Paper, "Russia No.1 (1919). A Collection of Reports on Bolshevism in Russia."

9. US Ambassador David R. Francis, in a report to Washington, 1918

10. Wilton, *Official Bolshevik Lists* 186-190

11. Reed *274*

12. Professor Pipes

13. Reed 275

14. Paul Johnson, *Modern Times* (1991) 47

15. Ibid., 48

16. Letter from Baruch Levy to Karl Marx, 1879

17. William Eleroy Curtis, "The Revolution in Russia" *National Geographic*, May 1907

18. Ibid.

19. Dr. A. B. Kopanski, "Ethnic Cleansing and Soviet Crimes Against Humanity" *The Barnes Review*, Dec 1997

20. G. Edward Griffin, *The Creature from Jekyll Island* (1994) 263

21. Johnson 48

22. David Irving, *The Barnes Review*, 1998

23. Arthur Koestler, *The Invisible Writing* (1940)

24. K. L. Billingsley, "Commie Dearest" *Heterodoxy,* Dec 1997

25. Abbe Augustin Barreul, *Memoirs Illustrating the History of Jacobinism* (1798)

26. Winston Churchill, *London Daily Telegraph*, 4 Dec 30

27. Pres. Clinton, *New York Times,* 22 Jan 99

28. Ibid., quoting Sec Def Cohen, Dep Sec Def Hamre, *Parameters*, Autumn 97, EO 12919

29. Briefing by "Mr. X" of Defense Dept., 5 Jan 00

30. *Reuters* report, 21 Dec 99

31. Richard C. Paddock, *Los Angeles Times*, 4 Jan 00

32. Ibid.

33. Ibid., quoting Marina Salye

34. Ibid.

35. Anton Surikov, *Zavtra*, Aug 97

36. Ibid.

37. Ibid.

38. Ibid.

39. Sergei Glazyev, *Pravda,* 8 Oct 97

40. Ibid.

41. Thomas W. Lippman quoting Strobe Talbott, *Washington Post,* 7 Nov 98

42. Ibid.

43. Paul Johnson, *Modern Times* (1991) 276

44. Lippman quoting Talbott

45. Ibid.

46. Ibid.

47. Lev Timofeyev, Russia's Secret Rulers (1984)

CHAPTER IV
FDR's Bloody Road

1. Garet Garrett, *Burden of Empire* (1938)

2. Ibid., 7

3. Ibid., 136

Louis Marschelko, *The World Conquerers* (1956)

Howard Sachar, *History of the Jews* (1992)

6. Whitaker Chambers, *Witness* (1952) 342-48

7. Ibid., 427

8. Ibid., 427

9. Ibid., 194

10. Marschalko 36

11. Henry Morgenthau, *Portland Journal,* 12 Feb 33

12. Forest Davis, *Saturday Evening* Post, 20 May 44

13. Rabbi Stephen Wise in *I Testify* by R. E. Edmonson (1956)

14. International Zionists and Combined Jewish groups, *The New York Times*, 16 Sep 32

15. Samuel Untermyer of the World Jewish Congress in *The New York Times*, 7 Aug 33

16. Vladimir Jabotinsky, 5 Jan 34

17. London *Sunday Chronicle,* 2 Jan 38

18. Rabbi Maurice Perlsweig, *Toronto Evening Telegram, 26 Feb 40*

19. Ludwig Lewisohn in the *Jewish Mirror,* Sep 42. See Issa Nakhleh's *Encyclopedia* of the Palestine Problem for a detailed analysis of what the Zionist and Israeli leaders have done since 1939 to the Palestinians, Lebanese, Syrians, Jordanians and Egyptians.
Nakhleh states: "The victims are called terrorists, murderers and criminals and the real

terrorists and criminals are being received as respectable representatives of a democratic society."

20. Marschelko

21. R. E. Edmonson, *I Testify* (1956)

22. *The New York Times,* 14 Mar 35

23. *St. Petersburg Times*, 14 Apr 34, quoting Mich. Gov Osborn

24. New York *Herald Tribune,* 8 May 37

25. Marschelko

26. Ralph Townsend, *There is no Halfway Neutrality (*1938), republished in *The Barnes Review*, Mar/Apr 98

27. George N. Crocker, *Roosevelt's Road to Russia* (1959) 164. Crocker quotes Lord Hankey and Hanson Baldwin commenting on FDR's "unconditional surrender" in *Great Mistakes of the War* (1950)

28. Ibid., John Gunther, referring to FDR at Casablanca 179

29. Ibid., Gen. J.F.C. Fuller on "unconditional surrender" 182

30. George Fowler, *The Barnes Review,* Jan 95

31. Ibid.

32. Ibid.

33. William B Breuer, *Unexplained Mysteries of World War II* (1997)

34. Ibid., 167

35. Crocker 186

36. Ibid., 189

37. Ibid, 190

38. Ibid., quoting Hopkins' top-secret memo 190

39. Ibid., FDR's role as "Master Builder" at Cairo 197

40. Dr. Eduard Benes, as quoted by Crocker 209

41. Ibid., on Truman assuming the presidency 211

42. Earl Browder, *Teheran and After*, quoted by Crocker 211

43. Ibid., regarding Browder's contacts with FDR 212

44. FDR's ideas on "The Four Policemen" under UN, as reported by Crocker 216

45. Bill Gertz article in *Washington Post,* 9 Jan 99

46. Elliott Roosevelt, *As He Saw It* (1946)

47. Count Leon de Poncin, *State Secrets*

48. Cordell Hull, *The Memoirs of Cordell Hull* (1940)

49. Henry L. Stimson, as quoted by Crocker 231

CHAPTER V
What Really Happened at Yalta?

1. Winston Churchill, *Triumph & Tragedy* (1952)

2. Ibid.

3. Molotov, as reported by Churchill

4. Churchill

5. Ibid.

6. Ibid.

7. Ibid.

8. Ibid.

9. FDR responding to a toast, as reported by Churchill

10. Josef Goebbels, article in *Das Reich,* 23 Feb 45

11. George N. Crocker, *Roosevelt's Road to Russia 241*

12. Arthur Bliss Lane, *I Saw Poland Betrayed* (1948)

13. Crocker quotes William C. Bullit 266

14. Joseph C. Grew, State Department Memo, 1945

15. F. J. P. Veale, *Advance to Barbarism* 352

16. Crocker 242

17. Ibid., quoting Adm. Chester Nimitz to FDR, Jul 1944 269

18. Ibid., 242

19. Ibid, 14-15

20. Ibid., 16-19

21. Churchill

22. Reed, *Controversy of Zion*

23. Quigley, *Tragedy and Hope* (1956)

24. Jean-Francois Revel, *How Democracies Perish* (1976)

25. Reed

26. Revel

27. Ibid.

28. Joseph E. Davies, *Mission to Moscow* (1939)

29. Dr. E. C. Blackorby, author and historian (the author's college professor of the 1950s), emphasized that World War I had three goals: (1) The destruction and dismemberment of Christian Germany to remove the chief obstacle to socialism; (2) The destruction and occupation of Christian Russia by *an alien and hostile force* to set up "socialism as dreamed of by Karl Marx"; (3) The establishment of an international League of Peace to make the world safe for democracy (socialism).

30. *The Conference at Malta and Yalta,* 1945

31. Reed 378

32. Ibid., quoting *Montreal Star* headlines 378

33. Ibid., 379

34. Ibid., quoting Mackenzie King 380

35. Ibid., 380

36. Ibid., 381

37. Ibid., 385

38. National emergency decree issued by FDR, 1933

CHAPTER VI

Nazi-Zionist Secret Alliance

1. Dr. Max Nordau, addressing the Sixth Zionist Congress convened at Basle, Switzerland in 1903

2. Litman Rosenthal published Dr. Nordau's speech in the *American Jewish News,* 19 Sep 1919

3. Klaus Polkehn, *The Secret Contacts: Zionism and Nazi Germany – 1933-1941* (1981)

4. Ibid., 71

5. Jon and David Kimche, in *Secret Roads* 75

6. Polkehn 81

7. Gerhart Holdheim, *Zionism in Germany* (1930)

8. Alfred Rosenberg, 1937 (Polkehn) 63

9. Polkehn 65

10. Chaim Weissmann, *Speeches & Essays* (1937)

11. Andrew Gray, review of Udo Walendy, "Truth for Germany: The Guilt Question of WW II" in *The Barnes Review,* Dec 97

12. Ibid.

13. Gregory Douglas in *The Barnes Review,* May 97

14. Ibid.

15. Richard Breitman in *German Studies Review*

16. Douglas

17. Top Secret document, 11 Jan 41

18. Ibid.

19. Ibid., document in its entirety

20. Ilya Ehrenburg, as reported by Polkehn

21. Salvador Borrego, *The Psychology of War and the New Era in 2000*

22. Ibid., *Numbers* 31: 8-18

23. Edwin Black, *The Transfer Agreement: The Untold Story of the Secret Pact Between the Third Reich and Jewish Palestine* (1984)

24. Ibid., 178

25. Ibid, 84-88

26. Ibid., 95

27. Ibid., 96

28. Ibid., 98-99

29. Ibid., 382

30. Warren Hough, *Spotlight*, 21 Sep 98

31. Ibid., Dennis Braham

32. David Hoffman, *Washington Post,* 19 Sep 98

33. Ibid.

34. Ibid.

35. While speculative, several signs point toward settling part of this massive exodus in Central Virginia. Several real estate agents state that, over the past ten years, wealthy Jews have purchased farms throughout Madison, Greene, Albermarle, Orange, and Culpeper counties totaling between 75,000 and 85,000 acres. This could end up as another pre-arranged "transfer agreement" similar to the agreement between the National Socialists and the Zionist movement in the 1930s which resulted in the transfer of at least 1.6 million Jews from Europe into Palestine and the Western Hemisphere, particularly the United States. If you think such a massive movement of people highly unlikely, consider the various "relocations" of all European peoples, which culminated in the fraudulent Nuremberg Trials after World War II.

36. Prof. Edward Said, "One State Solution" *New York Times,* 10 Jan 99

37. Ibid., Prof. Said quoting Zeev Sternhell

38. Ibid., Said quoting Ben-Gurion

39. Ibid.

40. Ibid.

41. Dietrich Bronder, *Before Hitler Came* (1964)

42. Henneke Kardel, *Adolf Hitler: Founder of Israel* (1974 & 1997)

43. Kardel quoting Eichmann
44. Ibid.
45. Rabbi Yitzhak Ginsburgh in New York *Jewish Week*, 26 Apr 96
46. Israel Shahak, *Jewish Fundamentalism in Israel* (1999)
47. Ibid., 62
48. Ibid., 63
49. Ibid., 64
50. Ibid., 64
51. Ibid., 91
52. Ibid., 64
53. Ibid., 65
54. Ibid., 74
55. Ibid., 75
56. Ibid., 76-7
57. Ibid., 77
58. Ibid., 125
59. Henry Kissinger's speech at Bilderberger meet, Evian, France, 21 May 92

CHAPTER VII
Nuremberg Trials as Fraud

1. Joseph E Persico, *Nuremberg: Infamy on Trial* (1994)
2. Harry Elmer Barnes, *Barnes Against the Blackout* 132
3. Ibid., 137
4. David Irving, *Nuremberg: The Last Battle* (1998)
5. U. S. Supreme Court Chief Justice Stone, 1945
6. Ibid., Justice William O. Douglas
7. Ibid., Justice Hugo Black
8. Prof Richard Pipes, *Russia Under the Bolshevik Regime* (1991)
9. Patrick Buchanan, syndicated column, 2 Jul 98
10. Ibid.
11. Irving, quoting chief judge for the USSR, Nikitchenko
12. Ibid.
13. Persico
14. Ibid.
15. Irving
16. Persico
17. Ibid.
18. Irving
19. *Book of Esther* (Chapter 9)
20. Underground *Bund* Report, 25 May 42
21. Jean-Francois Revel, *How Democracies Perish* (1979)
22. Prof. Arthur Butz, *Hoax of the 20th Century* (1976) 26-27
23. Ibid., 25
24. Ibid., 24
25. AP *New York Times,* 12 Jun 48
26. Capt B. H. Liddell Hart, *The Evolution of Warfare* (1946)
27. F. J. P. Veale, *Advance to Barbarism* 351
28. Montgomery Belgion, *Epitaph at Nuremberg*, first published in 1946, then updated and republished in 1949 by Henry Regnery under the title *Victors' Justice*
29. Eisenhower, of Swedish-Jewish heritage, whose ancestors came from Sweden in the early 1800s, would be somewhat snidely referred to

as "Dwight David Kerensky" by his military colleagues

30. Irving

31. Ibid., quoting Sec of War Henry Stimson

32. Veale, quoting Sen. Taft 240

33. Ibid., 238-242

34. Ibid., 238

35. Ibid., 239

36. Generals Clarke and Williams' statements to author

37. James Bacque, *Other Losses* (1989)

38. Editorial in *The Economist,* 5 Oct 46

39. Nahum Goldmann in his Autobiography, 1969

CHAPTER VIII
Rocky Road to Global Despotism

1. Evan Gahr, *Washington Times,* 1 Jan 98

2. Patrick J Buchanan, syndicated column, 16 May 94

3. Harvey Klehr, John Earl Haynes and Fridrikh Igorovich Firsove, *The Secret World of American Communism* (1995)

4. Book review by Philip Terzian

5. Harry Elmer Barnes, *Barnes Against the Blackout* 99

6. Ibid., 122

7. "Einstein on the Atomic Bomb" *The Atlantic Monthly,* Nov 1945

8. Ibid.

9. Ibid.

10. Ibid.

11. Ibid.

12. Bertrand Russell, *Bulletin of Atomic Scientists,* Oct 1946

13. Personal papers of Acting Secretary of State, Joseph C. Grew, 1945

14. Ibid.

15. Grew to Stimson in a personal letter, 12 Feb 47

16. Article 12, Potsdam Proclamation, July 1945

17. Gar Alperovitz, *The decision to Use the Atomic Bomb and the Architecture of the American Myth* (1995). Views of some of the key military officers involved in the dropping of the two atomic bombs on Hiroshima and Nagasaki in August of 1945 are contained in greater detail in Part VI "Military Necessity" of his voluminous work. See also *Wedemeyer Reports!* by Gen Albert C. Wedemeyer

18. Message sent to Japan on 24 July 45 from the Potsdam Conference

19. David Holloway, *Stalin and the Bomb* (1989)

20. F. J. P. Veale, *Advance to Barbarism* (see Ch. 6)

21. Ibid., quoting Sir Charles Snow, *Science and Government* 18-19

22. Ibid., 112

23. Ibid., British Government document *Strategic Air Offensive* (1961) 185

24. Fulton Oursler, "The Twilight of Honor" *Readers Digest,* July 1950

25. Prof. Robert Nisbet, *Roosevelt and Stalin* (1988) 10
26. Ibid., 20-21
27. Ibid., 24
28. Ibid., 110
29. Robert Dallek, quoted by Nisbet 25

CHAPTER IX
Fascism's Friendly Face

1. Dr John Coleman, *Socialism: The Road to Slavery* (1997)
2. J. P. Stehelin, *The Traditions of the Jews* (1865)
3. Wilhelm Marr, *Conquest of Germanism by Judaism* (1879)
4. Olivia Maria O'Grady, *Beasts of the Apocalypse* (1959) 8
5. Ibid., 25
6. Ibid., 48
7. Ibid., 115
8. Ibid., 161
9. Prof. Alfred Guillaume, *Zionists and the Bible* 247
10. O'Grady 108
11. Ibid., 173
12. Dr. Hans Eisele, *The Rulers of Russia* (1924)
13. Ramsay MacDonald, British statesman, 1918
14. Arnold Toynbee, *A Study of History* (1948)
15. O'Grady 354
16. Ibid., 366
17. Ibid., 369
18. Dr. Benjamin, *Freedman Facts are Facts* (1954)
19. Ibid.
20. Ibid.
21. Ibid.
22. World Jewish Congress (WJC) London Aug 45 (O'Grady) 383
23. Ibid., Ernest Bevin, British Secretary of State for Foreign Affairs, 13 Nov 45 383
24. Ibid., World Jewish Congress, 14 Nov 45 383
25. Ibid., Prime Minister Clement Attlee, 1 May 46 385
26. Ibid., Pres. Harry S Truman, counter-proposal, 4 Oct 46 385
27. O'Grady 386
28. Manachem Begin, *Irgun* leader, 10 Apr 48 388
29. Arnold Toynbee 388
30. O'Grady 388
31. Ibid., 389
32. Toynbee 389
33. O'Grady 390
34. Rabbi Elmer Berger, *Who Knows Better Must Say So* (1955) 393
35. Allan C. Brownfeld, *Washington Report on Middle East Affairs*, Dec 98
36. Ibid., quoting Joel Greenberg, *The New York Times*, 17 Nov 98
37. Ibid.
38. Ibid., quoting Aryeh Caspi in *Ha'aretz* paper
39. Ibid., quoting Leonard Fein, in *The Forward*
40. Ibid.
41. Ibid., quoting Golda Meir

CHAPTER X
Israeli Acts of Terror

1. Israel Shahak, *Open Secrets: Israeli Nuclear and Foreign Policy* 1
2. Ibid., 3
3. Ibid., 3
4. Ibid., 4
5. Ibid., 4
6. Ibid., 5
7. Ibid., 7
8. Dr. Noam Chomsky, of Shahak's earlier book, *Jewish History, Jewish Religion* (1994)
9. Ibid., David Ben-Gurion, quoted by Shahak 8-9
10. *Washington Times,* 17 May 99
11. Lee Hockstader, *Washington Post,* 13 Nov 98
12. Ibid., Binyamin Natanyahu
13. Ibid., Hassan Asfour
14. Ibid., Haim Ramon, Labor Party
15. Thomas W. Lippman and Bradley Graham, *Washington Post*, 13 Nov 98
16. Israel's chief chaplain writing in 1973
17. Jehovah's promise to Abram, as quoted by Olivia Maria O'Grady in *Beasts of the Apocalypse* 25
18. Ibid., 26
19. Avinoam Bar-Yosef, writing in Israeli newspaper *Ma'ariv,* 2 Sep 94
20. Ibid.
21. Ibid.
22. Ibid.
23. Eric D. Butler, *The New Times* (Australia), Feb 90
24. Ibid.
25. Victor Ostrovsky, *By Way of Deception* (1990)
26. CFR journal *Foreign Affairs,* Spring 1991
27. Pres. George Bush, TV speech, 11 Sep 90
28. Bush, TV, Dec 90
29. Bush in *U S News & World Report,* 7 Jan 91
30. Bush, press conference, 9 Jan 91
31. Bush signed *National Security Strategy,* Aug 91
32. John F. McManus, report of Bush *pax universalis* speech at the UN, 23 Sep 91
33. Livia Rokach, *Israel's Sacred Terrorism* (1980)
34. Ibid., 2
35. Ibid., from Sharrett's personal diary 3
36. Ibid., 4
37. Ibid., Sharrett's documentation 26
38. Israeli Prime Minister Moshe Sharett's "personal feelings" as expressed by him, 3 Jun 1955 46
39. Israeli Chief of Staff Moshe Dayan's explanation as expressed by him, May 1955 41
40. Ibid., Dyan, 26 May 1955 41
41. Rokach's summation of *Israel's Sacred Terrorism* 48
42. Ibid., 49
43. One of Sharatt's final entries, 4 Apr 1957 49

CHAPTER XI
Manipulating Public Opinion

1. Stephen Fay, "The Collapse of Barings," reviewed in *American Spectator*, Mar 97

2. Winston Churchill speaking in 1936, as reported by Conrad K Grieb, *The Balfour Declaration: Warrant for Genocide,* 1972

3. *The New York Times,* 24 Mar 17.

4. Ibid.

5. Ibid., NYC Mayor Mitchel

6. Ibid., Rabbi Stephen Wise

7. Ibid., George F. Kennan

8. Ibid., Jacob Schiff's message

9. Ibid., Pres. Woodrow Wilson's message

10. John Naisbitt, *Trend Report*

11. *Spotlight,* 25 May 98

12. Stephen Fox, *The Mirror Makers* (1984)

13. David Acker and John Myers, in *Advertising Management*

14. Walter Lippmann, *Public Opinion* (1922)

15. Edward Bernays, *Crystallizing Public Opinion* (1924)

16. Dr. Dennis Laurence Cuddy, *Secret Records Revealed* (1999) 45; quoting Bernays in his work, *Propaganda* (1928)

17. Rabbi Jacob Brafmann, *The Book of the Kahal* (1869)

18. Eliphas Levy, *Dogme et Rituel de la Haute Magie* (1872)

19. Ben Weintraub, *The Holocaust Dogma of Judaism* (1995)

20. Representative Louis T. McFadden, radio address, May 1934

21. Michael Kenny, SJ, *No God Next Door* (1935)

22. Ibid., 13

23. Ibid., Plutarco Calles address, 20 Jun 1925 26

24. Msgr. Francis Clement Kelley, *Blood-Drenched Altars* (1935) 37

25. Editorial, *Christian Science Monitor*, "The Jewish Peril" 19 Jun 1920

26. "The Fatal Discourse of Rabbi Reichhorn" appeared in the French newspaper *La Vielle France*, 21 Oct 1920 and 10 Mar 1921

27. Soviet text, *Psychopolitics* (1936)

28. Gunther Russbacher, *Mind Control in America: Five Easy Steps to Create a Manchurian Candidate* (1996). Russbacher, a former SEAL and CIA operative, was a Level 4 candidate; he is presently in prison.

29. Ibid.

30. Ibid.

31. Ibid.

32. Ibid.

33. Ibid.

CHAPTER XII
Defining the New Covenant

1. Bernard Grun, *The Timetables of History* (1946)

2. Ibid.

3. Dr. Benjamin Freedman, *Facts
    are Facts* (1959)
4. Robert D. Hickson,
    Chronicles, Dec 98
5. Ibid., quoting Tom Wolfe in
    "The Meaning of Freedom"
    Mar 88
6. Ibid.
7. Ibid.
8. Ibid., quoting Gen. Douglas
    MacArthur, 12 May 62
9. Hickson, quoting Whittaker
    Chambers, 1964
10. Hickson, quoting Augusto del
    Noce, 1976
11. Ivor Benson, *The Zionist
    Factor* (1986) 32
12. Lloyd Wright's foreword to
    Rose L. Martin's 1968 best-
    seller, *Fabian Freeway*
13. Benson 29
14. Ibid., 33
15. Winston Churchill, article in
    the *London Illustrated Sunday
    Herald,* 8 Feb 1920
16. Rose L. Martin 348
17. Ibid., 175
18. Pricilla Painton, *Time,* 5 Apr
    93
19. Ibid.
20. Ibid.
21. Ibid.
22. *Richmond Times-Dispatch*, 12
    Apr 93
23. Solzenhenitsyn's speeches,
    1975
24. James Webb, Asst. Secretary
    of the Navy, quoted in
    Richmond Times-Dispatch, 11
    Oct 92
25. Ibid.
26. Ibid.
27. Ibid.
28. Gov. Bill Clinton, Chmn, DLC
    convention, 1991
29. Ibid.
30. Thomas Hobbes, "The
    Kingdom of Darkness" in
    *Leviathan: Defense of Absolute
    Monarchy* (1651)
31. Ibid.
32. Ibid.
33. Ibid.
34. Quoting Terry Reed in
    Compromised (1996)
35. Ibid.
36. Ibid.
37. Ibid.
38. Sidney Blumenthal speech, 23
    Apr 98
39. Wesley Pruden editorial,
    Washington Times, 8 May 98
40. *Washington Times*, 9 Jun 99
41. *World Almanac* 703
42. Douglas Reed, *The
    Controversy of Zion* 503
43. *World Almanac* 704
44. *Washington Post*, 19 Jun 99
45. Dr. John Coleman, *Conspiracy
    Hierarchy: The Story of the
    Committee of 300* (1992) 236
46. Ibid., 236
47. Dr. Steven Powell, *Covert
    Cadre* (1987) 15
48. Frederick Rose, *Wall Street
    Journal*, 11 Sep 92
49. Committee on Un-American
    Activities, Rpt 3123, 21 Sep
    1950
50. Larry Abraham, *Insider
    Report*, Nov 92

51. Michael A. Hoffman II, "Hammered*" Revisionist History #5* (1998)
52. Ibid.
53. Ibid.
54. Bob Zelnick, *Gore: A Political Life* (1999) 268
55. Ibid., 269
56. Ibid., 257
57. Ibid., 258
58. Mark Weber, *Journal of Historical Review*, 28 Jun 82
59. *The New York Times*, 28 May 82
60. Ibid.
61. Weber
62. Ibid.
63. Zelnick 261
64. Ibid., 259
65. Ibid., 262
66. Cal Thomas, *Washington Times*, 5 Aug 99
67. Leonard Greenup, *Revolution Before Breakfast* (1947) 137
68. *Washington Post,* 13 Oct 99
69. Ibid.
70. Mrs. Nesta Webster, quoting Berkheim in *Secret Societies and Subversive Movements* (1923)
71. Ibid.
72. Carroll Quigley, *Tragedy and Hope* 73

CHAPTER XIII
Will Bolshevism Triumph?

1. Thomas Carney in *Los Angeles* magazine, Mar 99
2. Ibid.
3. Ibid.
4. Paul Findley, *They Dare to Speak Out* (1985) 143
5. Ibid., 159
6. Ibid., 161
7. Walter Isaacson, *Kissinger* (1992) 612
8. Ibid., 614
9. *Neocon* letter to Clinton, 29 Jan 99
10. Douglas Reed, *Far and Wide* (1951) 145
11. Ibid., 147
12. Jack Bernstein, *The Life of an American Jew in Racist Marxist Israel* (1984)
13. Ibid., 27
14. Ibid., 28
15. Ibid., 30
16. Ibid., 31
17. Ibid., 32
18. Paul Johnson, *Modern Times* (1991) 323
19. Ibid., 326
20. Ibid., 336
21. Warren Hough, *Spotlight,* 7 Dec 98
22. Ibid.
23. Paul Blustein, *Washington Post,* 21 Nov 98
24. Georgie Ann Geyer, *Washington Times,* 1 Dec 98
25. *Agence France-Presse,* 1 Dec 98
26. Pres. Hugo Chavez, AP report, 8 Dec 98
27. Ibid.
28. William Norman Grigg, *New American,* 7 Dec 98
29. Ibid.
30. *New York Times,* 1 Nov 98

31. Grigg
32. Christopher Mathews, *Washington Times,* 29 Nov 98
33. Ibid.
34. Ibid.
35. Patrick J. Buchanan, *Washington Times* Commentary, 22 Feb 99
36. Ibid.
37. Ibid.

CHAPTER XIV
The Coming Coup

1. Neil H. G. Glick, *Washington Times*, 21 Sep 98
2. Ibid.
3. Ibid.
4. Author's personal conversation with a division commander, 1992
5. Michael Collins Piper, *Final Judgment* (1998)
6. Edward Luttwak, *Coup d'état: A Practical Handbook* (1968)
7. Wilmot Robertson, *The Dispossessed Majority* (1981)
8. Ibid., 57
9. Fletcher Knebel and Charles W. Bailey II, *Seven Days in May* (1962)
10. Ambrose Evans-Pritchard, *The Secret Life of Bill Clinton* (1997)
11. Ibid.
12. Gary Allen, *None Dare Call it Conspiracy* (1971)
13. Barry M Goldwater, *With No Apologies* (1964)
14. Ibid., 24

15. Adm. Chester Ward and Phyllis Schlafly, *Kissinger on a Couch* (1961)
16. William Norman Grigg, *New American,* 23 Nov 98
17. Ibid., Statement by Eduardo Frei, 1972
18. Ibid.
19. Ibid.
20. Edward Luttwak
21. Gregory Douglas, *Gestapo Chief* (Vol. 2) 69
22. Ibid., 69
23. Ibid., 73-75
24. Ibid., 79-80
25. Carroll Quigley, *Tragedy and Hope* (1966)
26. Fletcher Knebel and Charles W Bailey II, *Seven Days in May* (1962)
27. President Eisenhower, 17 Jan 61
28. Fletcher Knebel and Charles W Bailey II, *Seven Days in May*
29. Ibid., 123
30. Ibid., Gen. Barney Rutkowski 124
31. Ibid., Gen. Scott, Chmn JCS 179
32. Ibid., 180
33. Ibid., Pres. Lyman 180
34. Ibid.
35. Mikhail Gorbachev (Kahn), taken from his speech on "World Forum" 1994
36. Dr. John Coleman, *The Road to Slavery* (1994)
37. Ibid., 9
38. Ibid., 11

39. John L. Spivak, *A Man in His Time* (Horizon Press: 1967)

EPILOGUE

1. Patrick Henry at Second Virginia Convention, 23 Mar 1775
2. Douglas Reed, *Far and Wide* (1951)
3. Patrick Henry
4. John Atkinson Hobson, *Imperialism: A Study* (1902)
5. John Swinton at an American Press Association dinner
6. David Rockefeller, speaking at the Bilderberger Conference at the Hotel Baden Baden, Baden Baden, Germany, June 1991
7. Donald S. McAlvany, *McAlvany Intelligence Advisor,* Feb 99
8. *Culpeper Star Exponent,* 12 Feb 99
9. Benjamin Franklin, at the time of the framing of the Constituion 1787
10. Gil Klein, *Richmond Times-Dispatch,* 17 Jan 93
11. Ibid.
12. Ibid., Lawrence Korb
13. Ibid., Robert Hunter
14. *Washington Post*, 12 Feb 99
15. Henry A. Wallace, *The Century of the Common Man* (1943)
16. Doug Thompson, *Capitol Hill Blue* web site, 29 Mar 99
17. William J. Corliss, *Chronicles*, Jul 98
18. Ibid.
19. John F. McManus, *New American,* 2 Aug 99
20. Charley Reese, syndicated column, 20 Apr 99
21. Ibid.
22. Samuel L. Blumenfeld, author of eight books on education, including *NEA: Trojan Horse in American Education*
23. STRATFOR's Global Intelligence Update, 21 Jun 99
24. Warren Hough, *Spotlight*, 28 Jun 99
25. Dr. William Pierce, *Our Revolutionary Right*, appearing on *American Dissident Voices* broadcast, 12 Jun 99
26. Bob Djurdjevic, *Truth in Media*, 5 Aug 99
27. Patrick J. Buchanan, *Washington Times,* 30 Nov 98
28. James Yaffe, *The American Jews* (1968)
29. Martin Mayer, *The Lawyers* (1967)
30. *The New York Times*, 6 Oct 46
31. Oscar Levy's letter to George Pitt-Rivers, July 1920
32. Ben Stein, speaking to pro-life group at Catholic University, 12 Nov 98
33. Rose L. Martin, *Fabian Freeway* (1968) 127
34. Ibid., 446
35. Robert Ardrey, Territorial Imperative (1966)

INDEX

AUTHOR'S BIBLIOGRAPHY
PUBLISHER'S BOOK LIST

Aldrich, Gary
UNLIMITED ACCESS

Alperovitz, Gar
THE DECISION TO USE THE ATOMIC BOMB

Ambrose, Stephen E.
RISE TO GLOBALISM

Andrew, Christopher
KGB: The Inside Story

Ardrey, Robert
TERRITORIAL IMPERATIVE

Arendt, Hannah
THE ORIGINS OF TOTALITARIANISM
EICHMANN IN JERUSALEM

Bacque, James
OTHER LOSSES
CRIMES AND MERCIES

Barbour, Nevil
PALESTINE STAR OR CRESCENT?

Barnes, Harry Elmer
PERPETUAL WAR FOR PERPETUAL PEACE

Barron, John
KGB: The Secret Work of Soviet Secret Agents

Beard, Charles
AMERICAN FOREIGN POLICY IN THE MAKING

Beaty, John, Col. (R)
THE IRON CURTAIN OVER AMERICA

Begin, Manachem
THE REVOLT: THE STORY OF THE IRGUN

Benson, Ivor
THE ZIONIST FACTOR

Bernstein, Jack
I WAS AN AMERICAN JEW IN RACIST-MARXIST ISRAEL
MY FAREWELL TO ISRAEL, THE THORN IN THE MIDDLE EAST

Billington, James
FIRE IN THE MINDS OF MEN

Bloomfield, Lincoln
A WORLD EFFECTIVELY CONTROLLED BY THE UN

Blum, Howard
WANTED: THE SEARCH FOR NAZIS IN AMERICA

Bober, Arie
THE OTHER ISRAEL: The Radical Case Against Zionism

Buchanan, Patrick J.
RIGHT FROM THE BEGINNING
A REPUBLIC, NOT AN EMPIRE: Reclaiming America's Destiny

Budenz, Louis F.
THE CRY IS PEACE

Burriel, Augusten
HISTORY OF JACOBINISM

Butz, Arthur R.
THE HOAX OF THE TWENTIETH CENTURY

Carmack, Patrick • Still, Stan
THE MONEY MASTERS (video)

Chambers, Whittaker
WITNESS

Chomsky, Noam
THE FATEFUL TRIANGLE: The United States, Israel, and the Palestinians

Coleman, Dr. John
CONSPIRATOR'S HIERARCHY: The Story of the Committee of 300
DIPLOMACY BY DECEPTION

Corti, Egon Caesar
RISE OF THE HOUSE OF ROTHSCHILD

Courtois, Stephane et al
THE BLACK BOOK OF COMMUNISM

Dawidowicz, Lucy
THE WAR AGAINST THE JEWS

Dilling, Elizabeth
THE JEWISH RELIGION: ITS INFLUENCE TODAY

Douglas, Gregory
GESTAPO CHIEF: The 1948 Interrogation of Heinrich Muller

Emerson, Steven
THE AMERICAN HOUSE OF SAUD: The Secret Petrodollar Connection

Fahey, Denis, Rev. Dr.
THE MYSTICAL BODY OF CHRIST IN THE MODERN WORLD

Findley, Paul
DELIBERATE DECEPTIONS
THEY DARE TO SPEAK OUT

Fry, L.
WATERS FLOWING EASTWARD

Golitsyn, Anatoliy
NEW LIES FOR OLD

Govlevitch, A.
CZARISM AND REVOLUTION

Grieb, Conrad K.
UNCOVERING THE FORCES OF WAR

Griffin, G. Edward
THE FEARFUL MASTER: A Second Look at the UN
THE CREATURE FROM JEKYLL ISLAND

Halloway, David
STALIN AND THE BOMB: The Soviet Union and Atomic Energy
1939-1956

Hart, Liddell
HISTORY OF THE SECOND WORLD WAR

Hayes, Tom
PEOPLE OF THE LAND (video)

Hendrickson, Paul
THE LIVING AND THE DEAD: Robert McNamara and Five Lives
of a Lost War

House, Edward Mandell
PHILIP DRU: Administrator

Hurley, Andrew J.
HOLOCAUST II? (cloth)
a.k.a. ONE NATION UNDER ISRAEL (paper)

Irving, David
CHURCHILL'S WAR: The Struggle for Power

Isaacson, Walter
THE WISE MEN

Johnson, Paul
MODERN TIMES

Kenny, Michael S. J.
NO GOD NEXT DOOR: Red Rule in Mexico and Our Responsibility

Kimche, Jon & David
A CLASH OF DESTINIES: Arab-Jewish War and Founding of the
State of Israel

King, Alexander
THE FIRST GLOBAL REVOLUTION

Klehr, Harvey; John E. Haynes
THE SECRET WORLD OF AMERICAN COMMUNISM

Knupffer, George
THE STRUGGLE FOR WORLD POWER: Revolution and
Counter-Revolution
THE RED SYMPHONY by J. Landowski,
translated by George Knupffer

Knuth, E. C.
THE EMPIRE OF THE CITY

Koestler, Arthur
THE THIRTEENTH TRIBE

Krylienko, Andrei
THE RED THREAD

Lee, Jeremy
UPON THE MILLENNIUM, "What Will We Tell Our Children?":
Dispossessing the World's Richest Nations

Lilienthal, Alfred M.
THE ZIONIST CONNECTION

MacDonald, Professor Kevin
SEPARATION AND DISCONTENT:
Toward an Evolutionary Theory of Anti-Semitism
THE CULTURE OF CRITIQUE: An Evolutionary Analysis of Jewish
Involvement in 20th Century Intellectual and Political Movements
A PEOPLE THAT SHALL DWELL ALONE:
Judaism as a Group Evolutionary Strategy

Marschelko, Louis
THE WORLD CONQUERORS

Martin, Rose L.
FABIAN FREEWAY

Morgenstern, George
PEARL HARBOR: THE STORY OF THE SECRET WAR

Nisbet, Robert
ROOSEVELT & STALIN: The Failed Courtship

O'Grady, Olivia Marie
THE BEAST OF THE APOCALYPSE

Ostrovsky, Victor
BY WAY OF DECEPTION

Perloff, James
THE SHADOWS OF POWER: The Council on Foreign Relations and the
American Decline

Pipes, Richard
RUSSIA UNDER THE BOLSHEVIK REGIME

Polkehn, Klaus
THE SECRET CONTACTS: Zionism and Nazi Germany 1933-1941

Poncins, Count Leon de
STATE SECRETS
THE SECRET POWERS BEHIND REVOLUTION
FREEMASONRY AND THE VATICAN
JUDAISM AND THE VATICAN

Pool, James and Pool, Suzanne
WHO FINANCED HITLER

Quigley, Carroll
TRAGEDY AND HOPE: A History of the World in Our Time
ANGLO-AMERICAN ESTABLISHMENT
THE EVOLUTION OF CIVILIZATIONS

Reed, Douglas
THE CONTROVERSY OF ZION
FAR AND WIDE (Part I) and BEHIND THE SCENE (Part II)

Revel, Jean-Francois
HOW DEMOCRACIES PERISH

Robertson, Wilmot
THE DISPOSSESSED MAJORITY

Rokach, Livia
ISRAEL'S SACRED TERRORISM: A Study Based on Moshe Sharett's Personal Diary

Schoenbaum, Thomas J.
WAGING PEACE & WAR

Shahak, Israel
JEWISH FUNDAMENTALISM IN ISRAEL
OPEN SECRETS: Israeli Nuclear and Foreign Policies
JEWISH HISTORY, JEWISH RELIGION: The Weight of Three Thousand Years

Shirer, William L.
THE COLLAPSE OF THE THIRD REPUBLIC

Singer, S. Fred
GLOBAL CLIMATE CHANGE

Snetsinger, John
TRUMAN: The Jewish Vote and the Creation of Israel

Stormer, John A
NONE DARE CALL IT TREASON

Sutton, Anthony C.
WALL STREET AND THE BOLSHEVIK REVOLUTION
WALL STREET AND THE RISE OF HITLER
AMERICA'S SECRET ESTABLISHMENT

Thomas, Gordon
GIDEON'S SPIES

Trent, Barbara
THE PANAMA DECEPTION (video)

Weinstein, Allen
PERJURY: The Hiss-Chambers Case

Wilton, Robert
THE LAST DAYS OF THE ROMANOVS: How Tsar Nicholas II and Russia's Imperial Family Were Murdered

Wormser, Rene A.
FOUNDATIONS: Their Power and Influences